DEATH
ON TWO
FRONTS

ALSO IN THE
History *of* Canada Series

*Death or Victory: The Battle of Quebec
and the Birth of an Empire*, by Dan Snow

*The Last Act: Pierre Trudeau, the Gang of Eight
and the Fight for Canada*, by Ron Graham

*The Destiny of Canada: Macdonald, Laurier,
and the Election of 1891*, by Christopher Pennington

*Ridgeway: The American Fenian Invasion
and the 1866 Battle That Made Canada*, by Peter Vronsky

*War in the St. Lawrence:
The Forgotten U-Boat Battles on Canada's Shores*, by Roger Sarty

The Best Place to Be: Expo 67 and Its Time,
by John Lownsbrough

Ice and Water: Politics, Peoples, and the Arctic Council,
by John English

*Trouble on Main Street: Mackenzie King, Race, and
the 1907 Vancouver Riots*, by Julie Gilmour

Two Weeks in Quebec City: The Meeting That Made Canada,
by Christopher Moore

SEAN T. CADIGAN

NATIONAL TRAGEDIES AND
THE FATE OF DEMOCRACY IN
NEWFOUNDLAND, 1914–34

DEATH ON TWO FRONTS

ALLEN
LANE

ALLEN LANE
an imprint of Penguin Canada Books Inc.

Published by the Penguin Group
Penguin Canada Books Inc.
90 Eglinton Avenue East, Suite 700, Toronto, Ontario, Canada M4P 2Y3

Penguin Group (USA) Inc., 375 Hudson Street, New York, New York 10014, U.S.A.
Penguin Books Ltd, 80 Strand, London WC2R 0RL, England
Penguin Ireland, 25 St Stephen's Green, Dublin 2, Ireland (a division of Penguin Books Ltd)
Penguin Group (Australia), 707 Collins Street, Melbourne, Victoria 3008, Australia
(a division of Pearson Australia Group Pty Ltd)
Penguin Books India Pvt Ltd, 11 Community Centre, Panchsheel Park, New Delhi – 110 017, India
Penguin Group (NZ), 67 Apollo Drive, Rosedale, Auckland 0632, New Zealand
(a division of Pearson New Zealand Ltd)
Penguin Books (South Africa) (Pty) Ltd, 24 Sturdee Avenue, Rosebank, Johannesburg 2196, South Africa

Penguin Books Ltd, Registered Offices: 80 Strand, London WC2R 0RL, England

First published 2013

1 2 3 4 5 6 7 8 9 10   (RRD)

Manufactured in the U.S.A.

LIBRARY AND ARCHIVES CANADA CATALOGUING IN PUBLICATION

Cadigan, Sean T. (Sean Thomas), 1962–, author
Death on two fronts : national tragedies and the fate of democracy in
Newfoundland, 1914–34 / Sean Cadigan.

(History of Canada)
Includes bibliographical references and index.

ISBN 978-0-670-06539-4 (bound)

1. Newfoundland and Labrador—Politics and government—1855–1934.
2. Political culture—Newfoundland and Labrador—History. I. Title.
II. Series: History of Canada (Toronto, Ont.)

FC2173.2.C33 2013   971.8'02   C2013-902700-9

Visit the Penguin Canada website at **www.penguin.ca**

Special and corporate bulk purchase rates available; please see
www.penguin.ca/corporatesales or call 1-800-810-3104, ext. 2477.

CONTENTS

The History of Canada Series   vii
Introduction: Death on Two Fronts   ix
List of Maps   xxviii

1   The Nature of Newfoundland and Labrador   1
2   The *Newfoundland* Sealing Disaster,
Spring 1914   32
3   War, 1914–1915   59
4   The New Front: Gallipoli, 1915–1916   93
5   Beaumont Hamel, 1 July 1916   123
6   Wars, 1917–1918   153
7   Progressives: Prussians or Bolsheviks?
1919–1920   188
8   The Failure of the Progressive Alternative,
1920–1923   217
9   Political Demoralization, 1923–1924   246
10   The Death of Democracy, 1925–1934   276

Conclusion   300
Notes   313
Bibliography   352
Acknowledgments   366
Photo Credits   368
Index   369

THE HISTORY
OF CANADA SERIES

Canada, the world agrees, is a success story. We should never make the mistake, though, of thinking that it was easy or foreordained. At crucial moments during Canada's history, challenges had to be faced and choices made. Certain roads were taken and others were not. Imagine a Canada, indeed imagine a North America, where the French and not the British had won the Battle of the Plains of Abraham. Or imagine a world in which Canadians had decided to throw in their lot with the revolutionaries in the thirteen colonies.

This series looks at the making of Canada as an independent, self-governing nation. It includes works on key stages in the laying of the foundations as well as the crucial turning points between 1867 and the present that made the Canada we know today. It is about those defining moments when the course of Canadian history and the nature of Canada itself were oscillating. And it is about the human beings—heroic, flawed, wise, foolish, complex—who had to make decisions without knowing what the consequences might be.

We begin the series with the European presence in the eighteenth century—a presence that continues to shape our society today—and conclude it with an exploration of the strategic importance of the Canadian Arctic. We look at how the mass movements of peoples, whether Loyalists in the eighteenth century or Asians at the start of the twentieth, have profoundly influenced the nature of Canada. We also look at battles and their aftermaths: the Plains of Abraham, the 1866 Fenian raids, the German submarines in the St. Lawrence River during the Second World War. Political crises—the 1891 election that saw Sir John A. Macdonald battling Wilfrid Laurier; Pierre Trudeau's triumphant patriation of the Canadian Constitution—provide rich moments of storytelling. So, too, do the Expo 67 celebrations, which marked a time of soaring optimism and gave Canadians new confidence in themselves.

We have chosen these critical turning points partly because they are good stories in themselves but also because they show what Canada was like at particularly important junctures in its history. And to tell them we have chosen Canada's best historians. Our authors are great storytellers who shine a spotlight on a different Canada, a Canada of the past, and illustrate links from then to now. We need to remember the roads that were taken—and the ones that were not. Our goal is to help our readers understand how we got from that past to this present.

Margaret MacMillan
Warden at St. Antony's College, Oxford

Robert Bothwell
May Gluskin Chair of Canadian History
University of Toronto

INTRODUCTION:
DEATH ON TWO FRONTS

Fronts defined the history of Newfoundland and Labrador between 1914 and 1934; they served as sites of suffering and sacrifice that subsequently helped give birth to national mythologies. For anyone unfamiliar with the province, the front that seems obvious in the context of 1914 is the one that an English-language dictionary defines partially as "a line of battle," "a scene of actual fighting," or "the foremost line or part of an army."[1] In Newfoundland and Labrador, however, "front" has another meaning: it may refer to "a stretch of coast facing the sea," but more commonly refers to "the seas east and north-east of Newfoundland, esp. the area covered by the leading edge of the ice which moves south in the spring and on which the sealherds whelp."[2]

The seal hunt took place on this latter front, which was often a site for struggles nearly as brutal and deadly as those that took place on the front lines of war. In folk tradition and popular culture, the dangers of the seal hunt fostered an image of the sealer as a rugged individual, a Viking of the ice, the son of hardy fishers, who battled the elements to wrest a livelihood in the form of the seal pelts and fat taken in the hunt during the spring. Such qualities of the sealer purportedly defined the

Newfoundland character—a proposition boosted by the emergence of anti–seal-hunt protests in the early 1970s.[3] These protests partly fuelled a local cultural revival that was otherwise a reaction against the modernization that took place during the years in which J.R. Smallwood held the office of premier. There was much provincial indignation towards the condescension of a protest movement that poorly understood the role of the seal hunt in Newfoundland society. The protests seemed to slight the historically vital role the hunt had played in the economy of coastal communities, and to be disrespectful and callous towards the tremendous danger endured by seal hunters at the ice. This front was also the scene of a terrible tragedy in the spring of 1914, the frightening reality of which was brought to life by Cassie Brown's magnificent account of the loss of seventy-eight sealers from the SS *Newfoundland* in *Death on the Ice: The Great Newfoundland Sealing Disaster of 1914*.[4]

Death on another front, during the Battle of the Somme two years later, has played an even greater role in the formation of public sensibilities about what it means to be a Newfoundlander. The first day of July is the anniversary of the most tragic battle in the history of the Royal Newfoundland Regiment in the First World War. More men fell in the other battles of that war combined, and the Regiment received greater public honours for other feats, but the battle at Beaumont Hamel, which took place on the first day of the Somme offensive, on 1 July 1916, was "Newfoundland's first encounter with mass death during wartime." The impact of that encounter was so traumatic that it "has been etched deeply into the consciousness of Newfoundland and has come to form part of the mythology of a land and its people, a symbol of its proud history and of its supreme sacrifice for King and Country."[5] In the acts of commemoration that followed in Newfoundland culture and society in the post-war period, this sacrifice became the standard against which surviving and subsequent generations were judged, and interpretations of the course taken by Newfoundland politics continually come back to this event as a touchstone. The state of Newfoundland's democracy has ever after been tied to questions of what is owed in commemoration to the sacrifices of the victims of war, and to both the talents and the worthiness of the post-war population.

One important myth of 1 July is that Newfoundland emerged fully as a nation through the sacrifice at Beaumont Hamel. In 1917, Newfoundlanders in St. John's observed their first Memorial Day on the anniversary of the Beaumont Hamel tragedy. It has subsequently become something of a cruel historical twist that people in the province celebrate Canada Day on the same day as the more sombre occasion. The first official history of the Royal Newfoundland Regiment during the war, written in 1964, observed that "while the rest of Canada light-heartedly celebrates July 1 as the anniversary of Confederation, to the people of the newest Province this day will always be one on which to fore-gather beneath the War Memorials throughout the land and renew their pledge of dedication, in proud memory of those of dauntless courage who fought and fell in Freedom's cause."[6]

In the years since the dominion's entry into Confederation in 1949, there has always been some ambivalence within the Province of Newfoundland and Labrador about its place within Canada, a condition that flares up in times of poor local economic conditions or of intense federal–provincial disagreement over jurisdictional and constitutional matters.[7] Statements drawing attention to the importance of Beaumont Hamel in the definition of Newfoundlanders' identities occasionally surface in the press, from satisfaction in 2006 that the Canadian government was extending greater recognition to Beaumont Hamel in national commemorative activities, through suggestions that 1 July should not be called Canada Day in Newfoundland, to a gardening columnist's recent frank aside that she never celebrates Canada Day because she believes "the date for it should never have been chosen in disregard of the fact that July 1 was already the date for Newfoundland's Memorial Day."[8]

The coincidence of Newfoundland and Labrador's commemoration of Memorial Day with Canadians' celebration of Confederation on 1 July is not as incongruous as it might appear. To many Canadians, the mythologies of military sacrifice during the First World War are just as important to their sense of national identities as the mythology of Beaumont Hamel is to Newfoundlanders. Although the historic Canadian advance at Vimy Ridge took place later, on 9 April 1917, it too demanded a tremendous sacrifice of lives. At least in English Canada, Vimy Ridge became no less a part of a national mythology of righteous, almost holy sacrifice than did Beaumont Hamel for Newfoundlanders. As one Parks Canada interpretation guide of the Vimy Ridge and Beaumont Hamel memorials in France put it, both battles were "the price we paid for nationhood."[9] Newfoundlanders, too, shared in the Canadian experience of Vimy Ridge. The local press took notice of the "glorious victory on Vimy Ridge" by the "gallant Canadians." Over the course of the war, nearly 3300 Newfoundlanders served in the Canadian Expeditionary Force, and one local newspaper editor thought it was very likely "that scores of them participated in the fighting and valiantly did their part in driving the Hun from his supposedly invulnerable positions."[10]

The many Newfoundlanders who served in the Canadian Expeditionary Force are an important reminder that Newfoundland's history in the nineteenth century and first half of the twentieth century was interwoven with Canada's as part of a larger British North American whole. A popular anti-confederate song of the failed campaign for Confederation in Newfoundland in 1869 said of the colony that "Her face turns to Britain, her Back to the Gulf, Come near at your peril, Canadian Wolf."[11] However, though the imagery has a persistent nationalist cachet, Newfoundland did not actually have its back to Canada. From the time of the American Revolution, Newfoundland settlers depended on trade with the other British North American colonies for provisions, livestock, and shipping tonnage. Many prominent British North Americans had ties to Newfoundland. Thomas Dalton, the brewer and Reformer turned Tory newspaper editor, began his mercantile career in St. John's in 1810, but bankruptcy in the post-1815 depression forced him to move to Upper Canada. Other people chose to move to Newfoundland, notably Henry John Boulton, the former attorney general of Upper Canada, who became chief justice of the Supreme Court of Newfoundland in 1833. In the late nineteenth century, Nova Scotian investors expanded into Newfoundland's west-coast lobster fishery and forestry industry. In the same period, many Canadians of Acadian, Mi'kmaq, and Highland Scottish backgrounds from Cape Breton established permanent residence on the west coast, giving Newfoundland a more Canadian-oriented demographic character by 1911. Overall, there were many links between Newfoundland and Canada in financial, educational, and religious institutions.[12]

The strengthening reorientation of the Newfoundland population towards Canada helps to explain why Confederation succeeded in 1949. Yet local nationalist mythology, of which Beaumont Hamel is an important part, often twists down another road, seeing union with Canada as the outcome of another process: the faltering of liberal democracy when Newfoundland surrendered responsible self-government for administration by a British-appointed Commission of Government in the early 1930s. David Macfarlane took this point of view in his well-received 1991 interpretation of his family's struggle with the memory of the Great War: *The Danger Tree*.

A prominent family of businessmen from Grand Falls, the Goodyears were Macfarlane's maternal line. His grandfather, Harold Kenneth Goodyear, who went by Ken, enlisted in the Regiment in 1914, and three of his brothers, Josiah Robert (known as Joe), Oswald Raymond (Ray), and Stanley Charles (Stan) also joined. A fourth brother, Hedley John, joined the Canadian Expeditionary Force. Only Ken and Joe survived the war. In Macfarlane's view, his maternal family members were examples of the best and the brightest that Newfoundland had to offer, and the family paid dearly in living up to the responsibility of Empire during the Great War.

The Goodyears believed that they were risking their lives in defence of a strong and independent Newfoundland, but their sacrifice was for naught. Almost thirty years after the beginning of the war, the Newfoundland House of Assembly supported the voluntary suspension of responsible self-government and its replacement by a Commission of Government that put political power in the hands of a British governor and six appointed commissioners charged with reforming Newfoundland's administration finances and economic circumstances, a development that prepared the way for Newfoundland's entry into Confederation in 1949. Ken was a proud Newfoundlander who despised his country's loss of responsible government and went on to oppose union with Canada. This stance is strong in Macfarlane's book, which gives voice to a critical element of Newfoundland's post-war mythology: that the war deprived Newfoundland of many of its finest sons and consequently diminished the capacity of its leadership. Macfarlane observed,

> The greatest change the war brought was one that no one could mea-
> sure. It was an absence…. The best were gone by 1917, or doomed, and
> what the world would have been like had they not died is anybody's
> guess. The war left their things unfinished: enterprises conceived, proj-
> ects initiated, routes surveyed, engagements announced. And that's
> where it ended. Their fiancées waited for them forever, their mail went
> unanswered, their deals never closed. Their plans were left in rough
> draft, their sentences unfinished.[13]

In Ken Goodyear's eyes, what would never be was an independent Newfoundland that might have lived up to the qualities of his lost brothers. The losses of the Great War had deprived Newfoundland of its best leaders, ensuring that its future would be in the hands of those incapable of maintaining its status as an independent dominion during the political crisis of the 1930s.

The myth of "the best and the brightest" is part of the understand-able pathos of the Great War. Of the 5431 Newfoundlanders and

Labradorians who served on the battlefields of Gallipoli and the Western Front with the Royal Newfoundland Regiment, there were 3565 casualties, including 1251 deaths; soldiers in service faced a 66 percent chance of becoming a casualty.[14] Bereft families and friends of those who died tragically needed to feel that the people they had lost were more important than most. It is also not hard to understand that such sacrifice inspired "a strong sense of national identity," which in turn later prompted a bitter speculation by people who opposed Newfoundland's loss of independence in the 1930s and 1940s: what if the best and the brightest had not been lost, but rather had taken their place at the helm of a better Newfoundland?[15]

The problem with this perspective is that it is just one invention, premised on a present-day revision of a number of other myths that arose immediately from the commemoration of loss in the Great War.[16] These other myths reflected the needs and struggles of the many thousands of Newfoundlanders who lived through the war as non-combatant volunteers, citizens who could not or would not fight, or soldiers and sailors who returned. About four thousand members of the Regiment returned home, as did most of those who served in the Royal Naval Reserve and the Newfoundland Forestry Corps, as well as at least fifty to sixty nurses who volunteered for overseas duty.[17] The myth of the lost generation demeaned, intentionally or not, the people who survived the war and, though often damaged in some way, nevertheless went on building their futures. Many of the myths of commemoration developed after the war were part of their struggle to do so.

The mythology of a national failure arising from the impact of the Great War needs to be reconsidered in the context of a broader re-evaluation of the reasons for the collapse of responsible government in the early 1930s. Scholars tended to see the Commission of Government as an imposition on the part of British authorities, perhaps in collusion with the Canadian banks that had become major creditors of the Newfoundland government, to secure the troubled public finances of

Newfoundland without regard for the political dignity of its people. By the late 1980s, however, historians were reassessing this conclusion and arguing that the rancorous political debates of the 1920s indicated that various groups in Newfoundland—whether representing rural people, members of labour unions, or mercantile and industrial elites—had lost faith in liberal democracy and were, in fact, open to the idea of government by an appointed commission.[18]

The political demoralization of the 1920s immediately set the stage for the Commission of Government in 1934. However, the point can be made that this demoralization was not solely a reaction to the immediate political problems of the 1920s. Instead, liberal democracy in that period foundered on the twin shoals of post-war crisis and commemoration. The themes that came to dominate the commemoration of the sacrifices of the Royal Newfoundland Regiment and other combatants in the Great War shaped the political response to the crisis of deepening post-war economic depression, worsened by the financial burdens of the war, and consequent social discontent. The particular idealizations of the fallen soldiers and sailors of the war were riddled with laissez-faire values and impossibly high standards of political purity that no pre-war govern- ment in Newfoundland had managed to live up to. Such commemo- rative values conflicted with another, more progressive, idealization of the fallen—the belief that the soldiers and sailors had sacrificed so that Newfoundlanders, through their government, might reconstruct the post-war world on a better footing. The association of laissez-fairism with political virtue triumphed and played a significant role in under- mining the legitimacy of attempts by government to manage economic and social problems in the context of a progressive ideology.

William Ford Coaker, the leader of the Fishermen's Protective Union (FPU), the first mass organization to represent fishers in Newfoundland, was the champion of such attempts. The terrible industrial disasters in sealing that had happened during the spring of 1914 intensified Coaker's fight for reform. Far from seeing the sealing disasters as examples of the hardy courage and noble sacrifice of men born to struggle, sometimes in failure, against the elements, Coaker saw them as instances of the terrible waste of life that went along with mercantile exploitation in Newfoundland. In the spring of 1914, Coaker was still an angry yet determined leader of a protest movement who spoke for the rights of what he saw as a downtrodden class of outport fishing people against the mercantile firms, St. John's industrial interests, and the politicians who represented them. The FPU leader directed the widespread anger about the sealing disasters of that year towards supporting the union's political movement. This movement was so successful that, by 1917, Coaker had become a minister in government and seemed poised to achieve some of the changes he felt would benefit the fishing people of Newfoundland.

Over the next fifteen years, in the wake of a series of post-war economic, social, and political crises, Coaker failed to realize the changes he had hoped for early on. Disillusionment accompanied disappointment as the FPU leader lost faith in the people his union represented. Coaker had started the FPU with tremendous faith in the inherent virtues of fishing people; in his view they were hard-working and God-fearing people who were downtrodden by grasping merchants. By the early 1930s, Coaker had come to see the same people as fallen ones—betrayed by their desperate need for relief from their poverty into reliance on the patronage of corrupt St. John's politicians and their mercantile supporters. These politicians and merchants had opposed Coaker's policies and, in his view, their patronage spending had financially ruined the government's ability to take any progressive measures to reform the economy or society. In consequence, Coaker lost faith in liberal democracy generally, ultimately embracing a much more authoritarian perspective on what the political future of Newfoundland should be. The trajectory of Coaker's political thinking was, in many ways, representative of the overall direction of post-war Newfoundland. It was shaped by a more general debate about the relationship between the state, social and economic inequalities, and the meaning of wartime sacrifice that had emerged in many of the countries that had been in conflict with each other. Over the long term, the twinning of free-market values and impossibly high standards of political morality in the ideals of wartime commemoration contributed to the suppression of the progressive impulse that had been so important in Coaker's early thinking.

One of the ironies of the Great War was that the complexities of its origins fostered much simpler moralizing explanations of what had led to the war in the first place. Broader, long-term economic and imperial rivalries between Britain, France, Prussia and its imperial German successor, Austria-Hungary, and Russia had set the stage for a particular set of armed nationalisms in Europe, in which Germany had been taking a leading role by 1914. The continental German Empire consisted of a relatively new alliance of Prussian landed aristocrats (the Junkers), newer economic, especially industrial, elites, and workers. Although the German Kaiser retained significant authority in military and foreign policy, the imperial government depended on a coalition of often competing interests. Courting an alliance of aristocrats with their martial traditions, industrialists who specialized in the new chemicals and metals that did so well in munitions, and working people who desired employment forced the German state to push outward. The German economy needed new resources and markets, and the Kaiser and his ministers desired the prestige that came from containing their main continental rival: France.

Abroad, Germany everywhere faced a British imperial obstacle, or so many Germans thought. While the sun might have always been shining on some part of Britain's empire, its workshops were old and its economy was sagging; it increasingly resorted to imperial accommodations with France, Russia, the United States, and Japan to restrain German expansion. Few allies were available to Germany except the Austro-Hungarian Empire, Italy, and the Ottoman Empire. Always a continental empire preoccupied with its ethnic and national complexities,

Austria-Hungary was not a significant threat to Germany, and was a counter-balance to Russia. Tensions between Austria-Hungary and Russia over the aspirations of Slavic peoples in the Balkans provided another possibility for conflict. Added to this was Turkey, an important commercial partner of Germany. The Turkish Empire had been a long-term participant in the conflicts of the Balkans, and continued to be at odds with Russia. Imperialist rivalries and emerging military alliance systems were the oxygen that gave life to the fires of war sparked by an archduke's assassination in 1914. While the move towards war was Germany's specific response to the complexities of international rivalry and domestic needs, the extent to which it bore most of the responsibility for war is still a matter of debate. Nevertheless, the belligerent posturing of the German regime made war appear to be the result of the Kaiser's aggression.[19]

It was difficult for Newfoundlanders, as part of the British forces fighting against Germany, to accept that there might be complex but understandable motives for their foe's desire to fight for a place in the sun in a world overshadowed by the British Empire and its allies. Newfoundland and Labrador men, by contrast, went to war for simple ideals ideologically derived from the "rigid set of moral standards" that was the ideological inheritance of British liberal democracy. "The ideals might have been a bit muddled," but they were nonetheless real: the war was between sacred British liberty and the dark forces of German militarism.[20] The soldiers of the Empire, Newfoundlanders and Labradorians included, could see themselves as the proud defenders of civilized tradition against the Prussian militarism unleashed by Germany's rapid industrial and urban expansion. British political culture valued duty as a form of restraint; liberty existed because law and justice restrained the sense of entitlement that went with rights. Without restraint, the insistence on rights was tyranny, and this was how many Newfoundlanders, like their fellows in other parts of the British Empire, perceived Germany's desire for expansion. British subjects went to war as a duty, to defend civilization against Prussian barbarism, which sought to tread on the smaller, defenceless countries of Europe.[21]

There was a clear sense in Newfoundland that the war was being fought for traditional British civilization against the modern barbarity of Germany. Prime Minister Sir Edward Morris, for example, in commenting on the war in 1916, argued that Germany had become Britain's chief imperial rival, and he dated this rivalry to the Franco-Prussian War of 1870. However, Morris would not concede that Germany had a legitimate claim to the same advantages of imperial wealth and power that Britain, or France for that matter, had enjoyed for much of the nineteenth century. For him, Germany's motivations were simply base, grounded in a Prussian desire to annihilate the world's greatest liberal democracy for its own self-aggrandizement. "Everyone knows," claimed Morris, "what has happened since. From 1870 starts the growth of German militarism, the education of her people to claims for a higher place for the nation, and to the acquiring by her people of that technical education which alone could fit them for what they have since won...."[22] In Morris's view, Germany's new industrial development was illegitimate because it threatened British power.

England stood for something nobler, a view captured in poetry in 1917 by the St. John's confection manufacturer, restaurateur, and poet Frederick B. Wood, who had come to Newfoundland from Nova Scotia in the 1890s:

O England, Our Brave England, —
Bulwark of Liberty;
Our hopes, our aspirations,
Are all bound up in thee!

O England, Our Brave England,
These are the times that test;
By strong-armed, ruthless tyrants
The world would be possessed!

O England, Our Brave England,
There is a noble part;
To those despoiled, down-trodden'
Hope, courage, strength, thou art![23]

By the time that Wood was writing, however, soldiers in the trenches and people at home were revising their views of what the war was about. Absolute disillusionment with previous ideals and a conviction of the futility amidst the horrors of the trenches might come later for some literary figures, but for men in the trenches, the ideals of duty become more intimate and practical. The soldier's duty was to the survival of his comrades, and to hope that people at home would not forget them.[24] For those who survived, the return home demonstrated that, far from forgetting the men in the trenches, people on the home front were obsessed with whether their part in what had become a total war had lived up to the contributions of those who had been wounded or killed on distant battlefields. Many people concluded that the war effort on the home front had failed those who made the sacrifices of the trenches.

The organization and conduct of the war effort had undergone dramatic change; voluntary leadership drawn from the commercial, industrial, and professional elites had been discredited amidst allegations of wartime profiteering and poor marshalling of society's resources for war on an unprecedented scale. In Canada, for example, and most notably in the industrial centres of Ontario and Quebec, people who worked in the industries vital to the war effort began to question the profits made by such magnates as Canada's bacon baron, Joseph Flavelle. The president of the Empire's largest pork-packing business, Flavelle was also the chairman of financial institutions such as the Bank of Commerce and the director of the Imperial Munitions Board.

Industrial workers were further angered by the federal government's willingness to use the War Measures Act, first passed without opposition in 1914. The act allowed the Canadian government to rule through orders-in-council rather than legislation approved by Parliament, and permitted the suspension of basic civil liberties for the sake of the war effort. Throughout the summer of 1918, the government used the War Measures Act to ban workers' collective action and intern labour and leftist leaders suspected of disloyalty.[25] Seeing such measures as Kaiserism or Prussianism in Ottawa, workers' organizations struggled for a new type of democracy at home.[26]

While this new democracy included the embrace of more radical industrial unionism and leftist politics in the immediate aftermath of the war, it was, by and large, moderate and reformist in politics. Its most successful political impulse, elements of which found their way into the Liberal and Conservative politics of the 1920s, was pre-war progressivism, the notion that the state could do more to ameliorate the worst problems of society so that capitalist development might proceed in a more orderly and consensual fashion.[27] Across the Cabot Strait from Newfoundland, some Maritimers had, before the war, become uneasy about industrialization, urbanization, and leftist radicalism. Health professionals, journalists, church leaders, union organizers, and women's rights activists argued that society, rather than individuals, must solve social problems. Consequently, they recommended a variety of voluntary and government interventions, especially in the areas of municipal health and sanitation reform.

Churches, particularly Methodist and Presbyterian, dominated the Progressive movement. The corporate organization of capitalism in the late nineteenth and early twentieth centuries was characterized by a movement towards consolidation and merger, and the Progressives offered a religion-based critique of the concentration of power and wealth that had resulted. Proposing a Social Gospel of bourgeois sympathy and responsibility for the plight of the poor, progressive Christians were prominent in urban reform.

Progressive and Social Gospel adherents throughout North America offered a variety of secular and religious views, often coloured by imperialism and racism, advocating that an Anglo-American and Protestant civilization had a duty to uplift the working poor, saving them from the degradation of unrestrained capitalism and the ignorance of their particular ethnic backgrounds.[28]

In industrial relations, the progressive impulse was to suggest that labour and capital had mutual rather than antagonistic interests; the duty of the state was to represent the public interest by requiring conciliation efforts between the two before strikes or lockouts might occur. In Canada, the most prominent accomplishment of the Progressive movement had been the federal Industrial Disputes Investigation Act of 1907, largely the brainchild of the deputy minister of labour, William Lyon Mackenzie King.[29]

In parts of Canada where industrial manufacturing and staple production were well developed, the impulse for a new type of democracy immediately exploded in what became known as the Labour Revolt of 1919. Workers across Canada experimented with more radical forms of unionism, general strikes, and radical leftist politics, taking their inspiration from a variety of socialisms and from the new Bolshevik regime in Russia. In doing so, they joined the alliance of miners, railways workers, and dockers who were organizing in Britain, general strikers in France, the workers who occupied factories in northern Italian cities, and the many participants in strike waves across the United States and throughout Australia and New Zealand.[30]

Conditions in Newfoundland, however, more closely resembled those in the rural Maritimes than the industrial areas of Canada. While agrarian discontent was widespread across Canada, society in the Maritimes, as in Newfoundland, was characterized by an uneven development of capitalism that had produced various forms of petty and household production in fishing, farming, and logging communities. Limited and fragmented industrial development, comparatively dispersed populations, and relatively low levels of immigration reinforced strong paternalistic ties between people across class lines.[31] While such fragmentation and paternalism were strong in Newfoundland, and tended to muffle or dissipate dissent, a particularly outrageous event could ignite far-reaching discontent. Such had been the case in the spring of 1914, when an unprecedented polarization of politics by class emerged in response to the deaths and injuries that occurred in the seal hunt that year.

And so the war began in Newfoundland with public sensitivities about social inequality heightened by a public debate about the extent to which sealers had suffered due to the negligence of ship owners and captains who cared more for profits than the safety of their crews. Coaker and the Fishermen's Protective Union led the criticism of the sealing industry and, as the war went on, earned further support by voicing additional concerns about profiteering and corrupt government. In commenting on the relationship between wartime profits and inflation, for example, Coaker charged the Morris government with being the dupes of "a handful of greedy speculators" who were becoming "millionaires" at the expense of working people.[32] Coaker pressed for moderate legislative measures to bring improvements in the living and working conditions of fishers and workers. Throughout the war, he became increasingly convinced that the government could play a more positive role in organizing Newfoundland's main industry, the fishery, a belief that culminated in his agreement to join the National Government in 1917, supporting its conscription policy despite the opposition of the FPU members to the measure in exchange for the chance to sponsor regulations for the fishing industry from 1919 through 1921.

Coaker's early political rhetoric, informed by his notion that the great mass of rural working people were being unfairly exploited by a small group of St. John's merchants and their political cronies, led him to challenge the right of the export firms to organize the fish trade; however, his fisheries regulations failed, and Coaker faltered in his commitment to progressivism.

Again, the Canadian case provides a useful contrast. The confluence of a powerful wartime idealism and middle-class social reform had led to a belief, at least at the federal level, that the state could intervene positively in areas such as public health to protect the public well-being. The Social Gospel, with its focus on bourgeois responsibility for those less fortunate, had been a powerful undercurrent in the manner in which people tried to make sense of the sacrifices being made during the war. The Canadian debate over conscription had produced a Union Government in 1917 composed of English-speaking Liberals and the Conservatives, and it promised more state intervention as a solution to social problems. Government, the Unionists promised, would rebuild the post-war world without partisan rancour and in the interests of the public. The Spanish influenza epidemic waves of 1918–1919 led to a focus of much of this energy on the creation of a federal department of public health. The department's emphasis on prevention of disease through the management of public hygiene conveniently challenged no dominant social or economic interests, but did provide a justification for managing the social mores of working people, immigrant communities, and returning soldiers in the interests of public improvement.[33]

The problem for Coaker was that his approach to the post-war reconstruction of the Newfoundland economy was perceived, at least by the mercantile community and their political allies, as a direct challenge to dominant social and economic interests. In Canada, state policy worked to suppress the more radical elements of the movement for a new democracy by greater regulation of industrial relations and the surveillance and harassment of radical leftist and union leaders. However, many people searched for meaning in the immediate post-war world without resorting to leftist radicalism. Disillusioned soldiers, in particular, returned to the home front to swell the ranks of those exhausted by the demands of the conflict, hard-pressed by the economic problems of inflation and post-war depression, and feeling betrayed by political leaders who seemed unable to deal with these problems. Coaker believed that, as a member of government, his policies were on the side of such people, but he was unable to convince them. His progressivism lost out to laissez-fairism and the association of state

xxvi Death on Two Fronts

intervention in the economy with political corruption and dictatorship that dominated public debates about how best to commemorate the casualties of the war.

In Britain and France, many veterans felt that they had been let down in the post-war period by governments and by the public generally, who did not care for veterans' social, economic, and health needs. In Canada, political, church, and community leaders quickly perceived the importance of containing such disillusionment by controlling how the war should be remembered. The public process of commemoration often drew on the ideals of British liberty and civilization potent early in the war. Monuments, buildings, literature, and theatre memorialized combatants as the embodiment of "Winged Victory," a symbol of justice triumphant, or as noble Crusaders ready to follow in Christ's path of the ultimate sacrifice. More and more, veterans participated in a commemoration that emphasized war as a purifying fire, the new sun at the dawn of a purer nation of Anglo-Canadians. Although often still carrying the mental and physical traumas of war, and poorly employed, if at all, veterans stood as the idealization of future civic virtue. That "civitas" continued to be British and "middle-class": personal industriousness and morality should inform public life. Although the Great War had prompted unprecedented centralization of British government departments responsible for the economy, especially in the supply of food, munitions, and labour, the government preferred to provide incentives to industry rather than to compel it directly through legislation to support the war. The new citizen was to guard against political divisions and subversiveness, especially anything that might be labelled revolutionary, such as the Bolshevism that had come to power in Russia in 1917.[34]

Coaker was put in the position of having to defend his political platform against such labels. The war initially bolstered Coaker's progressivism, but it also occasioned a rancorous political rhetoric. Coaker was the type of prominent political figure who had not actually gone to war and whose public virtue was, therefore, easily suspect—more so because, before joining the National Government, he was, like the rest of the FPU membership, opposed to conscription. Even worse, Coaker's belief in an interventionist state offended many of Newfoundland's mercantile elite, and they dismissed his fisheries regulations as a betrayal of the laissez-faire elements of the British liberal tradition that young Newfoundlanders had allegedly fought and died for between 1915 and 1918.

During the war, Coaker had begun to subordinate appeals to equity and fairness between classes to condemnations of his political and mercantile opponents by questioning their patriotism. Following the war, his opponents gained the upper hand in dismissing Coaker and his political allies as Huns and Bolsheviks, enemies of liberal democracy who sought to dissolve it in graft and corruption, polluting the legacy of Newfoundland blood left on the battlefield of Beaumont Hamel. Further, Coaker's enemies laid the entire blame for Newfoundland's post-war economic woes at the feet of his fisheries regulations. Embittered by such manipulative rhetoric, but in no way blameless for it, Coaker took a leading role in exploring more authoritarian solutions to Newfoundland's political woes.

Coaker's political enemies proved no more politically noble despite promises they made about a purer politics, and they cynically manipulated the rhetoric of commemoration. By 1932, the demands from the poor and the unemployed for relief frustrated all of them; a deepening contempt for the masses fuelled the commemorative trope that their laziness and selfishness had betrayed the noble sacrifices of Newfoundland's fighting men during the war. In other words, the people did not deserve the democracy these men had fallen for. What follows is a study of how the rhetoric of commemorating the Great War infiltrated the politics of post-war reconstruction, undermined local commitment to the possibility of a more socially progressive state, and ultimately contributed to the collapse of responsible government by 1934.[35]

LIST OF MAPS

1. Newfoundland and Labrador   xxix
2. The Gallipoli Peninsula in the Eastern Mediterranean   xxx
3. The General Area of the Western Front in France
    and Belgium, 1914–18   xxxi

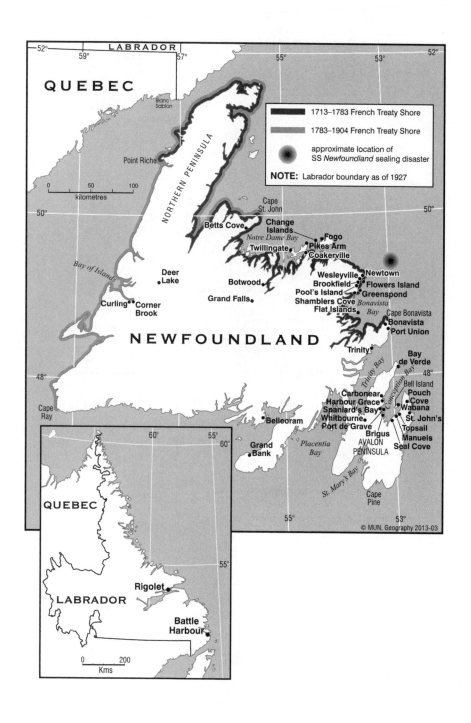

LABRADOR

QUEBEC

Blanc
Sablon

Point Riche

NORTHERN PENINSULA

Bay of Islands

Deer
Lake

Curling Corner
Brook

NEWFOUNDLAND

Cape
Ray

	1713–1783 French Treaty Shore
	1783–1904 French Treaty Shore
●	approximate location of SS *Newfoundland* sealing disaster

NOTE: Labrador boundary as of 1927

0   50   100
kilometres

Cape
St. John

Betts Cove

Change
Islands

Notre Dame Bay

Twillingate

Fogo

Pikes Arm

Coakerville

Wesleyville

Newtown

Brookfield

Flowers Island

Botwood

Pool's Island

Greenspond

Grand Falls

Shamblers Cove

Flat Islands

Bonavista
Bay

Cape Bonavista

Bonavista

Port Union

Trinity

Trinity Bay

Bay
de Verde

Bell Island

Carbonear

Conception Bay

Pouch
Cove

Harbour Grace

Spaniard's Bay

Wabana

Belleoram

Whitbourne

St. John's

Port de Grave

Topsail

Grand
Bank

Placentia
Bay

Brigus

AVALON
PENINSULA

Manuels

Seal Cove

St. Mary's Bay

Cape
Pine

© MUN, Geography 2013-03

QUEBEC

Rigolet

LABRADOR

Battle
Harbour

0   200
Kms

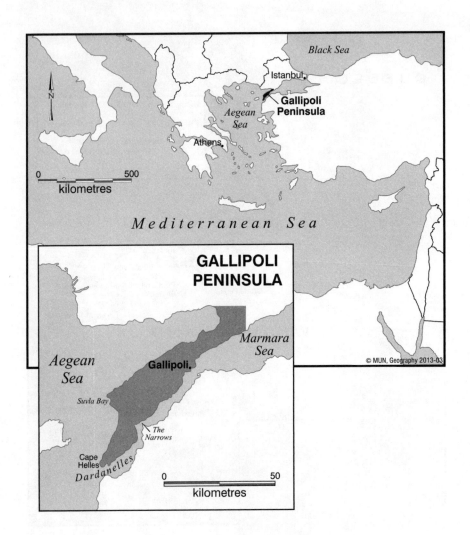

Strait of Dover

Poelcappelle
Langemarck · · Keiberg
Ypres · · Ledeghem
Bailleul

·Brussels

B E L G I U M

·Monchy-le-Preux
· Cambrai
Beaumont-Hamel · · Le Transloy
Gueudecourt

Somme River

G E R M A N Y

LUXEMBERG

Verdun·

Paris·

F R A N C E

© MUN, Geography 2013-03

EUROPE: 1914

20°W   0°   20°E   40°E   60°E

60°N

ATLANTIC OCEAN

NORWAY   SWEDEN   FINLAND

60°N

50°N

IRELAND   UNITED   NETHERLANDS   DENMARK

RUSSIA

KINGDOM   BELGIUM

50°N

LUXEMBOURG

FRANCE   GERMANY

SWITZERLAND   AUSTRIA-HUNGARY

PORTUGAL   SPAIN

ITALY   MONTENEGRO   ROMANIA

ALBANIA   SERBIA   BULGARIA   Black Sea

GREECE   T U R K E Y   40°N

Mediterranean Sea

0   1000
kms

ONE

The Nature
of Newfoundland
and Labrador

If human experience might be summarized as a constant struggle for resources that made possible the reproduction of families, kin groups, and communities over time, then the environmental setting of Newfoundland and Labrador has meant that its peoples have had a hard fight indeed. The interaction of millennia-spanning geological, oceanographic, and atmospheric processes resolved themselves into two conditions: the soils of the island and Labrador were scrubbed nearly bare by glaciers, and the weather systems that have prevailed until very recently in this part of the North Atlantic have brought fogs, rain, or snow that eroded soils and leached them of their thin nutrients. The region's sub-arctic, cold-ocean coastal ecology now consists of lands dominated by tundra, limited boreal woodlands, and scattered pockets of barely fertile ground. Compared to most of North America, very few land mammals are indigenous to Newfoundland, but the region's coastal waters and seas have (also until recently) teemed with life. The mixing of the Labrador Current and Gulf Stream off the Grand Banks produced a biologically rich environment, including zooplankton on which fed a variety of crustaceans and molluscs that in turn fed salmon, cod, and other fish that were prey for the larger predators: the seals, walruses, and whales that frequented the waters off Newfoundland or Labrador. Everywhere there were seabirds living off the wealth of the sea.[1]

The consequences of the marine largesse of the region for the development of human societies were profound. While the resources of the land were important, almost every society flourished on those provided from the sea. Until twenty years ago, the waters off the coast of Newfoundland were best known for their massive populations of fish, especially cod, which drew the attention of Europeans in the late fifteenth and sixteenth centuries. However, marine mammals were also crucial to the well-being of most of the human societies of the island and Labrador. Seals, the harp in particular, were vital from prehistoric times. The great herds of harp seals were abundant, coming close to shore with the pack ice that drifted southward through the Straits of Belle Isle into the Gulf of St. Lawrence and along the northeast coast of Newfoundland each spring. Seals provided meat, hides, and the all-important fat—a source of vital calories, nutrients, and oil for fuel. Whales and walruses additionally provided bone and ivory, especially to the peoples of Labrador. These marine mammals were such a rich source of oil that they attracted some of the most successful early commercial expansion by Europeans into Newfoundland and Labrador: the Basque whale hunting of the sixteenth century.

The Basques developed cod fisheries in association with their whale hunting, and in time other Europeans, most notably the French and the English, often in association with Irish fishers and merchants, began to migrate regularly to catch cod in the waters off the Newfoundland coast and on the banks off Newfoundland and Labrador. These migratory fisheries were complex, but those of the British came to dominate. Over the long term, this meant that the region would be washed by the tides of British imperial expansion. However, in the short term, the migratory fishery promoted small colonies that, while of limited success, proved vital to the development of settlement. By the Treaty of Utrecht with England in 1713, France had given up its claims to Newfoundland but had gained the right to fish and use shore facilities on the Newfoundland coast from Cape Bonavista to Point Riche during the fishing season. During the American Revolution, the British had excluded the French from these treaty rights. Although the French had regained the right to fish seasonally at Newfoundland by the Treaty of Versailles in 1783, the boundaries of what became known as the French Shore shifted from between Cape Bonavista and Cape St. John to between Point Riche and Cape Ray. These boundaries remained until France ceded its treaty rights in 1904, although Britain had again excluded the French during the wars with Napoleon.[2]

The wars of the late eighteenth century—the American Revolution, the French Revolution, and the subsequent Napoleonic Wars—which carried on into the first two decades of the nineteenth century, finally disrupted the migratory trade, fostered resident fisheries, and set the stage for longer-term colonial development. The North Atlantic became a theatre of naval warfare, disrupting the migratory trade. More important, Britain's episodic banishment of the French from the western North Atlantic fisheries in wartime, restrictions on American participation in imperial trade, and the capture of vital Iberian markets for Newfoundland cod produced high fish prices that were without precedent, encouraging many more Irish and English fishers to risk settling in Newfoundland in the period before 1815 when the Napoleonic Wars ended.[3]

The importance of the seal hunt can be understood in the context of just how big a risk such settlers took compared to those in most of the other regions of North America into which Europeans had ventured. Because Newfoundland's soil was shallow and infertile, and its growing season was short, wet, and cold, throughout the seventeenth and eighteenth centuries residents were limited in what they could produce. They had established kitchen gardens, with some farming of root crops, and raised some livestock, especially goats, but also some cattle, which could provide meagre amounts of milk and meat. During times of high fish prices, people working in the fishery could afford to satisfy their needs by purchasing imported goods. The fishery was embedded in the currents of transatlantic commerce, and the foodstuffs and capital goods required by residents were readily available as imports. In the seventeenth century, fishers were so well remunerated for their work that they could afford imported luxuries such as tobacco, wines, and brandy.[4]

However, as nice as a good pipe and warming draught might have been, there was a fundamental structural problem for future colonial economic development embedded in such a lifestyle. Kitchen herbs, potatoes and carrots, and the small amount of milk provided by free-ranging goats and a few cows were grossly insufficient to foster the industries based on the processing of agricultural goods that stimulated more diversified economic development in other parts of North America: no surplus cheese or butter would be produced for sale from local supplies of milk, no additional bread or biscuits for the marketplace would be baked from local flour, no beer made from local hops and grain, and no alcohol distilled from local grains. In good times, the fishery pumped out much of the wealth it generated into the import trades upon which it depended.

Newfoundland settlers remained dependent on the fishery—not a bad thing when fish prices were high, but not a good thing when they collapsed, as they did in the economic depression that followed the end of the Napoleonic Wars in 1815. Falling fish prices were a big problem for communities that depended on merchant credit to finance their fisheries and the import trades that supported them. The declining international value of salt cod after 1815 led most settlers to form household fisheries, using small boats and family labour, supplemented occasionally by servants. A few continued to hire larger crews to operate schooners. Settlers relied on fish merchants to import almost everything they needed to survive. British merchants supplied goods on credit against the settlers' fish and fish oil, and managed the risk of the fish trade by using credit practices that historians have called "truck." They had to give fishers credit at the beginning of the fishing season, long before they knew what quantity and quality of fish and fish oil they would get in return for export. More important, merchants did not know what the eventual prices for these products would be. Once they knew what markets would be like, merchants set the prices for fishers' purchase and produce to ensure their firms' success. Fearful of overextending credit, they advanced as little as possible.[5]

While fishing people resented "truck," it provided them with access to imported necessities for which there was no possibility of locally produced substitutes. By extending credit to fishing households, merchants avoided the risks and costs of participating directly in the production and marketing of saltfish. In addition to making saltfish, outport households engaged in wood-cutting, berry-picking, and what supplementary farming they might. Supplementary farming, meagre though it might have been, allowed fishing people to establish their own household production in the fishery, as garden produce filled shortfalls in provisioning caused by credit restrictions.[6] Fishers and their households did all the work associated with building, equipping, and maintaining fishing and household premises to satisfy their needs and limit the amount of credit they required from merchants in exchange for fish and fish oil. Fishing people exchanged labour, goods, and services with each other, but more on the basis of community values than the commercial ones that governed most of their relationships with the merchants or mercantile agents who dealt with their communities.[7]

The seal hunt was indispensable to settlers on Newfoundland's north-east coast in the wake of the post-1815 collapse in fish prices. Even in the days of the migratory trade, the fishing operations in Newfoundland required some year-round residents to protect the fish-processing facilities that were not used for part of the year and were needed to store the boats and equipment that would otherwise be costly to bring back to Britain. The people who stayed over during the winter turned to fur trapping, but the spring hunt for seals was more lucrative. Throughout the early nineteenth century, settlers' efforts to control access to coastal resources, including seals, disrupted the lives of the Algonkian-speaking Aboriginal people of Newfoundland: the Beothuk. Originally dependent on the same resources, the Beothuk were forced to retreat into the interior; the consequent loss of access to seals contributed to their demise as a people by 1829, a doleful reminder of the crucial role marine animals have played in the lives of the people of Newfoundland.[8]

The seal hunt became important during the Napoleonic era to settlers who had invested in schooners to fish areas that had been controlled by the French in northern Newfoundland but from which the British had excluded them in wartime. The return of the French with peace in 1815 meant that those fishers who managed to retain their schooners deployed them as dealers for merchants, carrying fishing families to the coast of Labrador. However, the Labrador fishing season was shorter, the voyage longer, and the conditions for drying fish poorer. The owners of schooners found that they could make extra money by deploying their vessels in an expanded spring seal hunt. The profits of the seal hunt, gained primarily from the sale of oil derived from seal fat—which had a value as fuel and industrial input similar to that of today's petrochemicals—offset low prices in the cod fishery. The seal hunt allowed outport communities to persist but did not provide enough income or stimulate enough activity to trigger much of an industrial transformation.[9]

The use of schooners reflected the fact that the seal hunt had been shifting from a shore-based to an offshore operation. The early seal fishery had been a small-scale land-based affair, in which people used nets to capture mature seals that wandered close to shore, but harp seals bred in large congregations on offshore ice. Hunters required larger schooners to go to the herds to kill the newly born white-coated pups whose hides and fat were of the highest value. Building and supplying schooners for the offshore hunt required capital resources beyond the ability of planters—settlers who owned all the shore facilities, small vessels, and fishing gear to operate independently of direct employment by merchants—and smaller outport merchants to supply; they turned to the larger merchant firms of Harbour Grace, Carbonear, and St. John's for credit. St. John's firms had the most resources, and they slowly consolidated their control over the industry by processing the seals brought by vessels from the many smaller outports of the northeast coast that did not deal with Harbour Grace and Carbonear firms. As a result, the limited economic linkages from the hunt increasingly benefited only the colony's capital.[10] The seal hunt continued to be vital to the economic survival of the outports, but the gulf between fishers, masters, and merchants, and the gap between the outports and St. John's, became even wider as the colony's largest merchant firms controlled most of the benefits of the hunt.

The seal hunt was dangerous work. Philip Tocque, a mid-nineteenth-century mercantile clerk, shopkeeper, and, later, Anglican cleric, claimed that the hunt was simply a bloody slaughter that coarsened the morals of the men who participated in it.[11] Tocque's observation appears to accord with more recent views of the seal hunt as cruel and inhumane. But his main complaint was that sealers had the temerity to hunt on the Sabbath. Toque's description of the dangers and hardships suffered by sealers suggests a more salient explanation of sealers' apparent callousness when it came to the messy work of killing seals. Sealers hazarded life and limb to provide for their families each spring by going to the ice, leaving the ships in work teams called watches, and hopping from ice floe to ice floe in search of seals to kill. Individual hunters routinely succumbed to frigid waters, but the crushing ice, the cold, and the unpredictable gales of snow and freezing rain that mark spring in the North Atlantic occasionally claimed entire ships and their crews. Many hunters died or suffered serious injuries because of the risks their captains took in sending watches out in bad weather, or because shipowners equipped their ships poorly. It was the understanding that few people cared about just how dangerous sealing was, rather than a contempt for seals, that hardened the hearts of many a sealer.[12]

Such contempt occasionally accentuated class distinctions between shipowners, shipmasters, and crews in the seal hunt. Yet distinctions were not as strong as the ties that bound outport people to their merchants. A paternalistic ideology, which drew on imagery of the household production that had come to characterize much of outport Newfoundland, affected the relationships between fishing people and fish merchants. People expected that merchants would behave ethically in extending credit, and they could take action against what they thought were unfair practices by merchants. Some fishers and sealers took legal action against their merchants, but others used extralegal means such as taking fish to competitors, threatening and assaulting merchants, or throwing agents or bailiffs into the harbour over disputes about court proceedings instigated by merchants. Such acts might force merchants into more paternalistic practices such as putting up with what might otherwise be considered insubordinate behaviour or allowing more favourable credit terms to their best clients to lessen the sting of exploitation, but they forestalled open conflict. Most fishers wanted to believe they were being treated fairly by merchants; they could be loyal to a merchant who lived up to their expectations, and might defend one threatened by forces from outside their community.[13]

Throughout the nineteenth century, merchants accepted paternalism because they needed reliable supplies of fish and oil in an economy almost completely dependent on two marine staple trades: fish and seal products. Trading by truck was, however, a gamble for fishers and merchants alike. Persistent poor market conditions in the fishery meant that merchants constantly risked overextending credit to fishing families by continuing to trade for their fish. Under such conditions, merchants might try to squeeze the people to whom they gave credit. Such was the case for merchants in Harbour Grace and Carbonear in the early 1830s. In 1832, local sealers were determined to get rid of truck, and agreed in

January to go sealing only on merchants' vessels for payment in cash. While Carbonear merchants quickly came to terms with the sealers, the Harbour Grace firm of Thomas Ridley did not. As a result, some of the sealers attacked a ship belonging to the firm. The authorities tried to intervene, but the sealers, led by people from Carbonear, continued to use violence to intimidate merchants and the planters commanding their vessels who would not pay wages by cash rather than in truck. Merchants yielded in March, and the seal hunt began.[14]

Although Newfoundland had long been settled by British people by the time of the sealers' action in 1832, it had only been officially recognized by imperial authorities as a colony since 1824. Before that year, the British had allowed naval officials to govern in Newfoundland. From 1824, Newfoundland had a civilian governor who considered the advice of an appointed council, but some colonists wanted further reform. The collective nature of service in the seal hunt provided sealers with a means of challenging merchants when they perceived that paternalism was compromised, and they demonstrated to colonial authorities that fishing people, when organized collectively, constituted a powerful political force. Throughout the mid-nineteenth century, political reformers—a constantly shifting alliance of Liberals, a nascent mercantile and professional bourgeoisie, and Roman Catholic and Methodist clergy—channelled this collective potential into the fight for colonial self-government against a supposed cabal comprising Church of England government officials appointed by London and the English merchants who exerted inordinate influence over their day-to-day decisions in Newfoundland. Local merchants and professionals desired more local control over government spending, patronage, and development policies; the clergy fought against efforts to have the Church of England effectively established in areas such as funding for schools and for patronage of members of their congregations; and both groups convinced fishing people that responsible colonial self-government would better control the power of merchants over their lives.

The long-term pattern of British migration to Newfoundland, which tapered off significantly in the post-1815 downturn in the fishery, fostered an ethnic and sectarian dimension in the struggle for self-government. Settlers tended to be of two types: West Country English Protestants of little means who were able to quickly establish their own household production in the fishery, and Irish Roman Catholics from Waterford and Wexford who sought waged employment as servants, and who clustered around areas such as the southern shore of the Avalon Peninsula or the seal hunting centres of Carbonear and Harbour Grace where such employment was available. Over time, Irish settlers established household production as well, and there were never absolute divisions between ethnic groups. But the overall pattern facilitated the Roman Catholic clerical appeal for sectarian support in the fight first for representative government, which succeeded in 1832 when Newfoundland gained an elected House of Assembly and an appointed Legislative Council, and then responsible government in 1855, by which the governor had to select his ministers, or Executive Council, from parties that enjoyed the confidence of a majority of the elected house. An alliance of Roman Catholic and Methodist interests was essential to the success of the fight for responsible government, a condition that suggests the difficulty of interpreting Newfoundland politics along a simple Roman Catholic and Protestant divide.[15]

Fishing people hoped that colonial self-government would bring about policies that were more responsive to their needs. In the fishery, it quickly became clear that local colonial governments had little appetite for developing regulations that reflected fishers' needs; such governments tended to reflect the views of dominant commercial interests—merchants who felt that there should be little regulation of their trade. Throughout the second half of the nineteenth century, for example, fishers and sealers periodically campaigned for conservation regulations for the fishery and seal hunt, but the colonial government bowed to mercantile desires to have few limits placed on either activity.[16]

Such inaction was a problem for the seal hunt, which had become marked by a cyclical pattern of resource depletion and overinvestment in capacity. By the 1860s, the depletion of readily accessible seal herds by sailing vessels meant that merchants had begun to invest in larger, more powerful steamers that could penetrate deeper into the ice in the quest for seals. As steam vessels roamed further, they dropped sealers onto the ice to kill and skin seals, piling the pelts and blubber for later retrieval by their ships in a practice known as panning. Weather and ice conditions meant that many panned seals were never picked up. The wastage sparked a public debate about the need for conservation in the exploitation of the marine environment, which extended into worries that the steamers sailed too early and pointlessly killed too many immature and breeding-age seals. The much higher overhead costs of the steamers meant that shipowners objected to any restraint on the hunt. The Newfoundland government for its part made few efforts to control the hunt. The legislature had passed laws in the 1870s that prohibited steamers from leaving for the ice before 10 March, but the powerful vessel owners ignored the ban. In 1887, the government passed laws considering unattended panned seals to be abandoned, and permitted each steamer only one trip to the ice to participate in the hunt. But mercantile pressure led to periodic relaxation of the regulations through the late 1890s.[17]

The advent of the steamers began to change the relationship between captains and crews in the seal hunt. Paternalism, reinforced by the shared dangers and close quarters of ships working among the ice floes of the treacherous North Atlantic in early spring, bound together the masters of fishing schooners and their crews. The importance of the household organization of the fishery meant that the authority of skippers on larger vessels became an almost organic extension of the familial patriarchy of households themselves. In smaller vessels, skippers required the consensus of their crewmates. In larger vessels, especially those of the seal hunt, captains were more autocratic. They took all the credit for successful hunts as if they had personally killed the seals. Yet, while these captains disciplined their crews, they worked hard to earn the personal loyalty of their men by dispensing favours and patronage, occasionally along family lines, and demonstrating courage and skill in the hunt.[18] A case in point was one of the most prominent sealing captains of the late nineteenth and early twentieth centuries: Abram Kean.

Born in 1855 at Flowers Island, Bonavista Bay, Kean's father, Joseph, and uncle William decided to pursue the seal hunt in partnership; Joseph hunted from the land while William took a ship to the ice. They built their first vessel, a schooner, and used it in the Labrador fishery as well. Kean joined his uncle in the fishery at the age of thirteen, and, ten years later, with a family of his own, became the master of a fishing schooner. He hunted seals every spring, advancing through the ranks to become captain of the Kean family's schooner in the hunt. Kean jumped into electoral politics, being recruited by the conservative Reform Party in 1885. Kean's political connections helped him gain command of his first sealing steamer in 1889, and from that point he built a career as the most successful sealing captain of his day. Constantly involved in politics, Kean's first love was nevertheless the command of a vessel; he continued to captain vessels in the fishery, as well as coastal and mail steamers, and to take part in the seal hunt. Kean's best years were those spent commanding steamers for the firm of Bowring Brothers (or Bowring as it was locally known), beginning in 1898. This firm began in 1816, when the watch- and clockmaker Benjamin Bowring, recently relocated from Exeter, England, to St. John's, established a shop. Finding a limited demand for his trade, Bowring and his family entered the mercantile trade. Bowring ships became important in the seal oil and cod oil trades by the early 1830s and, by the mid-1840s, had begun to operate vessels directly in the hunting of seals. The family businesses organized under the aegis of Benjamin's son Charles Tricks Bowring as C.T. Bowring and Company of Liverpool, England. By 1890, Charles Tricks's nephew Edgar Bowring had become the director of Bowring in St. John's, and Edgar's brother became the chairman of the Liverpool parent company.

Kean began to work for Bowring in 1898 at the invitation of Edgar Bowring, which was fortunate for the sealing captain. Edgar Bowring was a canny businessman who had steered Bowring safely through the turbulent economic waters of the Newfoundland Bank Crash of 1894. Politically influential, Bowring was also well known for his philanthropy and for his loyalty to those such as Kean who served him well. There is no doubt that Kean's association with Bowring was lucrative for the firm. As the firm acquired steamers, it operated them as the Red Cross Line, technically under C.T. Bowring and Company, carrying passengers and freight among St. John's, New York, and Halifax, and contracting vessels for the government coastal steamer service. Kean's uncanny ability to locate seals and return to port with record catches meant that sealers clamoured to get a berth on his ships. Under Kean's tutelage, his sons Joseph, Nathan, and Westbury learned the ways of the seal hunt, rising from common hand to second hand (the first mate of a sealing vessel) and eventually becoming sealing captains in their own right.[19]

In general, declining earnings in the fishery meant that most merchants began to withdraw capital from the shipping industry through the 1880s. A small number of St. John's and Conception Bay merchants, though, increased their investments—particularly in steam-driven vessels that were built outside the colony—and extended control over a greater portion of the colony's shipping fleet. Steamers, in the short term, had proven much more productive in the seal hunt, but their higher overhead costs meant that few firms could afford them. Further, their very efficiency exacerbated the long-term problem of diminishing returns due to their negative impact on seal herds. As well, owners were hard pressed to find profitable uses for steamers once the sealing season ended.

Many shipowners sought additional investment opportunities ashore, although this could be a complicated process. The Harvey Companies, for example, had begun as the late-eighteenth-century Bermuda Trading Company, which had branches in the West Indies, Quebec, New York, and Baltimore as well as St. John's. The St. John's branch evolved into Harvey and Company, and branched out from the fish trade into landward manufacturing in St. John's. One of the Harveys, Alexander J., established A. Harvey and Company Limited in 1865 to manufacture hard bread, a thick, oven-dried ship's biscuit still prized in Newfoundland kitchens to this day. This company expanded into what would have been a major market for its product: shipping. As in the case of Bowring, A. Harvey and Company deployed the steamers it used in shipping in the spring seal hunt.[20]

The concentration of steamers used at the hunt at St. John's and the practice of panning made the hunt more difficult. By the late nineteenth century, many outport men had to make their way to the capital to get a berth on a sealing vessel.[21] At the ice, sealing skippers often sent watches over the side to kill and pan seals, but that did not mean they would return to pick up the men. Captains might well expect their men to walk to the vessels, towing seals behind them. However, if bad weather or ice conditions changed for the worse, there was a danger that sealers might be stranded. Such was the case in 1898, when Captain George Barbour of the SS *Greenland* lost forty-eight men in a blizzard. The "*Greenland* Disaster" provoked public outrage about the dangers of the hunt, and about Abram Kean, when rumours began to fly that one of his crews had stolen pelts panned by the men of the *Greenland*, forcing them to stay at the ice longer and become stranded in the storm. Despite such disasters, men continued to go to the ice, often introducing their younger relatives to it.[22]

Overall, people put up with the risks of the seal hunt because there were few other options to supplement work in the fishery except permanent emigration or seasonal out-migration. Part of the popular support for colonial self-government had been an endorsement of colonial reformers' claim that, if given the reins of power in Newfoundland, they could better manage the colony's resources, foster industrial diversification, and make the place much more independent of the need for assistance from the Empire. Once in power, reformers, who increasingly

became known as Liberals, repeatedly tried to foster landward development through agriculture, mining, and forestry, pinning their hopes on
a railway across the island as a means of opening up interior resources.
The debate about development had influenced the heated campaign
about Newfoundland's possible entry into Confederation in 1869,
with the anti-Confederate side winning, partially by maintaining that
Canadians should not be allowed to gain control over Newfoundland's
untapped resources. The quest for economic development was an
important issue in blurring partisan politics. Nineteenth-century parties
were inchoate at the best of times. There was a political grouping of
Liberals, who were pro-development, and another group that might
best be thought of as pro-mercantile Tories, primarily interested in
ensuring that the colonial government did not have to tax the fish
trade more to pay for diversification. However, the Liberal Ambrose
Shea and the Conservative Frederick Carter had come together in
support of Confederation, hoping that union with Canada would spur
railway and economic development, while the much more conservative
C.F. Bennett led the anti-Confederates. Carter's fellow Conservative,
William V. Whiteway, was even more pro-railway, hoping that a line
across Newfoundland would consolidate St. John's control over those
portions of the west coast for which the French had treaty rights.
Whiteway became the Conservatives' leader, and prime minister of
Newfoundland, in 1878, facing mercantile opposition to the cost of his
railway policies. Whiteway's opponents coalesced into the New Party
in the early 1880s, while the prime minister made common cause with
remaining Liberal interests, becoming, in effect, the Liberal leader.

The development of universal adult male franchise in 1893 meant
that few politicians, whether Liberal or Tory in leaning, could ignore
working men's gendered understanding of their entitlements, as members
of the Empire, to good work and respectable incomes so that they could
provide properly for their families as the loyal heads of British households.[23] The Conservatives, in the guise of Sir Robert Thorburn's Reform

Party, had come to power in 1885, criticizing the expense of railway development and the lack of economic diversification arising from it. Nevertheless, popular demands for more employment drew Thorburn back to railway development, and Whiteway won re-election in 1889 by campaigning for even more. The Nova Scotia–born A.B. Morine, who had come to St. John's in 1883 to take up the editorship of the *Evening Mercury*, and who was mistrusted locally for his pro-Confederation views, was a strong influence on Whiteway. Morine alienated younger Liberals, most notably Robert Bond. Bond, a lawyer and developer, had served as Whiteway's colonial secretary, and had soured in his views of Canada as a result of the country's role in stymying a reciprocity deal he had negotiated on behalf of Newfoundland with the United States. A looming financial crisis in the colony, which reached a crisis point in the Bank Crash of 1894, led Bond to support Prime Minister Whiteway in investigating Confederation as a possible solution. The political instability that followed led to Whiteway's defeat in 1897, despite his trying to buy votes by awarding additional contracts for branch-line construction to Robert G. Reid's Canadian syndicate, which had received a new railway contract from the government. Encouraging expensive railway development did not lessen significantly the problems related to the overcapitalization of the fishery and consequent overextension of credit, and aggravated by higher tariffs to pay for assistance promised to the Reid syndicate. The opposition formed a government under the leadership of J.S. Winter, with A.B. Morine as the minister of finance. Faced with massive financial obligations, yet determined to proceed with railway development, Morine negotiated a deal that would hand over to the Reids much of the colony's new economic infrastructure outside the fishery in exchange for control of the railway.

Pro-railway Liberals, most notably E.P. Morris, liked the deal, which became known as the Reid Railway Contract of 1898, but Robert Bond despised it. He fought the 1900 election by campaigning against government collusion with big interests and for the defence of the common people against the dissipation of their national resources. Bond won, but continued support for the Reids by Liberals led by Morris limited the extent to which Bond could modify the agreement with the railway family, which remained one of the most powerful industrial interests in the colony. In the short term, railway building and France's surrender of its treaty rights to the shores of the west coast as part of the great *Entente Cordiale* with Britain in 1904 intensified a colonial "nationalism." At heart British and imperial, this nationalism emphasized Newfoundland's history as a crucible that tested and alloyed the rugged qualities of self-sufficiency born of "the sturdy and manly qualities of its fishermen and sealers."[24]

The building of the railway created some extra employment and the industrial diversification necessary for its operation. Much of the latter developed in St. John's, which, despite being the centre of manufacturing for the colony, was, with surrounding communities, home to only 39,995 people, or about 18 percent of the 220,984 people who lived in Newfoundland and Labrador in 1901.[25] The railway had a limited impact on the vast majority of the colony's people, who depended on the economies of coastal communities; fishing people were in constant need of extra sources of income. Some young men were able to find supplementary earnings through enlistment in the Royal Naval Reserve. As part of Britain's overall withdrawal of military forces from most of North America, the last British troops stationed in Newfoundland had shipped out in 1870, but no permanent colonial military force replaced them. As a mostly maritime colony of coastal communities dependent on seafaring trades and the exploitation of marine resources, and geographically separated from borders with any foreign power, Newfoundland had relied on the protection of the Royal Navy. Under the British Colonial Naval Defence Act of 1865, colonies could develop their own naval forces, which the imperial government incorporated into the Royal Naval Reserve.

Newfoundland, however, required more British naval attention than most of the colonies because of the existence of the French Shore. Britain patrolled the waters of the island to observe the French and ensure that there were no international incidents caused by Newfoundlanders. By the late nineteenth century, the cost of imperial administration, a desire by at least the colony's elite to contribute something in return, and the Navy's appreciation for cheap colonial recruits prompted interest in establishing a Royal Naval Reserve unit in Newfoundland. At the Colonial Conference in London in 1902, the governments of Newfoundland and Britain agreed to share the cost of a six-hundred-man reserve. Young outport men could join the reserve for a five-year stint, receiving pay in exchange for training and standing ready for service as general seamen when finished. The pay equalled that which a young man might earn for a season in the seal hunt, and the Reserve organized service so that it complemented work in the fishery.[26]

The desirability of naval service was one indicator that economic diversification was not alleviating rural dependence on the fishery and seal hunt. The tariffs used to raise money for railway development did protect some local manufacturing in consumer goods such as bakeries, confections, shoes, and tobacco products. The Bond government further encouraged secondary manufacturing through subsidies, premiums, drawbacks, and tax exemptions. The government reasoned that if Newfoundlanders spent most of their money on imported goods, capital would continue to drain away from the colony, while the purchase of local goods would not only retain capital but would also generate much needed employment outside the fishery. The whole strategy was premised on the success of what had become Newfoundland's national policy: the railway would open up interior resources, such resources would prompt industrial development and the growth of a consumer market, and eventually domestic manufacturing would not require protection. There were some successes, most notably in the development of iron-ore mining on Bell Island in the late 1890s, but this was not directly related to the railway. The railway did foster more sawmilling and, by 1909, pulp and paper development centred on Alfred and Harold Harmsworth's (later

Lords Northcliffe and Rothermere) massive pulp and paper complex at Grand Falls. Eventually, the Grand Falls development would generate significant employment, but in the short term the policy of fostering economic diversification through railway expansion, interior development, and protected manufacturing was proving more successful at creating public debt and higher costs of living for fishing people than at creating more work. The exception was in St. John's, where working people found employment in protected industries.[27]

Outport people continued to need employment in the seal hunt, but the tension between the hunt's increased capital requirements and the greater difficulty of finding enough seals to kill was changing the experience. Vessel owners tried to offset declining rates of return with more exploitative share payments and through a variety of means such as levying sealers with accommodation fees, billing them for their equipment, and charging them for coal to fuel the vessels and for cleaning the vessels after the hunt. Time spent working together and living under harsh and dangerous conditions encouraged sealers to see that they had much in common, leading to collective actions such as a brief strike in 1902. In that year, 211 sealers of the SS *Ranger*, a wooden-hulled steamer, left their vessel in St. John's to protest their wages, a move that sparked a wider strike by sealers from other vessels. On 8 March 1902, the international price for seal oil dropped so low that the sealers could not see how going to the ice would be worth all the extra fees and charges. Merchants were offering only $2.40 for every 112 pounds of seal fat, while the strikers wanted between $4.00 and $5.00. The men of each ship agreed to a compromise price of $3.25 and chose a delegate from each vessel, assisted by A.B. Morine, to meet with the owners, but the merchant firms—Baine Johnston, Job's, and Bowring—would commit only to looking into the matter. By 10 March, it was clear the owners would make no concessions. Tensions rose as some city residents began to support the strikers, while some sealers attempted to break ranks and go back to work. Morine eventually appealed to the prime minister for assistance; Bond brokered a settlement.[28]

Such industrial conflict did not indicate that sealers were becoming working-class radicals. Sealing remained something that young men who were part of families working in fishing households resorted to for a few weeks out of the year, and the share system militated against strong solidarity. Nevertheless, while shares continued to dominate the payment of wages, employment levels dropped. Working conditions became more industrial, but they were experienced by fewer people for a month or so once a year as overall employment in sealing declined. Crews continued to defer to their captains due to the deadly combination of masculinity and paternalism in the industry. Family structures remained very important as fathers often took their sons with them to the hunt, and young men went with their older brothers or uncles.

The persistence of payment by shares and the importance of earnings from the hunt meant that sealers admired skippers' reputation as "real seal killers," or as men who could find the "main patch" of the seal herds, thereby assuring a successful hunt for all.[29] Many sealers went to the ice with sealing captains who came from their own or nearby communities, and they were further tied to each other by a rich, church-centred spiritual life. About three hundred men from Wesleyville, an important centre of the seal hunt on the north side of Bonavista Bay, regularly went to the seal hunt each year in the early twentieth century. Methodism dominated the area. "We sang 'Eternal Father strong to save ... O hear us when we cry to Thee for those in peril on the sea,'" remembered one of the town's best-known ministers. "When the sealers returned, the church was filled again every Sunday night until our schooners left for the Labrador fishery, in late May or early June."[30] For Methodists at least, disaster on the ice may have been a personal trial that opened the road to salvation rather than a problem of industrial organization. Their spirituality included a profound sense of tragedy that was evident every day in the harsh maritime environment, tight-fisted merchants, and remote government. The world was hard, but the measure of true Methodists was the "varying degrees of humility and nobility" with which they bore it.[31]

Methodists worked mostly alongside Anglicans and Roman Catholics in the seal hunt, the latter denominations being by far the earliest and most important of the European religions to arrive in Newfoundland. Members of the Church of England tended to be English West Country fishers who dominated the settlement of Newfoundland's northeast coast, while the Irish of Waterford and Wexford brought their Roman Catholicism to the southern shore of the Avalon Peninsula, St. Mary's Bay, and Placentia Bay on the south coast. Methodism gained converts from the Church of England and the Roman Catholic Church, but it threatened the former more. The centres of Irish settlement on the Avalon Peninsula stood fast in their Roman Catholicism. The major population centres such as St. John's and the larger towns of Conception Bay had mixed religious composition, but these communities experienced the majority of deaths from the great sealing disasters of the late nineteenth and early twentieth century. The Roman Catholics and Anglicans who went to the ice each spring may not have embraced the fatalism of their Methodist counterparts in the seal hunt.[32]

The influences of paternalism and religion could provide a context in which fishers and sealers might hope to improve their working and living conditions. Many turned to William Ford Coaker and his Fishermen's Protective Union (FPU). The FPU originated in the contraction of merchant credit that followed the Bank Crash of 1894. Fishers who did not have credit had to work on shares for those who did, especially those who owned cod traps and the larger skiffs required to operate them. Successful trap owners, called trap skippers, were also those who could afford motors for their boats, allowing them to go further to set their traps. Most skippers hired relatives; community and family considerations rather than the market governed skippers' relationships with servants, and skippers and their crews depended on merchants' credit. Merchants recognized that cod traps, and later the motor boats used to tend them, served as adequate collateral that could be seized if clients defaulted on their debts. While some trap skippers prospered enough to trade as merchants, community identification continued to tie most skippers to their crews, particularly as it became clear that it was the merchants of Water Street who cut credit.

Over the course of the nineteenth century, Water Street, the main thoroughfare that snaked along the northern edge of the St. John's waterfront, had become the home of the main commercial firms involved in Newfoundland's maritime industries, many of which had consolidated their control over the seal hunt. Following the Great Fire of 1892, which had destroyed much of the city, these firms had built even more imposing edifices from which to conduct business and branch out into retail trade and financial services. Any outport people who came to St. John's, whether involved in the fishery or the seal hunt, were apt to associate the street with the firms that controlled so much of their economic lives. Water Street was an embodiment of mercantile exploitation; trap skippers, by contrast, were immediate and familiar, and were important paternalistic leaders in their own right.[33]

The fishery continued to be the economic mainstay of the island, making the restriction of credit all the more troubling. The fishers on Newfoundland's south coast worked in a highly competitive credit environment because of their proximity to merchants from Nova Scotia, the United States, and the French islands of St. Pierre and Miquelon, which also exploited those waters.[34] Discontent, therefore, was more acute on the northeast and west coasts, where credit restriction had eroded paternalistic truck practices. The slump during the 1907–1908 exporting season was particularly bad because of an oversupply of fish in the market, and merchants cut in half the price they had offered for fish the year before, threatening even trap owners. Trap skippers responded by taking a leading role in the formation of the FPU. By 1908, the FPU in turn mobilized the many more fishers who were brought together in the Labrador fishery and the seal hunt. The FPU's success among trap skippers, Labrador fishers, and sealers provided it with a strong base in communities such as Port de Grave, Bay de Verde, Trinity, Bonavista, Fogo, Twillingate, and in the District of St. Barbe on the west coast and Northern Peninsula.[35]

From the beginning, William Coaker's character was that of another patriarch competing for the fraternal loyalties of fishers and sealers. Born in St. John's in 1871, Coaker had worked as a fish handler on the waterfront, and had been involved in organizing boy workers on the docks for better pay when he was thirteen. Coaker was more a moderate Protestant than a political radical; at heart he believed in the right of every individual to participate equally in the pursuit of wealth. Hard work, honesty, a commitment to fair play, and a sense of duty, he believed, should be enough to ensure personal success. Coaker moved to Notre Dame Bay in 1887, where he took up farming on a small island he called, immodestly, Coakerville, and later tried to keep a small shop at a nearby community, Pike's Arm, but his ventures there failed during the Bank Crash. Having previously voiced support for Robert Bond in the Twillingate district, Coaker was given government work as a telegrapher, but he subsequently lost government employment when Whiteway's Liberals met defeat in 1897. In 1901, Coaker married Jessie Crosbie Cook of St. John's at Fogo, and they moved to Coakerville. The marriage was an unhappy one, and Coaker appears to have coped by turning to self-education, spiritualism, and religion for emotional satisfaction.[36]

Although Coaker regained a government appointment as a telegrapher in 1900 with the election of the Liberals under Bond, who had succeeded Whiteway as leader, he pondered the hardships of his neighbouring fishers and their families, identifying with them and believing they suffered from exploitation by a mercantile elite in St. John's. A devout Anglican, Coaker believed in a basic ideal: that all people should be equal in dignity before God. In Newfoundland, however, mercantile exploitation reduced hard-working and God-fearing fishing people to a state of undignified poverty.

In 1903, Coaker established a small newspaper that focused on the fisheries. His editorials argued that, given a fair chance, fishers should have been able to earn good livings, but the power of merchants and their government lackeys meant that such a fair chance never came.

Between 1903 and 1908, Coaker conceived of an organization of fishers that would counteract the influence of big merchants and indifferent governments in St. John's: the FPU.

The FPU's populist philosophy suggested that fishers should be independent, each having the right to accumulate the wealth from his labour. Embodied in the motto of the FPU, "To each his own," the ethic of Coaker's FPU was directed at merchants' use of credit to exploit the hard work of fishers. The FPU leader had little interest in socialism; his primary interest was in ensuring that merchants gave fishers a fair deal in trading for their fish and other related products such as cod liver oil. Coaker also believed in an imperialist and masculine sense of entitlement on the part of the men who joined the FPU. Fishers, and later the loggers and other outport workers organized by the FPU, had a right to fair treatment, he believed, because they were British men. In 1911, for example, Coaker attacked a Norwegian shipping firm, Park and Storm, for refusing to pay the wages of a worker from Change Islands who had been injured while loading one of its ships at Botwood. Coaker demanded that Newfoundlanders in Botwood refuse to work with "the Norwegian." "The men who endure Storm's insults to our countrymen," Coaker declared, "are not true sons of Newfoundland. They are unworthy of being called men, and are only fit to rank with Chinamen. Show Storm that you are Britons, and you never will be slaves."[37]

In 1909, the FPU held a founding convention; its constitution allowed any fisher, farmer, logger, or manual labourer to join a local in their community. Each local would then elect representatives to district councils that, in turn, would elect representatives to a supreme, governing council. The annual conventions of the FPU elected its president, with Coaker being acclaimed in the position at the first convention. In the same year, Coaker established an FPU newspaper, which went under various names but became known as the *Fishermen's Advocate*, to voice fishers' concerns, offer solutions, and politically educate their neighbours.[38] Along the northeast coast, Coaker became a charismatic hero.

In Wesleyville, for example, where the FPU organized a local council in 1910, and where Coaker attended a public meeting in 1911, people came together regularly to sing:

> We are coming Mr. Coaker from the East, West, North and South,
> You have called and we're coming to put our foes to rout;
> By Merchants and Governments too long we've been misruled,
> We're determined now in future that no longer we'll be fooled,
> We'll be brothers all and freemen, and we'll rectify each wrong.
> We are coming Mr. Coaker and we're forty thousand strong.[39]

The FPU spent much of its energy on giving fishers more control over the conditions under which they sold fish. The union wanted to see more government involvement in an impartial inspection and grading of fish quality, rather than leaving it in the hands of merchant-employed cullers. The FPU further criticized "tal qual" (the practice by which firms purchased all fish at one price, without regard for its quality) as a disincentive to the production of good quality fish. Most importantly, the FPU wanted fishers to control the marketing of fish.

Coaker wanted to organize fishers' participation in the market on a cooperative basis. He established the FPU's own mercantile enterprise in St. John's: the Union Trading Company (UTC). By using bulk buying, the UTC would be able to supply goods at prices below those offered by merchants and thus break their prices. The allegiance of the membership of the FPU to the UTC was impressive; by 1919, it was a successful mercantile venture. But while the UTC successfully competed with merchants, it did not precipitate reform of the fishery. The FPU's other business enterprises, the Union Electric Company and a shipyard, show the extent to which the union mobilized fishing people's dues to build a business empire. All of these enterprises were part of the FPU's town, Port Union, founded between 1916 and 1918.[40]

The FPU concentrated on improving fish marketing, but it also fought to improve the general conditions of outport Newfoundland, including

work in the seal hunt. Through the Union Party, Coaker made legislative reform of the hunt as well as of the fishery generally a centrepiece of
the FPU's presence in politics. Key to the Union Party's political success
were divisions within Bond's Liberal Party. The ambitious E.P. Morris left
the government in 1907 and founded the People's Party in 1908. Even
before he became prime minister, Bond had seemed more comfortable
in dealing with the high matters of state, such as when he negotiated a
convention exchanging American access to bait fish for the Newfoundland
fishing industry's access to the American market in 1889. The agreement—known as the Bond–Blaine Convention, after Robert Bond and his
opposing negotiator, James G. Blaine, the American secretary of state—
fell under Canadian criticism and a British veto in 1891. Bond faced
American opposition to a subsequent reciprocity agreement he negotiated
in 1902 with Secretary of State John Milton Hay. However, his pressure
on the British government to end French treaty rights to the French Shore
coincided with France's desire to seek a wider imperial entente with Britain
as both worried about German expansion. In 1904, as part of the *Entente
Cordiale* between Britain and France, the latter gave up its rights, except
to fish in Newfoundland waters during the summer. Under Bond's direction, Newfoundland's efforts to influence imperial policies were important
factors in the British government's decision in 1907 to concede to Canada
and the other self-governing colonies—some of which it had already
deemed to be dominions—the right to negotiate commercial matters with
foreign states on their own. While Newfoundland became known as a
dominion in that year, the meaning of this status was limited to international commercial matters and was in flux as it evolved against British
Foreign Office control over "matters of high policy."[41]

Bond was at home in the state rooms of the Empire and the United
States, but Morris, a man who was comfortable rubbing shoulders with
his working-class constituents, portrayed Bond as aloof and arrogant, a
patrician who had little sympathy with the sealers during their strike in
1902. While Morris claimed to be interested in fisheries development, it

was clear that his real interest lay in promoting the Reid enterprises and St. John's business interests generally. The People's Party's development policies were not all that different from the Liberals', except in Morris's support for the Reids.

Merchants, through the efforts of William G. Gosling, had recently organized in the Newfoundland Board of Trade to develop markets, regulate fish quality, support fisheries research, and lobby government on fisheries policy. Gosling's efforts had the sympathy of E.P. Morris; the People's Party platform called for better fish marketing and diversification. Leading merchants supported the Board's efforts, but they only wanted a voluntary inspection for saltfish, and preferred to cite fishers' supposed illiteracy and conservatism as the main reasons for the persistence of poor quality. The FPU, by contrast, wanted government control of a mandatory inspection process that would be free of mercantile influence.

Initially, Morris's image as the working man's friend appealed to Coaker, as did the People's Party's pro-development policies. Morris seemed to be the political leader most likely to take on the merchants of Water Street, especially as they tended to frown on government support for railway development. During the general election of 1908, Morris had angled for the support of fishing people and the FPU by promising fisheries reform and an old-age pension scheme. However, Morris opted to support merchants' preference for voluntary improvements over regulated change in the fishing industry.[42] The 1908 election resulted in a deadlock between Bond and Morris; a second election in 1909 provided Morris with a convincing victory. Coaker concluded that none of the St. John's-based parties were likely to represent the interests of fishing people adequately. The People's Party represented city capitalists, not fishing people, sealers, and loggers. And the Liberals' old association with the encouragement of manufacturing through tariff protection meant that they were largely a party of the city, not of the outports.

The FPU was a regional movement of the northeast coast. The way to gain influence over government policy, Coaker thought, lay in a balance-of-power strategy: the FPU should form a political wing to ally with whichever party was willing to promote the rights of fishing people, as articulated in the political platform of the FPU. The Union Party had an excellent chance of controlling the fourteen seats in the House of Assembly for the northeast coast. In a House of thirty-six seats, such control was critical in the balance of power but insufficient to allow one party to form a government. The full political program of the FPU shook the foundations of party politics in Newfoundland. It demanded that government provide free and compulsory education in non-denominational schools. In the outports, night schools should be made available to people who could not attend during the day because of their work. Local fishing people should elect individuals from their own communities to run school boards, but these boards should not be controlled by appointees of the church establishment in St. John's. Sectarian politics should also be removed from the composition of the boards that oversaw the provision of able-bodied relief through employment in the construction of roads. People in the outports should elect the boards rather than rely on the patronage of St. John's politicians. Further, the FPU advocated conflict-of-interest legislation and the use of referenda, both to ensure that the government in St. John's remained responsive to the people and to limit its corrupt practices. Finally, it required government to bring in universal old-age pensions and develop a program of rural hospital construction.

Such a platform clearly threatened the autonomy and power of merchants and industrialists in the economy. The union wanted tariffs on imports adjusted so that outport people could have access to cheaper imported goods, a direct threat to the factory owners and workers of St. John's. It wanted the government to legislate better working conditions and wages in the seal hunt and logging and, most threatening of all, it desired that the state take control of the marketing of saltfish to end the ruinous, competitive marketing habits of the colony's major exporting firms. The FPU demanded that the government guarantee the quality of its fish products to the foreign consumers by abolishing tal qual, by legislating a standardized fish cull (which would sort fish by grade and quality), and by appointing government cullers and inspectors. Further, the union insisted, Newfoundland must appoint overseas trade commissioners to take more direct responsibility for the promotion of Newfoundland products in foreign markets, rather than relying on British officials or agents of private companies to do so. While concentrating on fish marketing, the FPU was also interested in the conservation of fish stocks, and wanted the government to reorganize, and provide more financial support for, a professional fisheries department.

Having parted ways with Morris, Coaker approached Sir Robert Bond about the possibility of a Liberal–FPU political alliance. In 1911, Coaker proposed that any FPU candidates elected in the next general election would support a government led by Bond as long as it agreed to fisheries reform. Bond refused, arguing that he could not allow a specific interest group to "coerce" legislation from the Assembly, ignoring the fact that governments had acted on behalf of railway owners, manufacturers, merchants, and bishops in the past. Coaker organized a mass demonstration by sealers in St. John's in March 1912, but neither Bond nor Morris would bargain with the FPU. Morris, feeling cocky because of the better condition of the economy, openly attacked Coaker, as did Morris's allies in the Roman Catholic press. Coaker turned to organizing fishers in crucial Liberal districts such as Twillingate, which provided Bond's own seat, Bonavista, Trinity, and Fogo. Having lost a seat in a by-election the previous year, the Liberals' political fortunes looked bad indeed. Under pressure from his northeast-coast supporters in the House, Bond accepted an alliance with the FPU.

Although Bond had supported landward development, he feared the growing public debt and despised Morris's use of railway branch-line contracts to buy votes. He insisted that the Liberals could only enter the next election on a platform of government retrenchment. The Liberal-Union alliance, as it became known, survived only because Bond promised to attempt some of the reforms demanded by the FPU's own platform, and because of the efforts of more cooperative leading Liberals such as James M. Kent and W.F. Lloyd. At first glance, the result of the alliance in the 1913 general election was unimpressive. The Liberal-Unionists managed to gain only fifteen of the House's thirty-six seats, allowing Morris to hold on to power. The FPU's Union Party, however, had fielded nine candidates. Eight of these won their electoral battles, and the ninth, Nathan Barrett, lost by only nine votes to People's Party candidate John Chalker Crosbie (grandfather of the recent lieutenant governor of Newfoundland and Labrador, John Carnell Crosbie) in the district of Bay de Verde. The six Liberals elected in northeast-coast districts, including Bond, succeeded because the FPU had not run candidates against them. Thus, while the Liberals depended on the Union Party for electoral support, the Union Party depended on the Liberals for legislative experience and support in St. John's.

Bond could not accept his political dependence on a party of fishers, and so resigned his seat and retreated to his estate at Whitbourne to launch bitter attacks against the FPU. The leadership of the alliance was assumed by Kent, while Morris's political fortunes began to change for the worse. His St. John's constituents consisted largely of the Reid enterprises and all those workers who depended on the railway and its related enterprises for their livelihoods. Morris's use of branch-line construction to establish a broad base of support outside the city had begun to alienate the merchants of Water Street, who feared mounting public debt and higher taxes. Soon after the election in 1913, Morris again courted the FPU by promising fisheries reform. Morris agreed to a joint Union Party–Board of Trade call for a royal commission to investigate conditions in the fishery, but faced stiff opposition within the Legislative Council, where the influence of the St. John's merchants remained strongest. Morris refused to implement the fisheries commission's call for government regulation of quality standards, culling, and inspection. In consequence, the prime minister had little hope of support from the Union Party.[43]

By 1914, Newfoundland politics had sharply divided between town and country. Such divisions reflected the uneven and fragmented nature of the colony's economic development. Throughout rural Newfoundland, people remained dependent on the fishery, with the seal hunt serving as a crucial supplement. Government diversification policies fostered the growth of a more industrial St. John's, but largely on the backs of fishing people. Outport society was very paternalistic, but that did not fully mitigate the manner in which the tightening of credit in the fishery and the concentration of capital in the seal hunt had made the lives of outport people more difficult. A more class-based organization and politics had emerged in the support of northeast-coast people for Coaker and the FPU. However, class in Newfoundland meant something very different than in the more industrial and urban centres of Britain and North America. The most important relationship was not between waged working people and their capitalist employers, but rather between fishing people who often worked in household production and the merchant firms with which they traded through very paternalistic practices, usually seeking direct employment only for a limited time in the spring seal hunt. While railway development expanded employment opportunities for rural people, the wage workers of St. John's benefited most, as they did from tariff protection. The extremely sharp division between St. John's and the outports meant that fishing people were as divided from city wage workers as they were from merchants. Diverse local community and religious ties, and a shared sense of the danger of their work at sea, could unite fishers and sealers with the local representatives—often shipmasters such as Abram Kean—of the firms with which they dealt. The FPU aimed at St. John's as much as at merchants for reform, not revolution, and Coaker's balance-of-power strategy appeared to be integrating his political movement into the mainstream.

Death on the ice in the seal hunt of 1914, however, was about to change this situation by placing Coaker and the FPU in a much more antagonistic position towards the merchants of Water Street and their political allies in the Morris government, polarizing politics in the process.

TWO

The *Newfoundland* Sealing Disaster, Spring 1914

Sealers had reason to hope that their working conditions might finally begin to improve in the early spring of 1914. During the previous winter, William Coaker had introduced his Sealing Bill in the House of Assembly. In the aftermath of the *Greenland* disaster, popular support for some regulation of the hunt had prevailed against an extended period of mercantile opposition. Sealers and their supporters were not asking for much: the provision of safe and sanitary accommodations and food and the availability of proper medical assistance should injuries or illnesses occur during the hunt. Prime Minister Morris was still hoping to garner FPU support, so the Assembly passed Coaker's bill and, with some watering down, it made it through the Legislative Council. The legislation provided for better insulated and heated sleeping accommodations, medical assistance, healthier food, and cooks who would not be required to assist with the loading of seals.[1] Sadly, far from witnessing the birth of an improved industry, the spring brought one of the greatest tragedies in the seal hunt's history: seventy-eight sealers from the SS *Newfoundland* lost their lives by being stranded on the ice on 31 March. The public spectacle of the horrific event, popular indignation about the tragedy, and Coaker's anger with one of the major players in the event—Abram Kean—fuelled an unprecedented class-based political division in Newfoundland. Coaker was determined that the sacrifice of sealers' lives should not be in vain; out of the tragedy should come more careful public oversight of the seal hunt.

Although tragic, the *Newfoundland* disaster did not produce the most casualties in the seal hunt that spring. That dubious distinction belonged to a coincident event: the loss of the SS *Southern Cross* on 31 March. The entire crew of 173 people disappeared with the vessel on its way back to St. John's from the seal hunt in the Gulf of St. Lawrence. Captain George Clarke, from Brigus in Conception Bay, commanded a crew of mainly young men who had very little experience in sealing. There were wireless reports of sightings of the vessel during its return to St. John's, and the SS *Portia* sighted the *Southern Cross* about five miles from Cape Pine, laden down in the water with pelts. That was the last sighting, and the *Southern Cross* disappeared in the winter storm that had been raging. While there was much initial public speculation that overloading and design problems with the ship had contributed to the disappearance, the vanishing of the ship and its entire crew meant that there were no eyewitnesses and no testimony to contradict the final verdict of a public inquiry that the *Southern Cross*'s loss was "an Act of God." The *Southern Cross* vanished from public debate soon after it had disappeared beneath the waves of the stormy North Atlantic.[2]

The *Newfoundland* disaster, by contrast, remained at the centre of a political tempest. The presence of survivors and eyewitnesses meant that shipowners and captains would be unable to hide behind the notion that a tragedy at sea or on the ice was an act of God. In the spring of 1914, Abram Kean took the largest of the steamers—the

SS *Stephano*, belonging to Bowring Brothers—to the ice, while his son Westbury took the *Newfoundland*, which belonged to a competing firm, Harvey's. Westbury's brother Joseph also went to the ice that spring as master of the *Florizel*, the second largest of the sealing steamers. Sealers who had managed to secure a berth on the *Stephano* were fortunate; the ship was a modern, steel-hulled vessel that had been constructed in Scotland in 1911. The Bowrings used the ship to carry cargo and passengers as part of the Red Cross Line between St. John's, Halifax, and New York, but it went to the front in the spring as part of the seal hunt.[3] The *Newfoundland* was another matter. While the men who went aboard it that spring undoubtedly were glad enough to be working under one of the Keans, they were going to be hunting from a much inferior ship. The *Newfoundland* had been built in Montreal in 1872, and had been employed in the Allen shipping line, partially in the mail run between Halifax and St. John's. The ship made its first sealing voyage in 1893, under Captain J. Farquhar, who had assumed ownership of the vessel and registered it in Windsor, Nova Scotia. The 568-ton vessel was at that time the largest of what were known as the "wooden walls": wood-hulled steamers. The *Newfoundland* went to the ice in each following spring, but its hull was a liability in the deeper ice that the sealing fleet increasingly resorted to each year in search of seals. It had already suffered serious damage while at the ice on a number of occasions. In 1895, ice damage in heavy seas had forced the ship from the hunt, and in 1913, under Westbury's command and now owned by A.J. Harvey and Company, its stem had been "stove in" by ice and it stayed afloat only through constant use of pumps. The ship was aged and worn—it "was a tub, ancient, under-powered, too long and too narrow to manoeuvre safely in an ice-field without danger of breaking in two."[4] In consequence, the *Newfoundland*'s voyages were less profitable than its owners expected. In 1914, in an effort to reduce overhead costs, Harvey's removed the ship's wireless set because its use had not improved the captain's ability to locate seals.[5]

The crew of the *Newfoundland* might have worried about their captain. Westbury Kean did not have the experience of his father; he also did not have a master's certificate. In consequence, the younger Kean had to be accompanied by a navigation officer, Captain Charles Green. Westbury Kean appeared to have envied his navigation officer and the two barely spoke. The sealers were likely more comforted by the younger Kean's second hand—the person who ranked as next to the captain in command of the crew—George Tuff. Tuff was only sixteen when he first went sealing in 1897, and had been one of the survivors of the SS *Greenland* disaster in 1898. A hard-working sealer, Tuff had risen quickly in the ranks of the sealing industry in the years following the disaster, earning him the confidence of Captain Abram Kean. By 1914, Tuff had ten years' experience as master of a watch, the last three in the service of Captain Westbury Kean. The younger Kean relied on Tuff, who became his confidant during the hunt of 1914.[6]

Although the owners of their respective vessels were competitors, the Keans collaborated with each other to at least partially safeguard Westbury's ability to locate seals. Abram promised Westbury that he would signal whenever the "Old Man" (as Abram's crews called him) had found a patch. The *Stephano* had a radio, but this was now of no use to the *Newfoundland*. Instead, Abram arranged to signal Westbury by raising his ship's after derrick, the pole-like crane at the rear of the ship used for loading or off-loading cargo and supplies. The older, wooden steamer had difficulty in navigating through the pack ice. For two weeks, as his ship steamed and found nothing, the younger Kean confided his fear of failure in the hunt to Tuff. At the end of the two weeks, the *Newfoundland* had managed to come close enough to the *Florizel* so that Westbury could hail his brother, relate his lack of success, and have Joseph radio their father. Finally, when Abram found the main herd, he signalled Westbury, although the *Newfoundland* was jammed tight in ice five to seven miles away. With the *Florizel* also in the area, on 31 March Westbury decided to send his entire crew over the side to walk to the seal patch. The young captain had commented to Tuff that it was diffi-cult to see seals so close by but beyond the capacity of his ship to reach. Tuff volunteered to take command of the crew rather than leave them solely in the charge of the younger master watches, and to lead them to the *Stephano*. Westbury told Tuff that his men could count on staying aboard the *Stephano* for the night if they found seals to kill, something that the four master watches who took the *Newfoundland*'s men on to the ice—Jacob Bungay, Thomas Dawson, Sidney Jones, and Arthur Mouland—understood as their captain's intention. Captain Green later reported that he had heard Westbury say so, but Tuff, busy getting the men ready to go, did not hear.[7]

The second hand did not usually go over the side with the sealing crews. However, the seals found by Abram Kean were so far away that the four master watches would not be able to check back with their own ship should they require instructions. Westbury required someone to supervise and Tuff had volunteered. The second hand was busy ensuring that his crew took enough ropes and flagpoles to do the work of panning seals properly, but, perhaps now unaccustomed to actually going over the side himself, Tuff forgot to take his own compass.

The *Newfoundland*'s men went over the side at 7 a.m. At first, the weather was so warm that many of them took off their heavy outerwear and left it behind. Tuff borrowed a compass from one of the master watches, charted a careful course towards the *Stephano*, and started the crew out over some of the roughest ice he had ever travelled. Almost immediately the weather began to look threatening. After struggling four miles over the ice, thirty-four of the crew, tired, fearful of the worsening weather, and discouraged at having seen few seals, decided to return to the ship, although they faced calls of cowardice from their mates who continued on. Upon reaching the *Newfoundland*, the thirty-four were greeted by Westbury's angry glare from the deck. Not daring to climb up from the ice, the men took a tongue-lashing from the young captain, who called them a "crowd of grandmothers" for having abandoned Tuff.[8]

The rest trudged on, feeling that they were closer to the *Stephano* than the *Newfoundland*, but misjudging the difficulty and distance of the remaining trek. They reached the *Stephano* at 11:20, and Abram offered the men bread and tea. Tuff ate a better meal with the senior Kean, who informed the second hand that, despite the *Newfoundland*'s crew planning to spend the night aboard the *Stephano*, he would take them to seals but the men would have to walk back to their own ship once they had finished killing. Abram Kean later claimed that he had understood that the men of the *Newfoundland* had taken only two hours and twenty minutes to walk to his ship, when they had actually taken four hours and twenty minutes. He appeared not to understand how far the men really were from the *Newfoundland* or how exhausted they must have been. Tuff had hoped for better—that his men would not have such a walk back without a night's rest. He was further frustrated to find that his men would not even be able to work close by the *Stephano*. The closest seals were miles away; Abram Kean's ship took Tuff's men further from the *Newfoundland* to a patch of seals, and ordered Westbury's crew over the side in what looked like, at least to many of the sealers, worsening weather conditions. Some of the crew had not even had time to get something to eat.

Tuff had expected none of this, but would not dare challenge the Old Man's decision. Following Kean's orders, Tuff instructed his crew to go back onto the ice, and the men responded immediately, thinking that they would later return to the *Stephano*. As the crew went over the side at 11:50, Tuff remarked to the older Kean that the weather seemed to be getting worse. The Old Man told him not to worry, that the weather would be fine, and that the 132 crew members of the *Newfoundland* were to return to their own ship. At least some of the crew heard and feared what Kean said, but they also would not challenge his orders.[9] Kenneth Neil, a sealer from Spaniard's Bay on the nearby *Florizel*, had seen the *Newfoundland*'s men leaving the *Stephano* and "thought to himself, they must be crazy to be going after seals" in the weather that was developing. He further thought that Abram Kean "was nuts" for sending them off his ship.[10]

As the *Stephano* steamed away to pick up members of its own crew who were panning seals some distance away, the crew of the *Newfoundland*, by now seeing that a storm was coming on, turned to Tuff to ask what they would do. Frustrated and fearful, Tuff nonetheless told the men that they would follow the Old Man's orders and hunt seals. The second hand further indicated the crew would have to walk towards the seals in a direction that led them away from their own ship. Some of the men nearly mutinied, fearing that they could afford no more time and needed to make their way back to their ship. Tuff refused to give in and, believing that the *Stephano* had carried them closer to the *Newfoundland*, ordered the men to hunt. By 12:45, the snow was falling so heavily that Tuff decided the crew must return to the *Newfoundland*, hoping they would cross their original trail from the *Newfoundland* to the *Stephano*. Their crewmates who had turned back earlier asked Westbury to begin sounding the ship's whistle in fear that the men were lost, but their captain refused, believing that Abram would not have abandoned the crew to the poor weather. The men walked until about 2:30, when they discovered the original track and realized they still had a four-hour walk ahead of them. Dispirited, the men continued on, but the movement of the ice pans and the increasingly heavy snow made the track impossible to follow. At some point between 4:30 and 4:45, the *Newfoundland* sounded its whistle twice, which the men heard. Westbury had permitted the sounding only to assuage the fears of his boatswain, John Tizzard, and did not allow the whistle to blow again. On the ice, the men waited in vain to hear the whistle repeated. By now darkness was closing in fast and the crew realized that they were hopelessly lost, and much farther from the *Newfoundland* than anyone had thought. The trail had by now been completely obscured by the drifting snow. It was worse than the men originally apprehended, for no one knew the crew was lost. Without a radio aboard the *Newfoundland*, neither Abram nor Westbury could check with each other to see if the crew was safe on board the other's vessel.[11]

The result was calamity. Tuff tried to get the men organized for survival, ordering the watches to divide and find a large ice pan each, and then to build shelters. Master watch Thomas Dawson, who had been leading the men all afternoon, was exhausted but managed to get his watch organized in the shelter of a shoulder-high snow wall. Mouland's men built a better wall, while Bungay's built one similar to Dawson's. Jones's men failed to organize, and crowded onto the pans of the other watches. The effort was not enough, and the men suffered through rising temperatures, a rainstorm, and then freezing temperatures again. Most of the men were improperly clothed and had little food; now they were soaked to the bone and freezing. Many tragedies followed, but perhaps none more poignant than those involving fathers and sons. Through the first night on the ice, the men of the *Newfoundland* tried to keep each other's spirits up, both cajoling and capering in fun and jest and pushing and pleading in fear with their relatives and mates to stay on their feet and survive. The gale-force winds and the snow made constant movement difficult; many men tried to rest for a few minutes until their fellows got them moving again. One man, Edward Tippett, had been accompanied to the ice that year by his sons Norman and Abel. Fearful for them, Edward tried to use his own body to shield his boys from the cold. Dawn revealed that many had perished. Among them were the Tippetts, the father frozen stiff with his arms around his dead sons; they had clung to each other until the end.[12]

On Wednesday, it remained cold, but the winds picked up. Two ships, the *Bellaventure* and the *Stephano*, came close but did not see the men. Tuff, desperate to save his crew, struggled towards the *Newfoundland* with two of the sealers, John Hiscock and Richard McCarthy. He came close enough to sight the ship, but the wind had loosened the ice, allowing the *Newfoundland* to sail away. Stuck on the ice for another night, the men of the *Newfoundland* took shelter where they might.

Reuben Crewe and his son Albert John had survived the first night of the disaster. The two kept each other alive, but as morning dawned, their strength failed. Albert could fight no longer, and lay on the ice to die. Unable to leave him, Reuben lay alongside his son, took the boy in his arms, and lifted up his sweater to cover Albert's head. Father and son died together, frozen in their eternal embrace. The weather cleared for a second night, but became bitterly cold. Those of the crew who were still alive could see the lights of steamers in the distance, but none came near. Fathers and sons, brothers and uncles, and best friends from child-hood tried to keep each other going. As hypothermia and exhaustion worsened, men began to hallucinate about their loved ones at home; others sank to the ice in a stupor. Some simply walked off the edge of the ice into the sea. Friends and family tried to pick up those who had fallen to the ice, but often without success. They might return later to find only the dead, and face the gruesome choice of having to scavenge for caps, mitts, or food to stay alive.

On Thursday morning, Tuff, with some of the other men, struggled first towards the *Bellaventure*, which turned and steamed away without seeing them, and then towards the *Newfoundland*, seeing that it was stuck again. John Hiscock, having lost his brother Joseph to exposure in the night, joined him, along with Richard McCarthy. McCarthy and Hiscock were close friends from Carbonear, and McCarthy feared that shock, sorrow, and exhaustion were going to claim his friend. McCarthy had previously hauled Hiscock out of the water, and now kept him going by reminding him that he had a wife and children to return to. Westbury Kean could see the *Stephano*, and had climbed up to the barrel used for spotting seals to look for signs that his crew might be returning. He turned around to spot the distant Tuff and the others staggering toward his ship. Westbury raised a distress signal, and Abram, seeing it, sent men to find out what was wrong. In the meantime, part of the crew finally struggled to a nearby steamer, the *Bellaventure*. By 9 a.m. its captain, Isaac R. Randall, began to understand the magnitude of the disaster, and sent his entire crew out as rescue parties as he tried to get his vessel through the ice to the disaster area. When rescuers reached Richard McCarthy, they had to break him out of the ice that had encased him, but he was alive and ruefully remembered later that he received as pay for that season the grand sum of $2.09.

Many of the *Bellaventure*'s men wept when they found the crew of the *Newfoundland*, who continued to die even as help arrived. Later in the morning, men from the *Stephano* came to help. Men from the *Florizel* later picked up some of the bodies. Kenneth Neil remembered that the sealers were devastated to see what had become of the men of the *Newfoundland*, "and that all the men were saying at the time ... were calling Abe Kean an old bastard and that he should be shot for doing such a thing."[13] The rescuers stacked the frozen men like cordwood on the *Bellaventure*'s deck, including the bodies of Reuben and Albert, too frozen to separate. Although accounts vary, seventy-eight succumbed as a result of what they had experienced on the ice. Of the fifty-five survivors, many were seriously injured and proved later to be permanently disabled.[14]

The *Florizel* radioed authorities in St. John's about the tragedy on 2 April. A terrible period followed as rumours flowed and people rushed to Water Street to see if they could get more news from the telegraph offices, public bulletin boards, or the office of the Board of Trade. As the day unfolded, people's fears deepened, and they hoped at best for a full list of the dead. One newspaper reported, "no further information was available, the tension became almost unbearable. Our people moved about with gloomy faces and dragging steps that betokened their heavy hearts." By evening, more news whispered from the telegraphs: the *Bellaventure* had picked up fifty-eight bodies, thirty-five survivors were aboard but in hard shape, the *Florizel* had found five more bodies, while the *Stephano* had one body aboard but only two survivors. No colder fog had ever oppressed the city: "a murmur of dismay pervaded the crowd as the full significance ... dawned on them. Women wept aloud: strong men shed unwanted tears."[15] As night deepened, so did the sense of tragedy in the city. "Despondent" people wandered the streets close by the waterfront, and "among the groups who gave witness to the deep mourning of the community could be heard occasional whisper of how such a one was on board and had a wife and several children, and that another had a mother and several sisters."[16]

At the ice, other ships picked up the *Florizel*'s message. Coaker was aboard the SS *Nascopie*, an ice-breaking, steel-hulled steamer belonging to Job Brothers, ironically because he had wished to see first hand the impact of the sealing legislation he had introduced into the House of Assembly. During his time on the ship, the FPU leader had reported on infractions and felt there would have to be better enforcement in future. Coaker kept a log of his trip, intending to publish it later. On 1 April, he recorded, "Blowing a gale from the North during early part of the day veering N.W., in the evening, with very little abatement in the wind. Ice very tight. Freezing hard." The *Nascopie*'s men stayed aboard their vessel in what was "a stormy wintry day" enjoying themselves by singing and story-telling, but became upset by the *Florizel*'s message. The *Nascopie* tried to make for the *Newfoundland*, but could not get through the heavy ice. Members of the crew had relatives aboard the *Newfoundland*, and their spirits sank; the men "huddled together and talked in whispers about the awful calamity." Coaker was appalled, observing that the *Nascopie*'s men had been out on the same day that the *Newfoundland*'s men had first left for the *Stephano*, but Captain George Barbour, seeing the coming weather, would not let his men stray far from the ship. By 4 April, Coaker recorded, sealers throughout the fleet expected that the owners would order at least the steel ships back to port as a mark of respect. The owners did not, shocking the sealers, and leading Coaker to wire Job Brothers to ask that the fleet be recalled. The company replied that he was not to interfere with the hunt. The men of the *Nascopie* held a memorial service at sea, but there was a great deal of anger brewing

about the tragedy, especially when word arrived of the disappearance
of the *Southern Cross*.[17]

In St. John's, the rumours hardened into grim reality captured by
city newspapers on 2 April. "Death Stalks Unchecked Over Storm-
Swept Iceflows and Fatally Smites '*Newfoundland*'s' Crew," reported
the *Evening Herald,* whose editor observed fatalistically that this and
the tragedy of the *Southern Cross* were examples of the natural perils
of the sea faced by all seafarers; the "Grim Reaper" shadowed every
sealer, not just those on the two ships in question.[18] The *Daily Mail,* the
forerunner of the FPU newspaper the *Evening Advocate,* took a different
view, arguing that risking life and limb was a troubling and ever-present
part of working in such industrial enterprises rather than a matter of
fate or bad luck. Newfoundland had lost "scores of her most industrious
sons" because that was a price sealers were required to pay for making
a living. Foreshadowing the world conflict that was to come, the editor
of the *Daily Mail* wrote:

> The nations make boast of the heroes of stricken battle-fields. But there
> is a heroism of a far higher type and it is that which leads men to cheer-
> fully risk their lives in the hum-drum round of working for a living.
>
> The false and transient exhilaration of military service cheers on
> the soldier but the toiler is only kept young by his inborn courage and
> his sense of responsibility to dependent ones.
>
> And in such a way did our sealers risk and suffer and die.[19]

The city had come to a standstill, and the government asked Harvey's
to order the *Bellaventure* back from the ice so that the survivors on board
might receive medical treatment as soon as possible. As news spread that
the ship was carrying seventy-seven bodies, even more people gathered
at the makeshift morgue established at the King George V (or Seamen's)
Institute "to witness a scene of horror beyond the power of words to
depict."[20] The *Bellaventure* made port on Saturday, 4 April. Crowds
filled Water Street opposite the building; there were so many gathered

to watch the maimed and the dead unloaded from the ship that the police had to rope off the Seamen's Institute and nearby wharf to allow a detachment of Naval Reservists from the training ship HMS *Calypso* to help bring off the injured from the *Bellaventure* when it docked. As the dead and injured appeared, "a silence deep as death generally spread over the huge crowd and when men did speak it was in a deep whisper." It began to dawn on people that almost every part of Newfoundland— especially Bonavista Bay, Trinity Bay, Conception Bay, and the St. John's area—had lost people. Throughout the city, flags flew at half mast. While many in the crowd drifted away to their homes once the unloading was over, others stayed on through the night and into Sunday, despite cold and wet weather, to bear witness to what had happened. On Sunday, as other sealing ships such as the *Terra Nova* and the *Erik*, whose crews had not yet learned of the disaster, entered port, churches throughout St. John's held solemn services of mourning.[21]

Shock and confusion marked the return of the vessels. The resulting rumours and misreports could be quite distressing to families and communities. In Topsail, a small community on the shores of Conception Bay but very close to St. John's, ten men were lost in the sealing disasters. The father of Lemuel Squires was shocked to learn that his son was supposedly among the dead of the *Newfoundland*. He took the train to St. John's, where at the train station "to his great surprise and exceeding joy," Squires learned that his son, although suffering from severe frostbite, was alive at the hospital. Another member of Topsail's Church of England parish who had gone out on the *Newfoundland* was not so lucky. The parish buried James Porter, from nearby Manuels, "on a sunny morning, after a fresh fall of snow, the trees skirting the graveyard draped in a covering of pure white."[22]

Prominent government figures and politicians immediately wrote public notes of condolences to the family members of the dead and injured, but the letter from George F. Grimes of the FPU was different. While Grimes noted that people from all class backgrounds grieved for the fallen and wished to help survivors and dependents, he emphasized that it was only the "industrial soldiers," the sealers, who "went down in the fight."[23] In observing the many expressions of sympathy from the colony's elite, Grimes wondered what might have happened if they had shown as much concern for the sealers' welfare before the disasters of the spring had occurred. His description of the sealers as members of an "Industrial Army" suggested that sealers could well begin to think of uncaring shipowners and merchants rather than the elements from which they wrested livelihoods as their enemy.

Supporters of the government, such as the editor of the *Daily News*—a St. John's newspaper that had begun in 1894 as a conservative opponent of the Whiteway and later Bond administrations and that later threw its weight behind Morris and the People's Party—did their best to foster the impression that the *Newfoundland* disaster was a natural tragedy caused by weather rather than human negligence. Almost immediately, the paper attributed the loss of life to stormy weather, and emphasized that death under such circumstances was the inevitable price to be paid for Britain's "Lordship of the Seas," a maritime suzerainty for which Newfoundlanders, hardy "sons of the Empire," were always in the vanguard. The duty of the living, according to the editor, was to be charitable towards the women and children who belonged to the dead men, "but as to the dead, it is consoling to believe that after the first sharp struggle with the merciless storm, the tired limbs found welcome relief in unconsciousness and the Borean blasts became chariots on which they were borne to the land where the weary are at rest." The *Newfoundland* disaster, like that of the *Greenland* before it, was a piercing tragedy, to be sure, "but the bitterness of the draught was sweetened by the assurance that our sons and brothers had died as only good and true men could die."[24] This was cold comfort indeed.

J.R. Bennett, acting as prime minister while Morris was in England trying to raise money for further railway development, agreed with the *Daily News*, writing that the government was sure that Newfoundlanders would voluntarily subscribe funds to assist "widows" and "the father-less." The loss of so many men was sad, Bennett declared, but "our men, hardy and courageous in their calling, are continually wresting their bread from the very jaws of Death and occasions arise when Death conquers in the struggle."[25]

The Board of Trade quickly supported Bennett's declaration, having announced on 3 April that it was organizing a public meeting at the Casino Theatre for 10 April to raise a public subscription for the lost men's relatives. Small amounts began to trickle in: the Orange Order, under its grand master, Richard Squires, immediately offered one hundred dollars, and the Society of United Fishermen donated two hundred dollars, while the Knights of Columbus gave fifty dollars. The Reid Newfoundland Company volunteered five express wagons to be used as needed to help with the movement of the dead and the injured, while the Truckmen's Union promised all the teams that might be needed to help through the tragedy.[26] Although the acting prime minister urged the public to volun-tarily assist the relatives of the *Newfoundland* victims, Bennett would allow no commemoration through a state-sponsored public funeral for the dead, fearing that such a gathering might turn its sorrow into anger and protest against the government and shipowners.[27]

As public shock and grief gave way to anger, the *Newfoundland* disaster became a problem for the Morris government and the business community that supported it. John Alexander Robinson, the founder and first editor of the *Daily News*, continued nevertheless in his attempts to transform the sealers' deaths into acts of manly beatitude. Writing two days later about the unloading of bodies from the *Bellaventure*, Robinson exclaimed that people were surprised that the dead were "in a good state of preservation." "From the position of the bodies it was evident," he wrote, "that many had passed quietly away in their sleep. Many of the faces were calm and peaceful, and bore little trace of suffering. Some had the pink, rich glow of healthy manhood in their cheeks, and one wondered that they should have succumbed."[28]

Already, demands for an explanation of the tragedy had begun. The FPU quickly took the position that the men of the *Newfoundland* would not have been lost on the ice for so long if the ship had had a wireless on board. A wireless radio would have allowed the commanders of the *Newfoundland* and the *Stephano* to have queried each other about whether or not the men had reached one of the ships in the growing storm. The newspaper that was supporting the FPU, the *Daily Mail*, began to report popular rumours that condemned Abram Kean for not keeping the men aboard the *Stephano*, but the newspaper was not yet ready to give credence to them. Its editor, H.M. Mosdell, instead agreed that the absence of the wireless was a problem. The *Daily News* fought back against rumours that Westbury Kean had caused the tragedy, printing a notice from thirty-three of his surviving crew that their young captain had sent them over the side on a fine morning. The government, through its minister of justice and attorney general, Richard Squires, the selfsame grand master of the Orange Order, quickly established an inquiry under Judge A.W. Knight. The purpose of the inquiry was to head off the rumours that were beginning to coalesce around condemnation of the captains and owners of sealing vessels for neglect of their crews. Responsibility for the sealing disaster had yet to be proven, wrote the editor of the *Daily News*—it was only "British fairplay" to reserve judgment until there was a full investigation.[29]

Supporters of the Keans were already active in trying to deflect blame from the captains onto the crew of the *Newfoundland*. The editor of the *Evening Herald*, People's Party stalwart P.T. (Patrick) McGrath, interviewed Abram Kean and some of his crew, who suggested that the men of the *Newfoundland* had doomed themselves by trying to reach their own ship rather than returning to the *Stephano* once the bad weather had set in.[30] The *Daily Mail* reported that Westbury Kean "Believes Wireless Telegraphy Would Have Saved Life."[31] Abram Kean later maintained that the real culprit was the weather, which was "a sudden gale" that quickly became "a blinding snowstorm." While it did not help that there

was no wireless aboard the *Newfoundland*, the storm, which was unpredictable, had sealed the fate of the men.[32]

As the public anger about what had happened to the crew of the
Newfoundland combined with the anxious uncertainty about what had
befallen the *Southern Cross*, the civic and religious elites of the colony
held a public meeting at the court house in St. John's on 7 April. The
purpose of the meeting was to assist all of the dependants of the men
lost in both disasters and to consider whether Newfoundland required
a permanent marine disaster fund. From England, Governor Sir Walter
Edward Davidson—who had taken office the previous year following a
long career as a civil servant of the Empire in Ceylon and the Transvaal,
and as the governor of the Seychelles Islands—and Prime Minister Morris
raised a donation of five thousand dollars from Lord Northcliffe.[33] The
governor donated five hundred dollars and the Honourable George
Knowling, former cabinet minister and member of the Legislative
Council, came forward with a thousand dollars to start the fund.

More than a forum for charity, the public meeting was also an
opportunity for portraying the disasters as part of the inevitable
backdrop of danger that accompanied working at sea. Acting Prime
Minister Bennett repeated his view that the sealers "had fought life's
battles as true soldiers, and had died in harness." Church of England
bishop Llewellyn Jones stated that it was not for those present to apportion blame, a view supported by Monsignor Edward Patrick Roche, who
was about to become the archbishop of the Roman Catholic Church
in Newfoundland. Roche argued that tragedies at sea were the lot of
fishers. Since sealers in particular worked in an industry that was vital
to the colony's interests, it was, therefore, only right that people come
forward "irrespective of class or creed" to assist the families of the lost
ones.[34] Roche's fatalism about such maritime disasters could not compete
with Bishop Jones's effort to lessen the sense of public grievance that was
gathering force. The bishop invoked a story about a greater tragedy, a
storm in 1775 that had led to the deaths of three hundred fishers in the

colony and much damage to communities. As bad as the losses from the *Newfoundland* and the *Southern Cross* were, Jones suggested, they did not compare with the extent of the earlier tragedy.[35] The Rev. C.H. Barton, editor of the Church of England's monthly magazine, wrote that, while the "appalling double catastrophe" of the *Newfoundland* and *Southern Cross* disasters had "overwhelmed the scanty population of our island home," the tragedies were clouds with silver linings: they would allow the people of Newfoundland to demonstrate their generosity by supporting the relief fund. The parish at Bonavista had to bury twelve of the victims, and the parishioners donated all of their Good Friday service collection to the fund.[36]

The Newfoundland government clearly did not want to take any responsibility for the tragedy, but the repeated indignities visited upon the families of the lost *Newfoundland* crew members continued to provoke public outrage. For example, someone had to take responsibility for returning the bodies of the dead to their home communities. The government was unprepared to take on the duty, which therefore fell to the charity of merchant firms. Job Brothers agreed to return the remains of those who came from communities on the north side of Bonavista Bay via their steamer, the *Beothic*. However, its scheduled run would take it past the communities of Pool's Island, Shambler's Cove, and Greenspond without stopping. Families there could have to wait until motorboats would bring their loved ones home. William Coaker asked the government whether arrangements might be made to land the remains of those who had been lost more quickly, but the government replied that it had no responsibility for regulating such acts of private charity.[37]

Coaker was losing patience with such responses from the government, and was angry at the apparent complacency with which it treated the lives lost at the front. He began to demand a full inquiry by government into the circumstances of the *Newfoundland* disaster. The purpose of such an investigation would be to find ways to ensure that such disasters might not happen in future. In making his demand, Coaker readily offered his own thoughts about what action should be taken. "Men's lives are regarded too lightly at the sealfishery," he suggested. "If each owner had to pay $1,000 compensation for every sealer dying on the icefloe from exposure, through not being picked up by his ship, there would have been no *Newfoundland* disaster."[38] The FPU leader further stated that Wes Kean should not have rested until he was sure that his crew members were safe, and that Abram Kean should never have let the *Newfoundland* men leave his ship under such worsening weather conditions, and that the senior Kean should be condemned for not taking better steps to ensure the safety of the men once they had left his vessel.

In making his demand, Coaker was alleging that the inquiry by Judge Knight was "incomplete, unsatisfactory and superficial." The editor of the *Daily News* came to the defence of the Knight investigation, suggesting that the lawyers there were more than capable of ensuring a fair inquiry. C.H. Hutchings—the former deputy minister of justice and Liberal member of the House of Assembly, who was also the inspector general of the constabulary and fire department—represented the government, while William Warren, the prime minister's law partner, acted for Bowring and Abram Kean. A.B. Morine and Liberal William F. Lloyd, a teacher, lawyer, and editor of the *Evening Telegram* until 1916, represented the FPU.[39] The *Daily News* attacked Coaker for being too quick to apportion blame, stating that the shipowners involved in the matter faced serious charges and might well have to accept some blame, but that maritime disasters were everyone's responsibility. Citing a general failure by governments, the press, the public, shipowners, and sealers to have learned from the *Greenland* disaster, the *Daily News* asked people to unite in assisting the families of the lost and injured sealers and designing preventative measures for the future rather than wasting time on laying blame for what had happened.[40]

For George Tuff, caught in the larger battle shaping up between Coaker on the one hand and Kean, Bowring, and the government on the other, the anxiety must have been terrible. Appearing before Knight, Tuff observed that, while he had served on the *Newfoundland* for four springs, the ship only had a wireless for the first. The radio should never have been removed because it was the only means of certain communication about where crews were on the ice; its presence in 1914 would have saved the men of the *Newfoundland*.[41] A newspaper correspondent writing under the pseudonym "Mourner" agreed. The writer argued the wireless would have allowed Westbury Kean to determine the plight of his crew and call for the aid of the steel-hulled steamers in their rescue. While "Mourner's" letter was one type of reaction to the *Newfoundland* crisis, there were others. The same paper that printed the letter reported that the Journeymen Coopers Union had collected $150 from its members for the families of the lost. More worrisome to government and shipowners was the news that the crew of another of Bowring's sealing vessels, the *Ranger*, upon hearing of the disaster while at Catalina, refused to continue their work, and demanded passage home.[42]

Mutinies throughout the sealing fleet appeared to be a real possibility. On 4 April, seven men aboard the Job Brothers' *Diana* refused to continue with the seal hunt. Aboard the *Eagle*, a ship belonging to Bowring, thirteen men would hunt no longer. Most amazing, one of Abram Kean's men, Mark Sheppard, disgusted that the *Stephano* continued to hunt, led some of his mates in refusing to work. Sheppard did the unheard of: he cursed Kean, accusing him of being a cause of the *Newfoundland* tragedy and questioning his competence as a commander.[43] News also reached St. John's that the crew of the *Bloodhound*, angry that there might not be enough provisions for another ten days at the ice, had forced the vessel to return to port. Some of the crew tried to stand by their captain, but a fight against the majority broke out. The FPU newspaper wrote that such collective action would not be taking place if the government and the industry accepted the reforms Coaker had proposed in his Sealing Bill, and if companies would avoid the dangerous practice of dropping crews to pan seals.[44]

An apparent consensus quickly emerged that the absence of a wireless aboard the *Newfoundland* explained the severity of the tragedy. However, simply deciding to put the sets on all vessels was not going to satisfy people because the tragedy ignited a more general awareness among fishers and the wider public of the dangers that characterized their work and that these were not shared equally. The hunt made figures such as Abram Kean socially prominent, and therefore politically prominent, but it was clear they did not take the same risks in the hunt. Kean became a target for Coaker, a means for rallying his followers behind demands for improvements in their working conditions and stronger support for the FPU.

The political battle became personal and vicious. Coaker claimed that he had interviewed every survivor of the stranded *Newfoundland* crew, who laid "the blame for their suffering to Capt. Kean's lack of good judgement and common sense in sending them away from his ship at a time when they say they would not drive a dog out of doors." Abram Kean responded to such attacks by public letters that cast aspersions on Coaker, trying to deflect attention from the controversy over the *Newfoundland* disaster by drawing public attention to Coaker's family troubles. Coaker and his wife, Jessie, were estranged, and there had been a public accusation by Jessie's sister, Eliza Strong, against the FPU leader in 1912 that he had physically abused his wife. Although the matter became public, the parties involved settled the matter without trial in court.[45] The FPU newspaper's correspondents began a persistent campaign against Abram Kean. "Human Nature," for example, wrote that Kean had "slaughtered" the *Newfoundland* crew. "Talk about driving cattle to the slaughterhouse," the correspondent wrote, noting however that the cattle's "death would be a quick one, not like those poor creatures that were driven on the ice floe in a terrible snow storm to be frozen to death in slow torture." In answer to Abram and Westbury Kean's claim that each thought the other had the care of the crew, "Human Nature" wrote "what a sick excuse" and demanded an investigation into the *Newfoundland* crew's treatment while aboard the *Stephano*.[46]

The panning issue figured prominently in Coaker's mounting attacks on Abram Kean. Why in the world, he wondered, did the captain of the *Stephano* not return for the men of the *Newfoundland*? It was, the FPU leader alleged, because Kean was more interested in picking up the seals his own crew had panned. It was unbelievable, according to Coaker, that such an experienced sealing captain as the great Abram Kean could not have realized that bad weather was setting in; only callous indifference to the value of human life might account for what Kean had done. If the Keans did not value profits over lives, then the fishers of the northeast coast wanted "to know how it came to be that Capt. Ab. Kean and his son Westbury were clever enough to arrange a signal regarding plenty of seals, while they were too dense or indifferent to the risks to human life to arrange a signal intimating that men's lives were in danger."[47] The *Daily News* rushed to Kean's defence, calling Coaker's attacks "indecent and offensive," and maintaining that it would only be "British justice and fairplay" to await the outcome of the Knight inquiry.[48]

Abram Kean clumsily attempted to defend himself. In a letter to another St. John's newspaper, he denied any responsibility for the disaster and rejected Coaker's claim that hundreds of sealers would swear to his being a hard and negligent master. Kean used racist language, likening himself to an "old darkie," to suggest that Coaker was trying to persecute him.[49] The *Daily News* handled Kean's defence in a more subtle manner. It noted that the Knight inquiry was finding that there was little safety equipment aboard any vessel in the seal hunt. Few ships carried signal rockets, thermometers, or wireless devices. All shipowners, sealers, government officials, and the public were to blame for the absence of the latter because, while the wireless was expensive and hard to operate, the sealing fleet had simply "operated so many years without its aid, that neither sealers nor owners had realized its value." To general observers of the seal hunt, the wireless "looked an expensive luxury, rather than a necessity." Everyone had come to realize the error of such views, argued the paper, but "it is idle to blame individuals for the absence of the wireless. All share in the responsibility."[50]

Here was a dastardly dodge: the *Daily News* had managed to make the lost crew of the *Newfoundland*, their injured brethren, all of their families, and the public generally partially responsible for what had happened. Coaker was shocked, and argued that it was very unlikely that the Knight inquiry, established by Squires, the grand master of the Orange Order, would fairly assess the role of Abram Kean, a past grand master of the same order. Squires's position in the Orange Order was not a problem for Coaker; the Protestant organization was far more fraternal and less sectarian in Newfoundland than it had been in neighbouring places such as New Brunswick, and membership in the Order was very popular among the northeast-coast, largely Methodist and Anglican, communities that supported the FPU. Furthermore, Squires might have shared with Coaker the sense of being an outport outsider in the political world of St. John's. Born in 1880 as the son of a well-to-do grocer—and having received a good education at the Methodist College in St. John's and a law degree from Dalhousie University in 1898 with the help of a prestigious Jubilee Scholarship—Squires was nevertheless from Harbour Grace. He was not a scion of the great mercantile families of St. John's, but rather an outsider from the bays. Like Coaker, Squires was a johnny-come-lately in the political world of the capital.

Despite these apparent similarities, however, Coaker had little use for Squires, who had run unsuccessfully against Unionist candidates in Trinity in the previous general election, but by putting up such a strong fight that he had tied down the Union Party and prevented it from reaching further south towards the Avalon Peninsula. Furthermore, as a former partner of Prime Minister Morris's law firm and a loyal supporter of the People's Party, Squires received an appointment to the Legislative Council and his cabinet post.[51] The FPU wondered at a system of laws and judiciary overseen by such an attorney general as Squires that might well zealously pursue and imprison a starving child for stealing bread while allowing shipowners and captains such as Abram Kean to dodge responsibility for the appalling working conditions and treatment of sealers such as those who had died in 1914.[52] The *Daily News* continued to defend the integrity of the Knight inquiry, and noted that Harvey's had taken a twenty-thousand-dollar libel action against Coaker for his public attacks on the management and quality of their ship.[53] The FPU newspaper countered with a demand for a new investigation that would ask specific questions about the role of Abram Kean in the *Newfoundland* disaster, especially whether he had used bad judgment in sending the *Newfoundland*'s men back on the ice or had taken proper measures to ensure their safe return once they had gone back onto the ice.[54]

Coaker had previously been critical of George Tuff, especially when Abram Kean had claimed that Tuff deserved a medal for his role in the disaster. Coaker argued that Tuff's memory was at best convenient in that he could not remember what he had agreed upon with Westbury Kean. Coaker also claimed that Tuff bore some responsibility for leading his crew into danger, for not appreciating how poor the weather was becoming at the time, and for not noting correctly the direction in which the *Stephano* had steamed away from his group.[55] Tuff responded in writing from his hometown, Templeman, Bonavista Bay. Pointing out that he had suffered just as had every other man from the *Newfoundland* who had been stranded on the ice, Tuff claimed that he had done everything possible to save the lives of the men under his command. Admitting that he might have erred in some of his decisions, Tuff nonetheless claimed that many of the men who later complained that they knew stormy weather was coming had not been so vocal at the time, especially the men who had turned back to the *Newfoundland*.[56]

Coaker was more sympathetic to Tuff when Judge Knight finally made his report to the government on 16 May 1914. The judge concluded that Westbury Kean had passed on all legal responsibility for the crew of the *Newfoundland* to Tuff, who had assumed it by volunteering to lead the *Newfoundland*'s men onto the ice. Nevertheless, he noted, Tuff should not be judged harshly because "whilst he may have erred in his judgement, the fact remains that he took all the risks and shared all the terrible hardships with his fellows."[57] Knight further suggested that Abram Kean, while not legally responsible for the men, had a duty under the practice of the high seas to have rendered more care to them than he had. While Knight's report appeared to lay most of the blame at Tuff's feet, attributing minor fault to Abram Kean, his final conclusion was that nature had been the real culprit. The crew of the *Newfoundland* had "heroically fought the unequal battle with the Storm King of the North."[58] The editor of the *Daily News* agreed with Knight's report, but added that it had the status of a coroner's inquest, which could attribute no criminal liability to anyone. The editor noted that the Keans, Tuff, and the company that owned the *Newfoundland* had all exercised bad judgment, especially in the removal of the wireless from the ship. However, he defended the Keans by noting that they just did what sealing captains usually did: "it is the old story of familiarity with danger breeding contempt of danger."[59]

Coaker reacted much differently. He condemned the Knight report for trying to shift blame onto the shoulders of Tuff. The FPU leader accused Judge Knight of whitewashing Abram Kean's role in the disaster.[60] Cranking up the rhetoric, Coaker argued that the families of "those seventy-eight heroes" who had died at the ice now had to experience the political "farce" of an inquiry, established by Squires, covering up the guilt of Kean, a well-known crony of the People's Party.[61]

Other commentators were not as willing to place all of the blame on Abram Kean, but there was at least an implicit criticism of the Keans in their reaction to Judge Knight's findings. The editor of the *Evening Telegram*, for example, stated that the most important reason for the loss of the men of the *Newfoundland* was Wes and Abram Kean's ignorance about the whereabouts of the crew. Blaming this ignorance on the removal of the wireless set from the *Newfoundland*—which would have allowed the two captains to communicate and would have given Wes Kean the means of calling for the assistance of steel-hulled vessels in rescuing the crew—the editor nonetheless noted that the Keans had not demonstrated much interest in finding other means to communicate about where their crews might be on the ice.[62]

The *Evening Telegram*'s emphasis on the Keans' lack of concern for the men of the *Newfoundland* is not surprising. Abram Kean was an active supporter of the Morris government, and the *Evening Telegram*, having long been a supporter of the Liberal administrations of Whiteway and Bond, opposed the prime minister and the People's Party, especially for their close connection to the Reids. Coaker, however, was unimpressed by the *Telegram*'s perspective, and accepted nothing less than that Abram Kean should bear the responsibility for this disaster. The FPU leader continued to press for a fuller investigation of the factors that led to the deaths of the men of the *Newfoundland* throughout the late spring of 1914. When the local courts fined a Kelligrews man twenty dollars for the injury he inflicted on a sheep while driving it from his garden in June, Coaker remarked sardonically that it was hardly fair by comparison that a man such as Abram Kean could have his role in the loss of so many lives "whitewashed" by the law, in the form of the Knight inquiry. When Prime Minister Morris returned to Newfoundland later in June, Coaker expected that the government might act, but his paper's headline declared the unwelcome truth: "The Murder of 70 [*sic*] Sealers Still Ignored."[63]

Throughout the spring, people from the hometowns of the *Newfoundland* victims carried on with the business of helping the survivors and their families. In Newtown, Bonavista Bay, for example, the Church of England Women's Association held a "pie sociable," which raised $18.65 for the disaster relief fund. The people of the community collected further money to help. The minister of the local church wrote that his congregation realized that such money meant little to a mother or wife "compared to the giving back of a son to the one, of the husband to the other." Nevertheless, the people of his parish would pray for the bereaved.[64] Overall, the disaster relief fund gave many people a way to feel that they could respond usefully to the tragedy. The public subscriptions of people such as the parishioners of Newtown were very effective. As early as 27 April, the fund had accumulated just over $88,500 to help the victims.[65] In his 23 June address to the Diocesan Synod, Bishop Jones praised the generosity of the people of Newfoundland in raising money to help the relatives of those lost at the ice. The bishop made two additional points in his address. First, he suggested that such sympathy and charity would serve as a "balm" to the memory of a maritime tragedy. Second, he noted that although the people of Newfoundland were used to such tragedies, the sealing disasters of 1914 were "the greatest calamity as regards loss of life that ... [Newfoundland] has ever known within the memory of man."[66]

Bishop Jones contradicted his earlier claim that there had been greater tragedies in Newfoundland history. The bishop may have changed his view because of the manner in which politics had become so inflamed by the controversy surrounding the investigation of the *Newfoundland* disaster. By the early summer of 1914, Coaker had begun to use public anger to mobilize support for more government regulation of the seal hunt. While the sealing disaster may have been Newfoundland's greatest tragedy to date, that was soon to change. Like much of the world, Newfoundland would soon face disasters of greater proportion. War was coming, and it would further define Coaker's commitment to compelling the state to help lessen the suffering of working people in Newfoundland.

THREE

War, 1914–1915

By the early summer of 1914, the *Newfoundland* disaster appeared to be promoting a more class-divided tone in the public political battles of the colony than had occurred previously. In particular, the politics of the tragedy, under Coaker's leadership, tapped a mainstream of anger among fishing people weary of inequalities in the seal hunt. But the storm gathering in Europe soon began to overshadow local affairs, diverting attention from the question of who might have been responsible for what had happened to the crew of the *Newfoundland*. On the evening of 4 August, the British secretary of state for the colonies had informed the Newfoundland government that the Empire was at war with Germany. As the Great War broke out in Europe, the desire for debate about the sealing tragedies waned as patriotism waxed. Just after the beginning of the war, for example, rumours circulated that Britain had achieved a great naval victory over German forces in the North Sea. On 6 August, thousands of people poured into the streets of St. John's, congregated at the post office, and then marched to Government House to hear speeches by the prime minister and the French consul. Following this, they marched through the streets, singing patriotic songs. Even the FPU's paper declared triumphantly that the victory came from the hands of "the British tar," and condemned Germany for being an international bully that would have to answer to "the British lion."[1] On 7 August, the *Evening Telegram* heralded the news with the headline "Britannia Still Rules the Waves," but belatedly reported the next day that the victory had been merely a rumour. Preparations for the war effort got underway as the government appointed the Committee of Citizens (which was to include Coaker) to recruit a regiment to fight for the Empire. Formerly preoccupied by the sealing disaster, Coaker had a new problem to deal with. The FPU leader was opposed to the idea of creating a Newfoundland regiment because he felt Newfoundland could not afford it. The most cost-effective and realistic plan for Newfoundland's war effort would be to focus on recruitment for the Royal Naval Reserve and encourage any Newfoundlanders and Labradorians who wished to serve in land forces to join the British or Canadian armies.[2] In the short term, patriotic fervour and the debate over the nature of Newfoundland's participation in the war pushed the *Newfoundland* disaster into the background.

Coaker, however, was appalled that the Morris government was letting Newfoundland's war effort fall under the control of an unelected citizens' committee, and that Abram Kean might escape the righteous wrath of the people by hiding behind patriotic fervour. Seeing Kean as a government crony, Coaker kept up his demand that the sealing captain be held accountable for the *Newfoundland* disaster. The time had come for unity, declared Coaker's political foe at the *Daily News*, as the looming war effort demanded that any respectable citizen would put aside political differences and rally behind the government.[3] The war would be a titanic struggle for "freedom" against German "slavery" and "bloodlust," he asserted; it would also be a fight "for the liberties, the homes and the happiness of the people."[4]

Although patriotic fervour may have been widespread throughout Newfoundland, the dispersed and often isolated nature of the outports meant that organization of the war effort centred in St. John's. Newfoundland authorities had been anticipating the need for military plans, but the colonial government had little to offer in the way of military assistance apart from its small Royal Naval Reserve force which, nominally set at a complement of six hundred men, had only about fifty reservists in active training from year to year. The Newfoundland reservists trained aboard the HMS *Calypso*, and its men were commanded by the ship's captain, a British naval officer. The Admiralty called up the Newfoundland Naval Reserve on 2 August and on 7 August increased the reserve force to one thousand members. Recruitment restrictions had to be relaxed by the Admiralty to fill the ranks: originally the Reserve would take only men between the ages of eighteen and twenty-five, but it now accepted those as old as thirty-five; new recruits were supposed to have some fishing or seafaring experience, but recruiters chose to be more flexible about what this might mean. Even given these relaxed regulations, medical officers still had to reject about forty percent of those who volunteered.[5]

Coaker was right to worry about the cost of raising a land force. The perpetual economic troubles of the colony and the financial constraints of colonial governments committed to spending their funds on landward industrial diversification meant that Newfoundland had raised no local militia. The initial patriotism of the outbreak of war allowed Governor Davidson to take the initiative on 8 August, by promising the imperial government that Newfoundland would provide five hundred recruits for a land force, in addition to the extra naval reservists, although he later admitted that the Newfoundland government could hardly afford the cost.[6]

Prime Minister Morris supported the governor despite the financial strain that would result from creating a land force. War was a tragedy, but it also provided a screen for the prime minister. Morris's government had faced a serious challenge from the FPU in the general election of 1913, and the prime minister's support for the railway had burdened

Newfoundland with plenty of debt without much economic diversification. Furthermore, the Reids' enterprise continued to sink into a
financial quagmire. While Morris had previously opposed the idea of
confederation with Canada, by 1914 he quietly supported the Reids'
preference for union with Canada as a means of solving Newfoundland's
and the railway's financial problems. Always an enthusiastic imperialist,
Morris found the crisis facing Britain to be a convenient distraction from
Newfoundland's domestic troubles.[7]

On 10 August, Prime Minister Morris chaired a meeting between
the governor, Colonial Secretary John R. Bennett, and the church-based
paramilitary groups: the Church of England's Church Lads' Brigade
(CLB), the Catholic Cadet Corps, the Methodist Guards Brigade, and the
Presbyterian Newfoundland Highlanders. As extensions of the denominational educational system of the colony, the brigades were to shape
the character of young men. Representatives from other groups attended
the meeting with Morris. The St. John's Rifle Club was, as its name
suggested, an organization of the city, but the Legion of Frontiersmen
was unique in that it had first taken root in faraway St. Anthony. The
Legion was an imperial organization that had begun during the Boer War,
and had been transplanted to Newfoundland by Dr. Arthur Wakefield
of the Grenfell Mission. The Frontiersmen's original colonial members
were in Labrador and St. Anthony, but in 1912, it organized a St. John's
"levy." Joining these organizations and the brigades in the meeting were
the inspector general of the Newfoundland Police and the commander of
the HMS *Calypso*, the naval reserve training ship.[8] The meeting resulted
in the government's decision to support raising five hundred soldiers as
the basis of a Newfoundland regiment.

Although the Frontiersmen had a significant presence outside
St. John's, the meeting was a St. John's affair. The brigades reflected
the social hierarchies of the colony. Joseph Outerbridge, a leader of
the CLB, for example, was a prominent member of the firm Harvey
and Company in St. John's, and became its senior partner in 1902.

Eschewing partisan political ties, Outerbridge had been active in public service and charity work, including service in 1898 as treasurer of the committee established to oversee relief of the victims of the *Greenland* disaster.[9] His successor as commander of the CLB, William Franklin, was also in business, but on a much smaller scale than Harvey and Company. Originally from Liverpool, England, Franklin had come to St. John's in 1891 and begun Franklin Agencies, a small shipping company.[10] Newfoundland's war effort, then, was quickly falling into the hands of the same Water Street merchants and city industrial interests that the FPU had been organizing against.

The early enthusiasm for the war meant that few had the appetite for challenging the plans for a regiment. On 15 August, Governor Davidson held a public meeting at the CLB to announce his intention of raising a troop of five hundred men. On 17 August, the governor convened his Committee of Citizens as the Patriotic Committee, whose purpose was to raise the volunteer regiment to fight on behalf of the Empire. Comprised of prominent residents of the capital, the committee tried to balance Liberal, Union, and New Party interests. Davidson recorded, however, that Coaker and his *Mail and Advocate* editor, H.M. Mosdell, would not participate because the FPU leader opposed the creation of a regiment. Initially composed of fifty-five members, with a majority coming from the business community, the Patriotic Committee expanded on 18 August to include Prime Minister Morris, members of the legislature, local clergy, leaders of local unions and societies, doctors, newspaper editors, city councillors, and magistrates. Of the last group, rural members chaired outport branches. Again, Coaker and Mosdell would not participate because, as Davidson noted with chagrin, the FPU leader "says that the hour of danger is yet far off and that his followers will act when the hour of real need has arrived."[11] Arrogant and autocratic, Davidson had little experience in colonies with responsible government; he disdained partisan politicians, seeing it as his duty to participate directly in local political life. The governor felt that the assumption of the colony's war effort by such a voluntary committee would place it above partisan politics; however, the governor's view in fact placed Newfoundland's war effort beyond the control of elected government. Prime Minister Morris was just as happy because he hoped there would be less divisive debate about the war effort in the legislature.[12]

City union leaders were the first to suggest that there should be limits on the war effort. A letter to the editor about the manner in which working people would have to take wage cuts to help control inflation provoked the ire of James McGrath, the president of the Longshoremen's Protective Union (LSPU), one of the most important labour unions in St. John's. A determined proponent of better wages, fairer hiring practices, and collective bargaining rights for waterfront labourers, McGrath was a moderate whose commitment to unions and social reform grew out of his devout but progressive Roman Catholicism. As war dawned on the colony, he wondered why the burden for controlling looming inflation should fall on the shoulders of working people through reductions in their wages and working conditions. Such people were too poor already; perhaps, McGrath proposed, the local business community should demonstrate their patriotism by lowering their profit margins to control inflation.[13]

Coaker was sympathetic with concerns about business profiteering, but his main focus was on keeping the *Newfoundland* disaster before the public eye. During the summer, he had toured the communities of the northeast coast where, Coaker alleged, he had encountered a hue and cry for a better public investigation of Abram Kean's role in the loss of life at the ice fields. The FPU leader broadened his public criticism to include Bowring, angered at the company for having given Kean command of one of its steamers, the *Prospero*, for the summer, with which he provided coastal transportation and mail services on contract from the government.[14]

Coaker's and McGrath's efforts were reminders that, although enthusiasm for the war was building, the colony remained socially and politically divided. It was not certain that the people of the colony would rally behind a committee that, although publicly sanctioned, was a private body dominated by the business community of St. John's. The "holy" cause of a just war against "the modern Attila" was just, according to the editor of the *Daily News*, because it was a battle between liberty and tyranny.[15] The people of Newfoundland must unite behind the fight for liberty, the editor suggested, and many might well have agreed with Canon Smith, who wrote to the *Daily News* to remind them of their duty as British subjects: "We are warring in the cause of righteousness, truth and justice."[16]

Despite the calls for unity, the organization of the Patriotic Committee nevertheless reflected the social divisions of the colony. Most members of the committee were not from the big firms in the fish trade. Although Water Street helped to ensure that there would be no question about Newfoundland's support for the Empire, merchants tended to ignore the day-to-day requirements of operating government. They were no better at providing political leadership for the war effort; this fell to citizens drawn from the host of city business people, professionals, and journalists who made their money through government employment or by providing services to the railway and urban economy generally. Before the war, these were the people who had been firmly committed to the use of tariffs to protect local manufacturing in St. John's, and tended to see the outports and fishing people primarily as markets for St. John's products, not as places or citizens that the Newfoundland government should promote in their own right.[17]

Although small in number on the committee, representatives from the big trading firms held key positions in the organization. The Patriotic Committee's most immediate success was in establishing the war effort as a less partisan affair through recruiting the support of members of the Liberal opposition. Under the governor's direction, this citizens' committee formed sub-committees to raise money, recruit and equip troops, and expand the war effort beyond St. John's.

The governor asked Joseph Outerbridge to serve as vice-president of the Patriotic Association, and Outerbridge chaired its Reserve Force Committee for the duration of the war, which oversaw the recruitment of the Newfoundland Regiment.[18] The responsibility for financing the war effort fell to Edgar Bowring as the chair of the Finance Committee; Minister of Finance Michael P. Cashin served in his place when Bowring was absent.[19] Morris secured the legislature's approval of his war plans by calling the legislature together on 2 September to debate a War Measures Act similar to that of the United Kingdom and Canada, which passed on 4 September, the same day the government officially sanctioned the organization of the Regiment by passing the Volunteer Force Act.[20] Soon after, the Patriotic Committee renamed itself as the Patriotic Association of Newfoundland, often called the Newfoundland Patriotic Association (NPA). Although the government was willing to use its War Measures Act to enact the recommendations of the NPA, it never gave the citizens' committee any official regulatory status.[21]

Given the St. John's-oriented nature of the NPA, there was not much about it for Coaker to support, but the Union Party was willing to try supporting the Morris government's efforts. The FPU's party initially found that it was hardly possible to ignore the assertion that anyone who was truly British would unite behind the government's efforts for the sake of fighting the "German scourge."[22] Everyone appeared to be pulling together for the war effort. By the end of August, the governor's wife, Lady Davidson, had called on Newfoundland women to come together in the Women's Patriotic Association (WPA). Many of the women who answered the call were from the same professional and small-business component of the St. John's bourgeoisie as their male counterparts in the NPA, many having been active in pre-war social reform movements, particularly the Women's Christian Temperance Union, and the fight for women's suffrage. Lady Davidson also led in the recruitment of female nurses for the Voluntary Aid Detachment (VAD), an organization of such nurses originally formed in 1909 by the

Red Cross Society and the St. John Ambulance. Members of the VAD and other graduate nurses with fuller training would eventually serve overseas in British and military field hospitals.[23] In applauding the development of the WPA, one observer remarked that "the Empire to-day is one large family" in which the distinctions of class and gender had become meaningless.[24]

There was no doubt that Coaker was going to support the war effort; he was a strong supporter of the Empire and continued to be, at heart, a moderate reformer who felt that government should use its power to ameliorate the problems of inequality and to better regulate the fishery. Feeling that the Newfoundland government had a duty to shoulder the colony's war effort, Coaker had originally wanted a new government, composed of representatives from all the parties in the House of Assembly, to take charge of it. Such a union government, he argued, was the only way that the "Northern toilers" could have faith in the war effort. When it became clear that the NPA would manage the war effort for the Morris government, Coaker promised that he would take part in no partisan attacks on the government as long as its supporters reciprocated for the Union Party, although he still had not changed his mind about the formation of the Regiment being a mistake. Coaker promised to cooperate with the government in the convening of a special war session of the legislature on 2 September as long as it consulted the official opposition on war measures.[25] However, criticism of Coaker by R.K. Bishop in the Legislative Council ended the truce. Bishop, originally from Burin, was a prominent Water Street merchant in the fish trade, who had become a member of the Legislative Council in 1899 and had been appointed to cabinet by Morris in 1909.[26] Coaker now felt free to voice his concerns about the NPA and the expense of the Regiment.

The division between Coaker and the government did not dampen enthusiasm for the war effort in St. John's. On 21 August 1914, Governor Davidson had issued the first call for volunteers for the Newfoundland

Regiment. The call promised volunteers that they would have to serve for the duration of the war or one year, whichever came first. In Britain, the declaration of war had led enthusiastic early recruits to fear that it would be over by Christmas and before they got to fight. A similar enthusiasm, if not fully shared with their francophone counterparts, prevailed among Anglo-Canadians, and Canada's minister of militia, Sam Hughes, was just as optimistic that there would be an early victory for Britain.[27] Soon after the declaration of war, local theatres in Newfoundland began showing movies with stirring martial themes, and bookstores began to carry war-related books, helping to stir up patriotic sentiments. Many of the first recruits came from the St. John's area, while the pulp-and-paper town of Grand Falls quickly became another important source of recruits. In both places, industrial employers encouraged their workers to join up. Relatively isolated from the enlistment centre in St. John's, and with their labour in constant demand in the fishery, young outport men faced greater challenges in joining the Regiment. Greater unemployment among the wage workers in the capital and the pulp-and-paper town of Grand Falls, the promises of employers in those centres to top up the pay of enlistees and provide employment upon their return, and easier access to St. John's from nearby communities on the Avalon Peninsula made workers from this region more likely to join.[28]

St. John's was the seat of recruitment activity. A.J. Stacey, a young man known to his family and friends as "Jim," later reminisced about the heady patriotism of the time that led many local men to volunteer. Born in England in 1890, Stacey had come to Newfoundland in 1911 to join his brother Charles, who worked for the Bank of Montreal in St. John's. Jim Stacey worked for the Reid Newfoundland Company, but responded to the call for volunteers for the Regiment on 2 September.[29] There was also a commercial recession in the city, which led to unemployment and made many young men available for recruitment.[30]

The CLB Armoury became the recruiting headquarters for the Regiment. Within a week of Davidson's first call, 275 volunteers showed up and, by 2 September, there were 743 volunteers, of whom 250 had passed medical inspection. Overall, almost half of all the people of the colony who volunteered for military service were found to be medically unfit, likely because of poverty.[31] Jim Stacey feared that he would not be accepted because of his fallen arches, so he pointed his toes inward to hide the problem, and passed his medical exam. The offer of free rail or water transport for anyone travelling to St. John's to enlist meant that some recruits from the outports, such as the Dawe brothers of Bay Roberts, began to answer the call.[32] During the summer of 1914, the brothers had sailed northward to Labrador to fish for cod. They had known about the tensions in Europe upon leaving, but were surprised to hear the news of war in August from the crew of another vessel that had arrived on the coast from home. Frank Gilbert Dawe and his two older brothers decided to return home to enlist. One of these, Harry, failed to pass his medical exam because he had contracted rheumatic fever as a child, and the other, Will, failed his medical due to his bad teeth. Frank Dawe reported that Will felt so bad that he said, "'I knew we had to go overseas to fight the Germans. But I didn't know they wanted us to eat 'em.'"[33] Many people thought that the outports were impoverished places plagued by health problems, but Stacey's case and the fact that about a third of the first week's potential recruits were medically unfit for service are reminders that health problems were an urban as well as a rural problem in Newfoundland.

The Dawe brothers and Jim Stacey joined the Regiment because they felt it was their duty to answer the appeal for volunteers. Stacey remembered feeling especially motivated by the highly charged emotional and patriotic fervour prompted by the declaration of the war. In many ways, it was a juvenile response; many underaged men volunteered, looking for romance, adventure and, perhaps, an escape from the monotony and discipline of home life. Stacey recalled that, for the month following the call for volunteers, "there were Mothers, coming down to Headquarters, saying that their sons, who had joined up, were under age."[34] Throughout the war, the Regiment would receive a steady stream of underaged youths as volunteers, many taking advantage of free transportation to St. John's, free meals, and pay to get the chance to play a heroic part in fighting for King and Country. The youths were generally fitter than older recruits and game for anything that would prove their daring manliness. Oblivious to what fighting might really mean, the young were compliant and trainable—ideal candidates for service. By the end of the war, about 272 of the 1305 members of the Regiment who were to die in service were underaged soldiers.[35]

Hard-pressed to handle the volunteers, the Patriotic Association established a training camp for the recruits on the nearby shores of Quidi Vidi Lake under the command of William Franklin, billeting the men in a variety of tents assembled by the church brigades, local businesses, and Government House. The colony's major industrial forestry concern, the Anglo Newfoundland Development Company, provided the wooden flooring for the tents. The shortage of uniforms for the troops led the Patriotic Association to commission the manufacture of local uniforms, but a local shortage of khaki cloth meant that the uniforms for the first recruits included blue puttees. At first, the volunteers did not have their own arms to train with, but they eventually received five hundred Canadian Ross rifles. While hard training marked life in the camp, most soldiers knew nothing more than that they had volunteered to serve for a war that they thought would last only a year. Recruits such as Frank Dawe found camp life demanding: the training was physically tough, but more importantly the young men began to worry about leaving their families and homes. Fortunately, the St. John's community showed its admiration for the volunteers and kept them entertained with concerts and dances. Overall, a festive atmosphere marked the camp, and Dawe later recalled that the Regiment's commanders worked on the men's morale by instilling in each recruit "a feeling of pride. The King had called on him to fight for the mother country and what she stood for, and each man intended to do what was expected of him."[36]

The task of figuring out how the Regiment would be funded had fallen to the NPA, and it resorted to voluntary efforts. Aside from the FPU paper, the St. John's press enthusiastically supported the call. There was a great deal of popular support for the Regiment within the environs of St. John's, but many people in the outports were more lukewarm because they saw it as a military unit funded and administered by a St. John's elite, even though Coaker wrote favourably of any outport man who tried to enlist in the Regiment. However, he continued to be of the opinion that funding a regiment of five hundred was far too expensive a venture for a colony in Newfoundland's financial position, particularly with a relief problem looming following a poor season for the fishery in 1914.[37]

The FPU leader was not impressed by Lady Davidson's call for women throughout the colony to support the WPA, feeling that such women's efforts would be better directed towards relieving the families of the deceased and the injured survivors of the *Newfoundland* disaster. His position drew the ire of a correspondent at the *Daily News*, "An Indignant Woman," who argued that it was more important to raise money to assist the relatives of soldiers who would fall in battle than to support the families of a few sealers who had died at the ice.[38] Coaker had underestimated the extent to which patriotism had motivated women to become involved in the WPA. Further, while the "distaff" feminism of many of the WPA's members meant that they brought domestic work to the war effort, these women did so because they were asserting such work's public value and their own natural rights to respect and citizenship. They were not about to be denigrated by the FPU leader.[39]

Coaker was enraged by "An Indignant Woman's" rhetorical questioning of whether the lives of sealers could be compared to those who would die on the battlefield. The FPU leader pointed out that if the correspondent's son had been among the men who had died because a mercantile firm wanted to save the expense of a two-hundred-dollar wireless set, she might feel differently. The real issue here, Coaker argued, was that Britain had far greater resources to aid its troops than did a comparatively impoverished Newfoundland, which could barely aid its poor and unemployed. Such desperate local people deserved help before the WPA busied itself making "socks, pillows and pillow covers" for troops.[40]

Such a reminder that the acute social inequalities of Newfoundland had not simply evaporated in war fever made Coaker few friends in St. John's. The FPU leader nevertheless continued to promote enlistment in the Naval Reserve by outport men, as a way to demonstrate the loyalty of the FPU and "Northern toilers" to "the Empire and King and their love for the Flag."[41] Many people from the outports eventually enlisted because they fully supported the view that Newfoundlanders and Labradorians had a duty to support the imperial war effort.

Despite such views, St. John's interests continued to dominate the war effort. The initial enthusiasm for the war had led to the creation of forty-five branches of the NPA, with a total of three hundred members registering outside St. John's in 1914–1915. Within a year, most of these had lapsed, and the St. John's leadership of the NPA did nothing to revive them. Few of the St. John's business people, clergy, or professionals who were active in the NPA could be bothered with the affairs of the outports. The most important standing committees of the NPA continued to be chaired by members of prominent Water Street families: Outerbridge, Bowring, Harvey, Job, Macpherson, and Grieve. Almost all of the Regiment's officers came from the same St. John's mercantile, business, and professional elites, and had very little field experience. Politicians and other leaders outside the capital gave up trying to develop local support; it became clear that many outport people saw the efforts of the NPA as another instance of the manner in which St. John's interests developed programs to suit local concerns without regard for the outports. The NPA further proved less enthusiastic about organizing and recruiting for the Naval Reserve, in which more outport people were likely to join. The naval reservists received only about half the pay of enlistees in the Regiment, and tended to be looked down upon by government and NPA officials. As the war progressed, rising fish prices and the labour demands of the fishery dampened outport enthusiasm for the NPA's efforts.[42]

The founding of the Newfoundland Regiment forged a specifically Newfoundland dimension of a broader local imperialist sentiment, stronger among the elites of St. John's than the peoples of the rural parts of the island. While its attachment to the Empire remained the colony's defining element, this newer mood emphasized a special pride in Newfoundland's present and future potential role as a nation in imperial service.

Thus, although imperial strategy had originally called for Newfoundlanders to be part of the larger Canadian force in Britain, the upper-class officers of the Regiment, supported by the NPA, refused to accept this arrangement, and the Regiment was deployed as a separate force. There had been widespread support in the capital, and in government, for the maintenance of the Regiment as a distinct Newfoundland fighting force: the Regiment allowed only Newfoundland residents to join its ranks, or become its officers, but its senior commanding officers came from British military ranks. The news of the Regiment's impending embarkation led to celebrations in St. John's, and when the "First Five Hundred" recruits (later bearing the honour of being known as the "Blue Puttees" because of their uniforms) shipped out aboard the Bowring vessel *Florizel* on 4 October 1914, they did so to the ringing cheers of nearly the entire population of the capital. Accompanying the recruits were 25 officers and other personnel; altogether about 540 men boarded the steamer, of whom 400 were residents of St. John's.[43]

For many of the St. John's men, stepping aboard the *Florizel* might have given them their first intimation of what it was like to work as a sealer. The ship was not ready to leave port, having to wait a day so that it might rendezvous with the convoy carrying the First Contingent of the Canadian Expeditionary Force to Britain. The troops were quartered in the vessel's hold, in which hammocks had been slung for the non-commissioned officers and their men, with the accommodations normally used for the passenger trade between St. John's, Halifax, and New York reserved for the officers. One of the volunteers later recalled that "we were stowed away like so many seals on the steamer's last voyage to the ice only the March before."[44] Private J.F. Hibbs later recalled that the ship "had been out to the seal fishery that spring and she stank like hell."[45] The enlisted men were not thrilled by this treatment, or by their diet of black tea and "skilly," a boiled mixture of mutton and vegetables. However, they had the advantage of excellent weather and calm seas for most of their voyage, encountering bad weather only as they approached Plymouth Sound around 12 October. Throughout the voyage, the men could not drill because of the small size of the *Florizel*, but they had almost daily lectures from their company commanders, religious services, and ship's concerts for entertainment. Former private Owen Steele, just promoted to colour sergeant, recorded that there was ample opportunity for the men of the ships that convoyed with the *Florizel* to cheer each other.[46] There was little about the voyage to prepare the members of the Regiment for what they might encounter on the battlefields of Europe, and the landing at Plymouth Sound continued the festive atmosphere that had begun with the men's departure from St. John's. The Regiment disembarked on 20 October at Devonport and, along their route to the railway station from which they would leave for training on Salisbury Plain, were showered by gifts of candy, cigarettes, and apples from local residents.

Salisbury Plain on a dark autumn night was a different matter. The Regiment arrived at Pitney Station after midnight, and faced a seven-mile march in the rain to their camp at Pond Farm. The troops were cold and the ground soggy when they arrived, and they could not have been blamed for thinking over the next month or so that they would never be dry again. The Regiment finally received proper uniforms and, perhaps with some misgivings, their Ross rifles, which, although fine for sharpshooting, were longer and heavier than would suit trench warfare. The Regiment's members bristled at rumours that they might be merged with Canadian units and at the British for constantly confusing them with Canadians, who were also training on Salisbury Plain. For Owen Steele, the thousands of tents laid out across the plain were an inspiring reminder that many thousands of British subjects were training "with the object of fighting for the honour, and may be, the preservation of our great nation." Steele's nation was Britain and not Newfoundland; the distinction he was anxious to make was that the Canadians did not behave as well as his countrymen.[47] More miserable than affronts to colonial dignity were the conditions on Salisbury Plain. The Regiment's commanding officers subjected troops to constant training, especially seemingly endless marches. This toughened the Regiment's men, all the more so since it took place in almost constant cold rain, which turned the ground into slick mud that, while nearly freezing, never quite hardened with frost.[48]

Salisbury Plain was not pleasant, but it hardly yielded the kind of conditions that would worry people back home. Coaker continued to be more concerned about the far greater suffering that had occurred at the ice the previous year, but was nonetheless mindful of the discomforts experienced by members of the Regiment on their English training ground. The FPU leader had opposed the creation of the Regiment, but the fact of its existence now meant, in his mind, that its men were soldiers of the Empire who deserved no less than the full support of every Newfoundlander. In his address to the annual convention of the FPU on 16 November, Coaker called the war "the Armageddon of Scripture" and laid the blame for it "upon the head of the German Emperor." Attributing the war to the military buildup that had accompanied the rivalry between empires, Coaker associated the hope for a future of liberty, peace, and prosperity with the "best traditions of the glorious British past" and Britain's decision "to crush the 'mailed fist' which had terrorized Europe so many years." It was, he stated, every

Newfoundlander's duty to support the Regiment now, in the hope that this war would end all war. In the better world that must come from the war, the "vast wealth" previously used to support imperialist rivalries would "be utilized for the social improvement of the people. These improved conditions for the masses [would] be secured at a tremendous cost of blood and gold, far surpassing the cost of all former struggles known to history."[49]

On the surface, Coaker was accepting the argument that the war was a simple fight between traditional liberal British values and those of German modernism and Prussianism, but the FPU leader was really suggesting that the war justified a more progressive state in the post-war world. In the pursuit of such a goal, Coaker began to cheer on the WPA's efforts to raise money for gifts and cakes to send to the members of the Regiment for Christmas as a matter of loyal obligation.[50] There was, however, more than British patriotism on Coaker's mind. At a rally for the war effort in Catalina on 15 November, he argued that the war effort was waged in the cause of the working man's liberty: "It will be the end of war. It will release millions of toilers from the awful burden which they have carried for a generation, of providing millions annually for maintaining great armies and navies which filtered the life blood from the bodies of the toiling masses."[51]

While Coaker felt that every Newfoundlander must support the Empire, he was not willing to say that this meant having to support the Morris government locally. At the FPU annual convention in November, Coaker had condemned Morris for having appointed the defeated Richard Squires to the Legislative Council so that he could become minister of justice, and for having appointed another losing People's Party candidate, Sydney Blandford, in the same fashion to the position of minister of agriculture. Particularly antagonized by the latter appointment because Blandford had run and lost in Coaker's district of Bonavista, the FPU leader had previously written Morris to ask how an intelligent man could raise a defeated candidate in a general election to

a cabinet post.[52] Coaker argued that Morris's action offended the principles of British liberal democracy, and that, by accepting the prime minister's recommendations, "Governor Davidson has proved to be an enemy
of popular election and has trampled under foot practises followed by
all former Governors. If he can do so with impunity, we may as well tear
up the Colony's Constitution and make Sir E.P. Morris a Dictator."[53]

Late in October, Coaker publicly disagreed with the government's
decision to investigate the *Newfoundland* disaster more extensively by
appointing three Supreme Court judges to the task—on the grounds that
William H. Horwood, George H. Emerson, and George M. Johnson
were not properly qualified because they had little practical knowledge of the operation of the seal hunt. At the FPU annual convention in
November, Coaker declared that the government was failing to investigate the matter properly, although he also made clear that he felt Kean
was guilty already for failing to make proper efforts to rescue the men
of the *Newfoundland*. Having a single judge was acceptable, Coaker
maintained, but the two other members of the investigation should be
a qualified shipbuilder and a qualified sealer. The FPU leader feared
that the judges would be puppets of the government, whitewashing
the affair as Knight had before them. Furthermore, he wondered how
the judges would be impartial if they were also called upon to hear the
many libel and litigation cases that were bound to arise as a result of the
disaster. Coaker felt that there had been a devious delay by government
in announcing the investigation, which should have been established
immediately after the disaster in the late spring. Evidence was becoming
stale, and the beneficiary would be Abram Kean, who would be much
less likely to be found culpable. At its annual convention in November,
the FPU had reiterated its support for legislation to regulate the work
of sealing, noting Kean's opposition to such laws, and advocating even
more regulations such as prohibiting the sending of crews more than
two miles from their ships on the ice, allowing them to return for breakfast and dinner, and not having the crews wait on the ice to be picked up

by their ships.[54] While Coaker criticized the new investigation, the press generally supported it, arguing that the commission would ensure that the welfare of all sealers was properly attended.[55]

While Coaker and the FPU newspaper continued to focus attention on the need for a proper investigation into the *Newfoundland* disaster, other newspapers concentrated on the cause of working men, whether from St. John's or the outports, who were trying to enlist for the second contingent of the Regiment. All such potential recruits could only drill on a part-time basis because they could not afford to give up their jobs, and outport men could not afford the room and board that would allow them to stay in St. John's. One paper argued that all recruits deserved to be put on full pay immediately so that they could train properly, and that the government should finance a better recruitment drive in the outports.[56] Depicting the island of Newfoundland as the Gibraltar of North America, another paper called for more volunteers. If Britain did not prevail, it argued melodramatically, the Germans would be on Newfoundland shores in no time, pressing Newfoundlanders into their navy, and carrying battle to Canada and the United States.[57] Attending a war rally on 10 December at the St. John's Lodge of the Society of United Fishermen, Prime Minister Morris declared that all Newfoundlanders "should throw petty differences aside when the question of defending the Empire is at stake." Not to be outdone, Coaker got up on the same platform to agree with Morris, arguing further that if Britain had the money and ships for a war effort, then "surely it was an easy matter to get the men to stand behind the guns."[58]

Support for the war effort did not stop Coaker from attacking the "Sealing Farce," the title he had given the commission of investigation into the sealing disaster. As the judges turned to matters such as how the men were fed and otherwise accommodated at the ice, Coaker thundered that the people really wanted to know how seventy-eight men had come to be "massacred," and they wanted to know why Abram Kean faced much less legal sanction for the tragedy than would a poor man who stole bread to feed his family. The people, Coaker declared, wanted to know why Kean's political and business connections allowed him to continue to command steamers without paying any price for his role in the *Newfoundland* disaster.[59]

The case against Abram Kean, as put to the people in the pages of the FPU's newspaper, was that the sealing captain was guilty of manslaughter by having been unusually careless of the welfare of men working on the ice in favour of the profits of the voyage and his own family. The senior Kean, for example, had arranged to signal his son Wes Kean when the *Stephano* found seals, when his business was only the work of his own crew and not that of the *Newfoundland*. Having influenced Wes Kean's decision about deploying the *Newfoundland*'s crew, Abram ignored their welfare, allowing the men to risk straying further from the safety of a vessel than would any other captain in the sealing fleet, and taking no effective measures to ensure that the crew was safe.[60]

Other major newspapers provided little coverage of the investigation, likely because of its potentially embarrassing nature for the government—of which Abram Kean had been a prominent supporter—during a time of war. The Liberal *Evening Telegram*, for example, only commented at the end of the year that the disaster was the result of the lack of a wireless, and that new legislation passed during the fall requiring the equipment on all sealing steamers would safeguard against such tragedies in the future.[61] Coaker would not accept such apparent disregard for the importance of command decisions at the ice, and became even angrier when the commission began to look as if it was staking out George Tuff as the scapegoat for the disaster. Coaker had felt that Tuff bore some responsibility for what had happened to the men under his command, but this paled in comparison to the role of the "martinet" Abram Kean. Tuff was to be blamed for taking Kean's advice, but he was a sealer who had deferred to an experienced captain— it was this experienced seaman who failed Tuff and the other men of the *Newfoundland*.[62]

The new year opened with a convention of the FPU districts of the communities on the north side of Conception Bay, which passed a resolution condemning the commission. The convention claimed that the people of St. John's were underestimating the anger of outport people over the *Newfoundland* affair, a position echoed by Coaker. The FPU leader claimed further that ten thousand fishers were prepared to march on St. John's to ensure that Kean faced a proper punishment, and to prevent Bowring from hiring him again to command a coastal steamer. The people did not want to riot, Coaker claimed, but they did want justice for the fallen. He made the claim in language redolent of the rhetoric of war: let the people remember "that many a father lost a son, many a wife a husband, many a man a brother, many a son a father, and the blood of these 78 slaughtered heroes cry aloud to Heaven for vengeance."[63]

News from the war was not yet serious enough to overshadow the *Newfoundland* tragedy. In England, the Regiment's training had been going well, although there were rumblings of problems in some areas, especially reported delays in pay reaching family members of the soldiers because of poor organization by the Regiment's paymaster, Captain Henry Arthur Timewell. Timewell, a charted accountant from St. John's, had begun with the Regiment at Pleasantville in 1914, and had travelled to Britain with its men.[64] In the short term, conditions improved for the men when the Newfoundland Regiment left Salisbury Plain for Fort George in Scotland on 7 December. The men enjoyed better accommodations and food, and had begun to receive better arms training. They celebrated Christmas at Fort George, having an excellent time until the sad death of twenty-year-old Private John Fielding Chaplin of an abdominal condition on New Year's Day, 1915.[65]

Back home, people were keeping up with the news of the Regiment from the letters of Betts Cove native and volunteer Frank Lind. Lind's letters appeared regularly in the St. John's *Daily News*, and contained a mixture of news from the Regiment, reminders about supplies that might usefully be sent to the troops, and reassurances for friends and relatives back home. In February, for example, he wrote about how grateful the men at Fort George were to get Christmas parcels from home, and assured readers that the Regiment was anxious to get into the fighting at the front to repay their debt.[66] Owen Steele would have agreed with Lind; he was anxious to leave behind the relative monotony of training for the front—a distant, poorly understood place that had the appeal of excitement and achievement.[67]

Newfoundland soon experienced more directly war-related casualties. On 30 January 1915, the FPU newspaper reported the loss of the British merchant cruiser the *Viknor* off the coast of Ireland. The two-hundred-ton steamer had been a Royal Mail Steam Packet Company ship converted by the British Admiralty for naval patrol duties, although it was poorly designed for the rough winter waters of the North Sea. When it foundered on 13 January in waters recently mined by Germans, it was carrying as crew members twenty-five naval reservists from Newfoundland, including Fred Morgan of Seal Cove, Conception Bay, who were all lost. The FPU newspaper mourned the lost men, and asserted that their sacrifice was the price that Newfoundlanders were paying for the rights of democracy and citizenship in the British Empire.[68] The editor of the *Evening Telegram* agreed, stating that the lost men had come from every part of Newfoundland, and had "set an example which will be an inspiration to others. They have given their all for their King and Country."[69] More tragedy was to come on 9 February, when another vessel, the *Clan MacNaughton*, was lost with all hands, including twenty-two Newfoundlanders, among them Fred Morgan's brother John Thomas. The *Clan MacNaughton* had been a fast cargo ship equally unsuited to patrol duty in the North Sea. No one knew what happened to the ship, as it had not been heard from since 2 February, but wreckage found on 8 February indicated that it had likely foundered.[70]

The FPU newspaper was struck by the injustice of naval reservists receiving only fifty cents per day for their service while the new enlistees of the Newfoundland Regiment earned a dollar a day. Support from the FPU notwithstanding, it would be a constant struggle for the members of the Naval Reserve to receive the same admiration from the Newfoundland press. As in the case of the *Viknor* and the *Clan MacNaughton*'s crews, the Newfoundland members of the Naval Reserve were dispersed among the naval personnel of many British dominions. Consequently, it was hard to identify their exploits as being "Newfoundland" accomplishments. Furthermore, the Newfoundland government initially felt no obligation to the reservists' material well-being. Although it noted that the British government paid the reservists, the FPU suggested that the Newfoundland government should provide additional money so that reservists received the same pay as members of the Regiment. Otherwise, fishers, who comprised the bulk of the naval reservists, would consider the pay a "disgrace" and a "foul slap" in their faces. While private charities provided funds to help the reservists and their families, it would not be until 1917 that the Newfoundland government decided to top up the reservists' pay to the level of the men of the Regiment.[71]

The early naval casualties of war might have rallied patriotic sentiment in a way that would force the FPU to drop the matter of the Newfoundland tragedy. However, as the FPU pointed out, there was no equality yet in how servicemen were being paid, and the deck seemed to be stacked against the fishers of the Naval Reserve. Later in February, the senior partners of the Bowring family in Liverpool apparently agreed to a request by the FPU not to employ Kean as a captain in its sealing fleet during the coming spring seal hunt. The previous November, the convention of the FPU had agreed with Coaker that Abram Kean was to blame for the *Newfoundland* disaster and should not be allowed to command another vessel.[72] Never one to be satisfied with half measures, Coaker not only asked Bowring not to employ Kean again but wrote to the company in St. John's that he would stand by the FPU members no matter what they decided, and would lead sealers if they should decide to take Kean from a vessel by force.[73]

With Bowring's apparent acquiescence in the matter of Kean, the union decided it was time to drop the matter. It went so far as to reminisce about Kean's heyday as a sealing captain, wishing only that he had expressed "proper" remorse about the loss of the *Newfoundland*'s men. Kean later recounted that Edgar Bowring told him that his usual ship, the *Stephano*, would not be going to the ice because it was required for the war effort, not because of any reason related to the *Newfoundland* disaster.[74] On reading that Bowring had apparently decided not to employ him as a captain again, Kean demanded that the company respond. Within days, Bowring's directors, led by John Munn, threatened to resign unless Bowring reversed its decision. Bowring complied, incensing the FPU, and leading Coaker to demand that the governor intervene. Coaker argued that, while no judicial process had convicted Kean, it was the people's belief that he had caused the loss of the *Newfoundland*'s crew and, therefore, it was their will that he be punished. The people of Newfoundland were so angry, Coaker alleged, that the two machine guns recently donated by the Reids for the war effort were really intended to keep sealers in check should they rise against Bowring's action.[75] Governor Davidson had no intention of agreeing with Coaker's request, but he was worried that Morris felt the sealers might riot when they came to St. John's in March for the annual hunt, and he relayed to the Colonial Office Coaker's warning that Kean might be seized by the sealers. British authorities took no action, and Coaker later wrote to Munn and to Bowring Brothers again to demand that Kean be withdrawn as captain from any of the company's sealing vessels, but to no avail.[76]

Coaker's persistent demand that Abram Kean be held accountable for the *Newfoundland* tragedy had been drawing criticism from those who felt that he was sowing divisiveness during the crisis of war. A headline that had appeared in the 18 February 1915 edition of the *Mail and Advocate*, for example, raised the issue of Bowring's hiring of Kean under the headline "Toilers Fight for Liberty" and suggested that fishers might take action into their own hands by some sort of collective action such as a riot or strike. A correspondent from another newspaper, writing under the pseudonym "A Fisherman's Friend," argued that Coaker's article was unpatriotic and unfair to Bowring. "If the FPU thinks that through an error Capt. Kean was responsible for the lives of these men," the writer asked, "is it making matters better or worse, by talking strikes and such disorders to the fishermen?"[77] The writer thought that Coaker was making matters worse. Advocating collective action by and for any particular social group was viewed as a far more serious and potentially traitorous business in the context of war. In what were still the early months of the war, Abram Kean's defenders were not quite ready to call Coaker a traitor. Kean continued to be visible and gave public lectures while his supporters accused Coaker of pursuing a personal and vindictive campaign against the sealing captain.[78]

The opposition to Coaker might have made more of an impact if there had not been growing discontent about how war-related inflation was already beginning to drive up the cost of living for working people who had little income as it was.[79] The vast majority of the people of Newfoundland were either poor working people in the larger centres such as St. John's or fishing people. While Coaker represented the latter, he sympathized with the plight of all of the disadvantaged and initially stood ready to speak up for all of them against what he saw as a cabal of merchants and their political cronies in St. John's. Members of the NPA and the government could not afford to antagonize Coaker too much if they wanted to have the support of his followers for the war effort, so they remained silent about the controversy. Kean's advocates claimed that it was not Coaker's right to try to pillory him in public; if Kean had broken the law, they argued, then the judicial system was responsible for dealing with the transgression.[80] As the anniversary of the *Newfoundland* and *Southern Cross* disasters approached, the press tended to remember them alongside military naval disasters such as the HMS *Viknor* and the HMS *Clan MacNaughton*. Rather than dwell on the loss of life in the seal hunt, such coverage emphasized the heroism and patriotic sacrifices of the naval casualties.[81]

Coaker realized that the mounting tragedies of the war would cast a long and dark shadow over the public memory of what had happened to the crew of the *Newfoundland* on the ice the year before. Nevertheless, he insisted, the fact of the disaster should not be hidden by the war. The members of the FPU would not allow this to happen; indeed, petitions from local councils in Conception Bay and Trinity Bay began to appear in the pages of the FPU newspaper, all demanding the arrest and trial of Abram Kean for criminal negligence.[82]

Coaker's cause gained momentum with the report of the Supreme Court judges' investigation into the sealing disasters on 24 February 1915. Justices William H. Horwood and George H. Emerson filed a majority report that found Abram Kean guilty of "a grave error of judgement" and of failing to properly care for the men of the *Newfoundland*. The justices proposed that there were many circumstances that had led to the tragedy, but noted, "its primary cause was the sending of the men so great a distance from their ship that there was no expectation of their being able to do the work for which they were sent in time to return to their ship for the night." Wes Kean may have been unwise to send his men to his father's vessel, but the *Newfoundland*'s captain had claimed that he directed George Tuff to ask for shelter aboard the *Stephano*. Tuff denied hearing such instructions, but, for the justices, this did not excuse him for the error of not asking for shelter. Tuff had further erred, they found, by not expressing his reservations about the worsening weather when ordered by Abram Kean to take his men over the *Stephano*'s side to kill seals. But while Tuff had made mistakes, in the justices' opinion Abram Kean had made the most significant and puzzling ones. The senior Kean had misjudged the distance he had carried the crew of the *Newfoundland* from their ship. Most damning, in the justices' eyes, was the fact that it was Abram Kean's decisions that had fundamentally caused the disaster. The senior Kean had devised the original derrick signal that "invited" the *Newfoundland* crew to come towards him in search of seals. The justices contended that "The signal, well intended in the interest of the *Newfoundland* and her crew created *per se* relations between the captain of the *Stephano* and visiting crew, and placed him in a position of responsibility towards them." Once Kean had raised the derrick, the majority report argued, he had assumed legal responsibility for the sealers who walked towards it. The justices could not understand how such a seasoned captain could have sent men out in heavy snow and with the barometer falling. All of Abram Kean's claims about misunderstanding the position of the *Newfoundland*'s crew and their distance from their home ship were, the justices argued, simply admissions that he had not been as competent as one might expect of the Grand Old Man of the hunt. No matter what, Abram Kean should have arranged to have the *Stephano* shelter the *Newfoundland* men.[83]

The inquiry's minority report by Justice George M. Johnson, however, completely excused Abram Kean. Any mistakes in calculating the relative positions of the *Stephano* and the *Newfoundland* or forecasting the weather were accepted as simply the result of variations in ice, winds, and sea currents, natural forces that "baffle human calculation." Furthermore, the report argued that the *Newfoundland*'s men might have reached their own ship "if one or two of the weaker men had not added to their delay." The report also absolved Tuff of any blame by stating that "throughout the ordeal he played the man." Johnson fully accepted Abram Kean's account of the disaster, including that he had had reason to believe that the *Newfoundland*'s crew had safely returned to their vessel. Arguing that Kean's many years of success in the seal hunt made his expert testimony beyond reproach, Johnson stated that the disaster was an "Act of God, and in the circumstances inevitable."[84]

Abram Kean's defenders in the press were quick to spin the inquiry report to his advantage. The editor of the *Daily News* engaged in a peculiar mathematics, adding Johnson's minority report to the earlier Knight report. The result, he claimed, was a draw: two judges found that Kean had erred, while two others found that he had not. The draw meant that it was now up to each individual to decide for him- or herself whether Kean bore any responsibility for the sealing disaster.[85]

The FPU's reaction was explosive. Almost immediately, five hundred sealers who were gathering in St. John's to embark on the seal hunt in the Gulf of St. Lawrence passed a resolution calling for the arrest of Abram Kean. On 6 March, the government received petitions bearing two thousand signatures condemning Bowring, and Munn in particular, for employing Kean. Coaker proclaimed that the day was over "when a coterie of merchants and politicians can run the laws and the institutions of this country to suit themselves" and that the "game of the few overriding the will of the many is now exploded."[86] Although Coaker had originally claimed the commission of inquiry into the sealing disaster was a waste of time, he sided with the majority report, claiming that "the tenor of their findings read guilty Capt. Kean in almost every paragraph."[87]

Coaker's questioning of the manner in which class privilege and penny-pinching capitalism had led to the death of so many sealers in 1914 became lost in his mounting attacks on Abram Kean. It was becoming difficult to determine whether Coaker was fighting for a more just and egalitarian organization of the seal hunt or for the personal humiliation of Kean. Opponents of the FPU leader began to argue that he was manipulating his "20,000 of Northern Newfoundland" into a type of personal political vendetta that betrayed the democratic values people were going to fight for in Europe. Coaker's demand that the sealers try to force the government to have Kean arrested for criminal negligence suggested, according to one writer, "A Woman," that he was "a 'Kaiser' in our midst, who champions as his standard, Might is Right, and that the Law of Discretion and Right must give place to force and foolhardiness." "Kaiser" Coaker, she argued, was betraying the principles of "a true British-loving race." Furthermore, the FPU leader's demand was treasonous in that he was dividing Newfoundlanders at a time when they needed to rally behind the war effort.[88] The editor of the *Daily News* agreed, writing that Coaker's campaign against Kean "is cowardly, cruel, and un-British, an exhibition of personal vindictiveness, that none with a rudimentary notion of the principles of fair play, can contemplate without shame and disgust."[89]

The opponents of Coaker were probably worried because, despite the personal tone of the FPU's leader campaign against Kean, there were visible signs that he had the support of the union's membership. On the night when the *Daily News'* editorial against Coaker appeared, four hundred sealers rallied in support of him at the Temperance Hall in St. John's, encouraged by working men of the town.[90] At least some of these sealers might have been motivated by the manner in which Kean's defenders tried to shift the blame for the *Newfoundland* tragedy onto George Tuff's shoulders, as suggested by Justices Horwood and Emerson.[91] This attempt to saddle Tuff with the responsibility for the disaster was completely at odds with Justice Johnson's defence of Tuff and Kean. In addition, most sealers knew that their captains expected obedience, and that respectable and trusted crew members did not defy their superiors, especially such a senior and well-respected paternalistic figure as Abram Kean.

In almost every issue of the FPU newspaper throughout March, petitions in support of Coaker appeared from communities throughout Newfoundland. Over ten thousand people eventually signed them. On 10 March, Governor Davidson informed Morris that he had received the petitions from Coaker, but he also wrote to the FPU leader informing him that the two investigations of the *Newfoundland* disaster had provided no grounds for criminal proceedings against Abram Kean.[92] On the night of 11 March, eight hundred sealers— about half the men were FPU members—gathered at the Temperance Hall to rally in support of Coaker. About fifteen thousand people lined the city streets to witness a torchlight parade by the sealers through the city and back to the hall. There they heard an address from Coaker accusing Kean of criminal negligence, and a band ended the night with a patriotic anthem.

The sealers had gathered in St. John's to embark on vessels bound for the spring hunt. Coaker's opponents claimed that the sealers were ready to go back to the ice because, like good soldiers, they knew that facing danger was their duty. "It is said," claimed the editor of the *Daily News*, "that after the first few days in the trenches, men forget the terrors of the flying shells; fears fly, and the calm of fatalism, or shall we not say, of resignation, succeeds. And so it is with the Seal Fishery. Long immunity from danger breeds contempt of danger." It was good for the sealers to be fatalistically resigned to their lot, the editor argued—it made them worthy "vikings" who embraced battle with the elements just as soldiers rushed to engage the enemy. Working Newfoundlanders, in other words, were real men just as were those who had enlisted to fight the Germans. Like soldiers in the field, such men embraced danger willingly and without questioning their commanders. Loyal men rejected "violent appeals to passion" and "refused assent or approval to counsels of madness" such as Coaker's demand that they hold Abram Kean to account.[93]

The FPU newspaper, in the meantime, left no doubt about where it stood. Throughout March, the daily edition ran the same banner statements at the top of each page of each issue. The paper opened with the headline "Commission Find Kean Guilty of Error of Judgement," followed on the next pages by "The Bowrings Challenge the Power of the FPU" and "Supported By a Supine, Stir-pot Government." The fourth page proclaimed that "Twenty Thousand Freemen Take Up Challenge" and that "Bowring, Munn & Kean Must Be Taught a Lesson." The last page was so bold as to proclaim, "There Must Be An End To Class Rule in Nfld."[94]

Prime Minister Morris began to share the brunt of Coaker's attacks. The FPU leader argued that the government should have embraced the message of the petitions against Kean, but instead it had supported the sealing captain. Coaker marked the first anniversary of the loss of the *Newfoundland* crew by writing that "thousands of men to-day will think the same thoughts of the almost criminal indifference of the Prime Minister and some of his henchmen regarding their action in reference to the manner in which they have coddled and bluffed the Country concerning Kean and the slaughter of 78 breadwinners on March 31st and April 1st last."[95]

The *Daily News* editor disagreed. In his view, the tragedies of the *Newfoundland* and the *Southern Cross* were bound to be eclipsed by the greater calamities of the battlefield and war at sea.[96] The editor of the Church of England's journal did not want to suggest that the sealing disasters would be rendered any less tragic once war-related casualties made a greater impact on Newfoundland. However, he encouraged people to see both the disasters and the war as part of a greater martyrdom. The losses of each contributed to the building of a great empire, and must be borne in faith and patience.[97]

Sealers may well have taken issue with the view that they were inured to the hardships and dangers of their work. The crew of the Bowring vessel *Terra Nova*, for example, decided that the result of their sealing trip to the Gulf of St. Lawrence was so poor that it was not worth the risk. The crew demanded that the vessel return to St. John's, but its captain made for the port of Channel, where he had hoped to discharge the men. The crew refused to leave the ship, demanding instead that Bowring make arrangements to pay for their return home. The Newfoundland government stepped in to arrange passages, giving notice to Bowring that the company would have to pay the bill. The company responded by having six of the crew criminally charged for refusing their duty. Coaker wondered that the company was so quick to charge the crew members when it had taken no action against Abram Kean.[98]

As the struggle over the sealing disaster continued at home, the men of the Newfoundland Regiment stepped closer to war. On 19 February, the Regiment had been ordered to Edinburgh, where they would join a new company of 250 more recruits who formed C Company, and were now on their way from St. John's aboard the sealing vessel *Neptune*. Another 250 would come as D Company aboard the *Stephano* later in March. The troops drilled hard and were well thought of by local people. Frank Dawe learned to operate and repair a machine gun, earning a promotion to lance corporal for his efforts. Many members of the Regiment enjoyed the theatre, popular music halls, and other entertainments of the city, which people back home learned about from the letters of Frank Lind published by the *Daily News*. While the Regiment was developing an excellent reputation, earning the distinction of being the first overseas troop and the only non-Scottish unit to be allowed to guard Edinburgh Castle, the First Five Hundred were becoming restless, and many wanted to get on with it—to finally be sent into action. John Gallishaw, who had enlisted with the First Five Hundred, later recalled that his fellow soldiers had heard of the Australians being sent to Gallipoli and of Canadians going into action at Ypres. The members of the Newfoundland Regiment felt that they had been overlooked and wanted to follow the Canadians.[99]

In May, the Regiment moved to Stobs Camp, about fifty miles from Edinburgh. They experienced almost summer-holiday conditions there, despite intensive instruction in trench digging and in bayonet fighting with the more reliable Lee Enfield rifles that had thankfully replaced their Ross rifles. The only thing lacking, according to Frank Lind, was the sale of Mayo's tobacco at the local YMCA canteen "instead of the horrible weed we have to torture ourselves with."[100] Lind's letters led to a flood of donations from the readers of the *Daily News*, which the newspaper, in partnership with the Imperial Tobacco Company—the manufacturer of the local tobacco brand—organized as a regular fund to supply the troops with tobacco from home. Lind became popularly known as "Mayo" rather than Frank as a result.

By late July, the Regiment was at Aldershot as Army Troops Battalion of the Third New Army under the command of General E.T.H. Hutton, who had formerly been in charge of the Canadian Militia. The Regiment experienced its "final hardening" at Aldershot, and its members heard on 12 August that they were being sent to the Dardanelles.[101] Receiving the news in an address from Lord Kitchener, field marshal and secretary of state for war, during his inspection of the Regiment, the regiment cheered. "From eleven hundred throats broke forth wave upon wave of cheering. Then came an instant's hush, the bugle band played the general salute, and the regiment presented arms."[102] Not wanting to miss out on going into action with his mates, John Gallishaw, who had been transferred to London as a record clerk, surreptitiously rejoined his Regiment as it readied for departure.

During the first year of the war, Coaker had emerged as the de facto leader of the opposition in Newfoundland. He had broken with the NPA and the government on the issue of the Regiment's formation. More importantly, he had refused to yield to the notion that war required all differences to be put aside in order for Newfoundlanders to rally together behind the flag. He continued to fight for accountability in the matter of the *Newfoundland* sealing disaster, attacking class privilege and power. In many ways, however, Coaker was much like his nemesis, Abram Kean. Both seemed bent on making the issue a bitter but public battle. But whereas Kean stood behind the government, Coaker's attacks made him vulnerable to accusations of treason. The course of the war would soon force Coaker to moderate his views and to think more about how best to build a more just society for the outport people his organization represented.

FOUR

The New Front:
Gallipoli, 1915–1916

By the summer of 1915, the growing influence of the war effort in Newfoundland led Coaker to moderate his rhetoric of class, although he did not reconcile with Abram Kean. This shift did not mean that he abandoned his principles, but to find them one had to consider his statements very carefully. In his support for the war effort, Coaker continued to push for fairness and unity within society. For example, readers of the FPU newspaper early in June might have been surprised when Coaker wrote that "We Britishers, or perhaps we should say, Colonials, are ... so disposed to become very chesty when we discuss the prowess and patriotism of Englishmen, that the supposedly effete people of Southern Europe are dismissed with a sneer," even though the Italian parliament had supported Italy's total war effort.[1] Originally allied with Germany and Austria-Hungary, Italy's ambitions in the Adriatic, Mediterranean, and Asia Minor had led it to side with the Entente, especially as it became clear that Britain and France were going to open a front against the Ottoman Empire at Gallipoli in 1915. On 23 May 1915, Italy entered the conflict by declaring war against Austria-Hungary.[2] Coaker admired the Italian government's expectation that *all* its citizens obey its orders without question for the duration of the war, and its declaration that *all* male citizens were liable to military service. He was impressed, that is, by the government's insistence that all citizens serve and do their duty without regard for distinctions such as class. Throughout the next year, Coaker was to lead the way in redefining patriotism as an attack on profiteering and privilege, arguing that the state must do more to ensure that the rich as well as the poor did their part for the war effort.

War demanded patriotism, Coaker agreed, but true patriotism meant that the powerful and the wealthy should forgo the privileges of their class. In particular, the FPU leader argued that the business community of St. John's had been profiteering—inflating prices at the same time as government did little to provide funds for the widows and parents of the inevitable casualties of war. Government officials continued to draw their lucrative salaries, paid for largely by the revenues from duties on the imports required by working people and the poor. It was time, Coaker felt, to start taxing incomes and war profits.[3]

Coaker continued to be critical of the Morris government, but left no doubt about where he stood on the issue of the war. For example, he supported the view that the German Kaiser deserved to be hanged as the butchering leader of a barbarous nation.[4] Coaker declared that the war was a "holy" cause, and that every Newfoundlander should be proud to fight for "King and Country."[5] The war effort against the Huns would go better, he argued, if the Newfoundland government prepared the people for the economic hardships they were bound to face. The FPU newspaper blasted the newspapers that supported the Morris government's excessive reliance on voluntarism as a source of funds that might assist people. In its pages, Coaker criticized the government's development policies for saddling the colony with debt but not improving its economy. A strong colony would be in a better position to aid the war effort, the FPU leader suggested, and it was therefore Coaker's patriotic duty to point out how the government was betraying the noble cause of the war effort.[6]

While there had been casualties among the naval reservists, the Newfoundland Regiment had yet to see action; little had happened to its members to cause grief at home. This began to change in the late summer of 1915, however, with the news that the Regiment was being deployed to Gallipoli in the Dardanelles. The British experience of the first and second battles of Ypres in 1914 and 1915 had demonstrated that the war in Europe was likely to bog down in what one historian described as a "victory for defence" since "a combination of machine-guns, barbed wire and artillery defied all offensive moves." Turkey's entry into the war on the side of Germany and Austria-Hungary in the fall of 1914 had opened another front, which to the Entente seemed to be a weak point in the Central Powers' alliance that could be exploited. For some time before the war, Germany had used its influence as the main advisor and weapons supplier for the Ottoman Empire's army to encourage it to expand against Russia and its allies. In 1913, Turkish nationalism had surged in a coup by the Committee of Union and Progress, dominated by the military and Young Turk modernizers, against the old Ottoman regime. The new regime wanted to expand at Russia's expense in the Caucasus and regain influence in the Balkans. From Germany's perspective, Turkish ambitions gave it an ally in a possible Balkan bloc, along with Romania and Bulgaria, that would aid Austria-Hungary against Russia in the east. The Empire's Sheikh-ul-Islam issued the official proclamation of war on 14 November 1914 by declaring a jihad, or holy struggle, against Russia, France, Britain, Serbia, and Montenegro, calling on the Muslim faithful in their empires and territories to rise up against their colonial masters.[7]

The Turks opened up a front against Russia in the Caucasus. In early January, the Russians asked the British for a diversionary action against Turkey. The Entente decided on an attack on the Dardanelles, the strait that connected the Mediterranean with the Black Sea. Strategically, the

British hoped they could force a sea route to their Russian ally, ensure the safety of the Suez Canal, and perhaps force Turkey out of the war. However, First Lord of the Admiralty Winston Churchill also saw the action as a way to wipe out the British navy's humiliation at having allowed two German cruisers, the *Goeben* and the *Breslau*, to escape into Constantinople's harbour the previous summer and begin to cruise under the Turkish flag. The problem was that, while the amphibious assault Britain planned was in theory suited to its more maritime-oriented military, Churchill in 1911, and other British military officials as early as 1904, concluded that the British navy, even acting in concert with the army, lacked sufficient resources to succeed in such an assault.[8]

Nonetheless, the British agreed to engage in an amphibious assault on the Dardanelles to aid their Russian ally and to address their previous naval embarrassments in the Mediterranean. The members of the Newfoundland Regiment, equipped with immunizations and new uniforms, were deployed as part of the effort, and on 20 August, 1042 enlisted men and 34 officers embarked on the *Megantic* at Devonport, little knowing the dubious nature of the military adventure they were beginning. Although the newspapers at home reported that the Regiment was bound for Egypt, the soldiers themselves thought they were bound directly for Gallipoli. In Newfoundland, no one was certain about the viability of the Regiment's mission, but the *Daily News* assured its readers, "That they will acquit themselves like British heroes none need doubt, that they will do their duty whatever the cost, all are justly confident; and the universal prayer will be for their speedy return, crowned with peace and honour, and bearing their blushing honours thick upon them."[9] On 1 September, the troops landed at Alexandria and then travelled by train to a camp outside Cairo. Close by was a Canadian hospital unit operating a camp for convalescing Australian and New Zealand troops. "As soon as the Australians found out that we were colonials they opened their hearts to us in the breezy way that is characteristically Australian," John Gallishaw recounted. After training to get used to the heat, the men returned to Alexandria on 13 September for transport to the British base of operations at the port of Mudros on the Greek island of Lemnos.[10] There, they received ammunition, rations, and a single sheet of paper with an envelope to be used "for a parting letter home." As Gallishaw noted, "For some poor chaps it was indeed the last letter."[11]

By mid-September, people at home learned that the Regiment was being sent to the Dardanelles, and the local press began to concede that Newfoundlanders must prepare to hear news of casualties. Nevertheless, reports attempted to reassure readers: "the general opinion is that the Dardanelles, despite the difficulties they have offered, cannot much longer hold out."[12] The experience of Gallipoli, however, was soon to destroy such optimism and extinguish the air of festivity and adventure that had marked the early experience of the Newfoundland Regiment. Although trained in the basics of trench warfare, the Regiment was not prepared for the grinding nature of battle ahead.

The Gallipoli campaign seemed ill-fated from the start, for many reasons: Britain had hoped for the support of Greece and Bulgaria early in the year, but that did not materialize. Further, the amphibious campaign required both Royal Navy and land forces, but there was insufficient coordination between the army and navy. In addition, British forces had arrived to find that Turkish shore batteries were excellent and the Turks had well-mined their coastal waters. Naval bombardments began in February, but by the second half of March, the navy backed off without sufficiently denting Turkish defences, and in late May the British withdrew their capital ships after German submarine attacks, leaving only destroyers with smaller four-inch guns to support the campaign. Throughout the spring and early summer, French, British, and, most prominently, Australian and New Zealand Army Corps (ANZAC) forces—who had broken out towards the Turkish lines at Suvla Bay on 6–7 August—sank back into the stalemate of trench warfare. Though the ANZAC forces fought valiantly, they were disorganized. British management of the campaign was rushed and uncoordinated, giving Turkish forces plenty of time to develop defences and respond to the campaign. The British did not have accurate maps and, in the steep terrain, had inadequate means for observing the effect of their artillery fire—especially as they had few airplanes. And Entente forces spent much of the campaign facing almost as much risk from friendly fire as from the Turks.[13]

The Newfoundland Regiment was part of the 29th Division; it replaced the 1st Battalion of the 5th Royal Scots in the division's 88th Brigade. The Royal Scots had taken heavy losses in attempts to take a Turkish position at a place known as Scimitar Hill. On the night of 19 September, the Regiment began to land in the cold and dark, with the sands of Kangaroo Beach blowing all around them. As the men came ashore, they hunkered down in dugouts for the night, to be greeted by Turkish shells in the morning. Although no member of the Regiment died on the beach, the men experienced their first casualty on 22 September after they had moved forward into the trenches: the explosion of a Turkish shell killed Private H.W. McWhirter. A day later, sniper fire took the life of Private W.F. Hardy. This was now war in deadly earnest. By 30 September, the Regiment had taken responsibility for the fire and support trenches of a mile-long stretch of the British front. Unfortunately, it was stationed at a bulge (or "salient") in the British line, and was subject to Turkish fire from both flanks as well as from the fortifications of Tekke Tepe, which loomed above them.[14]

Of the Newfoundlanders serving in the Gallipoli campaign, the Regiment received the most attention from the press in St. John's, but there were other Newfoundlanders at this front. Members of the Naval Reserve had been on many of the ships of the Royal Navy's Mediterranean fleet when the campaign began in February. There were also Newfoundlanders serving on HMS *Cornwallis*, the vessel that ferried many imperial troops ashore. Until January 1916, Newfoundland members of the Naval Reserves took part in the bombardments and landings, and in dropping supplies at the beaches and evacuating the wounded, all of which marked the navy's contribution to the war.[15] By 23 September, the Newfoundland newspapers reported that the Regiment had landed at Suvla Bay and, by 1 October, there was news that it had seen its first action.

The main initiative to provide moral support to the Regiment as it was about to engage in battle came from the Women's Patriotic Association, which appealed for donations of money to provide items of comfort for the troops. The press asked all Newfoundlanders to buy a five-cent pin bearing the Regiment's emblem to show their pride in the boys overseas and to raise money for them. However, by 5 October so many rumours had begun to fly about large casualty lists that the papers had to begin responding to public requests for news. As the month wore on, the *Daily News* warned its readers against believing the rumours because, despite all of the hearsay about who might be sick or wounded among the troops, there was little real news to report.[16]

People at home feared that men would fall in battle, but the soldiers in the trenches faced more dreadful and insidious, if apparently more mundane, enemies than Turkish shells and bullets. Potable water was always in short supply and was contaminated by the gasoline containers in which it was carried. Jim Stacey remembered that the well from which the Regiment's water came turned muddy so that not only did their food and tea taste of gasoline but, when eating stew, "you would be cracking grit with your teeth."[17] The men had enough food to keep them going, but it consisted mostly of jam, hard biscuit, and bully beef, of which the latter two items were very difficult to eat without plenty of water. Personal hygiene was difficult to maintain: the men struggled constantly against lice and fleas, whose biting and consequent itch drove the troops to distraction, disrupting their sleep. No morning was complete without stripping to the waist in an effort to pinch off and kill as many of the vermin as possible.[18] As the weather warmed in October, the men faced another horror when flies began to breed in the dead bodies that littered the No Man's Land between their positions and the Turks'. Along with the lice, the clouds of flies, often swarming on the troops' food, brought dysentery, enteric, and jaundice, and there were also plenty of rats. By mid-October, about one-third of the Regiment was incapacitated by illness, with no reinforcements expected until 1 December. On 18 October, Lieutenant Owen Steele reported that almost three hundred members of the Regiment had been felled by sickness, with diarrhea proving most debilitating. By late October, Steele himself was ill, and wrote that there were too few men well enough for the Regiment to carry out its duty.[19]

Originally, members of the Regiment had spent ten days at a time in the front lines, with two companies alternating between the front and the support trenches. Simply living in the trenches was dangerous, but the troops had to get on with the business of fighting. That mostly involved waiting for the cover of darkness and then creeping out into No Man's Land to repair barbed wire, operate listening posts, or patrol the lines to seek opportunities to push against enemy positions. This was hazardous and nerve-wracking work; the slightest clatter of metal, a cough, or a scuffed stone could draw Turkish fire.[20] Even in the relative safety of the firing trenches, hazards abounded. Lieutenant Steele, directing a party of men in extending a trench on 6 October, recorded that "during the night one man must have come into contact with a buried body for the smell was terrible and two or three men were made sick."[21]

Few members of the Regiment were killed in performing such duty, but many were wounded. Even when the men returned to the rear of the British lines to rest, they faced shelling as the Turks concentrated their artillery fire towards the rear lines, hoping to disrupt communications and supplies.[22] The men began calling the shrapnel "Turkish Delight" when it arrived during their meals. Illness made soldiering more difficult, and from mid-October, cold and rainy weather added to the misery. Casualties meant that fewer men had to do more of the work of the Regiment: by mid-October, the number of men available for active duty was so low that the Regiment's commanders changed the duty rotation. Men had initially served four days in the front line and then moved to the rear for eight days of rest; they now served eight days up front and rested for four days. Conditions became so bad that some of the men began to hope for the kind of wounds that would require their removal from the lines. John Gallishaw recalled that members of the Regiment, when in low spirits, looked upon the wounded as lucky. "The best thing we could wish a man," he wrote, "was a 'cushy wound,' one that would not prove fatal, or a 'Blighty one.'" "Blighty" was the troops' name for England; a Blighty wound meant a trip back to a hospital there.[23]

Back home, the newspapers wanted to maintain public morale as news began to filter through about the hardships that the men of the Regiment were now facing and that the Women's Patriotic Association was attempting to alleviate. Coaker had to find a way to assure his followers that the FPU's ongoing fight with Abram Kean was not adding to morale problems and was not somehow unpatriotic. Kean had been fighting back against Coaker by successfully suing him and the FPU paper over allegations that he had stolen ship's stores from a vessel he had commanded. Kean also sued the Union Publishing Company, the owner of the *Mail and Advocate*, for printing a story alleging that Kean had received a wireless message from Captain Joseph Kean on 31 March 1914, when the crew of the *Newfoundland* had left the *Stephano*, asking Abram Kean to look out for the soon-to-be-doomed sealers. Although the wireless operator swore he had received confirmation of the reception of the message, Abram Kean stated that he had only been given a verbal summary that did not mention the *Newfoundland* sealers. Governor Davidson thought that Coaker's various public statements against Kean were outrageous enough that a court might sentence the FPU leader to jail or at least give Kean "heavy damages—unless the Jury consists of members of the FPU."[24] A verdict in favour of Kean outraged Coaker, because it came from Judge George M. Johnson, the very same justice whose minority report had earlier absolved the sealing captain of any responsibility for the disaster. Coaker (well aware that he might be accused of fostering discontent during the heightening anxieties related to the war) warned that the Morris government and the judiciary (by allowing conflict of interest in the courts), along with Kean himself, might kindle revolutionary discontent among the people.[25]

Abram Kean could not resist trumpeting what he felt to be his vindication by the courts, and began sending telegrams to people throughout the colony boasting of the verdict. Coaker responded in the FPU newspaper under the headline "Ignoramus" by stating that he would not be boasting if he had, like Kean, lost a ship, the *Rimouski*, which had been working for the Reid Newfoundland Company off the coast of Nova Scotia. In any event, Kean's gloating was premature for, in November, the Supreme Court, while upholding the verdict, reduced the damages owed to Kean from $1800 to $100.[26] At the annual convention of the FPU held in St. John's in November, Coaker insisted that, regardless of the government's lack of criminal proceedings against Kean, "the day will come when Abram Kean will have to answer before the bar of justice for his conduct in connection with the Sealing Disaster." In responding to Coaker's address, the FPU council reiterated its position that Kean should be arrested, tried for manslaughter, and never allowed to command a sealing vessel or coastal steamer again.[27]

Though the acrimony between Coaker and Kean would occasionally flare up, the sealing disaster was receding in political importance as people struggled with the meaning of the Great War for Newfoundland. Patriotism and imperial sentiment remained important, but the reality of battle in the trenches was changing soldiers' views of war, and this would have an effect on the debate about the meaning of the conflict. Throughout October and November, morale among the men of the Newfoundland Regiment plummeted due to what might best be described as the war's monotonous horror. Day by day, men hunkered down in the trenches. Often ill and constantly wet, the troops went about the business of maintaining trenches, dodging bullets, and taking cover from shells, all the while hoping to receive a letter from home or a bit of reading material to take their minds off what unfolded before them. The fighting at Gallipoli was as much a struggle against boredom, loneliness, and fear in the trenches as it was a fight against the Turks across No Man's Land. For the men, boosting their own morale could take many forms, such as enlisted men swiping supplies from officers for an impromptu scoff by raiding the field kitchens for anything that might improve the biscuit and bully beef. Most important, the enlisted men gathered together to hear the news from anyone lucky enough to get a letter from home. Frank Lind wrote of the daring of Tom Humphries, the men's orderly in chief for B Company, who ran out into No Man's Land amidst Turkish bullets to retrieve watermelons he saw growing there because "they would be a nice addition to the breakfast."[28]

The excitement Humphries provided for his comrades, and the fresh fruit no doubt, were means of alleviating the monotony of the trenches. More important, Humphries's reckless disregard for his own safety made a manly tale to be embellished and related over and again as a source of entertainment among the men. Talk of home was, however, their favourite subject. The men of the Regiment tended to avoid direct discussion of casualties, especially of fatalities. John Gallishaw remembered that his fellow soldiers would not even say that a comrade had been killed or had died; they rather said that someone "had 'gone west.'" "All the time I was at the front," he wrote, "I never heard one of our men say that another had been killed. A man killed in our regiment had 'lost his can,' although this referred most particularly to men shot through the head. Ordinarily a dead man was called an 'ashout'; or it was said that he had 'copped it.'"[29]

Over time, life in the trenches began to undermine the morale of even the most determined soldiers.[30] The men of the Regiment had all but lost any sense of adventure or patriotic zeal. In the night, unable to sleep, men's talk might turn to why they had bothered to join the Regiment in the first place. In response to the usual cant about duty and Empire, a voice might growl from the gloom that the men had enlisted because of their ignorance of the conditions under which they would be fighting. Gallishaw wrote that even the tone of the Regiment's singing changed as the battle wore on: "At first the songs had been of a boisterous character that foretold direful things that would happen to the Kaiser and his family 'As we go marching through Germany.' These had all but given place to songs that voiced to some extent the longing of home that possessed these voluntary exiles." More and more, as the men went forward into the fire trenches, they felt hopeless.[31] It was not that they shirked their duty; they were so immersed in the terror of the campaign that the "thought of being killed had lost its fear. Daily intercourse with death had robbed it of its horror, familiarity had bred contempt, or more simply a descent into apathy, as men waited for the day when their turn would come, when they would receive the bullet that had their 'name and number.'"[32]

Little real news reached home about the terrible experiences of the Regiment, possibly because of censorship, although Governor Davidson reported that censorship under the War Measures Act concentrated on preventing knowledge about the movement of ships leaking out "from this Colony." Newfoundland did not have an official representative in London until Edgar Bowring became its first high commissioner in 1918. Bowring kept the government informed of anything he learned while in Britain for business or family reasons, but much of this was not passed on to the public.[33] In the absence of accurate information, rumours abounded until reports of casualties appeared in the newspapers. It was not very hard to imagine what the members of the Regiment were going through in the fight for the Dardanelles, and the newspapers became very adept at ensuring that patriotism and pride in the British connection tinged the reports. The exuberance of the early days of the war was nonetheless gone, dampened by the growing casualty lists published in the colonial papers throughout the fall of 1915.

While the papers often published the names of the dead, injured, or wounded, they occasionally printed fuller accounts that combined a sense of pathos and a more maudlin patriotism. Such was the case, for example, in November, with the coverage of the death of Corporal Walter Tucker. Like so many soldiers, Tucker had survived an operation to remove shrapnel, in this case from his bowel, only to succumb to peritonitis afterwards. In his final hours, Tucker had been attended by Major Cluny Macpherson, who sent home a message to his mother from the dying corporal—that he was glad to have volunteered and that "he would rather be in the condition he then was than to have failed to fight for his country."[34] Macpherson, a doctor from a prominent St. John's mercantile family, had been named regimental medical officer in 1914, and would become renowned in 1916 as the inventor of the box respirator gas mask that became widespread in British troops' coping with the enemy's use of poison gas.[35]

Mounting casualties turned minds to the need for replacement troops. The editor of the *Evening Telegram* marvelled that recruitment was as good as it was, considering that the NPA had not established "a continued and sustained campaign for recruiting." The number of men joining the Regiment was all the more impressive "considering the heavy losses in life and limb sustained by Newfoundland at the sealfishery last year."[36] The same editor recounted the privations experienced by the members of the Regiment who were fighting in Gallipoli, noting that they were not receiving the warm clothing sent by the WPA, and that the men survived largely by the help of nearby Australian troops, who had established a very close, protective relationship with the Newfoundlanders.

Coaker was angry that the private administration of the war effort was leaving the men at Gallipoli without proper clothing, and demanded that the governor investigate the shortages. Suspicious of plundering among those responsible for arranging the supply of the troops, the FPU newspaper wrote that the Newfoundland government had a duty to ensure that the lives of the men fighting with the Regiment were no less comfortable than those of the Newfoundland men who had "stayed behind to drink whiskey, and amuse young girls."[37] In his view, the war effort and the noble sacrifice of the volunteers demanded the support of every Newfoundlander, and no lesser sacrifice should be expected from any able-bodied person. Coaker's particular blending of Christianity, patriotic duty, and populist egalitarianism led him to believe that the war was a crusade that would perfect British civilization by extending its freedom to the masses. The mobilization of all elements of society in the just cause of the war would mean that

> Wealth will be more evenly distributed, Governments will possess and operate public utilities and administer them solely to benefit the condition of the common people. Laws will be devised to prevent a few from becoming enormously rich at the expense of the common people. Education will become more general. The common necessaries of life will be cheaper. Work will be abundant and all will be made to work. Thus poverty, intemperance and crime will greatly decrease.[38]

The real significance of the war then, for Coaker, was that its conduct had required unprecedented intervention by government in economic and social matters; such interventions might well be turned towards building a more just society.

Although sanguine about what the war effort might actually accomplish, Coaker's contemporaries came to admit that it would outstrip the management capacity of voluntary organizations such as the Patriotic Association of Newfoundland or the Women's Patriotic Association. Earlier in September, the editor of the *Evening Telegram* had written an editorial in favour of the Newfoundland government's use of the War Measures Act to take control of the economy for the war effort. Calling "the safety of the State" the "Supreme Law," the editor wrote that the laissez-faire liberalism of Adam Smith and the Manchester School were out of step with the demands of war.[39] Coaker went further, arguing for a patriotism committed not simply to defending ideals embedded in the British form of liberal democracy, but also to principles that were progressive, or similar to those of the Social Gospel movement. Always a keen observer of events affecting labour in Britain, Coaker additionally accepted the sentiment growing there that the war had a transformative power to make the state into an instrument for the establishment of a more just and egalitarian society.[40]

The war, for Coaker, was directed against two enemies, one foreign and the other domestic: the Kaiser-led Central Powers and the merchants and political cronies who fostered gross inequality at home. The suffering and the achievements of the Newfoundland Regiment at Gallipoli meant that the foreign enemy currently loomed larger, and the incident that became known as Caribou Hill became a particular point of pride. The hill in question was a knoll from which Turkish snipers had good lines of fire into the Regiment's fire trenches, but since the hill was not within their lines, the Turks each night had to send snipers to occupy it. The Regiment decided to eliminate the threat, and the job fell to Lieutenant James J. Donnelly of C Company. On the evening of 4 November, Donnelly took six enlisted men and a non-commissioned officer to occupy the post before the Turks arrived. Donnelly's squad was successful, and they managed to fight off the three Turkish snipers who approached, killing two of them, while the Turks wounded the NCO, who returned to the Regiment's trenches for reinforcements. A party of eight, led by Lieutenant H.H.A. Ross, set out to reinforce Donnelly's position but encountered Turkish soldiers in the dark. In the fight that followed, Ross and four of his men were wounded; one of the wounded, Private James Ellsworth, was to die from his injuries. Ellsworth's NCO, Sergeant W.M. Greene, and Private R.E. Hynes, managed to keep firing on the Turks. By morning, Donnelly was able to report that they had held the position, and the Regiment reinforced it with machine guns. The Regiment was cheered by news that Donnelly would receive the Military Cross and that Greene and Hynes were to receive the Distinguished Conduct Medal.[41] Even John Gallishaw, having been wounded and sent back to Alexandria in Egypt before being sent to Wandsworth Hospital in London for convalescence, felt that the boost in national pride and morale from the success at Caribou Hill meant that the men who fell at Gallipoli had "not died in vain."[42]

By 17 December, the St. John's papers carried reports of the award of the Military Cross for Lieutenant Donnelly's role in the capture of Caribou Hill. Along with stirring accounts of Donnelly and his comrades' repulsion of repeated efforts by the Turks to retake the hill, and of Donnelly being deafened by Turkish bombs, the papers printed copies of a letter from Captain A.R. Bernard, the commander of C Company, congratulating Donnelly's mother for having raised "such a brave and tenacious son."[43] The papers further printed lists of the men who were dying at Gallipoli, identifying them primarily as terrible sacrifices to Germany's greed and ambition. Although Turkish snipers shot the bullets and Turkish artillery bombarded the trenches, the papers made clear that the tragedy of the war had been set in motion by Germany and its Kaiser. The men of the Regiment were soldiers in a crusade against "the ravenous beast who has issued from his cave," "a madman and a blood-crazed nation." Donnelly and the rest of the regiment were fighting for life and liberty against "the reign of Anti-Christ," and those who died in the cause were "giving to all of us, who remain in the safety of our homes, a truer sense of citizenship, and a deeper realization of what service means."[44] Indeed, even soldiers in the trenches continued to identify their main enemy as German rather than Turk. Two months earlier, for example, Frank Lind had written approvingly of how Turkish soldiers did not use gas and how they provided medical treatment and cigarettes to the British soldiers they captured, even occasionally returning the wounded to their own lines. "Just imagine the cultured (?) German doing this!" Lind exclaimed.[45]

While pride in the events of Caribou Hill grew at home, people were unaware of a natural disaster that was befalling the Regiment at Gallipoli. On 26 November, a severe thunderstorm brought heavy rainfall to the area around and including Suvla Bay. The rain lasted for five hours and was so bad that the trenches began to act almost like floodways, the waters overwhelming the trenches and dugouts of both sides all along the front. The men of the Regiment received a thorough soaking, and much of their clothing and equipment was destroyed or badly damaged. More distressing, much of the rain had fallen at night: the "men struggling in the higher parts of the trenches could hear despairing shouts and cries in the darkness. It was impossible to go to the help of any who might be drowning even a few feet away."[46] There was no hope of drying out as, by 27 November, temperatures plummeted, turning the rain to snow and the water to ice. Frostbite became an immediate problem; it was a major factor in 150 members of the Regiment being sent for hospital treatment. For the rest, even as the weather warmed, the water continued to cause casualties. In particular, the men began to suffer from trench foot, a condition marked by swelling and tissue damage to the feet as a result of constantly standing in water. At first an uncomfortable nuisance, trench foot could quickly lead to gangrene and possible amputations.[47] By then a patient at Wandsworth Hospital, John Gallishaw met comrades from the Regiment who had been evacuated because of such problems; they reported that what became known as the "Big Flood" carried with it "blankets, equipment, rifles, portions of the parapet, and the dead bodies of men who had been drowned while they were sleeping."[48]

As news from the battlefields reached Newfoundland, the problem for Coaker, and for anyone who was concerned about the ongoing inequities in Newfoundland, was that the war was shaping sensibilities about citizenship and service in such a way that the identification of problems on the home front, especially those worsened by the impact of the war, could be made to appear a betrayal of the holy cause of the war and the suffering of troops overseas. Plenty of local difficulties were arising. Throughout the first year of the war, it had become increasingly clear that there would be complex impacts on the colony's economy and, in consequence, on society. Although the pulp-and-paper and mining industries had become important, the economy still depended on the export of fish and the import of almost all provisions, other consumer goods, and capital equipment. By 1915, the disruption of shipping by the war, especially the diversion of tonnage from the fish trade for the war effort, meant that Newfoundland could depend on only one steamship line, Furness Withy, rather than the five that had previously been used. Tonnage shortages and rising insurance costs were contributing directly to inflation in Newfoundland, and many suspected that this was attributable to local mercantile profiteering since the colony had to rely more on locally owned shipping.

Water Street firms certainly took advantage of the great demand for tonnage to negotiate the sale of their best steel-hulled steamships through the end of 1916, leaving domestic shipping almost completely dependent on the older wooden-hulled ships that dominated the sealing fleet. The St. John's firms may be partially excused since they had developed their plan to sell the ships (which primarily ended up in Russian hands) in the early days of the war, when everyone expected the conflict to be over within a year. Nevertheless, the strategy had been to take advantage of the conditions of war to dispose of a fleet that had been increasingly unable to make good profits in the seal hunt. The Reid Newfoundland Company quickly sold two vessels, the *Bruce* and the *Lintrose*, while Job Brothers unloaded two prominent sealing ships, the *Beothic* and the *Nascopie*. Two of the vessels that had figured so prominently in the 1914 sealing disaster, the *Bellaventure* and the *Bonaventure*, disappeared from Newfoundland in a sale by a group of firms under the name of the Venture Steamship Company. A. Harvey and Company, made notorious as the operators of the *Newfoundland* in 1914, led the consortium, which also included many prominent members of the NPA. Alexander Harvey eventually justified the sales by explaining that attempts to make the seal hunt safer had made it unprofitable.[49]

By the end of 1915, the scarcity of shipping and consequent higher freight rates had resulted in domestic coal shortages and higher prices. Intense political debate began about the role of mercantile profiteering.

At first, Coaker did not object to the sale of the steamers: he thought that although it would worsen the tonnage freight problem, the seal hunt might well benefit by reducing the capital invested in steel-hulled steamers.[50] However, once he realized (early in January) that local coal dealers planned to raise coal prices to $10.80 per ton, he accused them of "barefaced robbery," and asked that the government "commandeer" all coal supplies so that they might be sold at cost, or $6.50 per ton. The next day, Coaker declared that it was shameful of Alex Harvey and John Chalker Crosbie to justify the higher price on the grounds that it would prevent the poor from wasting fuel. If it were a matter of enemy ships having sunk ore carriers, the FPU leader stated, then the price hikes might be understandable, but the higher prices stemmed from tonnage shortages arising from the sale of steamers.[51] Governor Davidson sympathized with Coaker's views, writing to the Colonial Office that, while St. John's firms might have been legally entitled to raise coal prices, the hikes caused much distress and came "with a bad grace from merchants, such as A. Harvey & Co, who were largely interested in a fleet of steamers—used heretofore to carry coal at certain seasons of the year—which had been sold to the Russian Government at prices which were practically double their original cost."[52]

Coaker felt that the war was providing the wealthy of Newfoundland, and Water Street in particular, with an opportunity for profiteering. Upon learning that W.D. Reid, whom he called one of the "Coal Barons," was to receive a knighthood, Coaker exclaimed that "there is not a more despised or disliked man in the Colony to-day.... He is simply hated by the masses." Coaker wondered if a knighthood was also on the way for Abram Kean or Richard Squires.[53] Other newspapers justified Reid's knighthood by citing his many donations to the War Fund and various local charities, as well as the fact that two of his sons served with the Newfoundland Regiment. Later in January, the *Daily News* came to Reid's defence by stating that he was supporting a convalescent home. The paper additionally came to the defence of people of Reid's class

by noting that one of Coaker's earlier antagonists, Edgar Bowring—
now Sir Edgar, having been knighted the previous year—had pledged
five hundred dollars per month for the rest of the war to aid sick or
wounded soldiers at a convalescent home he had established in the West
of England.[54]

The *Daily News* blamed the coal shortage partly on the sale of
steamers to the Russians; partly on the general commandeering of
ships for the war throughout the Empire, which drove up freight rates;
and partly on shortages caused by the war, although this position was
hardly a defence of the colony's merchants.[55] Coaker approved of the
government's arrangements to regulate the sale of coal and to charter
vessels to bring in more coal, so when Alex Harvey complained about
the arrangement, the FPU leader demanded that no weakness be shown
by the government in its dealings with "Coal Barons."[56] With the full
support of the opposition, the Morris government informed coal dealers
that they were obliged to sell their existing inventory at $8 per ton, and
that the government would charter the import of more, all under the
oversight of a committee composed of the prime minister, the minister
of finance, and Coaker. Coaker hailed the move, stating that a "few men
in this city have long enough lorded it over the people through their
combines in trade and their utilization of the tricks of the trade. This
action of the Colony will cause some of them to open their eyes and
realize that we are now living under war conditions, such as no generation before us had to contend with." The next day, the FPU newspaper
announced an expanded Committee of Citizens to oversee coal sales,
which included James McGrath of the LSPU.[57]

In contrast to St. John's coal dealers, owners and drivers of the many
carts and wagons that shipped goods and supplies to and from the city's
docks—truckmen—did not automatically pass on their rising costs to
the purchasers of their services. Their union, the Truckmen's Protective
Union, had, on 3 January, agreed not to raise their rates despite the rising
cost of animal feed. Coaker asked the people of St. John's to contrast

the truckmen's actions with those "of the Coal Barons, who in a cold blooded manner set to work and soaked the poor laboring classes of this City $2.80 per ton on coal which they had in their sheds for weeks and for which they were satisfied to charge $8.00 a ton up to the end of 1915." The truckmen stood revealed as "patriots in the true sense of the word," and the FPU would continue to defend every man among them and their fellow workers "because it is the laborer by the sweat of his brow which has enabled our Merchant princes to hand in their fat cheques to all the funds in which their names appear as our leading patriots."[58]

Meanwhile, in the early days of January 1916, the sacrifices being made by the Newfoundland Regiment at Gallipoli were coming to an ignominious end. Even as the troops had been suffering through the Big Flood, the Entente command had belatedly decided that the cause on the peninsula was lost. Bulgaria had allied with the Central Powers, threatening Serbia in the nearby Balkans and ending any hope that help might come from that quarter. On 23 November 1915, the British War Committee had decided that all Allied forces should be evacuated, and troops began to leave in December. By 19 December, most of the Newfoundland Regiment had been moved to Imbros, but it then returned on 22 December to the peninsula with the 29th Division in order to hold off the Turks while the French evacuated their position at Cape Helles. The Regiment worked under such dangerous shelling that the Greek Labour Corps used by the British refused to join them, leaving the Regiment to perform the manual labour that had been the duty of the Greek Corps. The British and the Newfoundlanders had all left the Cape by 9 January 1916.[59] Just before the final evacuation, on 7 January, Lieutenant Owen Steele rushed to aid men from the Regiment's B Company, who had been injured when a shell struck their cookhouse. While digging out the wounded and the dead, Steele heard another shell coming, which frightened him and his fellows, who dove for whatever cover they could find. The shell landed close by, but hurt no one, leaving Steele to observe,

It is very strange indeed, what trivial bits of shelter we make for under such trying moments. I have seen men, and have done so myself, dodge behind a small bush not larger than a gooseberry tree, being even worse than the proverbial ostrich, for such shelter would be no protection whatever, but under such a trying ordeal, one feels a great sense of protection and safety behind the least little cover.[60]

At home, Coaker had been defending himself from accusations that he was not properly supporting the Regiment or the war effort. In particular, P.T. McGrath, of the *Herald*, had suggested Coaker was implying that Roman Catholics were receiving preferential promotion in the Regiment. This, argued Coaker, was simply an effort by McGrath to undermine the FPU via sectarianism. McGrath had also objected to Coaker's continued hostility towards Abram Kean, to which the FPU leader replied that "McGrath will yet witness the sight of Kean standing at the Bar of Justice to answer for his conduct which left so many brave toilers to die like dogs on that never to be forgotten day of March 31st, 1914."[61] The news of the Gallipoli withdrawal fuelled Coaker's anger. "The Gallipoli episode," he declared, "has a sinister meaning for us, as many of our brave lads went down in the terrible slaughter which characterized the brief and inglorious campaign." Incompetency in command had caused the defeat there, Coaker argued, "and it is poor comfort for us to be told that the soldiers 'died without flinching.'"[62]

Coaker's claim that Gallipoli was a tragic waste of Newfoundland lives met with little support in St. John's. The FPU leader's inability to write without hyperbole likely did not help his case: though he referred to a "slaughter," only between forty-four and forty-nine members of the Regiment had actually been killed or died from disease. The more debilitating casualties, as far as the operations of the Regiment were concerned, were the three hundred or so ill and wounded who were in hospitals throughout the Mediterranean and in England. The wounded in England, although in British hospitals, were having many of their needs met partially by the Newfoundland War Contingent Association, a group of Newfoundlanders and their friends living in England and working under the chairmanship of the occasional object of Coaker's anger, Sir Edgar Bowring. While many people in the capital might not have shared Coaker's critical perspective on the war, his continued leadership of what had become the single most significant political movement in Newfoundland, and one that represented a largely outport constituency, suggests that the FPU leader's views reflected a significant body of public opinion in the dominion.[63]

Though the number of dead and wounded may not have been catastrophic, the experience of Gallipoli had gouged the shiny patina of adventure that had marked the Regiment's first year. The press had already been active in finding a nobler meaning in what the experience of trench warfare meant for the members of the Regiment in its treatment of the heroics of Caribou Hill. In their letters home and the presentations of returned soldiers at public meetings in support of the war effort, members of the Regiment further tried to romanticize what was otherwise an experience of horrific boredom. Stories became commonplace about the manner in which the Newfoundlanders, supposedly because of the rugged, cold climate of their home, had been better able to withstand the privations of the Big Flood and subsequent freeze of November. Owen Steele, for example, wrote home that, while there was much suffering among the other troops as a result of the flooding, "thanks to the general hardiness of the Nflders, not one death resulted in our Battalion."[64] Overall, a more heroic image of the Regiment's soldiers emerged: they were gallant crusaders in a noble cause, abler and more willing than most to stand up to the hardships of war.[65]

This romantic imagery was useful to the NPA, which was, in light of the casualties of Gallipoli, preoccupied with how to get the Regiment back up to strength. The original plan had been to keep five hundred enlistees in reserve to be deployed as needed, but the casualty rates of the Regiment in action had proved that this would not be enough. The NPA had taken some steps to increase enlistments—most notably, by the end of 1914, allowing reserve forces to receive pay before deployment, and providing additional money to assist enlistees from the outports with the costs of lodgings. By the end of the following year, 2744 men had volunteered for the regiment, although only 1418 were fit enough or of the proper age to be accepted.[66] Increasingly, support for recruitment sufficient to maintain the Regiment at the strength of two battalions—one active and the other in reserve—drew on the argument that Newfoundlanders were playing an important role in a great battle of civilization against "Prussianism," a battle for "Freedom and Liberty." One newspaper editor called for more enlistment and warned that bloodier sacrifices on the battlefield lay ahead if Newfoundlanders were to do their part in defeating the Germans. True British blood coursed in the veins of Newfoundlanders, he argued, "which will be freely sacrificed that we remain free. Better death than Prussian slavery. The call is now for men to do or die in the second battalion of the Newfoundland Regiment."[67] Another editor agreed, declaring that Newfoundlanders must be inculcated with the proper values of imperialism and patriotism in every school and from every pulpit. Real men must realize that they would face the contempt of their fellow Newfoundlanders for failing to enlist.[68]

Support for the war effort was important to Coaker, but he was not willing to say that it subordinated the rights of working people or gave anyone the right to denigrate the contribution that labour made to the war. For example, in commenting on labour unrest in Welsh coal fields and the Clyde shipyards, Coaker stated that it was unfair for anyone to think that workers who did not enlist were slackers. Wars were, the FPU leader argued, fought as much from work benches as from trenches. In Newfoundland, Coaker protested, it was all too easy to "hear some of our fishermen denounced as slackers in certain quarters. There are some people who have contributed very little to the cause of Empire who are very denunciatory of the fishermen because they are not falling over each other to enlist."[69] Those outport men in the Naval Reserve,

Coaker insisted, were doing more than their fair share of military service. Moreover, he suggested, more men from the outports would enlist if commissions were as readily available to them as to the sons of the gentry in St. John's.

The question of class privilege remained as important to Coaker as did the war effort. He continued to be angered by the status of Abram Kean, and was furious at the news that Kean was to be appointed to the Legislative Council. H.M. Mosdell, the former editor of the FPU's newspaper and now editor of Richard Squires's *Daily Star*, defended Kean, leading Coaker to declare that "Mosdell fairly loves Abe Kean. He is ever ready to lick him all over if the licking process can be done with any financial advantage." Too bad, Coaker suggested, that Mosdell did not care as much about the widows, orphans, and maimed survivors of the *Newfoundland*.[70] While Coaker took aim occasionally at Kean, he was even more concerned with what he felt was the profiteering by Water Street merchants, complaining that they were using the scarcity of tonnage and higher freight rates to drive up the price of coal and flour, and continuing to argue that "Big Interests" had caused the problem by selling the steel steamers to the Russians.[71]

Coaker maintained that by fighting against these interests he was fighting for the war effort. "If the public knew the one half of what is going on in official circles the past few months," he claimed, "they would stand appalled. They have been asked to send their sons to fight the foe. They have been asked to contribute to collections for patriotic purposes. They have been asked to make many sacrifices which they have done with true British spirit. But in returns for all this they find themselves at the mercy of a ring of commercial grafters...."[72] In arguing that Newfoundlanders had two fights on their hands—one against the Germans and the other against "Big Interests" at home— Coaker was turning the language of war to the advantage of the FPU cause, and was following in the path of a more general "democratic" challenge by workers and fishers to the "autocratic" domination of mercantile and industrial elites in Newfoundland, especially through profiteering.[73]

Coaker's opponents did not deny that the cost of living was going up, but argued that it was everyone's duty to economize as much as possible. "Patriotism without economy is not Patriotism," argued one newspaper. "These are days for sacrifice, but in what a cause! Britain and her Allies are fighting for Peace, for Liberty, for Right."[74] Another editor, in commenting on news of the German offensive at Verdun, argued that the enemy's gains were very small compared to the men and munitions expended on them. This war, he wrote, would be a matter of "Men, Money and Munitions," and Newfoundlanders must give their all, especially by enlisting or encouraging their sons and brothers to do so. This editor was ecstatic to learn that a recruitment drive aboard the sealing steamers had led to a number of Trinity Bay sealers giving up their berths aboard the *Bloodhound* to enlist.[75] His fellow editor at the *Daily News* argued that the operators and skippers of sealing vessels should refuse berths to any single man who was fit for military service.[76]

Coaker was unwilling to accept such a measure, but he did appeal to sealers to enlist during a meeting at the Mechanics' Hall of the men who were in town to join the spring seal hunt. The war required, he argued, nothing less than the complete breaking of Germany. People might be dissatisfied with the impact the war had made on Newfoundland, but that was due to the bad management of the Morris government rather than to the necessity of fighting. Voluntary enlistments were necessary—Coaker later called for two thousand volunteers for the front—to ensure that the government would not have to consider conscription, and to "protect our rights and to uphold the grand traditions of the British race."[77]

For Coaker, ensuring the proper conduct of the war from the home front meant demanding better government management of the war effort rather than leaving it largely in the hands of private citizens and entrusting the supply of Newfoundland's needs to private commercial interests without much regulation. The FPU leader would have agreed with the editor of the *Daily News* that there were enough sealing steamers and sailing vessels in Newfoundland to ensure an adequate supply of food and fuel if they were managed carefully. On 8 May, Coaker met with the prime minister, other representatives of government, and members of the Board of Trade, including Alex J. Harvey among the latter, to establish a number of shipping committees to oversee the supply of the colony's needs.[78]

By the late spring of 1916, Coaker could see positive signs that the government was paying more attention to the interests advocated by the FPU. The Seal Fishery Act, passed in May despite the complaints of Harvey, was an example. Among its provisions were a ban on allowing sealers to be left on the ice overnight; compensation in the case of death or disability resulting from being left out at night; the treatment of those who were responsible for such exposure as felons; the regulation of signalling equipment that would be available in the event that crews were in distress; limits on the total number of pelts that could be loaded; and the staffing of ships with proper navigators and doctors. The new bill also prohibited the use of steel ships in the hunt.[79] Coaker hailed the bill, but was disgusted when R.J. Devereaux, the People's Party Member of the House of Assembly for Placentia and St. Mary's, attempted an amendment in the House of Assembly to allow the *Florizel*, which would be commanded by Abram Kean, to participate in the hunt. The FPU leader attacked the president of the council, P.T. McGrath, refusing to call him by any other name than "Patsy," for defending Kean in 1914. As editor of the *Evening Herald*, McGrath had printed what Coaker referred to as Kean's "darky jokes" even as the dead of the *Newfoundland* still lay awaiting reclaim and burial in the Seamen's Institute.[80]

Whether in military service or civilian work on the home front, the problems of social and economic inequality did not go away simply because there was a war to win. A naval reservist made this clear in May when he protested at a meeting of the Legislative Council. One council member, John Anderson, had risen to speak about the service of local sailors and soldiers when the unnamed reservist interrupted him from the gallery, protesting the small pay afforded to the wives and families of his comrades. The Legislative Council expressed its sympathy, but pointed out that reservist pay was an imperial matter.[81] Later in the month, Coaker wrote an editorial asking why miners working at Bell Island were being so poorly paid that many decided to leave the island. It was unchristian, he argued, for men to be worn out in dangerous work and their families forced to live in poverty, while mine owners did well. "We have no doubt that some interested parties, before we are finished with the matter will cry 'Socialist and Disturber,'" the FPU leader wrote, but "we do not ask or seek the impoverishment of the capitalist. We recognize his rights, but in so doing, we insist upon his obligations, and one of them is that the industry in which his capital is invested, shall afford a decent living to his employees therein."[82]

A decent living did not seem too much to ask for, and the demand was certainly not intended as a program for overturning the existing social and economic order of Newfoundland. Coaker wondered why local newspapers felt that the working men of the colony should rally to the flag considering their mistreatment at the hands of merchants in the fishery and employers in the other industries of Newfoundland. Besides, he pointed out, plenty of people had volunteered for military service by the early summer—nearly five thousand—many of whom were fishers. Although working men came forward to offer their lives, Coaker wondered "how many of our local Croesuses have ever subscribed to our war loans?" If they were "as patriotic with their bank-rolls as they are with their oral appendages," he argued, it would not be necessary for the prime minister to be borrowing money in foreign markets to meet the colony's expenditures.[83] Concern about the cost of Newfoundland's war effort had been in large measure the reason for

Coaker's opposition to the formation of the Newfoundland Regiment. Prime Minister Morris had accepted a loan from the British government for one million dollars to assist with Newfoundland's war effort and would soon borrow more. By 1915–1916, the war was favourably affecting trade to the point that the Newfoundland government was able to run surpluses for the next five years. However, these surpluses were not sufficient to cover Newfoundland's burgeoning war costs, and the government continued to borrow in the New York and London markets, eventually adding directly about $13.5 million to its national debt and many more millions in interest to service the debt.[84] It irked Coaker that the people of Newfoundland were incurring the liability for money that was borrowed by the government but spent according to policies set by an unelected body, the Newfoundland Patriotic Association, whose members included people from the St. John's business community who appeared to be prospering in wartime.

As far as Coaker was concerned, working people, especially fishers and their families, were making much greater sacrifices than the wealthy elites of the colony, particularly the privileged merchants, professionals, and bureaucrats of St. John's. In the early summer of 1916, the FPU leader was still demanding, often stridently, that these elites, and the government they dominated, take notice of the plight of working people. While he continued to crusade against Abram Kean in the cause of the sealers who had died or been injured in 1914, the war had created other problems, especially inflation, for working people, and Coaker expected government to use its power to alleviate their problems. Coaker further demanded that merchants and employers treat their clients and employees fairly by affording them a decent living. At times it might have appeared that, by drawing attention to the social inequalities and divisions within Newfoundland, Coaker was detracting from the patriotic rallying that the war effort required. In truth, there was no doubt about Coaker's commitment to the imperial cause, but he had, to this point, assumed that the right to express dissenting views freely was part of the liberal cause for which Newfoundlanders were fighting, and he had at least the backing of the FPU membership. Few people had challenged Coaker's right to speak freely in the press. The events of 1 July 1916 would change that.

FIVE

Beaumont Hamel,
1 July 1916

Readers of the *Evening Telegram* opened their papers on 1 July 1916 to see the editorial headline "British Launch Great Offensive." There was little more on the story except that at 7:30 a.m. the British had launched an offensive against the German front line along a twenty-mile stretch of the Somme river in France. The newspaper claimed that British casualties were light, and that German prisoners described the British bombardment preceding the attack as very effective. Three days later, the paper reported "The Drive Continues," and that British forces had mastered all the elements of the new warfare: "heavy bombardments by large guns, blowing the trenches and the concrete reinforcements to pieces; trench mortars, useful particularly in demolishing wire entanglements; great aerial activity, in which we seem to have a complete ascendancy; and the final and most effective weapon of all, infantry assaults, leading to fierce hand to hand fighting."[1] The *Daily News* noted that the British had advanced five miles along the front despite determined German resistance, particularly at Gommecourt and Beaumont Hamel, where there was especially fierce action.[2] Although accounts of the casualties vary, the most common suggest that, of the 801 members of the Newfoundland Regiment who went into battle that morning, 324 (about 40 percent) had been killed or were missing and presumed dead, and another 386 (over 48 percent) were wounded.[3]

Beaumont Hamel redefined the Newfoundland war effort. The terrible loss of life occasioned by the attack on 1 July forced people to think much more about what the war was for, and to reflect on the nature of patriotism. The conclusion of officials and the conservative press was that the war had become a crusade in which "Our Noble Dead"—those lost between their own and the German lines on 1 July 1916—had sacrificed their "Manhood," demonstrating their patriotism by dying for freedom, liberty, and the "Motherland."[4] Running counter to the official interpretation were the views of William Coaker. He did not dispute the nobility of the sacrifice being made by the Regiment, but argued that such heroism demanded the re-dedication of Newfoundland to the war effort so that victory would be achieved and a better post-war world built. The state should, he thought, serve as the means of achieving such ends through more progressive intervention in the economy.

The tragedy of 1 July 1916 developed in the wake of the Entente's humiliation at Gallipoli. While disease had played an important part in the Entente's defeat, they had also faced a much stronger Turkish force that proved more than competent. The Allies were now decided on a strategy to defeat the Central Powers on three fronts in Europe: in the east, where Russia was fighting; in the Balkans; and in the west. Britain's main effort in partnership with France would be to engage Germany on the Western Front in a major offensive during the winter of 1916, in the hope that fighting in the east would draw enough German resources from the west to aid their goal. Britain and France anticipated striking together at the German lines first, but the Germans had other plans, and began a massive assault on the French at Verdun in February. Hard-pressed by the German offensive, the French had fewer resources to commit to the Entente offensive, even as France needed the action to begin earlier to relieve the pressure building at Verdun.[5] On 25 February, the commander of the Ninth British Corps ordered the 29th Division, to which the Newfoundland Regiment belonged, to prepare for deployment to France as part of General Rawlinson's Fourth Army. General Sir Douglas Haig, commander-in-chief of the British Expeditionary Force, along with the French commander-in-chief, General Joseph Joffre, planned the Entente assault for 1 July, to take place in the French department of the Somme, through which the river of the same name flowed.

Although the original plans had been for an offensive by three armies (two French and one British), the German attack on Verdun meant that the French could provide only one army; the British would have to provide additional units from their Third Army. The commanders of the 29th Division (the unit was known as the "Incomparable Division" for its previous efforts) had initially been dubious about having the Newfoundland Regiment join it as part of the 88th Brigade, but they had come to respect its troops, especially after their part in the evacuation from Cape Helles. On 14 March, therefore, 560 men and 23 officers of the Regiment left Egypt for Marseilles, arriving there on 22 March and spending much of the following three weeks travelling northwards by train and then marching to the front.[6]

The Regiment reached the village of Louvencourt, located to the south of the front lines in the Somme region, on 4 April, and stopped there for additional training, particularly in coping with gas attacks. Groups of officers and occasionally members of the Regiment could be afforded time for small excursions to the coast or England during that stay, they were told, but by 22 April, the Regiment was sent forward to the firing trenches of the front line, from which they might observe or engage the enemy. The original plan for an Allied offensive along a sixty-mile front had been tightened to twenty-four miles, of which the British were responsible for eighteen (between the Ancre and Somme rivers). The British troops, members of the Regiment included, faced well-trained

German soldiers who could fire machine guns from superbly fortified positions. The Germans had also constructed much better trenches than the Allied forces, and had developed a fine system of forts and villages to supply them. The men of the Newfoundland Regiment were particularly unfortunate, as they were stationed across from a strongly fortified German position on a steeply sloping area known as Y Ravine. The Germans had made the occupied village of Beaumont Hamel a strongpoint, putting an enormous amount of work into digging bunkers and trenches in the chalk ridges and heights of the surrounding area. It was one of the best fortified positions on the Somme front.

The Regiment arrived to find shallow, muddy trenches that they had to improve while subject to constant sniper fire. Worse still, the Entente troops, particularly driven by the French desire to yield none of their ground to invading forces, faced an enemy who was willing to retreat strategically to the best positions from which their guns might dominate the battlefield. Within days, on 24 April, the Regiment lost nineteen-year-old Private George R. Curnew, and Lieutenant Peter Cashin was wounded. Curnew's case was particularly poignant. Originally from the Bay of Islands, he and his brother had lost their parents when young and had been adopted by John and Sarah Leggo of Curling. The government, however, would not consider the Leggos to be next of kin and insisted that they return the Memorial Scroll and King's Message that marked Curnew's death so that these would be sent to his brother.[7] Cashin's wound was a deep laceration on his head, the result of having been struck by shrapnel from an exploding shell. The lieutenant had been on a night patrol that, as part of its many duties, strung barbed wire. He had returned from the patrol unharmed, removed his gas mask and helmet, and stepped outside his dugout at the moment when the shell struck nearby.[8]

The occasional shelling by the opposing forces was a reminder that the Regiment had rejoined the murderous boredom of trench warfare. The troops spent long days in the monotony of digging and drilling, broken mainly by shelling and the sporadic exchange of gunfire across No Man's Land. Nightly patrols broke up the routine, but they were nerve-wracking and dangerous. Otherwise, the men simply waited in varying degrees of discomfort, eating poor food and suffering from various pests, including visits by what they began calling the "Somme rat," a rodent "as heavy as cats"; Lance Corporal Frank Dawe, who had come through Gallipoli relatively unscathed, proved very handy with a revolver in shooting them. Sickness again began to take a toll on the troops, but their main fear was the peripatetic artillery bombardment, which was difficult to predict and almost impossible to react against except by ducking for whatever cover was available and hoping for the best. On 16 June, Dawe, who was in the front line, received a shrapnel wound in his shoulder while carrying an injured comrade to a first-aid station. The wound required Dawe's evacuation to London for treatment. He felt unlucky at the time, but the injury meant that the lance corporal would not be in battle on 1 July.[9]

Artillery fire was an enemy of the Newfoundland Regiment's men in more ways than they imagined. The fate of the Regiment at Beaumont Hamel depended partly on the faith of their British commanders in the effectiveness of artillery bombardments to weaken the enemy's lines. Haig gave the command for the infantry attack on 1 July to Sir Henry Rawlinson, who had admired the effectiveness of the German bombardments at Verdun, and believed that the artillery under his command could do even greater damage to the Germans at the Somme. Rawlinson and Haig also hoped that heavy bombardments could clear the way to the German lines for Allied infantry, who, when their turn came, would penetrate the lines and thus make way for Allied cavalry who would carry out the final victorious charge and chase down the fleeing Germans. The British commanders had faith in the resources under their command: British forces outnumbered the Germans by a ratio of about seven to one, and the British had a vast reserve of shells for the big guns—mortars and howitzers—at least one placed every seventeen yards along the German front lines under attack. Impressive as these resources might seem, they were not enough to effectively assail the depth of the enemy's fortifications. Moreover, the German troops were better trained and dug in so that the artillery bombardment did little damage, the British lacked sufficient heavy guns, and British mass-produced shells were of low quality. Although the British eventually fired more shells in the week preceding the attack than they had in the whole first year of the war, many—perhaps as many as a third—did not explode. Rawlinson, it turned out, overestimated the effectiveness of the British artillery barrage; he also did not accept Haig's advice to ease up on the bombardment at least three days before his men were to charge from their trenches, so as to avoid alerting the Germans to the possibility of attack.[10]

The Newfoundland Regiment was particularly unlucky. Rawlinson had ordered the Fourth Army to advance about 1.5 miles along a fourteen-mile-long front, but the section of the front across which the men of the Regiment would have to advance was further away from the support of British artillery fire, and the five hundred yards between the British and German lines was a mass of tangled barbed wire that had been churned up by artillery fire. Along with the rest of the 29th Division and their comrades in the 4th Division, the men of the Newfoundland Regiment had not received enough training to manoeuvre over the hilly terrain they would have to cross. Throughout June, as the men took their turn in the front line and worked to improve its defences, they saw constant signs that the Germans were anticipating and preparing for an attack in the valley at Beaumont Hamel. On 20 June, for example, Lieutenant Owen Steele wrote that the men were feeling "strangely pensive" about the coming battle, and a day later noted that "the Hun certainly appears to be expecting our visit, for they are, according to reports all along the front, hard at work."[11]

Despite their apprehension, at least as far as Steele could tell, the men were impressed by the sheer scale of the British preparations for the attack: "Everyone seems so cool about it all," he wrote on 23 June,

William Ford Coaker (1871–1938), c. 1896. Coaker was about 25 years old when this photograph was taken. In five years he would found the Fishermen's Protective Union (FPU), the first mass-based social and political protest movement in the history of Newfoundland and Labrador. Populist and progressive in nature, the FPU fought for the better treatment of outport fishing people by government officials and merchants based in St. John's.

265–281 Water Street (Bowring Brothers, Ltd.), St. John's, n.d. Bowring Brothers was one of the most important mercantile firms involved in the fishery and seal hunt. Most of these firms had their headquarters located on Water Street, St. John's. As a result, the mercantile firms were collectively known as "Water Street" and were the object of much of the FPU's criticism about the conditions that produced social inequality in Newfoundland. Bowring Brothers was often the subject of William Coaker's ire due to its association with the sealing captain Abram Kean.

Sealers with gaffs walking on ice, before 1916. The seal hunt was the most important supplementary economic activity for the fishing people of the northeast coast of Newfoundland. By the early twentieth century, large firms such as Bowring Brothers dominated the hunt by employing sealers on large steamers. These vessels carried men deep into the pack ice from which they would walk, often for miles, to reach patches of seals. The work was dangerous and vessel owners gave little thought to their crews' safety.

King's wharf, St. John's, Newfoundland, with flag half mast. Crowd awaiting
arrival of survivors of SS *Newfoundland* sealing disaster. One of the greatest risks
faced by sealing crews was becoming stranded on the ice in bad weather. Such
was the fate of a sealing crew from the SS *Newfoundland* between 31 March
and 2 April 1914. Seventy-eight men died as a result in a tragedy exacerbated
by the shipowners' (A.J. Harvey and Co.) removal of a wireless set and poor
communications between the captain, Westbury Kean, and his father, Abram
Kean, the captain of another vessel, SS *Stephano*, owned by Bowring Brothers. The
Newfoundland tragedy outraged the public and was an example of what William
Coaker alleged was the constant neglect of outport people by "Water Street."

Captain Abram Kean (1855–1945). For over forty years, Abram Kean was one of Newfoundland's most prominent captains in its merchant marine. Kean was most famous for his role as the foremost sealing captain of his time. Conservative in politics, Kean supported Sir Edward Morris's People's Party and was a bitter opponent of William Coaker and the FPU. Coaker attributed most of the blame for the *Newfoundland* tragedy of 1914 to Kean's role as commander of the *Stephano* during the incident.

Courtesy of the Rooms Provincial Archives Division, A 23-83/ J. Vey.

Sir Edward P. Morris (1859–1935). Premier of Newfoundland from 1909 to 1917, Morris was a proponent of the Reid railway interests and St. John's economic development. Despite early overtures for FPU support, Morris became one of Coaker's political nemeses, the latter seeing him as an agent of Water Street. Morris was a strong supporter of the British war effort, but his handing over of much of the responsibility for Newfoundland's participation to the Newfoundland Patriotic Association and his support for raising the Newfoundland Regiment further antagonized Coaker.

Volunteers with 1ˢᵗ Newfoundland Regiment Leave St. John's Aboard Steamer, 1914–1915. The soldiers pictured above were either members of the First Five Hundred who left Newfoundland aboard the SS *Florizel* in 1914 or of D Company, which left aboard the SS *Stephano* in 1915. The ships were identical, and both were used in the seal hunt. Despite the popular surge in patriotism that accompanied the declaration of war in August 1914 and the raising of the Newfoundland Regiment, the controversy about the *Newfoundland* disaster continued to dominate local politics.

Trenches, Suvla Bay after November Storm, 1915. News of the deployment of Newfoundland troops as part of the British campaign at Gallipoli in 1915–16 changed the political debate at home. The *Newfoundland* tragedy receded as people considered more the meaning of participation and sacrifice in the war. For the troops, the Gallipoli campaign revealed that disease, poor supplies, and exposure to bad weather were just as bad for morale and well being as was enemy fire. In November 1915, a severe rain storm, followed by freezing weather, flooded British trenches, causing much hardship.

"quietly preparing for what is going to be the greatest attack in the history of the world, and very probably the greatest there will ever be. We only hope that it may be a very strong factor in bringing an early end to the war."[12] Three days later, Major-General Sir Beauvoir de Lisle, the general officer commanding of the 29th, addressed the Regiment. Steele wrote in his diary that de Lisle acknowledged the danger the Regiment was about to face but emphasized the honour the soldiers were about to earn in battle. For the fearful, de Lisle stressed the Entente forces' supposedly overwhelming superiority in artillery and sheer numbers of men who might be hurled at the enemy lines. Death might come to some, but they would be remembered forever in glory by their friends in Newfoundland.[13]

On 24 June, Rawlinson's bombardments began, but these (and subsequent raids carried out by members of the Regiment and other units of the 29th) did not significantly reduce the German defences. The raids were very risky: on 27–28 June, for example, a raiding party from the Regiment tried to cross into the German line, but got caught in a firefight with the Germans in which four Newfoundlanders were killed and two more taken prisoner. Such risks were designed to assess the effectiveness of the artillery fire in opening holes in the wire, but the information gained at such cost was not well used. Haig, incredibly, decided the problem must lie with the raids—that they must be producing flawed accounts of the impact of the British artillery.[14]

The men spent a pensive last couple of days in the trenches, waiting for the battle. On 29 June, Frank Lind wrote a final letter, which contemplated the horrible dangers of trench life, but also told of how the men laughed at the incongruity of seeing the weather improve, revealing "a beautiful clear sky" while they gazed "across 'No Man's Land' to the enemy's lines." Lind signed off with the hope that he would soon write again, assuring everyone at home "that they may feel proud of the Newfoundland Regiment, for we get nothing but praise from the Divisional General down. With kind regards."[15]

A bright sunrise heralded the dawn of 1 July. However, since it had been raining heavily in the week or so preceding the attack, the clothing and equipment of the Newfoundland Regiment and the other British troops were damp, and the men faced a tough slog across the mud of No Man's Land. At 7:30 a.m., the first troops went "over the top" to begin their attack, charging into slaughtering machine-gun fire. The bombardment of the preceding week had hurt German troops both bodily and in morale, but had not been strong enough to open ways through barbed wire or significantly damage the Germans' dugouts, and the Germans had been able to keep their guns and grenades safe and ready for action. The force of the British bombardment had destroyed the landscape of the valley of Beaumont Hamel, and this had the effect of depriving advancing British troops of any cover from the devastating German gunfire: the No Man's Land between the Regiment and the Germans became "one great killing field." To make matters worse, the British had mined the crest of a ridge known as Hawthorne Redoubt, a protruding spur in the enemy line from which the Germans would have been able to pour machine-gun fire into the advancing British troops. Rawlinson rejected a plan to blow the mines nine hours before the attack, fearing that the Germans would be able to fortify the crater, and hoping that a later detonation would allow some of his troops to reach it first. The huge blast, which came just ten minutes before the beginning of the advance, provided not the defensive crater for the British troops that had been intended but rather a warning signal to the Germans, who were therefore able to reach it first.[16]

Other units of the 29th Division had gone over the top in the first charge and were being mowed down. In a further tragedy, divisional commanders mistook German signal flares for similar ones they had previously agreed would indicate that their own first units were achieving their objectives. The Newfoundland Regiment, held in reserve in a rear position known as St. John's Road, heard the sounds of battle. Scraps of news from the forward observations suggested to the men that the first charge was going badly, but A and B companies nevertheless advanced readily when ordered at 9:15 a.m. to do so. Major Forbes-Robertson remained behind, in command of a mandatory ten percent reserve around which the Regiment could be rebuilt in the event of disaster. Owen Steele, who had felt lucky to be appointed billeting officer in April (the person who would find billets for the Regiment once they were sent for a rest after the battle), was among the reserve forces. The men moved forward from the reserve trenches, facing enemy fire, their own barbed wire, and eventually the bodies of their fallen comrades before they could get to a point beyond their firing lines. They were heavily laden, so such a manoeuvre would have been difficult under the best of circumstances: each man carried about sixty-six pounds of equipment, including sandbags, shovels, picks, wire, stakes, bombs, and flares in addition to their guns, ammunition, rations, and emergency supplies. The Germans were aware of the precut holes in the British wire around which the Newfoundlanders had to cluster to get through to No Man's Land. As they gathered there, the men of the Regiment faced concentrated German gunfire, which killed or wounded many of them.[17]

C and D companies then followed their fellows. These newer companies had a much higher proportion of soldiers who had not been in action before, and their first chance to fight alongside their comrades was, for most, their last. The few who made it through had to move down a slope towards the German lines. Halfway down, about five hundred yards from the British wire, was a small cluster of blasted trees, one of which served as a rallying point for those left alive and able to move. Later known as the Danger Tree, this point was meagre shelter from the German fire, and it was there that Frank "Mayo" Lind met his end. Hardly any made it to the German wire, which was largely intact, and those who did were shot.[18] Another who fell that day was Mike Broderick, a fisher from St. Brendan's who had enlisted in the Regiment on Boxing Day, 1914, served at Gallipoli until laid low by dysentery, and recovered to rejoin his comrades. Lind spoke well of Broderick as a fearless and capable man who battled against the Big Flood of 1915 to secure rations for the men in the trenches at the Dardanelles, and wrote that Broderick had been one of the *Newfoundland*'s men stranded on the ice in 1914. "Mike got off with only a frostburnt finger," Lind recounted, and his enlistment record indicated that Broderick's only distinguishing mark was a "scar above left index finger." Despite Lind's claim, Broderick's name was not recorded on the crew list for the *Newfoundland*'s voyage in 1914. Broderick died of his wounds on 3 July 1916. If Broderick had in fact survived the disaster on the ice in 1914, his was a doubly tragic end.[19]

By 9:45 a.m. on 1 July, it had become clear to Colonel Hadow, the commander of the Regiment, that the men had met with disaster. Jim Stacey, serving as a messenger or "runner" for the Regiment's command, had not gone over the top, but stayed with Hadow, the signalmen, Red Cross volunteers, and other runners. One of the officers, Captain Arthur Raley, ordered Stacey to move along the front trench to get information from a soldier who had managed to crawl back. Stacey crept along the trench, "but it was filled with the wounded, and as I tried to push by the wounded, agonizing cries would come from them. It was too much for me so I turned and went back and told Raley it was impossible. We stayed there for a while because it was useless to go forward, as it seemed that everyone was wiped out."[20]

Hadow quickly reported to his brigade headquarters that the attack was a failure, but received the command to gather survivors and keep going. Hadow went forward to the firing line, but found none but dead and wounded. Beyond the line there was only carnage. Everywhere lay fallen soldiers. As evidence of yet another planning fiasco, the metal triangles that had been fixed to the soldiers' backs to serve as markers for British observers made excellent targets for German snipers as the sunlight caught them. The only hope the wounded had for survival was to lie still, praying to live until nightfall when rescue might come. Private Howard Morry, who had been lucky enough to be called back from the attack when the disaster became apparent, later recalled what he had seen as the Germans shot at the triangles: "It was a grand thing that mothers couldn't see how their sons died the way that they did. Boy! That was an awful sight; the front line was like a butcher-shop in hell, with our wounded dragging themselves in and falling down in the trenches. All day long we were watching through glasses, and any of our chaps moving from anywhere they were lying, the Germans would shoot them."[21]

Towards the end of the day, Jim Stacey went out with Jim Young to rescue "stragglers," mostly "shell-shocked" men who could not speak. With German shells and machine-gun fire all around them, the runners rescued as many as possible, working far into the night. Exhausted, Stacey crawled into a dugout and slept, later reporting to headquarters, only to find "they had me listed as missing."[22]

Hadow was relieved to have the order to fight on countermanded by a senior officer. Through the night, stretcher bearers worked hard to bring in the fallen, but many were never recovered. Reports vary on how many survived relatively unscathed physically, but the Regiment's war diary noted, "During the night and evening unwounded survivors managed to crawl back to our own lines and by next morning some 68 had answered their names in addition to stretcher bearers and H.Q. runners."[23] With the exception of the ten percent held back at the beginning of the battle to serve as the core for a regrouping, the Regiment had been almost annihilated, taking one of the most complete beatings of any British battalion in warfare to that point in history.[24]

The Regiment was relieved of front-line duty, but this did not mean the remaining men were safe. On 7 July, Lieutenant Owen Steele, who had travelled ahead of the regiment to arrange their billets at Englebelmer about 2.5 miles to the rear of the British lines at Beaumont Hamel, was struck by a high explosive shell while walking with Major Forbes-Robertson. The major guessed correctly, and dove for cover in a ditch on the right side of the road; Steele did not, and took cover under what he must have thought was more than a "trivial bit of shelter"—a barn to the left. The shell landed on the barn. Steele suffered a severe fracture of his thigh and died a day later, following a frantic effort by Jim Stacey to find a working ambulance that could carry him to a field ambulance unit.[25]

While the men of the Regiment coped with their wounded and tried to come to terms with what had befallen them on the battlefield of the Somme, people in Newfoundland anxiously awaited news, and rumours abounded in St. John's. The first reports of casualties suggested modest losses, but on 6 July Governor Davidson issued a statement confirming the heavy casualties of 1 July. Trying to give some meaning to the tragedy, the governor stated that "the world will ring forever with the imperishable fame of the heroes of Newfoundland, who have made sure for all time that the Loyal Colony is worthy of its ancient name." The editor of the *Evening Telegram* agreed with the governor, and further stated that the sheer magnitude of the Newfoundland losses suggested that the Regiment's charge had not been in vain. Rather, such losses must indicate that the Newfoundlanders had sorely taxed the German lines at the Somme: "The action of July 1st was no defeat. It was the first and greatest step towards the final victory that will crush German power and humble German arrogance."[26] The FPU newspaper agreed, trying to report positively on the Battle of the Somme by stating that the British had, overall, used artillery bombardments to good effect, and that the battle might well prove "the first step to ultimate victory, the crisis in the most terrible war of all time, the most momentous climax in human affairs."[27]

Throughout the next few weeks, the Newfoundland public had no idea about the sheer magnitude of the casualties of the Regiment. Public commentary focused partially on how Newfoundland would deal with the wounded who returned home: the editor of the *Evening Telegram* suggested that it was time for the government to introduce an income tax to provide a means for non-combatants to share in the burden of the war by providing the funds to care for those damaged, widowed, or orphaned by the fighting in France.[28] However, by far more common were news stories about the heroism and the gallantry of the Regiment on 1 July. The *Montreal Star* provided a much reprinted cable story to the St. John's paper, reporting that the Regiment had advanced when ordered into enemy fire calmly and without fear. The story alleged that one soldier told his commander to keep going if he was shot. Upon receiving a fatal wound, the same soldier told the men who tried to help him to leave: "Push on with it."[29] The same report told terrible stories about the Germans targeting the wounded with gunfire. Nonetheless, the Newfoundlanders had "pushed on with it."

The St. John's papers quickly seized on the image to make sense of the terrible tragedy, making the losses at Beaumont Hamel into something in which their readers could take tremendous pride. "We knew our boys would faithfully and fearlessly do their duty," wrote the editor of the *Daily News*, "but now we know that this highest tribute, one which seasoned veterans of a hundred fights might well hail with pride, was paid to Newfoundland's regiment. The cost has been terrible, but amid the heartbreak came the undying words, 'Push on with it.'"[30] Surely this sacrifice would inspire more young men to come forward to "prove their manhood" by joining the Regiment, while older people would "do their duty" by supporting the war effort in every possible way.

While the full scale of the losses of 1 July was still unknown in Newfoundland, people knew they were extensive enough to have touched families from every walk of life. Even Governor Davidson had lost nephews at the Somme, although they had belonged to other regiments. Wartime tragedy appeared to stalk equally the high and low, without regard for class. "This war has tested the manhood and the womanhood of the Empire as no other testing could have done," wrote one editor, "and neither in cottage or in palace has the test failed." Sorrow was the inevitable accompaniment, but it had to be faced: "the hearts of mothers and sisters are breaking, but if death must be the sequel of duty, not one would wish it otherwise. Better, far, death than dishonour."[31]

By the second half of July, news had filtered back to St. John's to the effect that the "Big Drive" along the Somme was slowing down. Coaker wrote that while it had probably set the Allies on the path to victory, a long road still lay ahead. "We must steel ourselves," he said, "to the painful fact that the present offensive must involve very heavy losses."[32] In his editorials, he took pride in recounting the courageous nature of the members of the Regiment at the Somme, and reported on news from the Canadian press about the fearlessness of the troops. Oddly, the FPU leader seemed unaware of the nature of the Somme battle, and the Regiment's role in it, writing instead that its men had "been specially selected for patrol and reconnaissance work, and they evidently are opening the eyes of their Commanders. It is said that there are no troops at the front that equal our boys, especially in this particular phase of warfare." In such light, he suggested, the relatives of the men in the Regiment could take "pleasure" in "the heroism of the brave 'little colonials.'"[33] Although Coaker did not seem to grasp what had happened, there were signs that something extraordinary had happened to the Regiment. The editor of the *Evening Telegram*, for example, thanked the *Montreal Star* for quoting, on 14 July, Haig's address to the Regiment's men after the attack, in which he consoled them for what they had suffered: "'Newfoundlanders, I salute you individually. You have done better than the best.'"[34] Victories tended to be celebrated quickly, but Haig's address mentioned none and portended dire news of the battle.

It was only on 26 July that a full list of casualties appeared in the Newfoundland newspapers. Coaker tried to blunt the trauma by citing a letter from one unnamed soldier of the Regiment, stating that he had no fear about going into battle; he placed his faith in God and was determined to do his duty.[35] While Coaker hoped that such heroism would inspire more young men to come forward to enlist, he was scathing in his attacks on Prime Minister Morris for being absent from the home front—having travelled to London, from which he had toured the Western Front and visited members of the Regiment on reserve in Scotland—while "agony is being piled on agony, and fresh wounds are being opened as the appalling truth of the sacrifice of our boys leaks out." Coaker reported that only ninety-five men of the battalion sent over the top on 1 July had escaped unwounded. "There is no section of the Empire which has been so hard hit as we have, as these soldiers were the very cream of our manhood," he wrote.

Without stopping his criticism of Morris, Coaker directed his anger at the manner in which British military commanders seemed to be following up on the failure at Gallipoli with another on the Somme: "One thousand of our bravest and noblest lads have fallen through bungling, and without as much as putting a dozen Turks or Germans out of action. It is a tale of woe...."[36] The staggering losses of 1 July suggested that the members of the Regiment had apparently been ordered to engage in a "suicidal" attack "by their English staff officers, who seemed determined to prove that their men were indeed 'lions led by donkeys.'"[37]

While many might have expected hard questions to be asked about what had happened at Beaumont Hamel, there was a quick effort by the local press, local and imperial officials, and the churches to control any potential damage to Newfoundlanders' commitment to the war effort. Hard questions might have led not to considerations of flawed military command but to an interrogation of the very nature of modern industrial warfare. Indeed, Beaumont Hamel, like the Battle of the Somme generally, simply revealed that the "conditions of warfare between 1914 and 1918 predisposed towards slaughter." Fighting was primarily about serving as cannon fodder.[38] It was hard to accept that men had become meaningless in war except in terms of their sheer number. The FPU newspaper apart, the local press worked hard to develop a greater meaning for the tragedy of Beaumont Hamel. The local newspapers, in a reaction common to the presses of combatants on both sides of the conflict, attributed a potent combination of motivations to the men who died in battle on 1 July: "bravery, determination, imperial loyalty, Christian devotion, and immortal achievement."[39]

Military leaders such as Haig could not allow the loss to be seen as a simple defeat, and it was hardly more glorious to suggest that the men of the Regiment had been sacrificed to allow British and French strategic objectives to be realized elsewhere. In consequence, the sheer magnitude of death was converted from a tragic loss of life to a noble example of sacrifice. The theme of sacrifice revolved around Haig's message that the Regiment, on 1 July, had "showed itself worthy of the highest traditions of the British race, and proved itself to be a fit representative of the population of the oldest British colony." If it failed in its assault, it was not because the men had quailed or shirked their duty, but rather "because dead men can advance no farther."[40] By August of 1916, the local press was largely repeating the message that Beaumont Hamel was a moral victory rather than a strategic loss, a position that found its way more and more into the letters that soldiers would write about their service.

The editor of the *Daily News* immediately offered the opinion that the losses at Beaumont Hamel were heavy but not unexpected. Further, "the gallantry of the leaders was equalled by the gallantry of the men. Newfoundland owes a deep debt of pride and gratitude to her heroic sons."[41] On 4 August, there was a war rally outside the St. John's court house to mark the second anniversary of the war. The attendees overwhelmingly supported a resolution made by William G. Gosling, now mayor, that the city's residents were determined to carry on with the war.[42] Governor Davidson addressed the crowd by saying that the Regiment's sacrifice was of an historic importance that equalled "the far-famed charge of the Light Brigade at Balaclava." Although the "Prussians" had thrown "every product of devilish and perverted ingenuity" at the advancing Newfoundlanders, the latter did not hesitate, and in so doing "incurred losses which exceeded the losses of any of the famed Canadian Regiments which held the broken line outside Ypres or of any of the gallant Anzacs who stormed the defences at Gallipoli." The heroism of the Regiment at Beaumont Hamel was not surprising, Davidson declared, because "'we at home knew, all the time, that the men who at home had braved the perils and dangers of the ice and the sea, and who had endured the hardship of the dreadful blizzard at Gallipoli, silently and uncomplainingly, these men would never waver before any enemy and under any condition.'"[43]

Coaker was impatient with rote patriotism; one of the reasons he had been wary of Newfoundland making a commitment to the Regiment was that he knew military action would produce wounded men and bereaved dependants who would require government assistance, and he was unsure how a dominion in constant financial crisis would be able to help them. Returned soldiers and their families would require practical help. Coaker argued that praise and platitudes about their heroism would not be sufficient to help returned soldiers resume their civilian lives, and would prove poor compensation to the wounded and the surviving dependants of those who had fallen in battle. "Ice cream socials" and similar fundraisers might raise some money, but veterans and their families required more: "[I]t is high time that something of a concrete nature be undertaken to meet the exigencies of the case."[44] The editor of the *Daily News* agreed, but did not suggest that government should respond by spending money. Rather, he argued that the Board of Trade, the Importers' Association, and local trade unions should cooperate in the establishment of a Returned Sailor and Soldier Employment Association. Such an organization would try to match returning soldiers with available jobs. The editor went further, arguing that the government should dismiss all men of fighting age so that they would be free to go to the front, and replace them with veterans. There is no evidence that such an association ever came to be, but the Board of Trade did make its secretary available to help find work for returned soldiers, and its council assured the public that it was likely that Board of Trade members would allow former employees who had left to enlist to have their jobs back upon their return.[45]

The FPU demanded a government pension plan. Its newspaper argued that most of the civil servants working in St. John's held Morris patronage appointments, so they were "leeches" unlikely to have the character that honourable military service would require. However, letting them go would free up the funds to pay for pensions. Coaker condemned the prime minister for being in London "enjoying the sweets of entertainment" but doing little for the soldiers and sailors who served the Empire other than giving them small comforts from home. "Cigarettes and boxes of candy are not very substantial rewards for heroic deeds," he argued, "wake up gentlemen of the Government! Wake up!"[46] Upon hearing a rumour that one returned soldier had no choice but to go to work in the mines at Bell Island because he was without an alternate source of income, Coaker was outraged. "It is an awful thing to realize," he wrote, "that a returned soldier should be forced to go down into the bowels of the earth to dig in order to earn a crust."[47]

Coaker was further worried about Morris's rash promises, especially his assurance that Newfoundland would be able to replace each soldier of the Regiment who fell in Europe. The colony did not have the resources to manage such war commitments, and the FPU leader feared the public debt that Morris was racking up through his efforts to raise war loans. Why, Coaker wondered, was the colonial government content to let the Newfoundland business community profit so much from the war effort without taxing their war-related earnings? The government should not be satisfied with the "few hundred dollars" businessmen donated to the war effort, when they were hauling in many thousands in excess war profits.[48] Coaker also condemned the new consumerism—"the code of the soda fountain" he called it—that was popular among the working people of St. John's, warning that it was their patriotic duty to save their money for the needs of their families and community. Overall, however, he thought that working people were not getting proper wage increases from their profiteering bosses, who were making lots of extra money off working people's backs by charging higher prices for imported basic necessities.[49]

The FPU began to question the commitment of the Morris government to the war effort. Coaker felt that Prime Minister Morris had abdicated the responsibility of his government by handing much of the war effort over to the Newfoundland Patriotic Association, which seemed incapable of basic functions. When news arrived that goods sent to the Regiment in December 1915 had only arrived during the summer of 1916, Coaker called for an investigation by Governor Davidson. It was hardly fair, he argued, that the goods people at home had collected to comfort men undergoing the hardships of battle should take so long to reach them while "the Government boodlers ... away on junketing expeditions to London" appeared to have no trouble reaching England in good time.[50]

By mid-September, as wounded or ill soldiers began to return home, it became apparent that voluntary employment placement schemes would not be enough to meet their needs. Early in September, eleven returned soldiers wrote to Sir Joseph Outerbridge, who was in charge of the NPA's recruiting efforts, that their pay had been ended on 14 August, though they had only returned to St. John's on 5 August and had yet to be discharged from the Regiment. "Now Sir," they stated, "surely this is not just to us. There are some of us who are not able to take up any employment just yet, and to be discarded so quickly seems to us rather harsh treatment." To add insult to injury, the NPA asked the men to help with recruitment on a voluntary basis despite their pay being cut off.[51] Such veterans began to complain that the NPA had developed no real pension plans for them, and that they deserved to live better than paupers.[52] The city's newspaper editors, who were usually leery of any demand for government rather than voluntary plans for aiding the needy, found the sight of wounded and invalided veterans begging help from the NPA to be unseemly. "We take the position that every soldier or sailor, whose wounds or sickness have been caused by his service to Home Land and Empire," wrote one editor, "is entitled not by privilege, nor by charity, but by Right, to adequate support." Further, he argued, "the safety of Newfoundland, the freedom of our people, the honour of our women, the lives of our children, are due to those who have donned the Blue and Khaki in the Empire's Defence."[53] The editor of the *Evening Telegram* wondered if the NPA had a legal right to establish pension plans and felt that the most immediate practical thing the association could do was find work for returning soldiers and sailors. However, the editor admitted that the pension issue was a pressing matter that demanded a solution. Late in September, the NPA met to deal with the issue, and agreed that needy cases would have to be assisted with funds raised for the Regiment until such time as the government developed a public pension plan for the veterans.[54]

Coaker's reaction to the military tragedy of 1 July shifted noticeably over time, from concern about the Regiment's military commanders' responsibility to a consideration of issues of class. One of the problems for the Regiment, Coaker suggested, was that class defined how it was run: in particular, the elites of St. John's dominated its command structure. Most of the officers of the Regiment, Coaker pointed out, were sons and relatives of the men who served on the NPA's Reserve Board Committee. Unfair promotion decisions influenced by religious denominational bias had already come under fire from P.T. McGrath in the pages of the *Evening Herald*, who alleged that Anglicans and Methodists found favour over Roman Catholics. Governor Davidson had flatly denied this in 1915, and further repudiated the notion that class was a factor in the selection of officers, even for positions such as that of the regimental paymaster, Captain Henry Arthur Timewell, which required the education and skills necessary for accounting. Not considering the connection between social background, education, and managerial experience, the governor dismissed additional allegations that Timewell received far better pay than other members of the Regiment by stating that his competent work was worth the pay he received. In March 1916, Edgar Bowring lobbied a sympathetic Davidson on behalf of Timewell for a promotion and, in April, the Reserve Force Committee of the NPA accepted the governor's recommendation that Timewell be promoted to the rank of honorary major, but declared that, in exchange, the paymaster would have to give up a daily subsistence allowance that had been supplementing his pay since he had gone overseas.[55]

The FPU leader's position on class preference in the Regiment led him into more open antagonism with the *Evening Telegram*. Under the editorship of William Lloyd—who, for part of his term, was sitting in the House of Assembly as a Liberal—the *Evening Telegram* had to balance its discomfort toward the hostility between the Liberals' ex-leader, Bond, and Coaker with the recognition that the Liberals would likely depend on an alliance with the Union Party for some time to come. Lloyd left the *Telegram* in June 1916 and was succeeded by H.A. Winter, a lawyer and brother of prominent lawyer James A. Winter, who had close professional ties with Coaker's occasional nemesis, Richard Squires.[56] Winter did not hesitate to defend the reputation of his fellow members of the St. John's elite who happened to be serving in the Regiment. Coaker consequently faced more hostility in the *Telegram*'s editorial pages, especially when he criticized Timewell's running of the London office of the Newfoundland Regiment, and attacked H.A. Winter for defending him. "The trouble with Editor Winter," Coaker wrote, "is that Timewell and Co. are known as the social end of the Regiment ... and as such the common herd must bow down and adore them."[57] The FPU leader subsequently rejected John Anderson's defence of Timewell and the London office of the Regiment, where his son Hugh Anderson worked as a second lieutenant (though disqualified from battlefield duty by poor eyesight), charging instead that the management of the Regiment's affairs had been bungled since its beginning. The FPU would now, assured Coaker, "stand by the brave lads who offered their all that their country might continue to possess its liberty and its British ideals of fellowship...."[58] Despite the controversies surrounding his service, Timewell received his promotion to major on 1 December 1916, later becoming a lieutenant colonel in 1918, and received the Order of the British Empire in 1919.[59]

Coaker's criticism of the way in which the elite of St. John's was running the war effort through the NPA was coloured by a general hostility to the social life of the town. He was appalled, for example, that on 28 September 1916, the Exporters' Association closed all shops in the city so that their employees could attended a festival of games and fireworks at St. George's Field, complete with a children's picnic and presided over by the governor. It was disgusting, he maintained, that hundreds of soldiers lay in British and French hospitals, and many more continued to enlist and serve in the trenches of France, "yet our ladies and some of their gentlemen friends must have a half day's sport in St. George's Field, surrounded by the Governor and others who love the glare of sport and pleasure and end it up, as though peace was declared and the German monster obliterated from off the face of the earth. It was a spectacle over which some men and women might weep. It will be highly appreciated by the outport citizens and the loved ones of the 500 boys whose bodies were buried in distant France and Gallipoli."[60]

The first anniversary of the sailing of the First Five Hundred on the *Florizel* led to remembrance of the many now dead or injured. The editor of the *Daily News* wrote that their names and deeds deserved "to be recorded in letters of gold on Newfoundland's Roll of Honour, a roll that shall endure so long as the great World War remains in the memory of man."[61] Coaker was all for praising the courage of Newfoundland's soldiers, but he questioned the sufficiency of only promising to remember the deeds of the dead and of the wounded. The returning soldiers required jobs and financial help, but "the only gratitude we have shown them, so far, is to give them a reception on their arrival, a few motor rides in the country and a few 'pink' teas."[62]

A new dimension of the war, which brought the hostile action closer to Newfoundland, added a further target for Coaker's criticisms. On 8 October, at 3 p.m., a German submarine sank the *Stephano*, with cargo and passengers, off the coast of Nantucket, the German commander having given the crew fifteen minutes to evacuate the ship before sinking it. Governor Davidson received a letter signed only with the pseudonym "Patriot," claiming that the people of the capital were in an "uproar" and were looking for "spies" in every corner. "Patriot" questioned the loyalty of a local gardener, who happened to be of German descent, and asked the governor to purge the civil service of anyone who were "real pro-Germans." The writer also asked that "all communications" leaving Newfoundland be censored.[63] Davidson turned the letter over to the colonial secretary, but the main response to the sinking lay in new regulations for the port. The submarine menace led the authorities in St. John's to forbid any ship to leave or enter after sunset. Coaker was amused that these same authorities wanted to assure the public that shipping was "amply protected" from submarines, when the working people of St. John's were not "'amply protected' from the sharks" who owned the shipping—the profiteers such as the "coal barons" who had raised the price of coal in December 1915.[64]

The sinking of the *Stephano* refocused Coaker's discontent about the conduct of Newfoundland's war effort, drawing his attention away from the problems of the Regiment and back to the question of mercantile profiteering. Every instance of inflation, he suggested, resulted from increases in freight rates that shipowners and the Reids justified on account of the war. However, these "Patriotic Czars" gave no thought to reducing their profits and personal incomes to offset some of the increases, a self-interest evidenced by the growing imports of luxury automobiles into Newfoundland and the consequent rising demand for gasoline.[65] It was time for government to begin regulating inflation, said Coaker, speaking in support of local seafaring firemen's demand for better wages.

Abram Kean, never far from Coaker's thoughts, drew more of the FPU leader's fire by spectacularly ignoring the new anti-submarine regulations for St. John's harbour. As captain of the *Prospero*, in mid-October Kean had tried to ram the vessel through a boom stretched across the narrows. Coaker pointed out that Kean knew the regulations, but decided to break them because he thought no one would object to such an action from one of the greatest shipmasters of Newfoundland. The government took no action against the sealing captain, but that was no surprise to Coaker, who reminded the public that the Morris government had declined to take any action against Kean for the *Newfoundland* tragedy of 1914. To make matters worse, Kean was working for the Bowrings' Red Cross Line, which had just announced a fifty percent hike in all freight rates. Sure that new rates would lead to more inflation, Coaker wrote sardonically that "this is the Patriotism that pays. These are the men that ask others to send their boys to die for the Empire on foreign soil." The Bowrings stood to make hundreds of thousands of dollars from shipping, from which Sir Edgar Bowring or J.S. Munn might give a thousand dollars to a charitable fund for the war effort, yet be called a patriot for doing so. The FPU leader demanded that Morris do something about the Bowrings' profiteering, but also said he knew this was unlikely.[66]

Coaker speculated that Bowring wanted to raise freight rates because it had expected to sell the *Stephano* and now wanted to recoup what would have been the proceeds of the sale. The FPU leader proposed that the government "commandeer" the *Florizel* to carry freight without the increased rates, justifying the action by saying that the Bowrings were no better than the Germans. "Is there any difference," Coaker asked "in taking $100,000 out of the people by forced levies, as the Germans did in Belgium, and taking $100,000 by increasing rates which the people must pay, because of the want of competition in freight?"[67] When the Red Cross Line refused to bargain with the Firemen's Union over wages, and the government did not intervene, Coaker condemned "our local Czars" for taking advantage of the war to enrich themselves. Since 1914, he argued, it had become clear "just how easy it is for the rich to grow richer and the poor poorer."[68]

The war effort had become a conundrum for Coaker. From his perspective, the British cause was righteous, but the direction of

Newfoundland's effort lay in the hands of a small group of venal, self-interested plutocrats who were taking advantage of the working people of Newfoundland. However, the FPU leader appealed for volunteers because it was clear that the war could not be won without the enlistment of more of these working people. While volunteers could take some comfort that the British cause was right, Coaker felt that they would have to face a fundamental lack of respect during their service in the Regiment. The FPU newspaper reported regularly on alleged instances of upper-class officers' mistreatment of soldiers in the Regiment.[69]

Coaker's editorial opponents at the *Daily News* and the *Evening Telegram* took up the issue of recruitment, but preferred to focus on the nobility of the British cause. The *Daily News* emphasized the righteousness of British resistance against German aggression and expansionism. It called on fishers to enlist because they were "needed to fight for something higher and nobler—for faith, for freedom, for righteousness and truth. These are the stakes in this terrible conflict, and they are worth fighting for, aye, worth dying for."[70] Coaker's continued attacks on local profiteering, by contrast, appeared to his opponents in the press to be an unpatriotic undermining of colonial resolve. Always a supporter of the Morris government, the *Daily News*'s attacks on Coaker were not surprising, but they had intensified with the appointment of John S. Currie as editor in 1916 (a position he held with little interruption through 1956). Currie had won the District of Burin for the People's Party in the general election in 1913, and had participated in Morris's attacks on the FPU as a socialist body and on Bond for having allied with Coaker.[71]

By November, Coaker was on the defensive, and the FPU newspaper denied that he was opposed to the British war effort. Rather, it claimed, Coaker had opposed the formation of a Regiment that Newfoundland could little afford, and which had been offered in the service of the Empire without local consultation. The FPU leader maintained that Newfoundlanders generally were best suited for naval service, but "the Naval service was slighted and overlooked while the regiment was lionized and worshipped." "That our opinion was well founded," observed the paper, "has been demonstrated from month to month since the days of Salisbury Plain and Ayr, down to Egypt, Dardanelles and France. We have sacrificed about 1500 of our best sons and $3,000,000 for what? How many Turks or Germans have our soldier lads been able to dispose of? A few have returned and what is their experience?"[72]

Coaker asked hard questions at a difficult time, since the Newfoundland Regiment continued to see action. On 14 July, having received reinforcements, the Regiment took up a position on the front line at the Ypres Salient in Belgium. The men also worked on the trenches in the reserve at the rear, and it was there on 8 August that the Regiment experienced its first attack by German cloud gas, although members had previously experienced gas by shelling. Equipped with the gas masks invented by the Regiment's own Major Cluny Macpherson the year before, the troops suffered not a single casualty. By early October, the Regiment had moved back to the Somme from the Ypres Salient and distinguished itself in the British attempt to break through the German lines at Gueudecourt on 12 October 1916. It was part of the force committed by General Haig in what became known as the Battle of Transloy Ridge. The Regiment received orders to capture German positions at Hilt Trench on the Green Line, just outside the village of Gueudecourt. With other British troops, the Newfoundlanders again faced withering machine-gun fire from well-placed German positions, but this time the men advanced under a creeping barrage, following British artillery fire. The idea behind such barrages was that the British guns would first clear an area into which infantry could then advance. The problem was that the artillery barrage was first directed at a line two hundred yards in front of the German line, and members of the Regiment, eager to move forward, often rushed into their own fire. Although 120 Newfoundlanders died in the battle, and another 119 were wounded, they advanced 600 yards (about halfway to their objective), killing about 250 Germans, taking 75 prisoners, capturing three

German machine guns, and fending off a German counterattack. The capture of the Hilt Trench was one of the few British Army successes during the battle, but unfortunately, among the Regiment's casualties was Captain James Donnelly, one of the heroes of Caribou Hill.[73]

Jim Stacey was at Gueudecourt, and remembered the trenches there as a nightmare of frosty mud and constant shelling: the men tried to sleep in rubber sheets and sometimes found that their trenches and dugouts were atop the bodies of hastily buried Germans. In December, Stacey was at the village of Méaulte, about twenty miles from the town of Amiens. He spent Christmas there, and recounted how Roman Catholic padre Thomas Nangle rejoined the Regiment following a leave. Nangle, with Methodist padre W.D. Stenlake, took charge of the alcohol and other extras of the officers' mess, and Stacey remembered Nangle arriving late in the evening, when Stenlake was in bed with the officers' whiskey as a pillow for safekeeping. "Padre Nangle remarked smiling 'I don't know what religion is coming to, a clergyman has a case of whiskey under his head and a bag of prayer books at his feet.'"[74]

The twenty-seven-year-old Nangle was a native of St. John's and had been ordained as a Roman Catholic priest in 1913. He had been determined to minister to the needs of his co-religionists in the Regiment, but did not have the support of his archbishop, E.P. Roche. The Newfoundland government had initially assured Roche that British Roman Catholic military chaplains would minister to members of his faith in the Regiment. Desperate to serve, Nangle had tried unsuccessfully to volunteer as a fighting member in October 1915, but Roche relented following the tragedy of Beaumont Hamel and news that British chaplains were not able to meet the survivors' needs. Nangle joined the Regiment at Ville-sur-Ancre at the end of October 1916. Captain Leo Murphy, in recalling the routine of a later Sunday in the trenches, wrote of Nangle that he was "beloved of the Regiment and always welcome for his genial personality and pleasant company."[75]

On 14 November, news reached St. John's that the British had finally captured Beaumont Hamel. This fuelled local pride in the Regiment, and led to calls for more enlistments as the Regiment's reserves were so low that its future had become uncertain. For the *Daily News*, Newfoundland's only chance to achieve glory in the war effort now depended on its ability to maintain the independence of the Regiment.[76] In answer to Coaker's rhetorical question about what the sacrifice of Newfoundland lives was for, the *News*'s editor would have one answer: glory. Such an answer was better than accepting what had become obvious by November—that the "Big Push" at the Somme had failed to achieve a breakthrough in German lines or to force a retreat by the enemy. General Haig eventually claimed that the Battle of the Somme had met three broader strategic objectives for the Allies: it had tied up German resources that might otherwise have tipped the balance in favour of the enemy at Verdun, had taken pressure off the Russians and the Romanians on the Eastern Front, and had begun a process of wearing the Germans down that would proceed over the next two years. Nevertheless, although the battle at Verdun had important consequences for the Somme, Haig had not planned British strategy with Verdun in mind. Further, the Germans continued to be able to send divisions to the east, using them to overrun Romania when it joined the Allied cause. Finally, the Somme might have begun a process of wearing the Germans down, but Haig had not planned for this. Whatever the positive strategic advantages might have been for Britain as a result of the Somme, they were accidental rather than planned.[77]

There was little romance or incentive in suggesting to young recruits that they should want to serve as cannon fodder in a type of warfare pioneered at a battle that demonstrated little intended strategic advantage. Local promoters of the war effort found that recruitment would be better served by suggesting that young men could seek the path to glory through enlistment. Coaker was happy to do so, proclaiming at the annual convention of the FPU in November 1916 that the men who now lay dead overseas had "gone forth to fight for Liberty and Freedom....

What noble boys! They went forth willingly at the Call of Duty and we rightly call them Heroes." Coaker pleaded for more volunteers, and claimed that he had been struggling personally with whether he should serve in the Naval Reserve. The FPU president had decided that he was more valuable to his country by remaining in Newfoundland at the helm of the FPU. Coaker asked the FPU to support his decision—fifty young men should come forward to serve in his stead as what would become known as Coaker Recruits.[78]

By the end of the year, despite the earlier debate over the importance of providing pensions to returned soldiers, the NPA had failed to develop a plan. This was an impediment to recruitment for the Regiment, leading the editor of the *Daily News* to call for the establishment of a "most generous provision" by statute.[79] Coaker had realized from the beginning of the war that service in the Regiment would lead to demands for better military pensions, but he felt that profiteering was now sapping the ability of the government to enact such policy. More important, the profiteering of shippers such as the Reids eroded the earnings of working Newfoundlanders: consequently, young men were reluctant to leave their families for military service. Further, trade suffered and deprived the government of the resources to afford such things as military pensions. The only way to recruit more men for the Regiment (of whom the FPU newspaper estimated two thousand would be needed in the next year) was to bring profiteering and inflation—and consequent public demoralization and unrest—under control, even though that would only be possible through an unprecedented degree of state regulation.[80]

The FPU leader was now prepared to go much further than suggesting that the government establish a pension plan for returned soldiers. Coaker had come to feel that the Great War had brought civilization to a crossroads. At a very superficial level, Newfoundland, as part of the Empire, was fighting against "Prussian" militarism. However, he felt there was a much more fundamental struggle being revealed by the sacrifice of war: Newfoundlanders were learning that the war effort required all loyal citizens to sacrifice their self-interest for the common good. While Germany must be dealt with in the short term, there was a greater struggle over basic economic inequality being revealed by the shameless profiteering of the business class at home. The antagonisms caused by such inequality, Coaker suggested, must be put aside in a "New Age of Brotherhood" that would emerge from the ashes of the war. It was the duty of the state to bring about this new age by regulating the management of key economic resources.[81]

By the end of 1916, political debate in Newfoundland had polarized around the meaning of 1 July. The newspapers that supported the government and the NPA argued that the tragedy of Beaumont Hamel had given Newfoundlanders the opportunity to demonstrate their patriotism and sense of duty. The lost soldiers of the Regiment had represented Newfoundland's coming of age in the Empire, and it was now every citizen's obligation to ensure that their sacrifice was not in vain. Coaker would not disagree with such sentiments, but he continued to argue that economic voluntarism and bourgeois charity were insufficient for running the war. Rather, it was time for the state to step in and use its power to marshal all of society's resources for the war effort, especially by controlling the greed of the business community. A war had begun over the meaning of patriotism, and there was little room for continued concern about the lost sealers of 1914.

SIX

Wars, 1917–1918

As 1917 began, Coaker took the position that, whatever his past reservations about the Newfoundland Regiment had been, its sacrifices in 1916 had "shed a lustre of glory on Newfoundland which will last as long as time."[1] The FPU leader was anxious to demonstrate his support for the men fighting overseas, as was evident in his call for FPU members to come forward for military service as Coaker Recruits. However, such backing of the Regiment also freed Coaker to attack the Morris government even more vigorously. In doing so, Coaker demanded that the government take back control over the war effort from the Newfoundland Patriotic Association and introduce more progressive taxation measures and policies to alleviate the hardships related to wartime economic conditions on the home front. If the Morris government was unprepared for such actions, Coaker made it clear that the Union Party desired an election or the formation of a government that would.

By early 1917, Morris was unprepared to put up much of a fight for the control of the government. Even as the war dragged on, Morris remained burdened by the underlying economic problems of Newfoundland, particularly the expense of the railway and the search for diversification.

His People's Party's close relationship with the Reids continued, as did government support for the railway. Public debt mounted, limiting the likelihood of further contracts for railway construction, the vital source of patronage Morris had used to cultivate the support of his working-class constituents. While Morris continued to explore the possibility of confederation with Canada in 1916—a move even his opponent Coaker was willing to consider—the prime minister knew that such a union would be unpopular with his St. John's constituents, if not people throughout the dominion. The leader of a government that had been in power for eight years, Morris was tired; he was content to leave the government in the hands of the acting prime minister, Colonial Secretary J.R. Bennett, in the summer and early fall of 1916 so that he could visit the troops in England and tour the Western Front on the continent. Morris had come back to Newfoundland in October, but showed more interest in returning to England than in dealing with Newfoundland's problems. The opportunity came in late December when the new British government of David Lloyd George established a special Imperial War Conference. Morris was invited to attend alongside the prime ministers of the other dominions, and to serve as a member of the new Imperial War Cabinet with them and five members of the British War Cabinet. Morris quickly accepted, suggesting that his presence in London was a sign of Newfoundland becoming a full partner in the war effort, and dashed off at the end of January 1917.[2]

The often absent Morris was an easy target for Coaker, who charged the government with economic mismanagement that undermined the war effort and with allowing profiteering while working people became poorer.[3] To remedy the situation, Coaker argued, the Morris government had a duty to become more progressive. In particular, it should introduce an income tax for Newfoundland such as the one Britain and the other dominions had brought in for the war effort. The war provided him with both ideological justification (patriotism) and the means to carry out his goal of unprecedented levels of state intervention in the economy, for Coaker's ambition was to make government the instrument of the people in developing a more equitable society. Coaker's progressive impulse—his belief that poverty and inequality were not individual failings, but were rather systemic problems that must be redressed collectively, especially through the power of government—was likely eclectic in origin. His early-life biographer, J.R. Smallwood, claimed that Coaker had no exposure to the main currents of socialist thinking at work in the British labour movement, but the FPU leader was familiar with the British and Australian labour movements, although he was less interested in their doctrines than in applying their organizational tactics to the Newfoundland case.[4]

While the FPU leader suggested that reforming government was an essential precondition for more enlistment, others emphasized that patriotism and glory should be enough to bring out new recruits for the Regiment. One newspaper editor wrote that too few men were volunteering and that those who did not had no right to share in the glory of sacrifice made by the true Newfoundlanders who were willing to fight.[5] Coaker thought that the number who were volunteering was surprisingly good, considering that the government had refused to tax war profits and had done nothing to save money to fund veterans' pensions and the ongoing care of the wounded. Taxing war profits would help to offset the negative impact of profiteering and acquire the funds that would be needed if, as had become the case in Britain in 1916, it became necessary to conscript troops.[6]

It must have been very difficult for young men to make the decision to enlist amidst the apparently contradictory tendencies they could see in the colony. The presence of more returned soldiers meant the constant display of maimed men who could not find employment: the NPA's Pensions Committee could find no work for them, and Newfoundland had no version of Canada's Military Hospitals Commission, which provided retraining for employment that accommodated war injuries.[7] At the same time, young people could thrill to the patriotic fervour aroused by giant parades such as one held on 7 February 1917, when units of the local cadet corps and naval reservists paraded the machine guns captured by the regiment at Gueudecourt. A huge crowd gathered at the Court House Square to hear Acting Prime Minister Bennett praise the Regiment for its work at Gallipoli and Beaumont Hamel, repeating General Haig's comment that they were "better than the best": "No regiment in the British Army could have done better, and their superiority over the Prussian was made manifest."[8]

Coaker supported enlistment, but not blindly. He encouraged young men and their families to consider what was likely to happen upon their return from the war if the Morris government was allowed to remain in office. The government continued to do nothing to control profiteering, did not bother to tax the proceeds of such activity, made no provision for the future care of returning soldiers, and was sinking the colony into debt by borrowing to pay for its war effort.[9] Under such circumstances, young men might have hesitated to volunteer had there not been more coercive incentives offered beyond the exhortations of patriotism. Ship owners in the sealing industry, for example, had decided to refuse berths for the spring seal hunt to unmarried men younger than thirty if they had not volunteered for service.[10] Richard Squires fielded a number of queries from men looking for berths for the seal hunt, but had to tell them that ship owners and sealing captains were not going to sign young men who were eligible for the army or navy.[11]

Such actions were cheap, according to Coaker, because they required little sacrifice on the part of the commercial houses of St. John's. The FPU leader continued to emphasize merchants' failure to retain enough tonnage in the colony to meet its shipping needs, and their related inability to keep enough supplies on hand for essentials such as coal. While the basic principles of laissez-faire economics had always marked the government's relationship with Water Street firms, the war effort, Coaker argued, had demonstrated the need for greater state control "and so we find daily, the British Government are taking control of industries from the hands of private industries."[12] Pointing to news of insurrection in Russia and mounting strikes in the United States, Coaker argued that the government must use its power to lessen social problems arising from economic inequality to avoid such unrest. "The days are full of movement and trouble," he argued, "but are not without hope. The spirit of brotherhood and humanity's rights is spreading its wings over a world that will no longer be satisfied with the 'laissez-faire' days of the past. We are content that that spirit should have its way with the world. The future is not without hope while this is so."[13]

Whether they supported Coaker or the Morris government, most people in Newfoundland likely agreed that the young men who died on the battlefield at Beaumont Hamel exemplified this new spirit of brotherhood and sacrifice. There would have been much less agreement that such tendencies animated the NPA and the business community that dominated it. Many people were beginning to contrast the sacrifice of Beaumont Hamel with the suspicion that the NPA represented a cabal of St. John's politicians, "patriotic profiteering merchants," wholesalers, and retail traders who fleeced ordinary people for everything from potatoes to coal.[14] The rising price of coal was a particularly sore point, and additional fears grew that fish merchants were creating artificial shortages of salt and fishing supplies to extort higher prices from fishing people. Popular mistrust of the manner in which the organization managed money that it raised to care for relatives left behind by soldiers going overseas contributed to the NPA's faltering efforts to maintain recruitment at a level sufficient to replace casualties.[15]

The growing tension over leaving the NPA in charge of Newfoundland's war effort and allowing the free market to determine the supply of local necessities meant that Morris, who had returned to Newfoundland in May, had to take back control of the war effort by July 1917. Coaker continued to demand that government restrain alleged profiteering and claimed that the close relationship between the Morris government and the Red Cross Line was unpatriotic, allowing excessive and uncontrolled freight rates. Even one of Coaker's usual opponents, the new editor of the *Evening Telegram*, Charles T. James, conceded that local merchants were marking up the price of flour unreasonably, and asked for an investigation. Thinking that a war profits tax might be the best solution, the editor condemned the Morris government for devolving obligation for the war effort onto the Newfoundland Patriotic Association, thereby abdicating responsibility for matters such as new taxation. Coaker supported the call for an investigation into high prices, and demanded that the government do something to support firefighters on strike against local shipping companies and city firefighters, both of whom were asking for higher wages to cope with wartime inflation. The Morris government showed no interest in intervening in labour disputes, but it bowed to public pressure by establishing the Commission of Enquiry into the High Cost of Living to investigate the high price of food. The commission was chaired by Coaker's long-time adversary and "Morris loyalist" P.T. McGrath, but Coaker hailed the move.[16]

Ultimately, the crisis that forced the prime minister to reconsider the management of the war effort arose from the reduced fortunes of the Regiment on the battlefield. By late March, news began to arrive in St. John's that the Regiment had taken heavy losses again. In late February, the Regiment had been temporarily assigned to support the British 86th Brigade, and on 2–3 March had taken part in fighting against a German counterattack north of Sailly-Saillisel, a village about thirty miles northeast of Amiens in the vicinity of the Somme front. Twenty-seven members of the Regiment died there, and forty-four were wounded. Such losses, small in themselves, added to the cumulative impact of casualties. Voluntary enlistments could not keep up: many feared the Regiment would have to be disbanded and the survivors redistributed among other British regiments.[17] On 28 March 1917, the 29th Division, including the Newfoundland Regiment, departed from Camps-en-Amienois for a small town close to the city of Arras with orders to relieve troops fighting at Monchy-le-Preux (Monchy), a village located on a strategically important point about six miles southeast of Arras near Vimy Ridge. On 14 April, the Newfoundland Regiment and the 1st Essex Regiment advanced under cover of a creeping barrage towards an objective known as Infantry Hill. The barrage was not as intense as the Regiment might have hoped, but the Newfoundland men reached their objective under heavy fire and faced a German counterattack from three sides. The Germans surrounded C and D companies, which fought on until heavy casualties gave them no choice but to surrender. Every Newfoundlander either died or became a prisoner, except for one member of D Company. The Essex Regiment fared little better, and the Newfoundland Regiment's commander, Lieutenant-Colonel Forbes-Robertson, learned that every member of his Regiment east of Monchy was wounded. The lieutenant-colonel gathered a party of sixteen men from his command post, including Private V.M. Parsons of the Essex Regiment, and they rushed to Monchy, picking up weapons from the fallen as they went. Nine made it (later joined by Corporal John Hillier of St. John's), dug in, and fought to hold off the Germans until reinforcements appeared. Although the Germans retook most of the ground they had lost to the Newfoundlanders and the men of the Essex, they could not retake Monchy, and Lieutenant-Colonel Forbes-Robertson's feat with his small party led to their reputation as "the boys who saved Monchy." The Regiment had once again displayed tremendous resolve in the face of heavy casualties.

Through the attack on Infantry Hill and additional action on the Arras-Cambrai road, casualties had reduced the Regiment's fighting strength to 221 men by the end of May. Monchy finished the war for Frank Dawe, who had won the Distinguished Service Medal for his machine gunning at Ypres in the previous July. Captured by German troops, Dawe spent the rest of the war as a prisoner, despite a number of escape attempts.[18] Jim Stacey had continued his duties as a messenger throughout the war, and bore grim witness to the horror of the fighting at Monchy. On the eve of the engagement of the enemy, for example, he had been moving through an area that had seen heavy fighting as he sought the Regiment's headquarters. While doing so, Stacey "saw a man, limping around, searching dead bodies. The dead was everywhere and looked as if they had just dozed into a sleep. Most looked so peaceful that I had an urge to wake them. The man was taking the rations and water bottles from the bodies. He used them to help keep six wounded alive. There were five of ours and one German who were in a cellar alongside." Stacey promised to send help. He remembered that the Regiment "was at low ebb—49 killed, 142 wounded and 296 missing after the Monchy battle," and was glad when they received orders to go to the village of Berneville for a rest.[19]

News of the Regiment's feats at Monchy and Arras meant that the local press, which had been fretting about the imbalance between casualties and recruitment, declared that Newfoundlanders could not allow the Regiment to disappear as a distinct unit. Less than two weeks later, it was in action again, winning battle honours for its role in the Second Battle of the Scarpe, south of Monchy on 23 April, having lost thirteen of its number to death and fifty others to wounds while under heavy shelling and machine-gun fire.[20] In commenting on the efforts of Newfoundlanders at Monchy, the editor of the *Daily News* wrote that, while the Regiment had been baptized in blood at Beaumont Hamel, it had now proved that it could fight "the Hun" and win.[21] The editor of the *Evening Telegram* agreed, and suggested that "our soldiers have done for their country what generations of politicians could not do. If we hold a higher and more honourable place than we have done among the dominions of our great Empire, it will not have been won for us in St. John's or London but on the fields of France."[22] Coaker agreed, but was concerned about the matter of recruitment amidst profiteering at home. The FPU leader was sure that Newfoundlanders would remain undaunted because their fight against Germany was a battle for higher ideals, for brotherhood over the "selfish, grasping aims of business." Coaker proclaimed, "We can but trust that the war will remove this blight on our civilization, that MEN will arise who will place the Christian Ideal right in the heart of business...."[23]

The problem for the Morris government was that even the most determined opponents of Coaker, such as the editor of the *Daily News*, were now admitting that merchant profiteering in the trade of basic provisions was out of control.[24] Coaker blamed the Morris government for allowing Newfoundland's public affairs to drift "aimlessly like a ship without a rudder."[25] Coaker became more aggressive in his attacks, suggesting that Morris and his supporters were just as much a problem as the Germans. The FPU leader liked to define the Morris government in contrast to the members of the Newfoundland Regiment. For example, in commenting on the Morris government's lack of interest in controlling inflation, Coaker asserted that "the practice of unholy profits must give way to the call of the sacrifice that the young men are making to-day in Europe. If we ask them to give their lives for the Empire, the least we can do is to prevent their parents from suffering hardships by reason of men who will not give up their monetary gains. It looks dangerously as if material interests were preferred to flesh and blood."[26]

Coaker's views struck a sympathetic chord with leading elements of the organized labour movement in St. John's. James McGrath of the Longshoremen's Protective Union (LSPU), for example, was unhappy that Morris had returned from London in April committed to conscription and that he was willing to suggest that the measure might be necessary to replenish the ranks of the Newfoundland Regiment. The Newfoundland prime minister, like his colleagues from other parts of the Empire, had been under pressure from imperial authorities to provide more men. The British government had also asked for men to serve in roles other than combat, especially to replace British men who had left logging and forestry manufacture for military service. Meeting such a need was relatively easy for Morris, as many of the outport men who were reluctant to enlist for combat were experienced loggers and were willing to serve in non-combatant roles. The government created the

Newfoundland Forestry Corps in March to provide five companies of one hundred men to work as loggers in Scotland and to supply labour required in British sawmills. The British government bore the costs of the corps.[27] The measure did not lessen the pressure to enlist fighting men, and Morris was willing to suggest conscription—without, however, doing much about inflation.

McGrath met with his union membership on 21 May 1917 at the LSPU Hall. The result of that meeting was a series of resolutions opposing conscription as undemocratic, a threat to the labour supply for staple trades such as the fishery, and an imposition on working-class families who were already providing most of the volunteers. The editor of the *Evening Telegram* disagreed, stating that conscription was becoming necessary throughout the British dominions. "A Union Man" wrote to the newspaper, claiming that very few LSPU members had been present to vote or were able to understand what conscription meant. McGrath was incensed, writing that well over five hundred members had been present at the meeting, and that the LSPU had maintained in good standing all members who volunteered for the Regiment and had provided financial support for the relatives of members who fell in battle. The LSPU leader was particularly angry at the suggestion that his union's members were too uneducated to understand the concept of conscription and argued that education seemed to be a poor stimulus to patriotism among the profiteers of Water Street.[28]

McGrath was not alone in his anger. The specific concerns of workers about merchant profiteering, inflation, and lack of proper government regulation of the economy resulted in unprecedented concerted union action. Other workers had begun to feel the need to join larger organizations that could better represent their interests—for example, a new organization had been started in April by railway employees. The railway was one of the first concentrated industrial concerns in Newfoundland to depend on skilled workers, most of whom belonged to unions, as well as large numbers of semi-skilled and unskilled workers who had previously been overlooked by skilled workers' unions. Although the Reids were determined opponents of unions, railway metal workers belonging to the International Association of Machinists (IAM), a skilled workers' trade union, determined to bring all company employees into one industry-wide union. In April, they had organized the Newfoundland Iron Workers' Association, which soon became the Newfoundland Industrial Workers' Association (NIWA). The NIWA's immediate concern was the manner in which wages were not keeping pace with wartime inflation. Initially, the NIWA had the support of the FPU's George F. Grimes, who had been elected in the District of Port de Grave in 1913 as a member of the Union Party. Warwick Smith, the well-educated son of a local Anglican minister, who had spent time working in the United States in steel mills and railway construction gangs, brought an interest in progressivism and the rights of workers to form unions recognized by the state and employers to the NIWA as a member of its executive committee. McGrath and the LSPU did not formally affiliate with the NIWA, but they worked closely in support of the new organization.[29]

By the early summer of 1917, then, support for the Morris government's war effort appeared to be declining, especially among his key St. John's working-class constituents. Morris responded by proposing that a general election be postponed for the duration of the war. Coaker and the Union Party found this unacceptable and threatened loud opposition in the House of Assembly. The FPU leader called Morris "cowardly" and "un-British" for making the suggestion. He said that Morris was setting a poor example for "our gallant soldiers" by stooping to such a subversion of the principles of British traditions and constitution, noting that Australia and Canada had managed to hold their general elections despite the war.[30]

It was bad enough that the Morris government was trying by underhanded means to extend its life, but the government also tried to pass protectionist legislation for two textile companies: Riverside Woolen Mills Limited and Newfoundland Knitting Mills Limited. The government proposed guaranteeing the two companies a five percent return on their capital investment; allowing anything they needed for their plants to be imported duty free; and placing a protective tariff on any competing companies' imported woollen goods, yarns, blankets, or underwear for the next twenty years. Both companies were already in operation, but it was the president of the second company, R.K. Bishop, still a Morris supporter in the Legislative Council, who had requested the measures. Coaker howled at this blatant favouritism, and pointed out that the Morris government was much more responsive to the needs of its monied supporters than to those of the men who were injured or fell ill and died in overseas battlefields and hospitals. Bishop, the FPU leader argued, received more favourable consideration from the government than did returned soldiers, who often found no work and lived with their families in poverty.[31]

Although the Morris government did not go forward with the knitting mills proposal, the report of the High Cost of Living Commission on the relationship between freight rates and the price of provisions such as flour had provided evidence that confirmed popular fears about profiteering. The Reid Newfoundland Company, for example, had increased its freight rate on a barrel of flour by about 655 percent, according to the report, while the Red Cross Line had increased its rate by almost 500 percent. Even the editor of the *Daily News* was shocked by the revelations of the commission and agreed with Coaker that importers and shippers were profiteering. The *Evening Telegram*'s editor lamely defended profiteering as being legal but could not deny that it existed, and he went so far as to propose a tax on excess profits.[32]

The time had come, Coaker argued, for Morris to disavow members of the business community's hypocritical profession of patriotism and practice of profiteering. The government should call an election to defend its record before the people. The Union Party, in cooperation with the Liberals, Coaker promised, would take a new approach whenever an election took place by fighting for a tax on war profits.[33] Coaker sympathized with working-class organizations such as the NIWA, which called for a board of food control to deal with food supplies. The conundrum for the FPU leader was how to persist in attacking the government that was responsible for Newfoundland's war effort without appearing unpatriotic. Coaker solved the problem by identifying the plight of the returned soldier with that of working people victimized by profiteering, writing of wounded veterans who were given jobs in plants, provision stores, or lumber yards that they could not physically handle.[34]

But try as he might to immerse his message in the rhetoric of wartime patriotism, Coaker could not compete with the powerful sentiments emerging around Newfoundland's war effort. Though the war was not yet over, 1 July had already emerged as Memorial Day in 1917, and provided a reason for newspaper editors to comment on the heroic sacrifice of the Regiment at Beaumont Hamel. Their editorials emphasized the need for all loyal Newfoundlanders to put aside their political differences and rally behind the Empire in remembrance of the fallen.[35] While Coaker might attack the prime minister, Morris was in fact issuing commemorative messages on behalf of the government, claiming that the Regiment's sacrifice at Beaumont Hamel had become "a beacon of light" for Newfoundland.[36] Under such circumstances, Coaker had to be careful about continuing to criticize Morris.

It was, however, becoming clear that the prime minister's usual newspaper supporters were now agreeing with Coaker and the NIWA that a war profits tax was necessary, but the *Evening Telegram* did so in part to justify the establishment of selective conscription for the Newfoundland Regiment.[37] As conditions in the fishery improved, outport people, who depended upon family labour, did not enlist in as large numbers as the working people of St. John's. But families in St. John's had already lost too many sons, and working people were now haunted by the suspicion that their suffering had been added to by the profiteering of the local business community. Very few fishing people or city workers appeared to support selective conscription, but more prominent community members such as clergy favoured the measure. The Methodist minister T.B. Daly, for example, wrote to Richard Squires that he hoped the House of Assembly would pass legislation to give effect to conscription.[38]

While many working people either felt that they could not spare more male relatives for fighting or that their families had already given enough, there was another basic problem that affected the war effort. Enlistment rates in the Newfoundland Regiment, the Royal Naval Reserve, and the Newfoundland Forestry Corps had been apparently very high by imperial standards: Newfoundland government data suggested that about thirty-seven percent of eligible males had volunteered. However, only about half of these had proved actually fit medically for service, and consequently the rate of effective enlistment was quite low—9.8 percent of the eligible male population. By way of comparison, the Canadian rate for enlistment was 18.5 percent, Britain's was 22.1 percent, and Australia's was 16.7 percent. Newfoundland authorities had relaxed the minimum medical requirements for enlistment, but casualty rates were still outstripping the availability of volunteers who proved fit for actual service.[39]

From the beginning of the war, the NPA had bungled its efforts to recruit from the outports by not providing sufficient assistance to young men who might wish to travel to St. John's to volunteer. The organization put little energy into developing direct means of recruiting outport people or of providing adequate financial assistance to rural families that otherwise depended on the labour of potential recruits. Such problems were particularly acute for potential volunteers from Labrador, which was very remote from St. John's. The much heavier casualties experienced by the Regiment in France in 1916–1917 made the NPA desperate for much higher rates of enlistment, but it would not accept that there were serious economic impediments to increased volunteering from the outports. Members of the NPA, and most St. John's newspapers, preferred to see the problem as apathy and a lack of patriotism. It was becoming clearer that Governor Davidson's original promise of a Regiment was beyond the ability of Newfoundland to sustain, given the Regiment's exemplary but deadly experience in battle, the economic and geographic realities at home, and the ad hoc and voluntary nature of the NPA. The time for change had come.[40]

Coaker was not about to alienate his most important constituency by supporting conscription, but by the spring of 1917 it was clear that the recruitment measures of the NPA could not keep up with the casualties of the Regiment. Following the losses of Sailly-Saillisel, Monchy, and the Scarpe, the Regiment had been taking more casualties again in the Third Battle of Ypres in July, fighting in wet, sodden, slimy mud that made it impossible to dig in properly.[41] At home, Morris was flailing about in a political morass: the prime minister had promised conscription to imperial authorities, but he knew that he would need the support of every party in the legislature to impose such an unpopular measure. None of the parties wanted to fight an election based, even partially, on the conscription issue. The solution, for Morris, was a coalition government, but Coaker was not willing to enter one if Morris was to continue at the helm. The FPU had always pursued a balance-of-power strategy: the Union Party would support, but not join, governments. In 1916, aware that the Union Party had taken on the role of effective opposition while the Liberals languished, Coaker had piloted a motion through the annual convention of the FPU, allowing Union Party MHAs to accept appointments to cabinet. With the support of the Imperial War Cabinet, Morris invited the Liberal-Union alliance on 16 July to join the People's Party in a coalition National Government for the sake of a united war effort. To facilitate the deal, Morris's People's Party government formally resigned, and Governor Davidson asked the leader of the opposition, William Lloyd, to form a government. Lloyd refused, but indicated that the opposition was willing to cooperate with Morris in the formation of a National Government for the sake of a united war effort. As if to underline that need, and the need for more men, in mid-August the Regiment took yet more casualties at the battle of Langemarck in Flanders.[42]

There were a number of conditions that had to be met before Coaker would agree to join the National Government as a minister without portfolio. First, the NPA had to surrender the administration of the war effort to a new Department of Militia headed by former Morris supporter J.R. Bennett. Second, the dispute around the profits tax approved by the House of Assembly had to be resolved. The original proposal had been for a twenty-five percent tax, but the government had settled on twenty percent on all net profits over three thousand dollars and half a percent on all bank deposits held as of 31 December each year. The editor of the *Evening Telegram* bitterly opposed the tax, claiming that only war profits rather than profits generally should be taxed and that the NIWA opposed it. The NIWA, however, disavowed the latter claim, arguing instead that it hoped for measures to prevent the tax being passed on to consumers. Coaker defended the tax, stating that it was less severe than the British excess profits tax, no less damaging to the economy than profiteering, and was a patriotic measure designed to raise money for the war effort. Although the tax bill had made it through the Assembly, the Legislative Council blocked its passage. Morris responded by threatening to appoint more members to the council to see it through.[43] Coaker's third condition was that the National Government must better manage access to shipping, deal with profiteering, and more effectively regulate the export of salt cod and provide minimum fish prices. The Union Party accepted the woollen mills deal with an amendment to limit the guaranteed annual dividend to five percent and a cap on profits of five thousand dollars per year. More importantly, the new government had passed a food control bill, establishing a board of three people with sweeping powers to investigate the price of food, fuel, and clothing. The government also established a Department of Shipping in an attempt to remedy the tonnage shortage.[44] The NIWA supported the establishment of the Food Control Board, although it was unhappy that the board was to consist of three people, and argued unsuccessfully for more working-class members.[45]

The new measures of the National Government confirmed Coaker's belief that the war was demonstrating that government could take more progressive measures to improve the lives of working people. Under Coaker's direction, the Union Party had not been fighting for any sort of radical socialist transformation of society. When the NIWA put its support behind a strike for better wages by the workers at a local boot and shoe factory, the FPU newspaper asked the government to appoint an arbitration board. The paper made clear that it did not want to take sides, but observed that the factory was "a very wealthy concern."[46] The Union Party's modest policy was that a worker deserved a minimum wage "sufficient to give him a decent home, and our civilization is a farce until we get down to this and see that every man gets it."[47] Governor Davidson, about to leave his post in Newfoundland to become the governor of New South Wales, Australia, reported that, although Coaker had become a "leading spirit" of the National Government, the governor was not worried that radicalism now coursed through the veins of office. Coaker's "outlook in the conduct of affairs has widened," Davidson reported, and the FPU leader had learned to be more tolerant of opposing views.[48]

Coaker accepted the National Government knowing that Morris was to go; the prime minister left St. John's quickly, supposedly to rejoin the Imperial War Cabinet. After a face-saving delay, Morris resigned as prime minister on 31 December and accepted a peerage appointment. Morris's resignation appeared abrupt and irresponsible at the time and, in retrospect, might seem "bizarre," but it was not surprising. All he had to look forward to locally was his connection with the debt-plagued railway and a flirtation with Confederation, neither of which were popular at the best of times, and wartime disgruntlement made popular support even less likely. By the end of 1917, a peerage and political retirement in Britain was a much more attractive alternative to the struggles that were likely to come in Newfoundland for the old People's Party warhorse. The freshly minted First Baron Morris took his place in the House of Lords, but Peter Cashin later recalled that the former Newfoundland prime minister's estate was not as honourable as he might have hoped. Morris did not have the income to match the style of his fellow Lords and began the humiliating practice of receiving funds for allowing new companies to use his name in the process of their incorporation; he passed away in London in 1935.[49]

As the senior politician, and free of the taint of the People's Party, William Lloyd became prime minister. Lloyd's main asset appeared to be his conciliatory character. Cerebral by inclination, Lloyd seemed better suited to his earlier careers as teacher or newspaper editor, but he had always got along with Coaker, and had been one of the Liberals who had tried to maintain the FPU leader's difficult relationship with Bond. Now, Coaker was content to work through Lloyd and, along with fellow Union Party member William Halfyard, joined the cabinet, as did three Liberals in addition to Lloyd. The newspaper opponents of Coaker immediately attacked the propriety of Lloyd becoming prime minister because he was the lawyer for the FPU, and they argued that Coaker should either resign as president of the FPU or step down from cabinet. Coaker defended his position by pointing out that no one had demanded that Richard Squires step down as grand master of the Orange Order when he had become a minister in Morris's government. The *Daily News* further needled Coaker for making common cause in the National Government with John Chalker Crosbie, whom the FPU leader had constantly denounced as a profiteer. Its editor suggested that Coaker follow Morris into retirement, slyly feeding the impression that Coaker's position in the FPU and the Union Trading Company (which provided goods for working people on the northeast coast) was giving him an opulent lifestyle beyond that of his "men of the North." He went on to suggest that Coaker "could spend the remainder of his days at Port Union, enjoying his bungalow, his thousand a year, and his gramophone and rewriting his famous diaries...."[50] When Coaker made clear that he was staying in cabinet, the editor warned that Coaker would use his power over the Union Party MHAs and FPU members to rule Newfoundland. The FPU president was "as great an autocrat as the German Emperor; his will is law."[51]

In the context of the war, the easiest way to smear anyone's name was to question his patriotism by calling him a Kaiser, even though Coaker's critics were attacking his commitment to using the powers of government to address the worst inequalities of Newfoundland society. The participation of a party with Unionist goals in government—better regulated public funding for social services and education, and public regulation of the fishing industry—threatened the nature of liberal democracy, at least as it had worked in Newfoundland in the past. Coaker's approach was said to be "German": "Mr. Coaker has no use for either aristocrats ... or gentlemen, and he has several times expressed admiration of things German." The profits tax was an example, and Coaker's willingness to support public investment in improving the railway meant that he was, according to one editor, selling out to the Reids.[52]

Coaker dismissed the jibes of his opponents but, as a member of Lloyd's National Government, found that he had to shoulder the burden of an increasingly unpopular war effort, even as the Empire demanded more sacrifice. While Entente forces had begun to enjoy more success on the Western Front, and had gained a new ally when the United States entered the war in April, victory did not seem to be within reach any time soon. Germany was still well entrenched in the west, and the Entente had suffered a severe setback in the east. For some time, the strain of war in Russia had been exacerbating pre-war popular discontent with the Russian monarchy, the unequal and exploitative system of landholding in the countryside, and an exceptionally brutal form of urban industrial development. In March, a revolution replaced the czarist regime with rule by a Provisional Government. The Provisional Government made the unpopular decision to remain in the war, fuelling more support for revolutionary leftist groups such as the Bolsheviks, who seized power in a second revolution in November—their leader, Vladimir Lenin, having received German assistance to return from exile in April. Upon seizing power, the Bolsheviks made good on their promise of peace, and negotiated a withdrawal from the war with the Central Powers, sacrificing huge territories in Poland, the Baltic, and the Caucasus, as well as losing Finland. Formally signed in Brest-Litovsk on 3 March 1918, the peace at first appeared to be a huge setback to the Entente, as it allowed Germany to concentrate its efforts in the west.[53]

The Empire required more soldiers, and conscription appeared to be the only way to get them in Newfoundland. Coaker had been dodging the conscription issue by claiming that it would be unfair to draft men before the government conscripted wealth through profits and income taxes. By the end of 1917, however, both taxes had been established. Throughout the fall, both the FPU newspaper and its opponents had constantly demanded that more men come forward to enlist.[54] The paper had hoped that voluntary enlistment would protect "Liberty," which would otherwise be infringed by conscription.

But such hopes were unrealistic. The Regiment had had just over a month to rest and rebuild following its last engagement at Passchendaele, or the Third Battle of Ypres—fighting on the Broembeek River at Poelcappelle in early October. The massive losses it suffered later at the Battle of Cambrai in November made futile any hope that the Regiment could be brought up to strength by voluntary enlistments alone. On 17 November, the troops were sent to Sorel-le-Grand to participate in the attempt on the city of Cambrai, and fought in the battle against the Hindenburg Line there, beginning on 20 November. They tried the new tactic, which the French and British had begun using earlier in the summer, of moving forward behind tanks, but took heavy casualties again. The battle finally ended in the first week of December with failure to capture Cambrai. Once again the Regiment distinguished itself by holding off a German advance at Marcoing Copse, but by the end of the battle, even with reinforcements, their numbers now stood at two companies instead of the usual four.[55] News trickled home of the casualties and suffering of the wounded in the letters of witnesses such as the Voluntary Aid Detachment nurse Frances Cluett of Belleoram, on Newfoundland's south coast. Cluett, a friend of John Gallishaw's sister Henrietta, who was also in the VAD, had gone overseas late the previous year, and had written her mother frequent and moving letters about the terrible suffering she had seen among the soldiers. In December 1917, for example, Cluett wrote, "Oh! Mother, if you could only see and hear all we do; I assure you it is not very nice, when you have to rip the khaki off them in bed; blood everywhere, and then to hear them tell what they have gone through; it is very sad to see troops marching daily to take the trains for the line; bands playing: yet they seem so cheerful; and call Good Bye to us who watch them over the camp fences."[56] News of this type was not likely to encourage more volunteers.

There were simply not enough volunteers to replenish the Regiment's ranks—an embarrassment considering that the imperial government had recognized Newfoundland, which had enjoyed a nominal status as a dominion since 1907, as being of the same rank as Canada, Australia, New Zealand, and South Africa in December because of its war effort, especially the sacrifices of the Regiment.[57] The news of casualties and suffering must have made it harder to recruit volunteers, but the FPU newspaper nevertheless continued to support voluntary enlistment, arguing that Newfoundland's new dominion status required it.[58]

The voluntary enlistment strategy pursued by Coaker ultimately failed to provide enough men, and his opponents accused the FPU leader of currying outport votes by identifying conscription as a Water Street measure.[59] The *Telegram* further wrote that Coaker's attempt to defend himself from such attacks by pointing to his efforts to secure "Coaker Recruits" was "too nauseating" and "execrable" because the real heroes were the volunteers and their families who, unlike Coaker, did not boast about their volunteering.[60] The fact was that, as a member of the government, Coaker had to support conscription despite widespread opposition to it among his outport constituents. Many fishers did not want to go to war when fish prices were so high, but even working people in the city were not keen on conscription. They had already seen their young men go to war, while their relatives at home suffered from the high cost of living. One newspaper correspondent wrote that "some people wonder why volunteering has ceased. The common people read the papers, and feel the grip of the profiteers, and is it any wonder that their enthusiasm cools off?"[61]

The FPU responded to such criticisms by trying to associate inequality and poverty with the enemy being fought against in the war. "It is not only German militarism that is being fought today," its newspaper argued. "The people, the common people if you will, are fighting for their proper position in the world." By paying unfair wages and by profiteering, business people were waging another type of war on the people. "This war will end, but the war against autocracy will continue until the people come into their own, and it will continue as long as public opinion holds to the truth that every wrong shall be made Right."[62] Coaker might be fighting for the common people, riposted his critics, but he shared less in common with them now that he was a minister of the Crown and could be seen riding up and down Water Street in automobiles with the very merchants he used to attack.[63]

Coaker tried to demonstrate that he was not losing touch with ordinary fishing people by continuing to fight publicly for the outport constituency of the FPU. In particular, he took up the cause of fair prices for sealers' shares in the seal hunt. Ship owners in the hunt had been trying to purchase shares at a discount from sealers before the hunt even began, but Coaker encouraged the sealers to hold out for better prices. As seal oil was used in the manufacture of glycerine and other components of ammunition, Coaker argued, sealers were engaged in patriotic work, and so deserved better pay. Later in April, the government stepped in to fix the price for seals at twelve dollars instead of the ten dollars that Job's, Bowring, and Baine Johnston wanted to pay, despite opposition from the *Evening Telegram* and the *Star*, and the companies asked the governor to veto the measure. News had arrived in St. John's early in March that the Newfoundland Regiment had been granted the right to use the honour of "Royal," partially as a result of the sacrifice at Cambrai, but enlistments were not sufficient to ensure the Regiment's continued viability as an independent unit. The *Telegram* criticized the government for being more concerned about the seal hunt than conscription due to Coaker's influence. Coaker continued to prefer voluntary enlistment and Prime Minister Lloyd wanted more concrete evidence of popular support for conscription, a position that antagonized Harold Mitchell, who had served with the Regiment at Gallipoli and been invalided there. Mitchell wrote to the *Daily News*, claiming that returned soldiers had to demand stronger men in government, "men with backbone. Where are we going to get them? The answer is obvious—THE SOLDIERS."[64]

The conscription issue was difficult enough to deal with, but Coaker was simultaneously being challenged about his commitment to unionism. In March, the NIWA had decided to take on the Reid Newfoundland Company, which had allowed its employees a meagre six percent raise in wages throughout the war, although the company was widely recognized for its ruthless profiteering. Having begun with only thirty-five members in 1917, the NIWA had spread its organization along the railway lines to Reid workers elsewhere in Newfoundland, building a membership of 3500—2800 of whom worked in St. John's— by organizing workers without regard for skill and including workers not employed by the Reids. The NIWA advocated political reform to benefit all Newfoundland workers, and established a newspaper, *The Industrial Worker*, under the editorship of Warwick Smith.

In the past, the FPU had given a friendly ear to the NIWA's concerns, but as a minister of government, Coaker had acquired a curious relationship with Harry and William Reid, who had been running the railway company. This had come about when, during 1915–1916, the Reids had courted Coaker's support for Confederation, because they wanted Canadian assistance for their railway. Coaker had always worried about the long-term financial liability of the war effort for a colony in persistent economic trouble, and feared the impact of railway demands on Newfoundland's public finances. But, while the war-related improvements in the economy and treasury meant that Coaker lost interest in Confederation, he continued to be caught up in the Reid brothers' rivalries with each other. William Reid, a more openly political and temperamental person than Harry, had been president and general manager of the railway enterprise, and stepped aside for health reasons in 1917. Harry, with the support of the People's Party, replaced William, but refused to yield control when the latter was ready to return. An ugly public battle followed in which William attempted to embarrass the People's Party by exposing Morris's previous investigations of the possibility of Confederation and Coaker's interest in it. Coaker unsuccessfully pursued libel charges against William, but his position in government meant that the FPU leader would have to restrain his attacks on the Reid enterprises. The Reids were finding the railway unprofitable, and were in constant discussions with government about the possibility of their company ditching its operation. Coaker now had to balance his sympathies with the NIWA and his anger at the railway plutocrats with his responsibility to the government in matters of railway policy.[65]

The strike between the NIWA and the Reid Company that erupted on 27 March 1918 sorely tested the FPU leader. He asked the two sides to work out a settlement for the sake of the war effort, while the FPU newspaper claimed that "in disputes of this kind our sympathies have always been with the wage-earners."[66] The Daily News demanded that the government use its powers under the War Measures Act to legislate an end to the strike, fearing that it would spread out from St. John's to paralyze the railway across the island. Correspondents of the paper claimed that Coaker was hostile to city unions, and that there were rumours that the FPU leader was siding with the Reids.[67]

The possibility of a Newfoundland-wide general strike was real. Unprecedented labour unity had emerged between the NIWA, the LSPU, and the Truckmen's Protective Union, and other workers began to offer their support. The NIWA had a Ladies' Branch, organized by women, which organized and fought for shorter hours, higher wages, and better working conditions for women in manufacturing throughout St. John's. In the case of the strike in St. John's, the government pushed the company to accept mediation by a committee of cabinet ministers composed of Coaker, Michael Cashin, and John Chalker Crosbie. By the end of the second week of April, the mediation succeeded: the Reid Company agreed to wage increases, union recognition, and various concessions on matters related to job qualifications, seniority, grievances, and dismissal. The company decided that it was best to accommodate the NIWA through a joint management–union committee. Coaker continued to be criticized for not doing enough to assist the NIWA during the strike, but the FPU newspaper claimed that he was pivotal in the decision to use government mediation.[68]

The National Government decided to implement conscription on 23 April 1918 amidst the crisis on the Western Front comprising Germany's April offensive, an attempt to break through Entente lines in Flanders in the vicinity of Ypres. The offensive put pressure on the Entente forces, and Germany gained territory, but the move ultimately proved to be an overextension of Germany's lines beyond its ability to supply. In the short term, however, the pressure from the Imperial War Cabinet for more troops, the popular belief at least in St. John's that the Regiment must be maintained as a symbol of Newfoundland's emerging nationhood, and Coaker's reluctant support for conscription in exchange for more influence over government policy prompted the National Government to act. By early April, the British Army Council had called for three hundred more men, and estimated that it would require sixty more each month to maintain the Regiment at strength. Prime Minister Lloyd therefore proposed the Military Service Act, which would call up all single men between the ages of nineteen and thirty-nine. At this point, the more autocratic elements of the FPU leader's personality emerged. Inflated by the importance of government office, Coaker did not consult the councils of the FPU in order to secure support for his repudiation of a long-standing FPU opposition to conscription, although he did send circulars to the councils explaining that married men would not be conscripted. In the meantime, organizations that had formerly supported the NPA, led by St. John's business people and professionals such as the Orange Order, the Society of United Fishermen, and the Methodist Church Conference, campaigned vigorously for conscription. Coaker felt that his duty as a member of government took precedence over his responsibility as leader of the FPU, but many of his followers thought that their leader had become a turncoat, supporting St. John's.[69]

In truth, Coaker considered that fishing people stood to lose a great deal if he and the Union Party broke with government on the conscription issue. The Union Party could not form a government alone, yet every other potential ally in the government supported conscription. If it opposed the measure, the Union Party would be open to accusations of cowardice and treason; the result would be isolation from the other parties and an end to the possibility of reforming the fishery or improving the lives of fishing people. The problem was that this political calculation was being made by a man who would not have to fight in a trench or crawl across a battlefield; he had no sons to worry about, or fishing debts to pay along with a boat crew to keep working. Such were the immediate concerns of fishing people, many of whom felt abandoned by Coaker when conscription finally became law. To such people, Coaker's bargain of support for conscription in exchange for a place in government seemed like a deal made with the devil: their noble champion risked appearing to be just another politician.[70]

Coaker found that fighting the "just war" for a more equitable society was not made any easier by having access to the instruments of government. He might have been a cabinet minister, but he now had to accommodate the needs and interests of dubious allies. However, even with government committed to the policy, the difficulties associated with conscription would not go away. Veterans of the Regiment, such as returned soldier Private Hubert J.W. Fisher of Bonavista, were disappointed that conscription was necessary at all. Fisher argued that the measure sullied the volunteer blood that had been shed at Gallipoli, Beaumont Hamel, and the other battlefields of France and Belgium. The young men of St. John's had responded "nobly" to the calls for volunteers, but "the outports can do better and must, otherwise that for which your comrades are fighting, the end for which in the past Newfoundlanders have painted the battlefields with their very life blood will never be attained and all this sacrifice will have been in vain."[71] In France, not far from Ypres, the Regiment was carrying on, but taking heavy casualties again in its fight against the German April offensive near Bailleul in the Battle of Lys in April. The Regiment had lost so many of its number without adequate replacements that, by the end of April, its commanders had withdrawn it as a battalion of the 29th Division. From early May, the approximately five hundred members of the Regiment began service as the personal bodyguard for Haig at general headquarters at Montreuil. They remained in this role until August, as new recruits slowly augmented the Regiment's strength.[72]

Soldiers in the field had a more complicated view of conscription. Lance Corporal Curtis Forsey, for example, was the son of a mercantile family from Grand Bank, an important centre of the fishery on Newfoundland's south coast. He had enlisted in the Regiment on 30 May 1917 after working in the United States and deciding to serve when the Americans entered the war. By 1918, the twenty-three-year-old lance corporal had been in heavy fighting in France, and had been wounded and nearly buried alive by the impact of a shell at Passchendaele. Forsey's letters to his parents suggest that his major concerns were to get enough to eat, stay alive, reassure his parents, and keep in touch with men in the Regiment who were from the area around his home. He did not want his younger brother, Sam, to be conscripted, feeling that he was too young to experience the hardship of battle. Forsey had heard of the decision about conscription by early May and, shortly after, reported that a comrade "got killed in the last racket we were in. He was killed instantly, a sniper got him through the heart as he was helping to get a wounded chap out of a trench." Forsey was, nonetheless, "glad I enlisted as a volunteer. It will be a consolation in future days all right to think you had not to be forced." Writing two weeks later, on 17 May 1918, he said that he would like his brother to replace him should he be killed, but that he hoped it would never come to that. On 29 September, Forsey received wounds to his thigh and foot that led to his evacuation to England for medical treatment, and the war would end before his release from hospital.[73] In Forsey's view, conscription was likely necessary, but conscripted troops were not as desirable or noble as volunteers. Furthermore, conscription was easier to support in theory than in practice when it might mean that a loved one would be forced into the trenches.

The government announcement of conscription included the promise that the measure would not be implemented until the end of the 1918 fishing season in the coming fall, to minimize disruption of the fishery. In St. John's, supporters of the Regiment were unhappy about the delay. For the *Telegram*, which supported the compulsory call up, this was "abominable treachery" by the National Government.[74] Unable to please St. John's interests, Coaker's messianic shine had also dulled in the eyes of at least some of the "men of the North." On 28 April, the people of Wesleyville stood up and left a local church service in protest against the Military Service Act when the preacher began a "patriotic sermon." The editor of the *Evening Telegram* was outraged. He had no problem with people leaving any gathering in which unpatriotic comments might be heard, but to speak openly against conscription was treasonous.[75] Coaker defended the Military Service Act in May as being necessary to the defeat of Germany and as a measure that affected rich and poor alike. It was important, he argued, for anyone who might think of opposing the act to avoid creating the appearance of living in a "coward land."[76]

Coaker tried to focus on what he had originally hoped to achieve by participating in government. The Union Party, for example, had wanted to better support widows and dependants who required poor relief, hoping that revenues from the profits tax could be used to provide them with more than the meagre thirteen dollars they received every three months.[77] The FPU leader found it peculiar that a dominion in which so many people were making a lot of money from the war could stand aside to watch the poor being treated so badly. He wondered what patriotism could mean under such circumstances, and puzzled more over the behaviour of people during the first official Memorial Day holiday, established by legislation, on 1 July 1918. He thought such a holiday was a mistake, because the anniversary of Beaumont Hamel was terribly painful for the families of those who had died or been maimed in that battle. Even more disturbing, Coaker thought, was the likelihood that many people would treat the holiday as a vacation day rather than as a time to participate in acts of remembrance. On 1 July, he noted, "even those intimately associated with patriotic work did not think it amiss to absent themselves from town."[78] He proposed instead setting aside the Sunday closest to the date as a day of national remembrance, to be observed primarily through church services.

In Coaker's view, there was something contradictory and impractical about what was passing for patriotism in Newfoundland. It was all well and good for people to indulge in any amount of anti-German rhetoric—particularly about how Germans would have to pay for the costs of post-war reconstruction—but Coaker wanted Newfoundlanders to think practically about what conditions might be like once peace had been achieved. He thought that a deep economic recession was likely, and that governments such as that of Newfoundland, which had borrowed a lot of money for their war effort, would find the post-war debt burden hard to bear. Ordinary working people would have to shoulder much of the load, especially "producers" such as fishing people, and their interests would require international economic cooperation even with former enemies such as Germany.[79]

Coaker's views earned him nothing but attacks from newspapers such as the *Daily News* and the *Star*. The FPU newspaper responded and singled out the *Star*, the newspaper of Richard Squires, as being "pro-German" because of the tone of its attacks on the National Government. Squires had stayed with Morris as colonial secretary in the National Government, but refused to stay on when the former prime minister, his patron, left for England, claiming that the Lloyd government was not really national in character because it was a tool of Coaker and the Union Party. In reporting the news to London, the new governor, Sir Charles Alexander Harris, who had replaced Davidson late in the previous fall, indicated that he felt Squires was insincere because Coaker's influence in Lloyd's government was no greater than in Morris's National Government.[80]

The *Star*'s attacks were especially egregious in Coaker's eyes because Squires had taken money from the Reids to finance the paper. Earlier in May, Coaker had observed that, if he himself had taken such money, "I would have been hounded out of public life long before this, and would probably find myself enjoying a rest on the banks of Quidi Vidi" (the site of the dominion's penitentiary).[81] At the time, the *Star*'s attacks on Coaker's role in the National Government became so strident that the government closed the paper under the authority of the War Measures Act, allowing it to open again on 10 June under the eye of government censors. Despite consequent grumbling in the press about censorship, the *Star* kept up the condemnations of Coaker's work in government, charging him with supporting a government that was "bossed" by profiteers such as Cashin and Crosbie, and of betraying the poor members of the FPU while living in his "palatial residence at Port Union."[82]

Coaker was particularly angry at accusations that he was hostile to the NIWA and that he was trying to undermine efforts to build affordable housing for working people in St. John's. James McGrath of the LSPU had, from 1914 to 1916, sat on a twelve-person Municipal Commission appointed to govern St. John's. That commission had been mired in a number of problems, but McGrath had taken a special interest in finding affordable, decent housing for working people, and had run unsuccessfully for the first municipal government in 1916 with W.G. Gosling, the successful candidate for mayor. The LSPU leader continued to fight for better housing in alliance with Legislative Councillors John Anderson and Michael Gibbs. Gibbs had been a co-founder, with Morris, of the People's Party and a cabinet colleague of Squires. As a lawyer, he had helped with the formation of the LSPU, serving as its attorney until he died in 1943; had supported organized labour in the past; and had provided legal counsel in the labour organization of other city tradespeople. Through McGrath, this group had been earning the support of the NIWA. The FPU newspaper charged that the *Star* attacked Coaker on the housing issue to build a political base for Squires among the working people of the city.[83]

The summer of 1918 was not a time for the sort of careful planning for a post-war world that Coaker would have wished for, but rather one for political rhetoric aimed at maintaining morale and strengthening popular resolve against Germany. The editor of the *Evening Telegram* cited Sam Gompers's address to the American Federation of Labor, which declared, "The lights of the world will be extinguished by a German victory. The lights of the world are Liberty, Justice and Truth. Can we afford to have even one of them snuffed out by the mailed hand of the Hun, let alone all three?" In answer, the editor cited instances of German atrocities, and asked readers if they were content to be lost in the darkness of German barbarity. If they were true Britons, Newfoundlanders would answer no and continue to support the Empire against Germany.[84] On 4 August, just as in the previous years of the war, a huge public rally affirmed Newfoundland's commitment to the war effort and the special mission of "Anglo-Saxons" to fight for "Liberty and Justice" against "the Hun."[85] Eighty Blue Puttees—the nickname the members of the Regiment had acquired as a result of the blue rather than olive drab cloth they had wrapped around their lower legs as part of their uniform—arrived in the city on 8 August. Another massive crowd gathered to greet the soldiers, who were the subjects of a public celebration and a motorcade through a cheering crowd to Government House.[86]

Patriotism did not extend to acceptance of the National Government, however—at least not on the part of the *Evening Telegram*. The paper singled out the work of the Press Censor's Department as an example of the autocracy that Britons were struggling against around the world, in part because the censor was supposedly benefiting papers that supported the government, most notably the *Evening Advocate*. In effect, the *Telegram*'s editor argued, the censor was simply trying to "muzzle" opposition voices.[87] The editor of the *Telegram* made it clear to its readers that Newfoundlanders owed loyalty to the entity that represented the best ideals of the war: the Royal Newfoundland Regiment, not the National Government. In commenting on news that the Regiment had gone into action again with the 9th Division and Scottish Regulars, the editor hailed the men's almost Christ-like sacrifice of blood as crusaders for peace in a holy cause. By contrast, Germans were rapists, cowards, butchers of women and children, and destroyers of churches. It was foolish for people such as Coaker to be speaking about the necessity of post-war cooperation with Germany; true patriots were only interested in the immediate issue of its complete subjugation.[88]

While these debates had been taking place at home, the Regiment had been fighting on the Ypres front, moving towards Ledeghem. Although conscription was under way at home, none of the 1573 conscripts actually taken into the Regiment reached the front in time to participate in the action. On 8 August, Entente forces had broken through German lines on the Western Front, and during the summer had begun to advance through what had been German-held territory. Through the early fall, Entente forces successfully advanced against the Central Powers in the Balkans, the Middle East, and the eastern Mediterranean. On 14 October, Private Thomas Ricketts, only seventeen years old, helped save his comrades by retrieving ammunition for the depleted Lewis gun they were operating, and then using it to drive back the men of a German battery who had pinned the Regiment down. Having lied two years earlier about his age in order to join, Ricketts had already been wounded at Marcoing. His exploits earned him the Victoria Cross: he was the youngest winner of that honour in the British Army. The Regiment continued to fight on through October in countryside near Courtrai on the way to the Scheldt.[89]

The Regiment was relieved of front-line duty on 26 October, and headed back to the rear for rest, later participating in the British advance into Germany in late November and early December. Perhaps the rhetorical excesses of newspapers such as the *Telegram* reflected the crisis point at which the war had arrived. Fighting continued on the Western Front through October, but it was becoming increasingly clear that the German forces—along with those of Austria in its battles with the Italians, Bulgaria, and Turkey along their southern frontiers—had lost heart. All were negotiating with the Allies, and Germany capitulated in the Armistice of 11 November.

The news of peace brought a joyous celebration. Another great procession took place in St. John's as a crowd of about five thousand people followed a parade of members of the Royal Newfoundland Regiment, the local church brigades, and motor cars carrying wounded Blue Puttees. The people paraded to the ringing of the city's church bells, and they gathered at Government House before the assembled members of government.[90] The National Government promised that it would improve on the War Pensions Act passed by the Morris government in 1917 by raising pensions for Newfoundland veterans to the higher levels provided by the Canadian government for its veterans, and asked the people of Newfoundland to help by providing as much employment as was possible to returning soldiers.[91] Coaker tried to redirect the idealistic imagery associated with the Regiment toward the reform of government that he had hoped for. It was time, declared the *Advocate*, for people to think about what would be born from the war: this should be a government that acted for all people. The paper was sure that "the Fishermen of this country, as the great majority of the population of Nfld., will unite in demanding that the House of Assembly shall, in its entirety LIVE for the country, just as the Royal Newfoundland Regiment, made up of all classes, were willing to DIE if need be for their Country and Empire."[92]

By the end of the war, then, the political scene in Newfoundland had changed dramatically. The experience of 1 July 1916 (at Beaumont Hamel) had transformed the rhetorical battles: Coaker and the FPU had shifted from the language of class to that of patriotism. The FPU leader still fought for the rights of those he saw as downtrodden, but he did so by attacking traitorous mercantile profiteers and inept government. His opponents, of course, retaliated by suggesting that such criticism was divisive at a time when the war effort demanded unity. When Coaker joined the National Government, his opponents in the press labelled the FPU leader as a hypocrite for his position on conscription and his hobnobbing with the elites of St. John's.

Two versions of patriotism had warred with each other in Newfoundland. One was expressed by Coaker: that the war effort had demonstrated that government could use its powers more progressively to build a better post-war world. The other, more liberal, view was that pre-war British liberal democracy and a commitment to as little government interference in the market as possible were the apogee of civilization, and any suggestion that government should intervene more in the economy or society except for the temporary expedience of the war was little better than Prussian in principle. Coaker compromised on the conscription issue, finding that the constricting realities of government limited his ability to completely support working people and fishers. Coaker's resistance to conscription had provoked a radical reaction among his opponents in the press. The FPU leaders' critics began to suggest that government had little legitimacy and that it required a thorough cleaning, possibly by soldiers as and when they returned. This was still only a minority view, however, and Coaker continued to hope his compromise meant that the people of Newfoundland would be able to enjoy the benefits of a more positive role for the state in post-war reconstruction. In particular, the time for fisheries reform had come.

SEVEN

Progressives: Prussians or Bolsheviks? 1919–1920

The rhetoric of war had promised Newfoundlanders much in return for the sacrifices made, whether overseas or at home, and they, like people in many other parts of the world, harboured great hope. With peace, the time had come for the reconstruction of a better world. For Coaker, that meant that it was time to use the power of the state to improve the lives of Newfoundlanders, especially outport people. The key to such improvement, he thought, was proper regulation of the fishery: better-quality production and more effective marketing would enhance the earnings of fishers and improve the overall economy of Newfoundland.

Coaker's commitment to state intervention clashed with more conservative beliefs that such developments violated the fundamental British liberties that men had died for. Coaker's opponents labelled him a "Newfoundland Kaiser," aggressively smearing the insult into what amounted to "red-baiting" by also calling the FPU leader a Bolshevik. It might seem oddly contradictory that his detractors would simultaneously label Coaker an autocratic imperialist and a leftist revolutionary. However, the FPU leader's opponents used both terms to identify him as a traitor and an enemy of Newfoundland. Despite this kind of opposition, and to further his goals for the fishery, Coaker agreed to become minister of marine and fisheries in the government of Richard Squires, his former nemesis. Unfortunately, the immediate post-war political climate in Newfoundland exhibited few of the nobler sentiments that had characterized the wartime belief in the possibilities of reconstruction. The increased involvement of the state in economic and social regulation for the sake of the war effort had suggested that government could intervene more to deal with social and economic problems, but the immediate post-war political battles in Newfoundland became an ugly, bare-knuckled fight to deny the legitimacy of a progressive state.

The end of the war allowed Coaker's opponents to directly challenge the National Government. The editor of the increasingly conservative *Evening Telegram* wrote that it was time for the people to do something about what it called an "autocratic" government. The paper condemned members of the government for cloaking self-interest in the guise of a "patriotic spirit": government members enjoyed the prestige and incomes of offices that had been preserved "for them by men who face the cannon's mouth, and whose deeds are unrecognized and unrewarded, while the wearers of such honors flaunt them in the faces of those who willingly gave their all, and are now passed by and overlooked, having served their turn."[1] Coaker's political enemies had learned a lesson from their nemesis, adapting the FPU leader's tactic of using wartime patriotism to attack their opponents as self-interested betrayers of those who had fallen during the war.

There was soon opportunity to smear the National Government as a group of Bolsheviks. The Council of the Board of Trade met early in the new year to begin considering post-war reconstruction in Newfoundland.

Identifying the relationship between capital and labour as a special problem, the council received a presentation by one of its more active members, R.F. Horwood, on the issue. Horwood, who, with his brother William, had founded one of the largest lumber and building supply companies in Newfoundland, argued that wartime economic conditions had made old industrial relations untenable. He felt that the very poor attitude displayed by organized labour and working people towards their employers would only be improved by collective bargaining, better communication between workers and employers, and a more systematic and informed approach to wage adjustment and profit sharing. He further advised that the risks were great if the business community did not take some action: "Our labour organizations are reeking with the ideals of the Bolsheveki. Our men are coming home from a fearful experience of war; all of them made better or worse by its influence, and the latter class brings a leaven of fearful possibility."[2]

The idea that Bolshevism was rampant among the Newfoundland unions was actually ridiculous. While an occasional public figure such as the Union Party's George Grimes claimed to have socialist sympathies, the party was clearly committed to labour reform, not Bolshevism. Throughout Europe and North America, revolutionary or radical leftist perspectives, including Bolshevist sympathies, had emerged in post-war labour movements. While such revolutionary or radical inclinations may not have appealed to large numbers of workers, they allowed governments, particularly in North America, to colour any desire for change in the same Bolshevik red. In Canada, for example, the federal government added Section 98 to the Criminal Code following the general strike in Winnipeg in 1919, which permitted the banning of organizations deemed interested in pursuing political or economic change "by force, violence or injury to persons or property" (the latter could be interpreted to include strikes) and allowed the imprisonment of people who even attended a meeting of such organizations. In the United States, federal authorities organized "dragnet" raids on labour organizations judged to be radical, focusing on rounding up, suspending the usual rights of due process under the law, and deporting immigrants they perceived to be radical leftist sympathizers in the "Red Raids" of 1919–1920.[3]

While Newfoundland observers might have feared movements abroad, there is little evidence that the radical or revolutionary left had any influence locally. The NIWA had taken great pains to distance itself from leftist radicalism, and prominent labour leaders such as Jim McGrath enjoyed close working relationships with more conservative political figures such as John Anderson and Michael Gibbs. McGrath's work with Anderson on providing better housing for working people had the support of the Roman Catholic archbishop E.P. Roche, and was in keeping with the anti-communist doctrines of Pope Leo XIII's encyclical *Rerum Novarum*.[4] Horwood's views were even more unusual in that, until the new year, much of the criticism of the Bolsheviks, and of Lenin and Trotsky in particular, was not particularly about their revolutionary Marxism but about the manner in which the Bolsheviks had extracted Russia from the war through the Treaty of Brest-Litovsk.[5] There was little to fear from Bolshevism in Newfoundland, and its nature as a form of revolutionary Marxist socialism meant little to the local press. Bolshevism was rather a term of abuse—a histrionic epithet to be hurled at Coaker or any other proponent of political, social, or economic change that, no matter how moderate, might upset the privileges of Water Street.

The opposition press was careful initially not to single out specific organizations or individuals, but the concerns expressed about the spread of Bolshevism left little doubt that it was tarring Coaker with the same brush. The *Telegram* called Bolshevism "a disease or mania," or a "complete Radicalism in politics" that led to a Soviet-style "red terror." While the paper made much of the Bolshevik seizure of private property and a government acting on behalf of workers and peasants, its goal was really to attack anyone locally who advocated for "some new social reform."[6] Socialist revolution, then, was not what essentially defined

Bolshevism for the *Telegram*. Rather, any interest in change, especially any that required a more interventionist state, might be considered, according to the conservative press, to be on par with the work of Lenin or Trotsky. With the end of the war, at least in the eyes of his political enemies, Coaker, as the major proponent of reform in Newfoundland, could now just as easily be smeared as Comrade Coaker as he had, in wartime, been called Kaiser Coaker!

The attempt to create a Red Scare in St. John's did not augur well for Coaker's hopes for a more progressive government. These tactics were yet another opposition weapon to be added to the constant criticism of Coaker for not giving up his presidency of the FPU or his role in managing the Union Trading Company while in government. His continued work in the FPU made Coaker appear to be using the power of government to advance special interests. The *Daily News* constantly labelled the National Government unpatriotic "grafters" whose profligate spending had betrayed those who fell during the war.[7] The editor called for disinterested politicians who possessed the political will to protect Newfoundland from mounting public debt through retrenchment. He wanted the involvement of supposedly unbiased men who felt that participating in government was a "sacred duty."[8] Fighting Coaker's influence over the National Government, the paper argued, was as much a duty of true patriots as combating the "Huns" had been during the war. This rhetoric was important: it reinforced the groundwork that had already been laid for associating state intervention with Bolshevism and Prussianism, and established that there were no legitimate political differences of opinion with the conservative ideology as articulated by the *Evening Telegram* or the *Daily News*. Politicians of like mind were fellow patriots keeping faith with the noble fallen of the war; their opponents, regardless of actual political persuasion, were exploitative reactionaries, traitors to the nation, or wild-eyed radicals.

In the short term, politicians tried to position themselves on the side of patriotism by vying with their opponents for the loyalty of returning troops. A very real problem continued to be finding a way for those troops to make a living, especially men whose injuries meant that they could not return to their former work. The press suggested that the National Government should be doing more to place returned soldiers in the civil service. In Grand Falls, the local Patriotic Association passed a resolution asking the government to establish a permanent war fund to assist veterans. Some employers, most notably Ayre and Sons, Ltd., hired back all the surviving Blue Puttees who had been in their employ before volunteering, thus keeping their promise to preserve the jobs recruits had left to support the Regiment. In February, the company provided each of the rehired men with an additional bonus cheque as an expression of its appreciation for the men's service.[9]

The FPU newspaper did not press the government to provide any long-term financial commitments to veterans, but was more engaged in suggestions that all who served in the war deserved a memorial to their struggle. This memorial, it felt, should take the form of a building to house a technical education and normal school for the training of teachers in St. John's. While uncomfortable with recommending spending in St. John's rather than in the outports, the FPU paper acknowledged that teacher training was most practically situated there, and would still benefit all of the communities of Newfoundland. To ensure this, the paper argued that the government should provide outport people with special "memorial grants" to allow them to attend the new school. Levi Curtis, the superintendent of Methodist schools, and Vincent P. Burke, the superintendent of Roman Catholic schools, brought together the proposal for more technical education and a normal school in a proposal for a Memorial College at a public meeting in St. John's in late January 1919. The editor of the *Telegram* hailed the proposal as the means to "engage in the work of educational reconstruction with the same desire to win as animated those in whose honor and to whom immortal fame the building will be erected."[10]

By linking post-war reconstruction with education, and by

proposing better educational facilities as a key act in memorializing those who fell in battle, Coaker associated his commitment to more progressive reform with the noble ideals of the war rather than with Bolshevism. While the *Evening Telegram* suggested that education was the most important means of ensuring that people would not be taken in by the Reds, Julia Salter Earle (the president of the Ladies' Branch of the NIWA) was less interested in seeing education as a way to fight off Bolshevism.[11] She saw free and compulsory education for all working-class children as the way to deprive future employers of the ability to use workers' relative lack of education as a justification for paying them low wages. Earle suggested that returning soldiers, having been educated by their experience of their travel abroad, would demand further formal learning. "They have earned with their blood the word 'Dominion' for us. Some have not liked the change 'Island Home' to 'Dominion.' I say, by all means be glad of any change that will help to advance us, but seeing they have had to pay such a price as 'human blood' to make us worthy of the word 'Dominion,' the least we can do is to join hand in hand with them and see that those growing up around us will receive proper education, so they will make us all prouder than we are of the 'Dominion of Newfoundland.'"[12]

Julia Salter Earle questioned the extent to which the impact of Newfoundland's war effort on its dominion status reflected meaningful change within the country. There had been great pride in Newfoundland's participation in the Imperial War Cabinet and the Imperial War Conference. In April 1917, the latter body passed a resolution affirming the status of Newfoundland and the other dominions as autonomous nations of an Imperial Commonwealth, and of India as a lesser but still important part. The dominions and India were supposed to find an "adequate" voice in imperial foreign policy. When Prime Minister Lloyd left St. John's to attend the Paris Peace Conference in January 1919, there were high expectations that Newfoundland was taking its place in equal stature with the other dominions. However, while the United

States and Britain agreed that Canada, Australia, New Zealand, South Africa, and India could be represented separately in the plenary session of the conference, the Americans would accept Newfoundland only as a member of the British delegation because of its small size and economic insignificance in the matters being addressed at the Peace Conference.[13]

At home, people were worrying more about the return of the Regiment than the finer points of an evolving but murky dominion status. The imminent return of the Regiment's members on board the *Corsican*, which arrived in St. John's harbour on the night of 7 February 1919, brought into sharp relief the distinction between Coaker's views about what the state should be trying to accomplish and the aims of his critics. Newfoundland's war hero, Thomas Ricketts, was on board; Coaker's opponents felt that Ricketts's Victoria Cross was a fine example of the type of honours that members of the Regiment should receive for helping to save the world "from the brutal domination of Prussianism." W.W. Blackall, the superintendent of education for the Church of England in Newfoundland, proposed that the dominion should recognize Ricketts by building a school in his home town in honour of his medal. The *Daily News* editor agreed, but felt that all of the returning soldiers should be recognized by more than the gold watches and chains that were being provided by the local chapter of the Daughters of the Empire. The Women's Patriotic Association immediately raised a Victory Bond worth $250 for Ricketts.[14] The FPU newspaper felt that the government should finance a grant for Ricketts, who had indicated that he wanted to pursue his education upon his return to Newfoundland. The *Telegram* protested, however, against such "government intervention in this entirely national matter," suggesting that the people could best express their gratitude and patriotism through voluntary subscriptions for an education fund.[15] The debate extended to the proposal for a memorial college, but in this case, the critics of government spending had to accept that public funding would be necessary. Even if donations were to supply enough funds for the building of a college or some other educational institution, only the government would be able to provide the resources for its annual operation.[16]

Coaker saw the debate about funding a college as a disappointing instance of penny-pinching in a dominion where far greater public sums were spent on private enterprises such as the railway. His moderate reformism did not even remotely resemble socialism: Coaker did not advocate public ownership of the means of production, but he did not see a problem with the government providing moderate regulation of key economic sectors, implementing public services such as education, and representing the public interest in industrial relations. Coaker was, as always, committed to the notion that working people deserved better treatment from their employers. To continue to allow citizens to live in poverty was, in his view, to permit "unrest, disorder and eventually anarchy of the sort which is attributed to Bolshevism." The FPU president did not even think better treatment was merely a matter of paying working people more. Primarily concerned about the fishers who made up the membership of the FPU, who mostly traded with merchants rather than working for wages, Coaker saw that profiteering and high prices were also culprits.[17]

Unfortunately for Coaker, his fellow Unionist, George Grimes, made a speech at a meeting of the FPU District Council at Port de Grave in February in which he asked the council to consider the Bolsheviks within the historical context of oppression and inequality in czarist Russia, pointing out that they seemed to have a lot of popular support and were pioneers in the social ownership of the means of production. Richard Squires's newspaper denounced Grimes and asserted that the Unionist had only brought out into the open that "Coakerism stands for Bolshevism," a new socialistic autocracy that ran counter to the democracy men had fought and died for in the war.[18] The editor of the *Daily News* had a fit, calling the Bolshevik regime murderous. Grimes was a Bolshevik sympathizer, the editor maintained, and a hypocrite who used to denounce government members for taking government funds but was now happy to take a cheque for his work as a Union Party MHA who sat on the Food Control Board. To make matters worse, Grimes justified drawing his pay by saying "that is merely 'social' ownership—in which the Bolsheviki of Russia lead the way."[19]

The controversy about Grimes extended into the beginning of the annual seal hunt. The FPU newspaper chose not to respond to charges that Grimes and the union were Bolshevik, preferring instead to emphasize how sealers had benefited from the sealing legislation passed in 1916, and underscoring how important sealers (all staunch FPU supporters) were as "the men who undergo the dangers of the deep that Newfoundland may prosper."[20] Coaker's detractors were not deterred, however, and these supporters of retrenchment had a field day when it became clear that the Union Party members of the National Government were going to support plans to provide further financial assistance to the troubled Reid Newfoundland Company's railway so that it could repair the worst of its crumbling infrastructure. "Bolshevism has broken loose in the *Advocate* office," proclaimed the *Daily News*, whose editor charged Coaker with hypocrisy for supporting the same sort of railway spending for which he used to castigate the Morris government, adding that he was probably up to the same vote-buying patronage tactics. The result was likely to compound a looming post-war crisis: "Only sheer ignorance or the wildest type of Bolshevism could advocate any other course" than retrenchment, he charged, and directed the public's attention to Grimes's admiration of the Bolsheviks.[21]

The editor of the *Daily News* was so adamant about the need to restrain public spending that he advised against government spending on the vocational education that would allow returning soldiers and sailors a better chance to reintegrate into society. In its retort, the FPU newspaper brought all of its opponent's arguments together: "The *Daily News* has said it will not support any big expenditures for good railroads and good roads and now it advises Economy in fitting the soldiers for re-entering civil life. A Policy of Despair from a Party of

Despair!" The Union Party was not yet ready to worry about government deficits, preferring instead to see spending on infrastructure and education as investments in the future, and noting that all of the spending it recommended would not be as expensive as the People's Party's railway policy, which the *Daily News* had supported.[22] Even if Newfoundland had to pay back war loans and fund pensions, the FPU paper argued, it would be unfair to returning soldiers to say that their efforts in the war had put the government in a financial hole so that it could not afford to stimulate employment.[23]

The retrenchment issue revealed the contrast between Coaker and his critics. The FPU leader had faith in the ability of the state to marshal the resources of society against the grosser inequalities of class, especially as expressed in the regional divisions between town and country, and between the mercantile and industrial elites of Water Street and outport fishing people. The war had demonstrated that the state could intervene directly to regulate industry and profiteering, among other things. Coaker's opponents, however (while conceding that the working people of the pre-war world had enjoyed too few of the fruits of their labour) held that the same state regulation of industry and taxing of wartime profits that the FPU leader had observed in Britain and had encouraged in Newfoundland were simply part of those larger costs of war that now threatened to plunge even the victors into an appalling post-war recession. The only way "British people," Newfoundlanders included, could effectively address the economic uncertainty, claimed Coaker's opponents, was by increasing their productivity and spending less. Coaker's opponents associated class inequality only with the inheritance practices of the aristocratic families of Europe, maintaining that, in Newfoundland, privilege had to be earned. "Businessmen" enjoyed higher social status because of their merit: they demonstrated the most efficient practices of production and trade. Patriotism in peacetime was a simple thing: "The most pressing duty of every citizen of the Empire is to work and save, so that the Empire's resources may be quickly developed to meet the world's needs, and that the war debts may be paid off, and commerce be quickly restored."[24]

Coaker, despite his continued faith in the ability of government policy to improve the lot of most Newfoundlanders, was starting to face a lot of opposition. To make matters worse, the relatively new and conservative Roman Catholic archbishop E.P. Roche—a strident man originally from the community of Branch in St. Mary's Bay and known as the "Borgia of Branch" for his ruthless politicking—began to work against Coaker. Roche had, the year before, asked Sir Michael Cashin, the senior Roman Catholic member of the People's Party rump, to either convince Bond to come out of retirement—an unlikely outcome considering Bond and Cashin had been bitter political enemies for at least fourteen years—or form a government himself rather than allow a coalition to persist with the Union Party as members. Cashin had no opportunity to form a government in 1918, but the forces of resentment against the FPU continued to grow. Long-time People's Party supporters such as Squires, and more conservative politicians such as Cashin, squirmed as it appeared that the Union Party was gaining more power, for while the Assembly seethed with factions, the Union Party was enviable in its unity and discipline.[25]

Prime Minister Lloyd, who had returned from participating in the Paris Peace Conference, suggested a quick spring election in which the Union Party and the Liberals, along with any other members of the National Government who were willing, would campaign as a single party. Coaker agreed: the Newfoundland economy was still buoyant from the war, and the people were feeling confident that Newfoundland had gained more recognition as an important partner within the Empire, despite the fact that Newfoundland, like the other dominions and India, had been allowed to participate in the actual negotiations for peace only as a member of the British Empire delegation. (Unlike the other dominions and India, however, Newfoundland chose not to be a signatory to the Treaty of Versailles in June 1919.[26]) The *Evening Telegram* responded to Coaker's announcement by accusing the government of misrepresenting the financial health of Newfoundland in the spring throne speech, which, it alleged, was full of false promises and evasive statements. Such falsehoods "could only be expected from a Bolshevik administration, such as at present controls and strangles the promise of Newfoundland's future."[27] The Cashin faction in the House of Assembly charged that Coaker and Lloyd were engineering a "coup d'état" by offering a "dictator's slate" premised on Coaker's "assumption of the role of dictator."[28] The *Telegram* charged that Coaker was "mentally debased and depraved" for his "Bolshevik" tactic of trying to pit the interests of the outports against St. John's by criticizing the role of protective tariffs in raising the cost of living, and condemning the role of Water Street in Newfoundland politics and economy.[29]

Squires unsuccessfully tried to get Bond to come out of retirement to take on Coaker, his newspaper alleging that the FPU leader treated the fishers of the north like serfs.[30] One self-described old Liberal hoped that Squires would be able to unite Bond and A.B. Morine, along with the *Telegram*, the *Daily News*, and the *Star*, in a great coalition to halt the FPU influence in government.[31] Cashin's supporters in the government— representing the business interests of St. John's and supported by Roche (who reluctantly accepted that Bond would not come out of retirement)— also wanted the Union Party's influence over government to end. Cashin tried to bully Prime Minister Lloyd into abandoning the Union Party for a different coalition dominated by Cashin, but when he tried to bluff the prime minister into submission by moving a non-confidence motion in the Assembly, the prime minister called Cashin's bluff by seconding the motion. Tired of the political manoeuvring, Cashin felt pressured by Lloyd's tactic to form a government before he was adequately prepared. This, according to the *Telegram*, was a "burlesque" that it hoped would be the closing act of the coalition National Government.[32]

Cashin cobbled together a "National Ministry" with old colleagues and supporters of the People's Party such as Morine and Liberal A.E.

Hickman. A Grand Bank merchant, Hickman had originally entered politics in 1913 as a supporter of Bond. Although he had served in opposition as part of the Liberal-Union alliance, and entered into the National Government alongside Coaker as a minister without portfolio, Hickman was uncomfortable with the idea of government regulation of the fishing industry, and sided with Cashin to serve as his minister of militia. Liberals such as Hickman who did not want to support an administration in which Coaker was a force would have preferred that Bond emerge from retirement, in part because he would have enjoyed the support of the Returned Soldiers' Association as a leader who, being a true patriot of Newfoundland, was above party interest.[33] His refusal left Hickman with an old People's Party warhorse, Cashin, who, it transpired, failed to shake his image as a wealthy, self-serving agent of Water Street.

Coaker was livid when John G. Stone defected to become Cashin's minister of marine and fisheries, calling him a "traitor to the FPU cause," "a Judas and Oath Breaker." The former boatbuilder from Catalina had joined the FPU in 1911 and quickly rose up through the ranks, winning election to the House of Assembly as a Union candidate in 1913. He had served as the minister of marine and fisheries in the National Government, but apparently was unprepared to give up high office for party loyalty. "Those who knew him well in the Party," Coaker claimed, "never considered that he could be relied on where his personal interests clashed with his duty to the fishermen's cause." Claiming that the FPU was a great "patriotic organization," Coaker proposed that the name of anyone so foolish as to abandon it "will stink in the nostrils of every honest fisherman throughout Newfoundland."[34] Stone probably did not think he had much to worry about since (at first) Cashin appeared to have a lot going for him as prime minister. The economy and government finances were still buoyed by the impact of the war, and Cashin had a solid working-class base in St. John's. He was also popular on the southern Avalon Peninsula, whose population, like that of the working-class neighbourhoods of St. John's, was heavily Irish and Roman Catholic in origin. In these constituencies, the prohibition of alcohol consumption—a measure that Coaker had embraced as progressive and patriotic and that had been established through a plebiscite in 1915—had very little appeal.

Morine's continued advocacy for the interests of the Reid Newfoundland Company proved to be a liability for Cashin. While Morine had been a solicitor for the FPU since 1914, his relationship with Coaker had become testy over the lawyer's desire to run in the District of Bonavista as an Independent without the blessing of local FPU councils. Squires had suggested in 1918 that Coaker wanted Morine to leave Newfoundland because Lloyd would be more susceptible to Union Party influence. By returning to support another administration, Morine "might save the country from ignominy ... if he would clean up this bunch of grafters."[35] When Morine joined Cashin's administration, Coaker criticized him rather than declaring that the FPU would remain neutral. Morine wrote to a Coaker supporter that the FPU leader's attacks were "madness."[36]

Morine's long association with the Reid interests was a liability in terms of whether people might perceive him to be the man to clean up Newfoundland politics. Many people continued to see the Reids as profiteering speculators, and this allowed Coaker to step up his attacks on Cashin, suggesting that the prime minister was a puppet of the Reids. The *Daily News* in return accused Coaker of being "autocratic," and when Coaker defended the Bowrings in a dispute with the government over a coastal steamer contract, the paper charged him with hypocrisy because of the FPU's bitter attacks on the firm in 1915 for its employment of Abram Kean.[37] The editor of the *Daily News* called Coaker vindictive, as Cashin's assumption of the government had deprived the FPU leader of the chance to establish Soviet-style control by FPU councils over government bodies such as road boards. If Cashin had not won government, the editor continued, "the Government would be under the control of a species of Bolshevism, with him [Coaker] playing the role of a Trotsky or Lenin."[38]

The newspapers' rancorous political criticism of the early summer only partially ceased for what was becoming the standard homage to those who were lost at Beaumont Hamel on 1 July. In the editorials that appeared in the issues immediately preceding that date, they "were the best blood of Newfoundland spilled over the battle field" but even the memorializing took a partisan turn.[39] The *Daily News* claimed that Coaker aspired, in his arrogance, to be a dictator, but that "the sons of our Empire and those of our Allies in winning the war have swept into oblivion from the nations all individuals of arrogant traits, so that the possessors thereof will be powerless henceforth to do any further harm."[40] Coaker had a ready response. Morine, as minister of justice, had become identified with the heavy-handed use of a British cruiser to arrest moonshiners in Bonavista Bay during the fishing season, even as it became known that Cashin himself had broken wartime prohibition laws to obtain alcohol for a private party. The government had requested that HMS *Cornwall* cruise to Flat Islands late in June to arrest the moonshiners, and the plan was that they would be brought to St. John's for trial on 1 July. Coaker had a field day with this: the FPU paper asked people to imagine the men being brought into port "when the ceremony of commemorating the valour and sacrifice of our men on sea and land was to take place." As it was, fog delayed the arrest, but the ship brought seven men to St. John's on 5 July.[41]

The advent of the Cashin government indicated that Newfoundland had entered a period in which the old party allegiances of the People's Party and Liberal-Union years had failed. Rather than parties, there were now "political warlords," of which Cashin and Coaker were chief. From the sidelines, the wily Squires, who enjoyed both Protestant support and the friendship of Roche, saw an opportunity for his own political ambitions. Having a taste for the high life, and having previously enjoyed the financial benefits that accompanied political office,

Squires was determined to return to government by grabbing the prize of the prime ministership. Enjoying many of the same ties to St. John's working people as had Morris before him, Squires was a formidable opponent for Cashin. Squires had few potential political allies, but his ambition for power was boundless, and he was willing to make a deal with almost anyone, including old Liberals and, somewhat surprisingly, even Coaker and the Union Party. Despite their past differences, Coaker and Squires were both populists and Protestants who came from outside St. John's—conditions that were considerable assets in a dominion in which resentments against both St. John's, with its large Roman Catholic and protectionist working-class constituencies, and Water Street were always important factors in politics. In June, Squires's paper began to adopt a more conciliatory tone, dropping the accusations of Bolshevism, and suggesting that Coaker was simply inexperienced in government.[42] In August, Squires wrote to Coaker, recommending Alexander Campbell as a mediator between the two. Squires made very clear that Campbell's purpose was to build a political coalition that would fight "graft and corruption" in the Cashin government and clean up "the public life of this Colony."[43] The outcome was a new Liberal-Reform Party led by Squires.

Coaker disliked Squires, but was committed to the notion that the state could play a positive role in fostering better economic and social conditions for his constituents, and that the likelihood of a post-war recession in the fishing industry meant that its reorganization was a matter of pressing concern. He therefore accepted an alliance with Squires, based on the understanding that their government would be able to develop a means of guaranteeing good fish prices. Squires allowed Coaker to believe that he supported this goal, but was careful not to be fully open or sure that such a guarantee was possible. William Warren, a former legal partner of E.P. Morris and supporter of the People's Party, led a small group of Bond Liberals into the campaign alongside the unlikely alliance of Squires and Coaker.[44]

As the general election of November 1919 loomed, Squires began to attack Cashin's party, now known as the Liberal-Progressives, as a tool of the Reid monopoly. At the same time, Coaker stepped up his attacks on Morine and Cashin, blaming them for not taking enough action to end a strike by blacksmiths and boilermakers at the Reid Company's dry dock: he thought that the government should appoint a board to provide a disinterested arbitration to settle the strike, but that it would not do that because of control by "Big Interests."[45] The antipathy of the Liberal-Reform alliance towards the Reid interests, Coaker's hostility towards tariff protection of manufacturing, and his prohibitionism (which often appeared to be militantly Protestant in nature) meant, of course, that the alliance had little support among the membership of the NIWA. The industrial organization, therefore, with the support of Jim McGrath, organized a labour party to fight government corruption in September. The subsequent Workingmen's Party appears to have had strong Roman Catholic influence, but it failed to see any of its candidates elected in the 1919 election.[46]

Squires's campaign asked electors to choose him as the candidate who stood against graft in government. Newspapers that supported Cashin scoffed at this, pointing out that, as minister of justice in the National Government, Squires had billed government for almost $4600 in legal fees for services that were part of his job.[47] As minister of justice under Morris, though, Squires had been subject to Coaker's scorn over his handling of the investigations into the sealing disasters of 1914. The alliance must have been awkward for the two men, even though Coaker had come to terms with Squires over natural-resource development policies—particularly as Abram Kean had decided to run for Cashin in the District of St. Barbe on the Northern Peninsula. Unsurprisingly, Coaker once again began to make what the *Daily News* called "Ghoulish Attacks" on the sealing captain's record in the *Newfoundland* tragedy. The editor reminded readers that Coaker had mended fences with the Bowrings, and that he had been willing to make common cause with his

206 Death on Two Fronts

old nemesis, Squires: the implication was that Coaker was willing to do anything for power.[48]

Coaker's response was to attack the government for not supporting better pensions or employment strategies for returned soldiers. He singled out A.E. Hickman, often identified as a Liberal but now serving as Cashin's minister of militia, for outbidding a returned soldier by five dollars for a surplus typewriter from his department—the informal policy of the department being that returned soldiers and sailors would have the opportunity of first purchase if they made a reasonable offer. Hickman yielded the machine, but the veterans were unhappy with him.[49] The FPU newspaper also reminded readers that Morine (who was running for Cashin in Bonavista, Coaker's district) was "the Leading Spirit in the Infamous Reid Deal of 1898." The Liberal-Reform Party, the paper stated, would "Give the Reids Fair Play, but Morine, Cashin, McGrath, Higgins, Kean, Cannot be Trusted in a New Reid Deal."[50] The paper further charged Hickman, Cashin, and the recently knighted Sir John Chalker Crosbie (who was running for Cashin in Port de Grave) with wartime profiteering. Cashin, the paper explained, had done little as prime minister to control the cost of living because he was "in the money class." Coaker claimed that Cashin's pro-mercantile stance had led him to refuse to use the War Measures Act (still in effect) to stabilize post-war fish prices.[51]

That Coaker was willing to use legislation that had been designed to support the conduct of war and apply it to fisheries regulation revealed the basis for the Squires-Coaker alliance, in the opinion of the Evening Telegram. Squires had become the tool of Coaker, "whose sole ambition it is to grasp the Government and maintain absolute power, and whose one desire is to rule the country with all the autocracy and tyranny of a Kaiser."[52] The Daily News agreed, calling Coaker's regulatory approach "German": a violation of the liberal freedoms people had fought for in the war.[53]

The Evening Telegram disagreed with the Daily News only in

that it called Coaker's interest in price regulation "bolshevist," blackening Squires with the same name and claiming that both would ruin Newfoundland financially.[54] Uninterested in splitting hairs, the *News* agreed, claiming that "Coaker has shown himself to be a Bolshevist of the most dangerous type," and that his lieutenant, George Grimes, had publicly supported a Russian regime that despoiled women and religion, and in which "murder, starvation and desolation" were rampant.[55] Formerly at odds with the *Daily News*'s support for the People's Party rump, the *Evening Telegram* had drawn closer to it as a result of the Squires-Coaker alliance. The *Daily News* editor, John Currie, had briefly served as a minister without portfolio in Cashin's government. Charles T. James, the editor of the *Evening Telegram* in 1917, had run for the Liberals in the District of Burgeo and La Poile in 1913, but had met defeat at the hands of the People's Party candidate Robert Martin. Now in 1919, James could not accept Squires, who was after all an old People's Party member. The *Telegram* editor preferred to see Cashin's Liberal-Progressives as the true successor to Bond's party, and decided to run for them in Burgeo and La Poile.[56]

Coaker took the position that it was hypocritical for people to charge him with betraying the principles that veterans had fought for during the war when the government and its supporters paid lip service to the rights of ex-soldiers and their fallen comrades. To demonstrate the point, the FPU newspaper publicized a dispute between A.E. Hickman and the Roman Catholic military chaplain Thomas Nangle over the amount of money the government should provide to build war memorials in England and France. Nangle had served with the Regiment until the end of the war, having been wounded on 24 April 1918. In 1919 he had become the champion of Newfoundland's interests with the Imperial War Graves Commission (IWGC). His role there was to ensure the proper identification and re-burial of Newfoundlanders who had fallen overseas, and to see that proper monuments were erected in honour of the Regiment. Travelling across the battlefields of Belgium and France to find and exhume hastily buried bodies was a solemn, although disturbing, duty, and Nangle made his preliminary recommendations about memorial sites on what he called the "Trail of the Caribou," including Caribou Hill at Gallipoli; Beaumont Hamel, Gueudecourt, Monchy-Le-Preux, and Marcoing in France; and Keilberg Ridge in Belgium. With the addition of smaller memorials for those who had died in England, the total bill, he estimated, would be about £6400—British pounds being the currency in which the IWGC budgeted its proposed work.[57] Nangle claimed that £1000 per memorial in France was needed, but Hickman, as minister of militia, offered £100. Nangle—exhausted by the gruesome work in which he had been engaged, and mortified about how the families of the fallen might feel about such a response—was incensed. In a report to the government, he claimed that if Hickman's offer was the best government could do, "I recommend that we erect nothing at all. Let us forget we ever had a regiment."[58]

The *Daily News* responded to this story by stating that Coaker was behind the dispute, using the issue of how to remember those who had fallen in battle with "ghoulish malignity" and for political purposes. It reminded readers of Coaker's early opposition to the formation of the Newfoundland Regiment, and asked "What ... did Coaker ever do for our men overseas, in any manner or fashion?"[59] The answer, its editor maintained, was "nothing." The *Telegram* agreed, and argued that Coaker wished to subvert the political morals of Newfoundland by fixing fish prices, a "danger that all honest and patriotic Newfoundlanders must do their utmost to combat and overcome, and Newfoundland can only rid itself of the possible incubus by voting for the Cashin party, the men that are able to guide the ship of state safely through the perils of Coakerism, Squirism and Bolshevism."[60]

The *Telegram*'s editor also condemned Coaker for allowing John Scammell, his private secretary and later organizer for the FPU, to run against Abram Kean in St. Barbe, because Scammell, although unmarried during the war, had not volunteered for service: "He is now jumping into the fray when there are no Germans around, and when the fighting is a bloodless one."[61] Coaker responded by suggesting that a new Cashin government would cancel the profits tax on the rich and divert funds for pensions to support the Reid interests, but the *Daily News* appealed directly to veterans to help vote against "a Kaiser in the person of W.F. Coaker," asking, "Will those who fought on the fields of France and Flanders for the liberty of the world now prostitute their manhood by supporting the Coakerite doctrine of political domination?"[62] J.T. Meaney, one of Squires's major political organizers, wrote that members of the Naval Reserve were being asked by their commanders to oppose Squires at the polls.[63]

Despite all this backbiting and name-calling, Squires made enough political capital out of the accusation that the Cashin government was in the pocket of the Reids to win the election of 1919 handily.[64] Even so, there were costs. John Stone had met defeat at the hands of Union candidates in Trinity, Morine fell to Coaker, and other Union candidates won in Bonavista. However, John Chalker Crosbie, who had held a seat for the District of Bay de Verde since 1908, had switched to take on George Grimes successfully in Port de Grave. Without Port de Grave, Squires, a prominent Orangeman and Methodist, and Coaker, who already had the enmity of Archbishop Roche, found very little support in the remaining Roman Catholic–dominated populations of the Avalon Peninsula, including St. John's.[65] Coaker and Squires immediately tried to cement the defeat of their opponents by disclosing alleged misuse by Morine and other Cashin candidates of public-works money to buy votes. "Before the new Government can commence any reforms," claimed the FPU newspaper, "it is necessary to clean up the Departments and to show up the actions of the grafters."[66] Squires commissioned an investigation of government spending during Cashin's prime ministership, but it revealed no evidence of corruption, although plenty of patronage and poor accounting practices in government departments were brought to light.[67] Squires and Coaker kept up their attacks on the Reids, the largest industrial employers in St. John's, thus alienating working-class support, as did Coaker's open contrast of outport and urban interests. Consequently, by the end of the year, William Linegar—a member of the defeated Workingmen's Party, which had been independent in the 1919 election—had agreed to support the much more conservative Cashin party in future, although other members of the NIWA hoped to preserve the party's independent stance.[68] While the *Daily News* had long openly opposed Coaker, Currie's loss of his seat in the election ensured the hostility would continue. More important, Charles T. James's resounding defeat in Burgeo and La Poile, by a vote of 1428 to 231 for Liberal-Reformer Harvey Small, ensured that the *Evening Telegram* became an implacable opponent of Squires and Coaker through the early 1930s.[69]

Coaker became minister of marine and fisheries in the new Squires government, which took office on 17 November 1919. The prices for saltfish had begun to collapse in the wake of a worldwide post-war recession, encouraging Coaker to feel he had to act quickly if he were going to have much hope of reforming the fishery. The Italian government had organized the purchase of codfish in 1917 through a national agency, the Consorzio per l'importazione e la distribuzione dei merluzzi e stoccofissi. The Italian market was important for Labrador fish, a key product of the northeast-coast fishers who formed the backbone of the FPU, but until 1919 the Consorzio was effective in ensuring that Italians got fish for the lowest possible prices, which translated into poorer prices for Newfoundland suppliers.[70] The FPU now had an additional, institutional, interest in the reform of fish marketing, as the Union Trading Company (UTC) had been successful at playing the same game as the other fish-exporting firms. The membership of the FPU had invested much in the UTC, which in turn had extended a lot of credit to fishers during the war, but now that prices were collapsing, the UTC risked failure.[71]

As minister of fisheries, Coaker imposed regulations over the entire fish trade to forestall glutting and further price drops. In 1918, the

National Government had passed the Imports and Restriction Act to give the government broad powers to regulate trade for the war effort. Coaker now used this authority to require that all exports of fish be subject to the approval of the minister of marine and fisheries in terms of quality and price. There was a precedent for this: in 1918, fish exporters had accepted similar regulation by a committee of government chaired by John Chalker Crosbie, then minister of shipping. Coaker, however, was the bête noire of the mercantile community, the administrator of their successful competitor, the Union Trading Company, and was possessed of an aggressive and arrogant management style that was out of tune with the more solicitous approach to government favoured by Squires.[72] He had to be opposed and so, from the beginning, his critics portrayed his regulations as a betrayal of the principles the men of the Regiment had fought for during the war. The *Daily News* called the measures "A Vicious Policy" that would, in the long term, make Newfoundland fish unattractive to international buyers. It was part of a new order (the newspaper argued at the end of the year) that really marked the beginning of the twentieth century: "These are the days of uncertainty and unrest. The old order is giving place to the new. Liberty, fraternity, equality, glorious ideals, are struggling with licence, conspiracy, and the clannishness of class." The answer, its editor felt, was for the young to act as had the men who had fought in the Regiment, "with the same singleness of purpose, the same unselfishness, the same devotion, the same loyalty and love, the glorious, ennobled and ennobling TRAIL OF THE CARIBOU."[73]

Coaker's fisheries regulations fell quickly, victims of a January 1920 Supreme Court challenge by the Newfoundland fishing brokerage and exporting firm of Smith and Shipman, whose export of fish to Italy via New York Coaker had refused to permit.[74] The *Daily News*, vigorously supporting Cashin, called the regulations "incomparable bungling" that would have little chance of influencing international fish markets. The newspaper suggested that something much more sinister was at work in Squires's and Coaker's reaction against opposition to the fisheries regulations. The minister of justice had discussed the Smith and Shipman challenge at a public meeting at the Majestic Theatre, and announced that the government would use the still active War Measures Act to reinstate the regulations. The correspondent "Fair Play," who attended, "was horrified to hear a flippant, schoolboy jeer at those gentlemen, who were referred to as Jews"—Smith and Shipman were in partnership with the New York firm of J. Aron and Company. The *Daily News* condemned the anti-Semitism as "un-British conduct," and tainted Coaker and Squires by their association with the regulations.[75]

The parliamentary practice in Newfoundland at the time, as it was in the other dominions, was for those members of the House of Assembly who accepted appointments to cabinet to seek the approval of their constituencies for such appointments through by-election. Although these were often uncontested, Cashin's party, now called Liberal-Labour-Progressive as a result of the alliance with union leaders such as Linegar, decided to contest the re-election of Squires and H.J. Brownrigg in the St. John's West by-election set for January 1920. The Cashin party had no hope of successfully challenging Coaker in Bonavista, but it turned the St. John's West contest into a referendum on Squires's alliance with Coaker. The *Evening Telegram* declared that Squires "is Prime Minister of Newfoundland ... by the permission and grace of Hon. William F. Coaker, President of the Fishermen's Protective Union, Minister of Marine and Fisheries, and Dictator of the Government of Newfoundland."[76] William Linegar, who had changed allegiance in the 1919 election, came forward to run with James T. Martin for the Cashin party, claiming that Coaker had proven too hostile to the economic interests of St. John's and that organized labour must use the by-election to defeat "the tyranny and menace of Coakerism."[77] Linegar was the president of the Journeyman Coopers Union and a prominent supporter of the NIWA, while the export trade of St. John's was a major market for the products of coopers and directly employed many of their number. Linegar feared that Coaker's attempts to regulate the fish trade would hurt exporters and, through them, his members, as well as the general economic well-being of St. John's: it was his duty to help stop the "juggernaut of Coaker."[78]

Coaker fought back, pointing out that Cashin had always been a Tory in principle: he was a Roman Catholic conservative, pro-mercantile and anti-labour. The FPU leader suggested that the NIWA and the LSPU had decided to back the Squires-Coaker alliance because Squires had agreed to support their desire for minimum wage regulations, the eight-hour day, regulation of child labour, control of the high cost of living, and the provision of better housing for working people. The FPU newspaper printed a letter from Michael Foley of the NIWA, which claimed that Cashin had used sectarianism to court Linegar and John Caldwell, two members of the NIWA's political committee, who had then convinced the committee to support Cashin, leading Jim McGrath of the LSPU to disavow any connection with it. It is, however, more likely that Cashin had promised to bankroll labour candidates in St. John's as long as they opposed the Squires-Coaker alliance. Financially exhausted from the 1919 campaign, the embryonic labour party needed money and this offer would give them further reason to be discontented with the Squires-Coaker alliance.[79] Moreover, though Squires had promised to support organized labour, his government had come to power during a period of considerable inflation in the prices of basic foodstuffs, and a significant beneficiary of that price inflation had been Squires's running mate, Brownrigg, a major St. John's grocery wholesaler.

Coaker's opponents then intensified their attack on the FPU leader's supposed dictatorial nature. Under the headline "No Tyrant for St. John's West," the editor of the *Evening Telegram* claimed that it would be unpatriotic for voters to help Coaker by electing Squires and Brownrigg. It would be folly, the editor claimed, to support "the wild ambitions of one solitary individual, who has no more right to place himself in a dictator's chair, than the German Kaiser was justified in plunging the world into the horrors of war." Just as people had stood up against the Kaiser, so should the electors of St. John's West stand up against Coaker, who really called the shots in the Squires government.[80]

The editor might well have been calculating that this rhetoric would appeal to the Great War Veterans' Association (GWVA), which had been formed in late August 1918 under the presidency of Harold Mitchell, and represented every Newfoundlander who had served with a Newfoundland or Imperial military unit during the war. The GWVA sought to foster a special sense of national pride among its members by romanticizing their service, and to encourage the people of Newfoundland to feel that the status of their members had been elevated by the heroism and nobility of their military sacrifice. In 1919, they had taken over the organization of the Memorial Day program for 1 July, organizing parades of veterans and the civic brigades to church services, and thence to a state ceremony in Bannerman Park.[81] They had also taken a special interest in planning for a Newfoundland war memorial, of which the FPU newspaper had initially been critical, stating that the people of Newfoundland would not benefit by "statuary" in St. John's, and that money would be better spent on funding a memorial normal and technical school.

The GWVA's ultimate goal was to lobby for better pensions and employment for its members since, while initially committed to being non-partisan, many of its members were working men who faced the same problems of poor housing, poor incomes, and high cost of living that had motivated the NIWA to take political action in 1919. The NIWA had provided organizational support to the veterans, and the GWVA reciprocated by cooperating with the Workingmen's Party candidates.[82] Although Grimes's earlier positive comments on Bolshevism had proved to be an exception to the usual rhetoric supporting better conditions for workers, it proved very damaging now, because there was little interest on the part of the labour movement in the kind of industrial militancy or leftist radicalism that had, in parts of Canada, made the Canadian GWVA hostile at times to much of the labour movement.

Late in the war, for example, the members of the Canadian GWVA had spoken out against revolutionary socialism and, when labour radicals called for a general strike in reaction to the assassination of union leader Albert "Ginger" Goodwin in 1918, veterans and soldiers attacked the Vancouver Labour Temple. The Canadian GWVA tended to be critical of militant organizations such as the One Big Union in 1919 as being the influence of foreign radicals, although the Winnipeg General Strike in that year had the support of many returned soldiers because of the largely Anglo-Canadian nature of the strike's leadership. No matter how much the local GWVA wanted to remain free of political affiliations, then, it would have been very difficult for it to resist calls that all "freemen and liberty-loving subjects of the British Empire" would have to reject "Coakerism, Czarism, Bolshevism, all [of which] are synonymous terms."[83] Although the GWVA was a major supporter of reform in areas such as the better provision of medical services and housing, its cooperation with the political allies of Michael Cashin clearly signalled that the association had little sympathy for Coaker. It wanted benefits for association members before government channelled its resources to other goals.[84] Thus, Coaker's 1919 fisheries regulations—the supposed evidence of his Bolshevism—also became important in the by-election.

Coaker ignored any attacks associated with the regulations, focusing instead on Cashin's relationship with Linegar. The Liberal-Labour funding agreement was, the FPU newspaper claimed, nothing more than Tory bribery that typified corruption in the Cashin administration. As a result, despite the implication of anti-Semitism that had been part of the attack on the fisheries regulations, Squires and Brownrigg won the by-election handily, an event marked by the FPU newspaper with the verse "For Squires and Brownrigg are our Men, To Keep the Grafters Out."[85]

In the short term, then, the by-election appeared to have opened the way for Coaker's fisheries regulations, since the FPU leader was minister of marine and fisheries in Newfoundland's first full-fledged post-war administration, whose election success appeared now to have been reaffirmed in Squires's and Brownrigg's victory.

However, the costs of the victory were important. The St. John's by-election revealed the sharp divide between Coaker and prominent working-class leaders in the city. Many of these leaders, through the NIWA, had been supporting the GWVA. The veterans' organization, although non-partisan, could not fail to notice the manner in which Coaker's opponents had labelled him a Prussian and a Bolshevik. Coaker faced an impossible task: he would have to show that his fisheries regulations could immediately revitalize a Newfoundland economy that was slipping into post-war depression. Failure to do so would appear to confirm the nasty rhetorical excesses of his opponents, who held that Coaker was doomed to fail as nothing more than a Prussian fool or a dupe for Bolshevism. The FPU leader had set a high standard by which to be judged because he could not resist the temptations of gutter politics, and the FPU newspaper had proven just as capable of excess, especially in accusing Cashin's supporters of graft. There was little hope that Coaker's regulations could fulfill their promise quickly enough to survive the continued onslaught of conservative attacks on the probity of their author.

The Failure of the Progressive Alternative, 1920–1923

The need for fisheries reform seemed unimportant compared to the problems arising from Newfoundland's participation in the Great War. Time and again, the men of the Royal Newfoundland Regiment had spilled their blood for the Empire. At home, people had suffered the loss of loved ones in battle and struggled through wartime inflation. The crisis of war had made the problems of the fishery seem distant in most people's minds, but not in Coaker's. The FPU existed to lessen the exploitative nature of the seal hunt and fishery's mercantile organization. In the FPU's political platform, the state always had a key role to play in improving social and economic conditions by providing better public services to people and by regulating key industries, especially the fishery. The war had revealed that governments could intervene to address social and economic problems; Coaker had joined the National

Government and gambled by supporting conscription so that he would have the opportunity to use the power of government to deal with what he felt was most important: putting the fishing industry on a sounder basis. By 1920, conditions could not have been less favourable for Coaker's attempt at fisheries regulations. A deepening post-war depression in the fish trade produced unfavourable economic conditions in Newfoundland and provided Coaker's opponents with a basis for attacking his policy. His regulations actually came to be blamed for the depression, and the opposition, when it suited them, accused him of corruption, or of making common cause with Squires. In their view, a new menace had joined Prussianism and Bolshevism in the local political lexicon: Coakerism.

The stakes for Coaker were much higher than simply the fisheries regulations, for the post-war recession was making it almost impossible for the Squires government to satisfy the demands of veterans for the support that reintegration into society required. The government faced growing demands for public relief from the unemployed and the poor, demands it was poorly equipped to handle. The frustration of veterans and the unsatisfied needs of the unemployed meant that there were growing numbers of willing ears to hear the opposition's potent labelling of the administration as corrupt, treasonous, Prussian, and Bolshevik. Unable to deal with the searing criticism of his regulations, Coaker seemed determined to live up to his critics' slanders, advocating the use of the War Measures Act to silence them through press censorship. In short, by 1923, Coaker had become willing to use undemocratic methods.

The St. John's by-election win in 1920 had indicated that there was public support for Coaker's efforts to regulate the fishery, although there was no doubt of mercantile opposition. Walter Baine Grieve, the principal of Baine, Johnston & Co., had already stated that the regulations imposed under the War Measures Act were an assault on free trade, a basic principle of the British liberal order.[1] Although Grieve had led the charge against fisheries regulations in a meeting of the Board of Trade in February, other mercantile figures—most notably R.B. Job of Job Brothers, who sat on Coaker's advisory board for fisheries regulation, and a director of Job Brothers, Brian Dunfield—defended the need for a more organized approach to marketing. Coaker claimed that Newfoundland was now engaged in a "'Trade' War which has inevitably followed the Great War," and that it was unpatriotic of Grieve and the *Daily News* to oppose measures that asked the mercantile community to cooperate for the sake of all Newfoundlanders.[2] Coaker's critics used war-related imagery and concepts in their attacks, but the fisheries minister did not hesitate to respond in kind. The FPU newspaper, for example, lauded Coaker's support for the regulation of the seal hunt by drawing on Haig's earlier description of the men of the Regiment. It argued that the seal hunt's "successful prosecution demands the best characteristics that manhood can supply. It demands *men*, in the truest sense of the word; such men of whom it was said: '*They were better than the best.*'"[3]

The problem for Coaker was that Prime Minister Squires had a knack for becoming embroiled in disputes with the Great War Veterans' Association (GWVA). Squires was not unsympathetic to the hardships experienced by veterans, and he tried to help them individually. In the summer of 1920, for example, he wrote to Coaker on behalf of B. Murphy of the GWVA, who had served at Gallipoli and in France and Belgium. The prime minister hoped that Coaker could find work for Murphy in the Department of Marine and Fisheries.[4] The veterans' organization wanted more than such individual acts and asked the government to increase the pensions it paid out to veterans and survivors. The prime minister refused, and seemed remarkably insensitive to the political position of the GWVA. Although Coaker was supportive of the GWVA, the government of which he was a member was unable to make itself the veterans' choice. In its first year, moreover, the Squires government had become embroiled in allegations of bribing William Woodford (a Cashin supporter in the previous House of Assembly) to abandon Cashin, while Coaker became involved in a bitter dispute with Abram Kean over the latter's treatment of sealers in the 1920 hunt. What was important about these ongoing disputes was not so much their content as their public and scandalous nature, which tainted Squires with corruption and Coaker with vindictiveness, hardly noble qualities worthy of veterans' support.[5]

The disputes also provided an unfavourable backdrop for Coaker's efforts to establish a more permanent regulation of the fishery in the legislative session of May and June 1920. Coaker proposed two measures. The Codfish Standardization Act established a commission to improve the quality of the Newfoundland product by regulating all aspects of the catching, processing, culling, warehousing, and shipping of saltfish. The establishment of a national system for the grading of fish should, Coaker thought, prevent foreign buyers from continuing to be able to offer low prices because of the poor nature of the cure. The Salt Codfish Exportation Act established an advisory board composed of four licensed exporters and two more chosen by a majority of all those holding export licences, but chaired by the minister of fisheries. Only firms granted a licence by this board could export fish. The goal was to end the fish merchants' practice of undercutting each other's prices and glutting the market. To that end, the main condition for receiving such a licence was observance of minimum conditions, fixed by the board, for the maximum amount of fish that could be sold in any season, and the minimum prices for which such fish could be sold. In the long term, Coaker thought, Newfoundland's fish markets would become much more stable. He also introduced other measures, such as the Codfish Information Act, to provide better information on the nature of the fish trade, and proposed a bureau of fisheries science.

Despite Coaker's efforts to secure mercantile support, Sir John Chalker Crosbie spoke against the Exportation Act in the House of Assembly on 20 May, the day after the minister introduced the measure. He claimed that the regulations were not British, declaring "they are not what this war was fought for." Much of the legislative debate that followed revolved around the issue of whether or not state regulation was "British" and thus permissible—leaving to one side whether a given regulation was well founded or wise. The *Daily News* accused Coaker of placing complete power over the fish trade in his own hands at the expense of other exporters who were (in Coaker's capacity as the overseer of the Union Trading Company) his competitors. Given Coaker's "fondness for assuming the role of dictator, there can be little doubt that power would be exercised," the paper averred.[6] Anxious to secure mercantile support for the initiative, and perhaps as a price for Squires's continued backing of his efforts, Coaker agreed to leave most of the discretionary authority for making regulations in the hands of the advisory board, which was now dominated by fish exporters.[7]

The fisheries regulations were not developing in a political vacuum: the issues of assistance for veterans and their families and commemoration of the war effort were important at the time, and in this context, Squires continued to be a difficult ally for Coaker. The prime minister had become embroiled in a dispute with Harold Mitchell, who had recently finished his term as president of the GWVA and had approached Squires about additional assistance for a widow of a member of the Regiment, suggesting that Newfoundland provided miserly pensions. The GWVA estimated that Newfoundland pensions were about fifty percent lower than those received by Canadian veterans; under the War Pensions Act, 1917, for example, a private of the Royal Newfoundland Regiment classified as one hundred percent disabled would receive an annual pension of $480. A Canadian private would, by contrast, receive $900 per year. To the outrage of the opposition press, Squires had brushed off Mitchell's claim, suggesting that most of the Regiment's recruits had originally joined not for patriotic reasons but for money.[8]

The FPU newspaper worked hard to counter the resultant impact of Squires's negative press by associating itself with the better world promised by the terrible sacrifices of the war. On 2 July 1920, it announced a special non-partisan issue to be published the next day, "devoted to the Commemoration of July First 1916, when our own Regiment received its baptism of fire and played the gallant part at Beaumont Hamel." Many of the articles in the special issue echoed the themes in J. Alexander Robinson's "Virtue Treads Paths That End Not In the Grave." Robinson, the conservative founder of the *Daily News* and People's Party stalwart, argued that the character of the people of Newfoundland had evolved through struggle against exploitative merchants and uncaring colonial governments, but their fearlessness and will to prevail was "displayed in storm and tempest on sea and land, and Arctic ice and furious blizzards." British authorities could no longer neglect Newfoundland after 1 July 1916 because of the deeds of the members of the Regiment—the "Crusaders of the Twentieth Century"— whose sacrifice at Beaumont Hamel was "the baptism of blood" that "changed the status of the self-centred colony to partnership with the Empire." W.J. Carew, a prominent civil servant and the prime minister's secretary, voiced similar sentiments in his article "Beaumont Hamel," but emphasized that every Newfoundlander shared in the sacrifice that had been made on 1 July. Many people lost relatives at Beaumont Hamel, but the men of the Regiment were "our fellow countrymen, blood of our blood and bone of our bone."[9]

The Squires-Coaker alliance could not afford to ignore the growing political engagement of the GWVA, whose members were becoming increasingly vocal on matters related to veterans and had come to feel that they had a privileged voice in post-war Newfoundland.[10] Coaker had to be careful about how his regulations might be perceived in such a political environment. However, he tripped up in several ways. In July, in an effort to keep exporters and critics of the regulations in line, he had, as minister of marine and fisheries, asked papers such as the *Daily News* not to print news of fish prices unless authorized by his office. He was anxious to control access to information about fish prices in Mediterranean and Iberian markets, fearing that news of low prices being offered for fish could panic exporters into breaking with the regulations. The editor called the request "dictatorial" and, when Coaker announced on 2 September that newspapers would not be allowed to print reports on meetings of the fish exporters unless authenticated by his office, the *News* protested his attack on the "freedom of the press."[11] While Coaker might have intended to use the authority of the War Measures Act, he did little more than threaten censorship.

Coaker then ran into more trouble in trying to deal with the impact on the fishery regulations of the banks operating in Newfoundland, particularly the Bank of Nova Scotia. The banks disliked the government's attempt to regulate the market, and restricted credit to firms that cooperated with the Exportation Board. Reluctant investors in the fishing industry, the banks lent money to exporters against the security of their inventories, and expected those to be sold as quickly as possible. Coaker considered that better investment in cold storage facilities and in a national marketing structure would allow Newfoundland to hold fish caught on the southwest coast of the island. There, ice-free waters permitted fishing in the winter and provided catches that had to be shipped to market well in advance of the later summer and fall fisheries run by the base of the FPU, the northeast-coast fishers. Coaker suggested that Newfoundland would benefit from having a national bank for such investment purposes, and mused publicly about using the War Measures Act to set one up. The *Evening Telegram*'s editor responded that such a measure was exactly the type of thing Lenin would implement in Russia, and Coaker was "our would-be local Lenin." The FPU leader, he suspected, was out to destroy merchants and independent fishers through a "Bolshevistic-Communistic-Socialistic programme."[12]

The intemperate language that his opponents used to attack Coaker suggests a political situation that, already inflamed by the rhetorical excesses of wartime, had become mired in hysteria over the perceived radicalism of the FPU leader's more progressive fisheries policies. The

Telegram's attack on Coaker was a gross misrepresentation of his intentions for the fishery, and it also contradicted the opposition newspapers' constant claim that Coaker, as president of the Union Trading Company, was in effect a merchant who was trying to use the fisheries regulations to undue personal advantage. The problem was that the intemperate polemics surrounding the controversy of Coaker's attempted reform of the fishery were becoming so common in the newspapers that they were creating an air of perpetual crisis.

Not one to prefer even-tempered debate over bombast, the FPU leader responded in kind. The FPU newspaper called Coaker's critics at the *Evening Telegram* unpatriotic "Tory heelers" and idiots for opposing the fisheries regulations, under the headline "Who Is Bolshevik? Coaker or the Telegram?"[13] The *Telegram* maintained that Coaker's regulations were an experiment in "communistic theories of trade," and its editor continued to call Coaker a "self-constructed dictator" who wanted to destroy the liberty of capitalists in Newfoundland.[14]

Such use of the term "dictator" reflected a contradiction in post-war Newfoundland attitudes. On the one hand, Coaker's opponents used it as an insult when referring to his belief that the state could intervene positively to address post-war problems such as worsening fish markets. On the other hand, the term could have positive connotations if it was applied to a forceful authority figure on the British side. In printing a message of congratulations on the 1920 foundation of *Veteran* magazine from William Goode (a Newfoundlander who had become the British director of relief missions with the Supreme Economic Council, British Department in Paris), the editors of the magazine noted that Goode "to-day holds the high office of Allied Commissioner in Austria, which means, under present conditions, that he is practically Dictator of that Country."[15] Dictators were good when they pursued goals and held values compatible with one's own views, or when they were a symbol of Britain's military victory; they were bad when they pursued any opposing agendas.

Coaker was advocating an approach to state intervention that was clearly at odds with the liberal market views held by the opposition press, and he needed to treat the editorial position taken by the *Telegram* cautiously. Liberty, after all, was a key principle that the Regiment's members had fought to preserve during the war. Unfortunately, Coaker was not careful in his *Evening Advocate* attacks on Charles T. James, the editor of the *Telegram*. James, according to the FPU newspaper, was smarting because he (a Cashin candidate) had lost in the District of Burgeo-La Poile in the last election, and was now making "a consummate ass of himself" by opposing the fisheries regulations.[16] Since Coaker felt that he had the best of motives for controlling access to information about fish prices in Mediterranean and Iberian markets, the FPU newspaper editor thought he could accuse James, and any other critic of the fisheries regulations, of disloyalty.[17] "Disloyalty," indeed, was another term that was used indiscriminately by Newfoundland political parties and their attendant newspapers in their attacks on each other.

The war of rhetoric continued through the fall. In September, the Italian Consorzio made it clear that it did not wish to purchase Newfoundland fish. At the same time, the devaluation of the Portuguese escudo against the British pound sterling hurt the important Iberian market for Newfoundland fish. The FPU newspaper again argued that the opposition newspapers' printing of the Consorzio decision so damaged the trade that the government should use its powers under the War Measures Act to impose censorship on the press. The recommendation "inspired, if not actually written by Hon. W.F. Coaker, that censors be placed in the offices of newspapers for the purpose of controlling (suppressing) all utterances and comments relative to fishing matters, is of the very latest type of Prussianism," argued the *Telegram*. "It is authority gone mad and a threat against the very fundamentals of the constitution, the right of free speech, and the freedom of the press, as well as the muzzling of public opinion."[18] The *Daily News* disagreed with the *Telegram* only in that it felt that Coaker's demand was more

Bolshevik than Prussian, but agreed that "Mr. Coaker, as actual, if not nominal, premier, would clothe himself with the powers of a dictator and crush and destroy all who stood in his way." Newfoundlanders would not tolerate such dictatorial methods as the use of censorship during peacetime.[19]

The FPU newspaper maintained instead that the government had every right to use censorship because the fisheries regulations were in the interest of the people of Newfoundland. The *Daily News* and the *Evening Telegram*, it argued, weakened Newfoundland's position with the Consorzio. The papers' criticisms of the fisheries regulations led the Italian agency to believe that resolve in Newfoundland was weak, and the constant discussion of market conditions provided the competitor with too much information about local conditions in the fishery. Furthermore, the regulations had been duly promulgated as law, making the opposition attacks on them little better than treason; it was the opposition who were the real Prussians and Bolshviks.[20] The *Advocate*'s position was that information on fish markets was as vital to the national interest of Newfoundland as was information about the movement of shipping to Britain's interests during the war. Disseminating such information hampered the fisheries regulations. As the measures were manifestly in the national interest, it declared, if anyone "is against such an object let him say so openly and then get out of the country quick!"[21]

Coaker's efforts to intimidate the opponents of his regulations achieved little but his own discredit. By October, it was becoming clear that exporters were getting ready to sell in spite of the regulations, particularly as the price for fish in the Italian market dropped from ten dollars to eight dollars—or at least that was the information printed by the *Daily News*. The FPU newspaper warned exporters that they were obliged to observe the law, that the "[r]egulations are the law of the land, and as such should command the support of every full-blooded Newfoundlander. To fight them is to injure every man, woman and child in the country."[22] Coaker defended the regulations as a means of protecting mercantile firms from their own worst marketing practices. The *Daily News* thought that it was disingenuous for the FPU leader who had for so long attacked merchants to now, as minister of marine and fisheries, be solicitous of their well-being and, as minister, to spend so much time hobnobbing in their company, forgetting the fishers who belonged to the FPU.[23]

The FPU newspaper, in defence of Coaker, accused the *Daily News* and the *Evening Telegram* of being the press representatives of the Consorzio in Newfoundland. The *Advocate* charged the opposition papers with taking delight in the Italian fish market problems encountered by the Exportation Board, and called them "the communist press" for their editorial policies against the Coaker Regulations. "They have revealed the cloven hoof," declared the *Advocate*, "and any intelligent man who possesses reason who in future is influenced by claptrap uttered by these papers, is just as great an enemy of Newfoundland as was the bitterest German carrying a gun during the years of the war."[24] Not to be outdone, the *Telegram* called Coaker's regulations the policy of a "loud mouthed dictator, whose sole notion and idea is unrestricted and untrammelled rule. Are fishermen not already cognizant of the desires and wishes of this local Kaiser?"[25] The *Advocate* referred to James and the editor of the *Daily News* as "Dangerous Lunatics" for their opposition to Coaker.

Such mudslinging indicated Coaker's frustration, but it could not disguise the fact that the minister of marine and fisheries had gone too far in trying to silence the press's comments on his regulations. The *Telegram* appeared to be on higher ground in claiming that Coaker's desire for press censorship was incompatible with the values of a liberal democracy.[26] Coaker's and the *Advocate*'s attempts to bully the opponents of the regulations, especially by threatening press censorship, allowed them to be portrayed as representatives of the kind of authoritarianism that true Britons, Newfoundlanders included, had fought against during the war. Brushed with the tar of Kaiserism, Prussianism, and Bolshevism, the FPU newspaper tried to clear the name of the union and its leader through patriotic appeal. Armistice Day was always an opportunity to burnish battered reputations, but even then the newspaper could not resist political engagement on the issue of the regulations. The *Advocate*'s Armistice Day editorial complained that offering two minutes of silence was a poor commemoration of the lives lost in the war. In the context of a worsening post-war recession, surely, the editorial argued, it was better to build prosperity by ensuring that working people, especially fishers, received a fairer share of the fruits of their labour. In late December, the *Advocate* reported on the 19 December opening of the "Soldiers' Memorial Church of the Holy Martyrs" in Port Union, emphasizing the stained-glass windows installed in memory of the lost Coaker Recruits, Coaker's donation of the altar and reredos, and the donation of the pulpit by Coaker's political friend Harry J. Crowe in memory of his son Lieutenant Lawrence Crowe, who had died in the service of the Royal Flying Corps during the war. Altogether, 130 men had answered Coaker's call, of which 68 proved medically fit to serve. Ten of the fallen were memorialized by the church windows at Port Union. The church, proclaimed the *Advocate*, was "another milestone in the life of Mr. Coaker and Port Union and the FPU."[27]

The *Advocate* also supported the Christmas appeal from Thomas Nangle of the GWVA that the government get on with building a memorial to the men who had served in the war, although the paper made it clear that it wanted public money spent on an educational facility.[28] The eventual decision was to have two memorials: a monument, which the GWVA actively supported, and a government-sponsored college, which would open its doors in 1925 as Memorial University College. Coaker was well acquainted with Nangle, having toured the battlefields and gravesites of the Regiment in France with him in February 1920, looking for possible memorial sites. He appreciated Nangle, and had secured Squires's consent that the priest be authorized to spend up to ten thousand dollars to purchase the Beaumont Hamel site for a memorial to the fallen of the Royal Newfoundland Regiment and the Royal Naval Reserve. The amount from government eventually rose to fifteen thousand dollars, and the Ladies' Auxiliary of the GWVA and a Beaumont Hamel Collection Committee engaged in vigorous fundraising to cover the remaining expenses of building the memorial.[29]

However, such efforts, in the short term, could not undo the damage caused to Coaker's public image, which continued to take a beating as his fisheries regulations fell apart. A stunning loophole in the regulations allowed companies to avoid the rules about minimum prices for fish sales because, should one firm lose its licence by underselling, it could always acquire another issued in the name of the company's general manager. By November, merchants such as Crosbie and A.E. Hickman, and later W.A. Munn, began to sell fish at prices below those set by the Exportation Board. In the context of a deepening depression, individual firms, whose business practices had been based on competition with each other rather than cooperation in marketing, were encouraged to break the rules, as their banks pressured them to sell fish as quickly as possible so that they had money to repay loans. Not surprisingly, many export companies did so. These exporting firms defended themselves by saying that it was beyond the capacity of the Newfoundland industry to control conditions in international fish markets. Coaker had not actually been willing to make the Exportation Board more authoritarian in its dealings with the exporters, and the nature of his alliance with Squires did not provide him with a secure enough political base from which to force exporters to obey the law. He had tried to meet them halfway by offering them considerable influence over the effective implementation of the regulations, but the exporters declined. They had decided to break with the fisheries policy, and so, in the FPU newspaper's view, their firms were responsible for the regulations' failure.[30]

The public battle over the fisheries regulations had damaged Coaker's reputation. Far from being the champion of the toiling masses or the "men of the North," he had become known as a dictatorial extremist whose views on the state threatened the liberty that men had struggled and died for in the war, and as a hypocritical unionist who claimed to speak for fishers while enjoying the lifestyle of a merchant. Worsening economic conditions and his continued presence in government made it difficult for Coaker to improve his image, and international fish markets continued to deteriorate. Although critics of the fishery regulations had undermined them partially by asserting that the small dominion of Newfoundland could not hope to influence global market conditions, they did not hesitate to lay the blame for these same conditions at Coaker's feet as he attempted to do something to improve the price of fish. Prices continued to drop, and the Squires government found that Newfoundland's public debt and obligations to the railway left it with very little room to manoeuvre.

The Newfoundland war debt was about $34.5 million, of which $13.4 million had been incurred by direct borrowing for the war effort and another $16 million was the capitalized cost of pensions owed to veterans and dependants. The government also had an annual financial commitment of $1.3 million to service its railway debt. Overall, Newfoundland's debt was becoming a burden too heavy to carry. The problem was especially bad in the post-war depression of 1919 through 1921, but Newfoundland continued to have deficits in its annual budgets from 1921 through 1933, with the exception of 1925. From 1920–1921 to 1931–1932, the average annual revenue of the dominion was $9,250,000, while its average annual expenditure was $11,250,000, leaving an average annual deficit of $2,000,000. Newfoundland borrowed in London and New York to meet these deficits, but increasingly it relied on Canadian banks, of which the Bank of Montreal was chief.[31]

Little economic diversification had transpired because of all the debt related to the railway, and depression in both the fishery and the markets for newsprint from Grand Falls resulted in weak demand for the manufactures of the capital, and hence led to lower wages and labour force layoffs. Nonetheless, and although the Squires government had come to power in part by campaigning against the Reid interests, their railway and related enterprises were still too great a component of the small dominion economy to ignore. In 1920, the railway company required further financial support, a need Squires could not ignore without risking the company's collapse, consequent economic disruption, and even higher unemployment. Unwilling to simply provide more support, the government formed the Railway Commission to oversee its relationship with the Reid railway during the summer of 1920, with Coaker as its chair. The government lent the railway $1.5 million to improve its infrastructure and develop local coal fields so as to reduce the cost of relying on imported coal (unfortunately, local coal fields never proved feasible). Financial assistance to the Reids was very unpopular with most Newfoundlanders and, to make matters worse, the railway operated at a loss of $1,335,000 in the first year of operation under the new commission—the greatest loss so far in the railway's unfortunate history, and a great embarrassment to the government.[32]

It was further mystifying to many people that a company with such wealthy directors, with extensive holdings, and with rights to so much of Newfoundland's natural resources could require so much government money. During yet another by-election in Harbour Main in February 1921, the *Evening Telegram* attacked Squires and Coaker for using the Railway Commission as a way to funnel money to the Reids without improving the railway system, and for allowing the Reids to import supplies for their operations that might otherwise be manufactured in Newfoundland. Allowing such imports drew the ire of the NIWA. The *Telegram* suggested that, through appointments on bodies such as the Railway Commission, Squires, Coaker, and their political friends enjoyed fine salaries and lifestyles while the people descended into "beggary."[33]

Demands for public help for the poor grew even as the government's financial ability to provide it declined. In February, Julia Salter Earle, the president of the Ladies' Branch of the NIWA, had written about the need for a greater government response to poverty in the city. Earle attacked critics who argued that such government help would be "Bolshevism," arguing instead that assisting the hungry was a Christian obligation.[34] The *Telegram* argued that the government could act indirectly by forcing the railway company to construct locomotives locally rather than importing them, thereby creating more work for NIWA members. The paper took the opportunity to attack the government as "heartless and cruel" for stating that it could not afford to pay the bill for men who stowed away on sealing steamers to get work at the hunt while it could give good employment to its own "gangs of grafters."[35] The paper further placed Newfoundland's economic depression squarely on Coaker's fisheries regulations and, with the *Daily News*, demanded that Coaker resign from government.[36]

The *Daily News* had, in January, argued that the main instrument that had allowed Coaker to do so much damage, the War Measures Act, must be brought to an end. The government had retained the act to facilitate the fisheries regulations as a post-war reconstruction measure, but the apparent failure of the regulations meant that there was now no need for it to continue. At a public meeting for the unemployed of St. John's held at the LSPU Hall on the evening of 16 April, attendees agreed that the War Measures Act and the fisheries regulations must be ended. Julia Salter Earle, who was present, supported their views. Throughout late April and early May there were a number of marches and public meetings by unemployed men and women in St. John's, which demanded an end to the regulations and greater assistance for the unemployed. Michael Cashin and Sir John Crosbie showed up at these gatherings to make sympathetic noises, but gave few actual promises of assistance. The meeting of 16 April passed resolutions calling for the removal of the War Measures Act and the abolition of the fisheries regulations, blaming them for the economic woes of the city. On 7 June, the government finally lifted the War Measures Act, which the *Daily News* likened to taking a "loaded revolver" out of "the hands of incompetents."[37]

On 3 May 1921, Coaker introduced the motion asking for the repeal of the Exportation of the Salt Codfish Act. It was becoming clear that the Squires, Coaker, and Warren factions in government were not getting along with each other, but Coaker's relative strength, in terms of the number of Union Party seats he controlled in the House of Assembly, meant that he continued to be called the "dictator" of the coalition by the opposition newspapers. These attributed Squires's motion for the House's adjournment in May as the prime minister's attempt to free government from the deepening rifts between the three groups there.[38] It is actually probable that Coaker thought that Squires was no worse than any other politician in St. John's: he had flirted with a new political alliance with the conservative opposition when the government struck down his regulations, but neither Crosbie nor the other Union Party MHAs could stomach such a move. Bitter at the failure of his regulations, Coaker did little to help the government as it flailed. The Liberal-Reform alliance began to drift more into Squires's hands and, when the FPU leader bothered to look about, he saw Squires and the opposition caught up in a corrupt contest of political bribery, each trying to shore up its support with unemployed and desperate voters by promising more spending on relief and public works, all of which the government could ill afford.[39]

It was bad enough for Coaker to have suffered being tainted with the opprobrium of Bolshevism, Prussianism, or Kaiserism, but he had, in Squires, a political partner who seemed determined to make matters worse. The GWVA had continued to fight for better pension benefits for veterans and the families of deceased servicemen, and in March the FPU newspaper assured veterans that "the best interests of the soldiers have been and will be at all times faithfully served by the present strong and trusted administration."[40] Although Squires had conceded that pensions should be raised to Canadian levels that month, GWVA President J.G. Higgins and Dominion Secretary Gerald J. Whitty wrote to the press in November that they were having trouble getting the government to make the additional payments.[41] Even worse, Newfoundland's naval reservists were upset: they were entitled to shares of the prize money realized from the disposal of captured enemy shipping during the war, and imperial authorities had turned funds over to the individual dominion governments to pay their veterans' shares. By 1921, however, it had become clear that the Squires government hoped to keep the money, arguing that the reservists had got their share when the Newfoundland government agreed to top up their pay to the level of those in the Royal Newfoundland Regiment. On 16 March, at the LSPU Hall, and on 21 March in Bay Roberts, veterans of the Reserves held patriotic protest meetings against the government, being careful to always end with "God Save the King." On 11 July, the ex-reservists marched on the Colonial Building, the seat of the House of Assembly, to demand their pay.[42]

The editor of the *Evening Telegram* reported that the newspaper had received many letters from reservists complaining about the situation. In 1920, the GWVA had organized a membership drive partly in response to the perception that the government was not assisting veterans properly: in particular, the organization felt that qualified veterans should receive preferential treatment in hiring for the civil service over people who had not served.[43] While reservists protested throughout the spring of 1921, other unemployed veterans drifted to Bell Island in search of work. Cutbacks in employment there forced the Wabana municipal council to provide relief to the "aged men, and women with invalided husbands" who "formed the floating population." Captain Leo Murphy of the GWVA wrote to Squires asking that the council be compensated for the relief it provided.[44] The *Telegram* reported that veterans continued to be passed by for government appointments in favour of those who had not served in the war.[45]

Squires yielded the prize money later in the summer of 1921, but complaints continued that the government was not doing enough to aid veterans. Although Squires had supported Thomas Nangle, backing his promotion from major to lieutenant colonel in 1920 (the governor continued to have the authority as colonel-in-chief of the Regiment to make promotions under the authority of the minister of the militia), the worsening financial circumstances of the government did not allow the prime minister to provide as much employment for veterans as he might have liked.[46] It must have stung Coaker to witness the FPU being associated with the neglect of veterans' interests, particularly considering that the war had taken his nephew and namesake, William Coaker Christian, who had enlisted in 1917 and died of gunshot wounds on 26 October 1918.[47] Further, it had been Coaker to whom Nangle had complained by writing in 1920 that Squires was not properly recognizing the priest's work, which Coaker responded to by recommending Nangle's promotion to lieutenant colonel.[48]

While Coaker had a good relationship with Nangle, the FPU leader's views were becoming more incompatible with the dominant approach to post-war commemoration. Coaker accepted the need to give meaning to tragedy, and he would have connected the many deaths on the fronts of Gallipoli, France, and Belgium with the ideal that the soldiers of the Regiment had gone to war to prepare the way for a better post-war world. However, Coaker had embraced the idea that the best form of commemoration was for the state to take more progressive measures to transform the economy and society to build that better world. The more conventional approach was to build monuments to the fallen.

In 1921, the warrant officers and sergeants of the 2nd Battalion, Royal Newfoundland Regiment, established a monument to their comrades who had fallen in the war. They, along with the GWVA, organized a memorial ceremony on 3 July 1921 to unveil the Celtic cross and plaque that was to be their monument, placed in Anglican Cathedral Square. Governor Sir Charles Alexander Harris gave the panegyric, in which he observed that the fallen "gave all up that they might make the world better for you and for all of us," although this was "a cause which they may have seen but dimly at first." This ability to fight for a purpose of which they were not conscious at the time flowed, according to Harris, from a higher, divine power that had ensured victory. Such divine purpose might not be subject to scientific verification, but it was the consequence of faith, and Newfoundlanders had a duty in faith to carry on the tradition of the Regiment's fallen and keep working to build a more harmonious and prosperous post-war world.[49] This task of reconstruction, argued J. Alex Robinson in an essay accompanying photos of the Sergeants' Memorial ceremony in the GWVA magazine, would be the real monument established by veterans to the memory of their fallen comrades. Reconstruction, however, was not to be forced by a more interventionist state, but rather to be inspired by the noble example of those who had fallen in defence of the high ideals of British civilization, and monuments would be a constant physical expression of such inspiration.[50]

Coaker agreed with the need for reconstruction, but insisted that it required putting aside the belief that it was unwise for the state to intervene against social and economic inequality. The opposing view was that liberalism was one of the noble ideals of the war but that this great ideal stood in direct contradiction of the approach favoured by Coaker: the duty of the peace was to ensure the full restoration of laissez-faire economics.[51] Thomas Nangle was not so ready to agree that a laissez-faire approach was best; he wrote, later in 1922, to congratulate Coaker on his attempt to regulate the fishery, stating that the current method of marketing fish "is a national disgrace and therefore requires a national remedy."[52]

By late November 1921 members of the GWVA sent a delegation to meet with the minister of public works, W.B. Jennings, on behalf of "200 unemployed sailors and soldiers who are walking the streets of St. John's in search of employment." The GWVA "authorized" the men "to ascertain the number of men who are holding Government positions and who never served. It is only reasonable to expect that at least 25% of those employed in Government jobs should be discharged and their places occupied by eligible returned men." Jennings was appalled at this blatant coercion and responded by writing to the prime minister that "as far as I am concerned, while I remain in the Office, I shall never consent to such an outrage."[53] In December, Squires met with another delegation from the GWVA, who repeated the same demand and additionally called for the "dismissal of all persons now in the Civil Service who were appointed since October, 1914, and who were eligible for Overseas service." The delegation threatened to send a letter, a draft of which they gave to the prime minister, to the American Legion claiming that the Newfoundland government was keeping veterans in poverty. Squires responded by writing to J.G. Higgins, the president of the GWVA, that he was not going to give in to such threats or fire people from their jobs to hire members of the GWVA. The government's policy was to give preference to qualified veterans in the hiring for any vacant positions.[54]

Unemployed veterans were not the only people unhappy with the government; throughout the winter of 1921–1922, Squires faced increased demands for relief of the unemployed. The government responded with the usual form of poor relief, providing money for able-bodied relief on public works, especially road building. The government had also decided to provide more poor relief, usually in the form of small amounts of foodstuffs and other provisions, in exchange for pitprops or pulp wood cut by outport people. Poor relief payments were small and were provided to men on behalf of all their dependants. The government expected people to otherwise shift for themselves by scrounging whatever food or money they could from relatives or charities. The opposition newspapers were not happy that the government was borrowing money to assist the unemployed, but the *Evening Telegram*, at least, was becoming concerned about political agitation by the unemployed. In January 1922, delegates of a committee of the unemployed approached the St. John's government about relief work, only to learn that the city had no money. The prospect of 1600 unemployed men milling about the city had the *Telegram* warning about the prospects of "revolution and Bolshevism," and it uncharacteristically praised Squires for finding the resources to provide some relief. Meagre though the relief provisions may have been, the loans saddled the government with about two million dollars in extra debt in 1920–1921.[55]

The split between Squires and the GWVA remained, however, and the GWVA opposed the government's intention to have the Regiment's flag installed in the Legislative Council chamber when the legislature opened in the winter of 1921. The veterans' organization wanted its flags installed at Government House, the home of the governor. Squires objected to what he saw as the undemocratic tendency of the GWVA because it was in the legislature "that the Conscription Bill was passed, without which the Newfoundland Regiment would have been withdrawn. It was there that the funds were provided for the Regiment, and it is there that year after year funds will be provided for disabled sailors and soldiers." The prime minister was annoyed with the GWVA, but felt that "I should not be pressed as against the views of those who actually enlisted in the Royal Newfoundland Regiment and have a very strong personal sentimental interest in the flag."[56]

Although the *Telegram* tipped its hat to Squires's assistance to the unemployed, it hammered away at Coaker's role in the government, supporting A.B. Morine's proposal that the Union Party should be eliminated from politics because it privileged class interests over the public good. The *Evening Telegram* began to call the FPU president "Juggernaut Coaker" for his threat to bring the weight of the FPU to bear against anyone who opposed a new pulp-and-paper scheme for the west coast of Newfoundland.[57] Although disillusioned with the Liberal-Reform alliance because of the failure of his regulations, Coaker was determined to stick with Squires and see him through the general election that would have to be held in 1923, largely because he felt that the west-coast forestry development on the Humber River was the only means of economic salvation for Newfoundland in the wake of the failure of his fisheries regulations. By turning to another large-scale forestry industry project, the Squires government returned to the earlier

Liberal national policies based on interior development, policies that had originally saddled the colony with a huge railway debt. Desperate to attract foreign investment to the forest industry to justify that debt, the Squires government courted large international investors to the forestry industry with tax and royalty breaks, subsidies, and Newfoundland's cheap labour. Coaker lacked enthusiasm for this initiative, but he saw that it was necessary either to make the attempt or else be forced to accept the impending destitution of the rural population. Sadly, the limited enclave industrial development that followed would do little to alleviate Newfoundland's debt or provide significant alternative employment to the fisheries. A few international corporations were gaining control over much of the island's forest and mineral resources without providing much of a return to labour or government that would allow Newfoundland to shake off its economic problems.

The FPU leader was lukewarm in his support for Squires, who liked to travel and spent as much time as possible overseas in Britain, such as when he left for five months in 1920–1921 under cover of the need to discuss an ongoing boundary dispute with Canada over Labrador.[58] Deputy Prime Minister Alex Campbell was usually at the helm, doling out relief money in the districts of Liberal-Reform members of the Assembly to shore up support. When Squires was active—as in his negotiations to acquire timber rights from the Reids for potential industrial development on the Humber River—the prime minister's actions seemed dishonest. The Reids controlled most of the timber rights not controlled by the Anglo-Newfoundland Development Company. Throughout the war, the railway had been heavily used and had generated a profit, but the Reids had invested little in its maintenance. The Reid Newfoundland Company, moreover, owed about one million dollars to the Bank of Montreal, and members of the Reid family owed personal sums to the bank. The Reids wanted to either renegotiate their contract yet again, or develop the resources they had been given to build the railway in the first place. The problem was that the Reids did not have the capital to

develop projects such as pulp mills themselves, and the Squires government was not about to commit political suicide by giving them any more
assistance. The *Daily News* suggested that the Humber development
might be a means by which the government could further benefit the
Reid interests financially.[59]

As a general election appeared to draw near, Squires became more
devoted to a proposal by the Reids in partnership with the British
engineering firm of Armstrong Whitworth & Company for the development of a pulp mill at the mouth of the Humber River, as well as
a hydroelectric plant upstream at what was to become Deer Lake.
The government negotiated a financing arrangement with the British
Treasury in 1922, but the Reids continued to demand more money for
the railway's operation, and actually closed it that year knowing full
well that neither the British government nor Armstrong would be interested in an industrial development that depended on the railway and
other Reid assets. The Squires government had to purchase these rights
for the sum of $2 million. It certainly looked as if Squires had hypocriti-
cally participated in another speculative act of profiteering by the Reids,
although his government had bargained them down from their initial
asking price of $2.4 million. Throughout the year, as the government
worked to put a financial deal in place, the opposition papers hammered
away at Squires and Coaker, accusing them of being in the Reids' pockets
and driving Newfoundland towards financial ruin in their quest for the
Humber development.[60]

The watchword of the opposition papers was retrenchment. They
portrayed Squires and Coaker as spendthrifts who were willing to buy
votes with poor relief. The *Daily News* maintained that relief would
not have been necessary if Coaker had not destroyed the local economy
through his fisheries regulations. Now, with its resources dissipated,
the Newfoundland government had fewer means of post-war economic
reconstruction other than the timber project. The current government,
the paper argued, was incapable and must be gotten rid of.[61] The FPU

newspaper responded that Michael Cashin and his "Tory clique" opposed relief spending because they were the puppets of Water Street. The paper reminded its readers that businessmen such as Cashin and Crosbie had been profiteers during the war.[62] The *Daily News* responded by asking if the Squires government was serving the common people any better. The answer, it felt, was no, and Coaker was the chief reason because, like Squires, he spent so much time travelling outside Newfoundland.[63]

Disillusionment followed disappointment in Coaker's political outlook. In commenting on the Memorial Day ceremony to take place at the Sergeants' Memorial in Cathedral Square on 1 July, the *Advocate* stated that it was important to remember the men who fell at Beaumont Hamel, although "whether the War has justified itself is a debatable question" in light of the level to which public debate had fallen.[64] Earlier in the spring, the editor of the *Daily News* had, in commenting on an appeal by Thomas Nangle for funds for his war memorial efforts, written that "it is true that the world is disillusioned. The war to end war has not yet won its claim. The new Heaven and Earth are not visible. Pre-war problems remain unsolved and post-war problems are more insistent and more in number."[65] Such disappointments were not the fault of those who had fallen in war, but rather remained the challenge of the living. Commenting on Memorial Day, the *Daily News* argued that people had to learn the lesson of sacrifice revealed at Beaumont Hamel and embrace a new "spirit of citizenship and of service."[66]

From the perspective of the FPU, there was no question that Newfoundland needed such a spirit, but an even greater question was what exactly did this declaration mean? Did it mean that people would be more patriotic? If so, then what did that mean during a deepening recession when merchants were cutting credit to fishing people?[67] The *Daily News* conceded that "the feverish post-war years have left behind a trail of greed and gracelessness, in public, industrial and commercial life alike. The high ideals of the war years have disappeared in callous disregard and the sacrifice of honesty and duty to expediency and ease."[68]

Coaker, however, was, in the *Daily News*'s view, just as greedy as any merchant. The hypocrisy of partisan editorials emerged in the *Daily News* and the *Evening Telegram*, which condemned Coaker's supposed influence on government spending while at the same time demanding that the government provide more relief projects to aid the unemployed.

The *Advocate* found itself in the position of arguing against government relief as a strategy for dealing with unemployment. It preferred private-capital investment in projects such as the Humber development, and accused the opposition papers of being "unpatriotic" in their refusal to support the government's efforts to get the Humber project under way.[69] The *Evening Telegram* responded by stating that the Squires-Coaker alliance was an example of "despotism of the worst kind" for imposing higher taxes on Newfoundland while spending money badly. "Let the right men, those who are guided by patriotic instincts, and not by the desire for self-advancement come forward," the paper urged.[70] The *Daily News* agreed, repeating that Coaker had ruined the economy through the fisheries regulations, and that the government had depleted the treasury through "extravagance, waste and corruption." Retrenchment, it argued, was the only possible course for Newfoundland.[71]

The opposition in the House of Assembly had regrouped as the Liberal-Labour-Progressive Party under J.R. Bennett in the spring of 1923. Using Jesse Winsor as a figurehead, and acting on the legal advice of A.B. Morine, the opponents of Coaker had tried to found a competing organization, the United Fishermen's Movement (UFM), which adopted a platform of lower taxes, retrenchment, and a more open legislature. The *Evening Telegram* lauded the UFM, arguing that it would provide a "moral force" to clean up government in a way that other countries in the era had achieved through the armed overthrow of governments.[72] The *Daily News* shared the *Telegram*'s view, praising the UFM for deciding to back Bennett against "the common enemy today ... the Squires-Coaker combination."[73] In reaction to the new configuration of the opposition, the FPU newspaper pointed out that the old Tory crowd—including Cashin, Crosbie, Higgins, and Morine—were still behind Bennett. In the *Advocate*'s opinion, it was "absolutely ludicrous to think of such men in control of the country. While in power some years ago they exhibited no capacity whatever except to collect enormous revenue from the earnings of the people, and spend it on themselves. Cashin and Crosbie acknowledge that they made piles of money during the war."[74]

In preparation for the general election due in the spring, the *Evening Telegram* launched a full assault on Coaker under the headline "To Arms! Patriots," calling for electors to rise up against Coaker, their local "Bolshevik" and "the Hun." Bennett, the paper noted, was by contrast "the St. George ... fighting the Dragon exemplified in Coakerism, and that the efforts of he and his associates for Clean Government will be blessed is the sure wish of all true patriots."[75] To emphasize the point that opposition to Coaker and Squires was a patriotic duty, the *Daily News* stated that the government had betrayed veterans by providing them with meagre assistance and that some of the unemployed "today are obtaining their livelihood breaking stones" on government relief projects in St. John's. "Lest We Forget," stated the paper, Squires broke his promises to returned soldiers and sailors.[76] William Linegar came forward to run for Bennett in St. John's, and Cashin, who was running again, made a point of visiting the rock sheds in the West End, where able-bodied men requiring relief were employed.[77]

The FPU newspaper fought back by asking "How Can We Elect Tory Grafters?" It pointed out that A.B. Morine remained prominent in the Bennett party, and that Cashin and Crosbie "Grew Fat in War Times."[78] Coaker's supporters may have done much more; reports surfaced that they had prevented or disrupted speeches by Walter Monroe and Lewis Little, who were campaigning against the Union Party candidates in Bonavista District. The *Evening Telegram* singled out the reports as examples of Coaker's lack of respect for the "British liberty of free speech," and called for every good Christian to rise up against him.[79]

Coaker and Squires nevertheless prevailed, largely on the strength of their Humber development platform, although Squires's group lost St. John's West to Cashin, who had decided to run there with Charles E. Hunt. Cashin's son Peter (who had been transferred to the British Machine Gun Corps following his injury in France in 1916, and promoted to major in 1918) won his father's seat in Ferryland for the Liberal-Labour-Progressive Party.[80] The *Telegram* was appalled at the Coaker-Squires victory, complaining that the "new generation seems to be satisfied to have the charter of our liberties and our rights torn to shreds, as long as the Government that does so gives them the loaves and the fishes and divides a share of the spoils amongst them on the eve of an election."[81]

Squires's win did not prevent trouble from building. The Humber deal was complex, and involved the Reids. The new government passed legislation guaranteeing mortgages for Armstrong Whitworth & Company. As part of the deal, the Reids would get $1.5 million from the engineering company, and royalties and dividends on developed water power and newsprint once they transferred their timber lands to the new company. The government got an export tax of one dollar per ton on newsprint and a water-power royalty. The Armstrongs' licence to operate otherwise was the same as that of the AND Company. To facilitate the deal, the government agreed to buy and operate the railway, coastal steam service, gulf ferry, and dry dock. Coaker had won a seat in the District of Bonavista and received a knighthood on 1 June 1923 as part of the celebrations for the King's birthday, and in recognition of his patriotism for having supported conscription in 1918.[82] However, the honour was not enough to maintain Coaker's interest in participating in government; the FPU leader concentrated on running the Union Trading Company, becoming increasingly more autocratic and mercantile in character.[83]

Although Coaker and Squires had won the election, a month and a half later the newspapers suddenly announced that Squires had been forced to resign and that a member of his government, William Warren, was to form a new administration. The opposition papers called for an investigation, but the people were left with a mystery. By the summer of 1923, Newfoundland had indeed approached a political precipice. The promise of a better post-war world had already degenerated amidst an economic depression into a bitter fight about what practices should guide reconstruction. Conservatives argued that men had fought for traditional British liberty, and that patriotism demanded a return to the pre-war status quo. Coaker argued that the war had been a battle for a better world than had existed before, and that the war effort demonstrated that the state could use its power progressively to promote prosperity and equity, noting that he had tried to put his beliefs into practice through his fisheries regulations. Mercantile opposition frustrated the regulations, as did a deepening post-war recession, but the persistent bickering over who was a patriot and who was a traitor did not help matters. The political battle between Coaker and his opponents had degenerated into vicious mudslinging, with the opposition press label-ling the FPU leader as a Prussian and Bolshevik. Over time, living up to the ideals fought for in the war had come to mean defeating Coaker. In turn, Coaker had been reduced to arguing that it was the government's prerogative to curtail political rights, especially through press censor-ship, to achieve its lofty new goals, while Coaker's ally, Squires, had managed to alienate veterans. The result of the increasingly hysterical political mudslinging from 1920 through 1923 was not only the discred-iting of fisheries regulation and the more progressive use of government policy generally, but Coaker's profound disillusionment with democracy in Newfoundland. Without realizing it, everyone was chipping away at the edifice of liberal democracy, but matters were about to become much worse. Now Squires had resigned, and the revelations that would arise from his stepping down proved to be a hammer blow.

NINE

Political Demoralization, 1923–1924

In the late summer of 1923, the public learned that Squires had resigned because of allegations of political corruption, much of it involving possible improprieties on the part of his supporters, who were accused of using relief funds as patronage. The scandal grew in the fertile ground of deepening economic recession, which Coaker's opponents had already associated with his "Prussian" or "Bolshevik" fisheries regulations but which he blamed on mercantile opposition and "treasonous" criticism by the opposition press. The investigation and political turmoil that followed in 1924 accelerated the erosion of liberal democracy that had begun in the vitriolic debates over the fisheries regulations, which included Coaker's threat of press censorship. While Squires and his more intimate political cronies were culpable, Coaker's publicly expressed political anger and disillusionment made him an easy target for the opposition, led by Walter Monroe and supported by prominent veterans' leaders.

They argued that the relief system reflected morally bankrupt politics: true patriots would rather starve than take government assistance. While the inquiry into Squires's alleged misdeeds brought such views into the light, it was not the investigation that caused the widespread political disillusionment. The growing lack of faith in Newfoundland politics was the bitter harvest of the failure of post-war reconstruction, including the acrimonious debate about Coaker's fisheries regulations. The immediate fruit would be Newfoundland's flirtation with the more authoritarian political tendencies of Europe during the inter-war years—on almost every part of the political spectrum.

Richard Squires was in a precarious position despite having secured a major industrial development. He had originally become prime minister in 1919 as the candidate who would save Newfoundland from the graft associated with the old People's Party's close connections to big corporations such as the Reid Newfoundland Company. But Squires had found it difficult to cope with the public debt and poverty without also seeking the goodwill of these same corporations, and he was a past associate of the People's Party. The financial support and later buyout of the Reids' interests were not in fact corrupt, but many voters felt that Squires offered no better alternative to the People's Party remnant, now calling itself the Liberal-Labour-Progressive Party. The latter's disorganization lost the party the 1923 election, or so it seemed.

Squires's lieutenant, Alexander Campbell, lost his seat in the election. Unwilling to lose him in cabinet, Squires appointed Campbell to the Legislative Council. This action rallied the opposition, for they saw Campbell as the patronage mastermind behind Squires's victory. Cashin openly accused Campbell of buying votes with relief spending during the election, and a prominent St. John's lawyer, W.J. Higgins, digging deeper, found evidence suggesting that Squires might have been directly involved in political bribery and the embezzlement of government funds. Higgins represented J.T. Meaney, the long-time organizer for Squires who had run as an unsuccessful Liberal-Reform candidate in the 1919 election.

Meaney had been acting liquor controller (an office of the Department of Public Works, of which Campbell was minister) and had engaged in the practice of lending money to Squires personally in exchange for the prime minister's IOUs. Meaney thought that Squires would appoint him permanently as the controller, but opponents in cabinet prevented this. As the potential liquor scandal came to light, the disgruntled Meaney, who lost his job, began to suspect that Squires was going to set him up to take responsibility. He approached Attorney General William Warren with papers incriminating Squires, but Warren was not keen to act. Meaney then hired Higgins. With three other cabinet ministers, Warren approached Squires and demanded that the prime minister fire his political bagman, but Squires refused to sacrifice Campbell.

Higgins had also approached Coaker. The FPU leader was incensed to find out that Squires had probably accepted a forty-three-thousand-dollar campaign donation from Dominion Iron and Steel Company (in the process of being incorporated into the British Empire Steel Corporation from 1919 through 1921), which had owned the iron ore mine on Bell Island, on the understanding that the prime minister would reopen a 1919 contract Coaker had negotiated pertaining to royalties, working conditions, safety standards, and workers' housing at the company's mine. A number of Squires's supporters in the House were already unhappy that the government had taken over operation of the railway on 1 July 1923. The additional scandals concerning Meaney, Campbell, and Dominion Iron and Steel then began to break, and on 23 July, Warren and his followers, with Coaker's support, revolted against Squires and forced him to resign.

The governor asked Warren to form a new government. Although the new prime minister had hoped to build a non-partisan administration, he could not entice the opposition to join with Union Party members. This left him in the embarrassing position of having to appoint a commission of inquiry, announced on 28 July, into alleged wrongdoings by members of his own government. In order to make sure that such a commission was beyond government interference, the new prime minister turned to the British government to suggest a commissioner. The British suggested the Recorder of Derby, Thomas Hollis Walker, whom Warren duly commissioned on 22 December 1923. A well-respected barrister, Walker possessed penetrating cross-examiners' skills tempered by courtesy and wit. Working without condescension or pre-judgment, Walker earned local respect in Newfoundland for the conduct of his inquiry. The prime minister asked Walker to investigate five charges: that improper payments had been made to private individuals from the Liquor Control Department; that Dominion Iron and Steel paid money to Squires during government negotiations with the company; that misspending related to pitprop accounts and those of a model farm established on Topsail Road just outside St. John's occurred in the Department of Agriculture and Mines; that there was misspending of public relief in 1922–1923; and that there were problems in the Department of Public Works related to able-bodied relief.[1]

Although they had been critical of Coaker's supposedly dictatorial control over the Squires government, the opposition papers reacted to the scandal by arguing that good government required a strong leader. At first, the FPU newspaper rejected this view by arguing that Newfoundland required instead a "strong people" who would back the tough decisions that good leaders would have to make. Unfortunately, the paper contended, recent history demonstrated that Newfoundlanders stood ready to burn or crucify their "patriots."[2] In response, the *Evening Telegram* backed a call by the *Daily News* for a strong leader, proposing as a model Italy's Benito Mussolini. The Italian fascist leader had been consolidating his hold over government in Italy throughout 1924, and the *Daily News* thought that Newfoundland could use the same sort of leader: a man with the ability to simply remove anyone who opposed a program of government retrenchment.[3]

It is not surprising that interest in the Italian reaction against the emergence of post-war leftist radicalism and industrial strife had grown in Newfoundland. Newfoundlanders were aware of the surge in socialism, industrial unionism, and independent labour politics, particularly across the Cabot Strait. Many Newfoundlanders, such as Silby Barrett, worked in the Maritimes, especially in the coal and steel towns of Cape Breton. Having gone to work in the Cape Breton mines in 1908, by 1916 Barrett had become president of the United Mine Workers of Nova Scotia and, in 1919, became an international board member of the United Mine Workers of America, which organized Cape Breton miners in its District 26. Although socialists were active in Newfoundland, the Newfoundland Industrial Workers' Association (NIWA) and the Longshoremen's Protective Union maintained more moderate political stances. Nevertheless, concern grew in the St. John's newspapers about the various working-class organizations and leftist political movements that were involved in general and sympathetic strikes, not only in Canada, but in the United States, Britain, and continental Europe. The potential for working-class radicalism and labour unrest in the 1920s scared people in St. John's. Anything that smacked of working-class independence in Newfoundland was likely to draw a charge of Bolshevism. In St. John's, Julia Salter Earle, the organizer for the Ladies' Branch of the NIWA, wrote, as "The Working-Man's Friend," that there was little to worry about. She felt that local workers were interested in a Christian progressivism; they only wished to be consulted more on public affairs, not to acquire political power.[4] However, as Coaker knew by bitter experience, many in Newfoundland were not interested in distinguishing between Bolsheviks and labour moderates. The Red Scare was on, and the heroes of the day had become Mussolini and his Black Shirts.

The *Evening Telegram* had openly declared its admiration of Mussolini for his coming to power by beating up on unions and socialists in the northern industrial cities of Italy. While the newspaper admitted that the violence used by the Black Shirts seemed distasteful, it maintained that the labour movement and the political left had asked for it by interfering with industry through strikes. Mussolini's cool attitude towards Britain, the *Telegram* argued, should not allow people to overlook the fact that many Fascists were young men who came from the very best families in Italy and enjoyed the support of the Italian business community for busting strikers' heads.[5] In the days following the general election of 1923, no less a personage than Lieutenant Colonel Thomas Nangle of the GWVA gave a glowing address in St. John's on the Italian Fascists, openly admiring their use of symbols and rituals to foster national solidarity, and their use of Black Shirt Regiments to engage in "combat with the Reds." The *Daily News* noted that Nangle was "evidently a warm admirer of the autocratic energetic Mussolini, and of his methods."[6] Admired in his day as a minister to the needs of the Regiment's men and as a public advocate for veterans, and later appreciated for his role in the commemoration of the Newfoundlanders who had fallen in the Great War, Nangle's more disturbing political views have received less attention. The soldier priest was no devotee of liberal democracy. In Nangle's view, people had the right to assent only to his vision of post-war order; it was perfectly legitimate to subject dissenters to ideological retraining backed up by a little fascist skull-cracking when necessary.

Nangle was not alone in this political hypocrisy and naiveté. The FPU was, at first, reluctant to embrace the idea that someone like Mussolini was a model of civic virtue for local politicians. The *Advocate* was nervous about the Fascist leader because of his international policies. In particular, Mussolini had been playing "the strong man" with Greece in Italy's bombardment and occupation of the island of Corfu in 1923, an incident ostensibly arising from the murder of Italian participants in a commission investigating a border dispute between Greece and Albania, but that most likely resulted from Italy's desire to control the strategic island. Mussolini's disregard for the League of Nations over the incident suggested that he had become a major threat to international peace.[7]

However, like Nangle, Coaker sympathized with Mussolini. The FPU leader had come to admire Mussolini's domestic policies, gullibly accepting whatever he was told or shown about Fascist Italy during his visit to Mediterranean and Iberian fish markets during the late fall and winter of 1923–1924. Flattered to receive the attention of an official, Coaker recounted his visit with the prefect of the Italian port of Civita Vecchia, who was "a close friend of Mussolini, the Italian Dictator." He observed, "The new master of Italy is generally popular and his rule has completely changed conditions in Italy. Laws are being enforced and order is completely restored everywhere." Noting that the Fascist leader had established a militia of about two hundred thousand troops to back up his rule, Coaker admired the fact that Italians "appear to realize that it is their duty to work with him and support his policies. There are no communists now to be heard. All pay their taxes without grumbling...."[8]

It is not surprising that there was open admiration for Fascism in St. John's at the time. Throughout Europe and the Americas, many people thought that dictatorship or some sort of non-democratic regulation by appointed experts was a reasonable response to the mounting social and economic crises of the post-war world. In Europe, political culture increasingly became dominated by the view that the Great War and the troubled peace that followed had "broken" the common understandings about what was legitimate in politics and culture. People did not lose faith in their ability to fix what had been shattered, but rather considered that liberal democracy or leftist alternatives were not the solution. Many looked to the rise of Mussolini as a way to put right the world without revolution, including many in Britain who were willing to turn a blind eye to the Fascist leader's politics of brutality. In Canada, in the context of deepening recession in the 1920s, hostility to leftist radicalism (especially communism) and immigrants (especially those from Eastern and Central Europe) fostered a variety of fascistic and anti-Semitic organizations such as the Ku Klux Klan and Quebec journalist Adrien Arcand's Parti national social chrétien during the 1930s. Newfoundland was no different.[9]

It might seem ironic that veterans such as Nangle, who had otherwise worn the cloak of crusaders for democracy in the Great War, would now flirt with dictatorship. The appeal of dictatorship in the 1920s, however, was that it promised to break the hold of self-interested classes on government, clear away their dishonesty, and ensure that the state acted for the good of the whole. Such an appeal implied that there was a national interest that was more important than any special one; indeed, such an interest was a key element in the exhortations to unity and patriotism that had been vital to marshalling public support for the war effort. Veterans were vulnerable to the appeal because the experience of the trenches had isolated them from their fellow citizens who had not served. The constant strain of a form of battle that combined boredom and terror had produced a solidarity among soldiers in the trenches that remained with veterans after the war, making it hard for them to empathize with the particular needs of other groups. Throughout the war, public officials, military leaders, and the press in all participating countries had assured soldiers that they were valued for the manner in which they were fighting for the noble cause of their nation. Now they found that their governments seemed less noble, and that no one valued their sacrifices enough to ensure that veterans would be cared for properly in the peace.

In Britain, veterans had found the state unprepared to deal with the needs of the demobilized and the injured, and the result was profound political demoralization and a search for alternatives. Even before the war had ended, returned British soldiers had been exposed to the strident claims, often made by Lord Rothermere in his family's London *Daily Mail*, that the war was dragging on because of decadence and disloyalty within the ranks of the nation's government. Rothermere became a leading apologist for Mussolini, suggesting that his high ideals of nationalism and patriotism outweighed their sometimes messy international consequences and often violent elimination of domestic dissent. While better state pensions and employment programs quieted many, in the 1920s some veterans became an important constituency for fascist organizations, although, over the longer term, most would not embrace fascist politics in Britain. The appeal of dictatorship was strongest in countries where government had been most weakened by the war, especially if there was no deep-rooted tradition of liberal democracy.[10]

The sad fact was that, in Newfoundland, there was concern about Mussolini's international policies only insofar as they might embroil the world in war again. Figures such as Nangle and Coaker, and institutions such as the major newspapers, could not claim that they did not know about the brutality and authoritarianism of the Fascist regime, and they did not simply overlook it—they openly admired the political thuggery as long as it was aimed at people who were even moderately on the left. On the one hand, the *Daily News* agreed with the *Advocate* on Mussolini's international policies. It feared that Mussolini's continued aggressive posturing towards Greece could touch off another war in Europe, as had the tensions between Serbia and Austria in 1914.[11] On the other hand, however, the paper made it clear that it liked leaders who took strong measures on the domestic front and that, in particular, it appreciated the Fascists' suppression of the left in Italy: "Mussolini with his Black Shirts, and his castor oil saved Italy from Communism, and to that extent deserves national and international gratitude."[12]

The *Evening Telegram*, now edited by C.E.A. Jeffrey, the former teacher from western Newfoundland who had chosen to serve with the Canadian Expeditionary Force during the war, was not to be dissuaded from its admiration for Mussolini. "Italy has had a new birth as a result of the war," the newspaper argued, "and directed by the vigorous, determined if somewhat reckless dynamo of energy, Mussolini ... has become fired with the desire to ... restore prosperity among her people."[13] Through strong-arm tactics, Mussolini would end the corruption and Bolshevism that supposedly mired Italy in an economic mess. The *Telegram*'s editor lauded Mussolini's reform of the Italian civil service, his retrenchment, and his supposed preference for appointing experts rather than cronies to manage government departments. Particularly appealing was the manner in which Mussolini had "applied himself to the educational problem, re-introduced religious teaching, [and] insisted upon the inculcation of patriotism." In all this, Mussolini was such a fine "benevolent tyrant" that it should be obvious that only "Government parasites" opposed him.[14]

The need to put the government's financial house in order, to end graft and corruption, to inculcate "patriotism" so that people would be more self-reliant, and to use merit rather than cronyism in civil service appointments—these justified fascist dictatorship in the view of the *Evening Telegram*, but they were also the conditions that supposedly lay behind Newfoundland's greatest political scandal. Hollis Walker began an immediate and thorough investigation of the liquor control board, but held off on probing the issue of more general corruption, which might have tainted many politicians on both sides of the House. The opposition did not push Warren very hard to broaden the scope of the inquiry, probably because Michael Cashin had, in 1919, imported forty cases of whiskey and three octaves of rum without paying duties. The ex-leader of the opposition had also been selling liquor to the Department of Liquor Control at inflated prices with Meaney's help in 1922 and 1923. According to its editor, however, the *Evening Telegram* did not pursue its interest in fascism more vigorously because it had faith that Hollis Walker represented the very best of the British liberal tradition.[15]

Hollis Walker began his hearings on 7 January 1924, and the proceedings were published regularly in the local newspapers, although the papers that had formerly identified Coaker as the main problem of the Squires government did not find much ammunition for attacks on him or the Union Party. Instead, they declared, Hollis Walker was finding that government became corrupt because it succumbed to the temptation to rule in the interest of classes or other narrow sectional interests. "The day has passed when any class or section can control," the *Daily News* argued. "Democracy implies government by the people, and by the people is meant not merchants, not professional politicians, not intellectuals, so-called, not fishermen, not lumberers, or farmers or labourers, not by any of these exclusively, but through the wisdom, experience and aspirations of all."[16] But despite its advocacy of government in the interest of all, the *Daily News* called for a government with more business-minded goals. The *Advocate* took this view as a jab at Coaker.[17]

The papers harped on about the need for retrenchment as the workings of the Hollis Walker inquiry unfolded. The moderate view came from the *Daily News*, which supported the view of the Board of Trade that Newfoundland's finances should be subject to cuts by a committee of businessmen.[18] The more extreme view came from the *Evening Telegram*, which continued to promote the Italian Fascist method of cutting public employment, taxing more, and stifling opposition. "The arbitrary system of Government operating in Italy may not meet with the approval of those countries which have struggled to secure the privileges of democracy," the paper argued, "but the success which appears to have resulted from Mussolini's methods cannot but win the respect of those who have watched developments."[19]

While the *Evening Telegram* would not go so far as to say that Newfoundland needed a Mussolini, it advocated strong leadership that would be able to define a public or national interest and pursue it ruthlessly without bowing to popular demands. The paper singled out poor relief to make its case, arguing that, based on the findings of the Hollis Walker inquiry, there were too many people working in the rock sheds of St. John's, where stone was prepared for use in local road construction and other public works by men on able-bodied relief—at least some of whom were using relief income to supplement earnings from the fishery. The paper also argued that the government used the civil service for patronage purposes, preferring to hire two unqualified people at higher total salaries than to allow one competent person to do the work for less money. The *Daily News* agreed that patronage had become a political disease in Newfoundland.[20]

Amidst the concern about the relationship between government spending and the supposed weakness in the moral fibre of

Barbed wire, Beaumont Hamel, 1916. Members of the Newfoundland Regiment participated in the attack on German lines at the Somme in the vicinity of Beaumont Hamel on 1 July 1916. A combination of heavily fortified German positions (including the use of barbed wire shown above), over-confidence about the effect of British artillery bombardments, and a number of other command errors resulted in tragedy: over 88 per cent of the 801 men who went into battle died or were wounded. The news of the near-annihilation of the Regiment had a profound impact on political discourse at home. Over the long term, competing views emerged about how best to remember the fallen as either martyrs to laissez-faire and liberal democracy or as heralds of a newer, more progressive state. William Coaker was a proponent of the progressive view.

Coaker Recruits. (From left to right) Top row: 3618 J. Bradbury, 3660 T. Stone, 3608 J. Mate. Bottom row: 3662 E. Quinton, 3544 N. Samson, 3372 W.J.S. Stratton, 3626 F. Spencer, 3631 R. Dawe. Anxious to avoid criticism that he was unsupportive of the Newfoundland war effort because of his criticism of the Morris government's wartime policies, William Coaker called for members of the FPU to volunteer for service on his behalf late in 1916. About 130 men came forward over the course of the war, of which 68 were fit for military service. The above recruits served with the Newfoundland Regiment.

Coaker Recruits. (From right to left) Top row: A.J. Windsor, K. Crews,
W. Fowlow, J. Pelley, E.J. Thornhill, J. Bungay. Middle row: W.P. Vincent,
A. Crews, Henry Tulk, J. Thornhill, G. Hillier. Bottom row: H.V. Hunter, F. White.
Many of the Coaker Recruits served with the Royal Naval Reserve. Coaker had
initially opposed the founding of the Newfoundland Regiment because he doubted
that the Newfoundland government would be able to afford its cost, including the
ongoing financial burden of pensions for wounded soldiers, their dependents, and
the dependents of soldiers who died in service. The British government bore most
of the costs of the Naval Reserve and, Coaker thought, maritime service was more
suited to outport men who worked in the fishery and seal hunt.

Thomas Nangle with Richard Squires and Helena Squires, France, 1922. Nangle (on the far left above) was the Roman Catholic chaplain for the Newfoundland Regiment for much of the war. Very popular among the men of the Regiment, Nangle was a key figure in the Great War Veterans' Association (GWVA) and worked with the Imperial War Graves Commission. Richard Squires (on the far right above), became prime minister in 1919 based on an uneasy alliance with William Coaker. Although supportive of Nangle's efforts to have fallen soldiers and veterans remembered properly, Squires had a difficult relationship with the GWVA. In 1923, Squires fell from power amidst charges of political corruption.

William Coaker (far right) with C. Mursell and Aaron Bailey at the Forum, Rome, January 1924. Coaker had allied with Squires so that he might implement progressive reforms as Minister of Marine and Fisheries, especially the regulation of the fishing industry. Coaker's regulations coincided with deepening post-war recession and he faced stiff opposition from mercantile firms and banks. Facing accusations of Prussianism and Bolshevism for his efforts, Coaker became more authoritarian and disillusioned with local politics. Following the failure of his regulations in 1921, Coaker spent more time abroad, visiting important fish markets such as Italy's, where he became enamoured of Fascism.

Unveiling the National War Memorial, St. John's, 1 July 1924. Richard Squires's fall from power in 1923 coincided with local efforts to fund and construct a national war memorial. Squires's opponents, led by Walter Monroe, alleged that Squires and Coaker betrayed the British liberal principles that Newfoundland men had sacrificed their lives for between 1915 and 1918. Monroe's Liberal-Conservatives won the 1924 general election by promising to clean up corruption in government and to make local politics conform to the noble ideals embedded in memorialization of those who had fallen in war.

Field Marshall Haig's Visit: Inspection of the Troops, Headquarters of the Great War Veterans' Association, 1924. Haig participated in the unveiling of the National War Memorial. The GWVA was prominent in Newfoundland politics at the time. Some of its members, most notably Nangle, flirted with Fascism. More common, however, was support for Walter Monroe and a rejection of the policies associated with William Coaker. As Newfoundland's public finances worsened through the late 1920s, the GWVA opposed spending on poor relief, although it continued to demand more spending on pensions for veterans and the dependents of soldiers and seamen who fell during the war.

**Crowd Gathering at Colonial Building to Listen to Speakers Prior to Riot,
5 April 1932.** Monroe's government proved no better than the previous Squires
government. In 1928, Monroe resigned and a Squires-Coaker coalition won the
next general election, although, by now, Coaker had little faith in democracy in
Newfoundland. Squires had become prime minister in a local political environment
demoralized by constant allegations of corruption and the betrayal of ideals
associated with those who had fought for Britain in the war. This demoralization,
economic depression, worsening public finances, and growing poverty meant that
further allegations of public misdeeds by Squires in 1932 led to rioting, his final
fall from power and, ultimately, the established of government by an appointed
commission.

Newfoundlanders, there appeared the unlikely model of manly independence: the sealer. The supposed romanticism and the rugged individualism of the seal hunt were themes that had been emphasized by Alex A. Parsons the year before in the pages of the GWVA's magazine. "The perils and hardships to be encountered, the skill and courage required in battling with the 'drift-ice,' and the possible rich prizes to be won," all for the well-being of families at home, were the basis of this romanticism. In this, sealers were like soldiers "going out to do battle for those who remain at home. In this case the enemies to be encountered are the hurricanes, the icebergs and the blinding snow storms." The dangers were worth it if the sealers had a good hunt; they returned home to "thundering cheers, like returning conquerors," and were "the heroes of the hour."[21]

On 7 March, commenting on the departure of the fleet for the spring hunt, the *Evening Telegram* depicted sealers as the descendants of the hardy "Elizabethan sailors" who had discovered Newfoundland for England. Sealers lacked "none of the qualities which their forefathers possessed. Theirs, too, is the love of adventure, theirs is the disregard of danger. Let perils crowd in upon them, they rise supreme to the emergency, and laugh with glee and forget risks as soon as they are past."[22] Sealers were now to be thought of as rugged individual adventurers who revelled in danger and required none of the state protection that Coaker had demanded in the wake of the disasters of 1914. This view was brought into sharp focus within days, with the news that three men belonging to the SS *Terra Nova* had drowned en route to the hunt. The *Daily News* reacted by stating that the 1914 tragedies, like that of the *Greenland* before them, proved that danger was a constant companion in the seal hunt. The *Advocate* reacted similarly, commenting on the heroic bravery of the sealers, but making no demand of government on their behalf.[23]

The independence of the idealized sealer stood in sharp contrast to the newspapers' depiction of a politically enfeebled and corrupted population whose demands for public relief were pushing Newfoundland towards financial ruin. Throughout the "white" British dominions, particularly in Australia, New Zealand, and Canada, nationalism and patriotism from the late nineteenth century had been bound up in the notion that the dominions' peoples were "New Britons," peoples made superior to those of "Old Britain" by their comparatively new environments. The vigour of New Britons had been revealed in the heroic sacrifices of their young men during the Great War and proved the growing importance of the dominions to a Greater Britain.[24] Such sentiments had been part of the rhetoric in St. John's newspapers during and immediately following the war, but the persistent relief crisis, public scandals, and debt problems of Newfoundland exposed their insubstantial nature. Commenting on the high interest Newfoundland was being charged for a recent loan of three million dollars from Canada and the relatively low rate of interest the dominion could earn from its own bond issues, the *Daily News* suggested that the "orgy of waste" discovered by Hollis Walker revealed the demoralized leadership and society of fallen Britons that might only be restored by a purge of government and the emergence of a strong leader.[25]

Relief financed by borrowing especially troubled the opposition papers. The *Daily News* took the view that the Hollis Walker inquiry had revealed that borrowing for public works—such as at a new suburban road development in St. John's West End—was of doubtful benefit. All relief work was prone to corruption, particularly in the form of patronage by government members.[26] The *Advocate* responded that although the inquiry suggested that there were a lot of management problems in the relief system, there was little evidence of corruption, and none that could be associated with Coaker.[27]

The FPU leader appeared worried that his good name might be sullied by the findings of the inquiry, but Hollis Walker's report, submitted on 21 March 1924, appeared to absolve Coaker of wrongdoing, as did early newspaper reaction. The *Daily News* printed the full report under the headline "Exhaustive Findings on all Counts, Sir Richard Squires Found Guilty of Wrong-doing, Dr. Campbell Raked on Pitprop and Model Farm Accounts, Relief and Charities Gross Waste of Public Money and Used to Corrupt Electorate, Conduct of Departments Strongly Condemned." The report revealed that Meaney had inappropriately taken one hundred thousand dollars from the liquor department, of which twenty thousand probably went to Squires. Further, the Hollis Walker report found that Squires had taken the money from the mining company on Bell Island while the company was renegotiating the taxes it paid to the government and the benefits it provided to Bell Island miners and their families. Moreover, Campbell had misused monies from the departments of Public Works and Agriculture and Mines to secure votes by awarding able-bodied relief contracts.[28]

The findings were "a damning indictment not only of the persons involved but of the political system under which they were able to flourish,"[29] but subsequent analyses suggest this was an overreaction to Hollis Walker's report. Most of the findings, while revealing numerous instances of petty mismanagement, more importantly exposed a government totally unprepared for the scale of the public relief crisis it had to deal with beginning in the fall of 1921. It had been caught on the horns of a dilemma, facing rapidly escalating demands for public relief at the same time as it found itself without the means to expand its capacity to manage a relief system. Mounting public debt and an overburdened civil service appeared to show that the particular problems of Squires and Campbell were the rule rather than the exception in Newfoundland.[30]

Corruption and poor administrative practices were not, however, the nub of the problems plaguing Newfoundland, according to the Hollis Walker report; it pointed out that terrible unemployment and actual hunger, caused by the post-war economic depression, had forced the government to create able-bodied relief through pitprop contracts as well as employment on the model farm and in the rock sheds. Campbell had certainly dispensed these contracts and given out employment to ensure support for the government, and these practices had intensified as the election had approached, but none of this would have happened, the report argued, were it not for the "deplorable spirit shown by the people themselves." If the people had not demanded relief, then it could not have been abused—although Hollis Walker also established that the initial demands for relief had been voiced by a non-partisan Citizens Committee of Fifteen in December 1921, and had received the support of the GWVA. Further, the report asserted, if the people had conducted themselves honourably, demonstrating a sincere desire to pay back to government the relief they received, then they would have set a good example for government and lessened its financial burden. So, while Hollis Walker blamed Campbell for not running the relief-related matters of his department in a businesslike fashion, he also stated that the department's "record is in the main a record of bad bargains, rendered disastrous by the conditions of the times and the temper of the people, and of public money poured out in alarming profusion without care and without safeguards." If the people had "shown a little patriotism," then politicians would not have been able to get away with their suspect practices.[31]

As far as Hollis Walker was concerned, the GWVA had helped to pressure the Squires government into providing the relief spending that had proven to be so problematic. The GWVA's 1921 annual report observed that the government had responded positively to its request for assistance in finding employment or relief for unemployed veterans in St. John's. The GWVA also took "an active interest" in the government's use of pitprop contracts as a form of able-bodied relief in the outports, "and a large number of ex-service men were placed in jobs both from the City and the Outports."[32] To be fair, the veterans' organization had supported Governor Harris's efforts to respond to the growing relief problem by coordinating private charities and providing employment through churches, unions, the Board of Trade, and other organizations.[33] In the 1923 general election, the GWVA had pressured for more financial assistance, and made it clear to all the candidates that pensions paid to veterans or dependants must not be affected by retrenchment.[34]

Despite Hollis Walker's findings, the GWVA was exempt from criticism in the opposition papers' reaction to the release of his report. The *Evening Telegram* wrote only that the people should feel shame at the problems caused by Squires, Campbell, and their followers, who were "parasites" that had to be removed.[35] A.B. Morine, in an address to the Methodist College Literary Institute in St. John's on the night of 21 March, argued that pauperism was the problem that generated the crisis, but providing poor relief aggravated it. "We are moving towards socialism; towards the abyss over which we may plunge as Russia did," warned Morine, noting that the main culprits were Coaker and the FPU. Coaker's "Red microbe" had to be opposed by decent people and the churches, and the government must treat any advocacy of extra spending on poor relief as "treason." The carping about Bolshevism was Morine's way of appealing to people to never again prop up governments that depended on Union Party support. Morine attempted to undermine popular support for Coaker, not by offering concrete policy alternatives, but by making platitudinous calls to a higher duty, a legacy of the Great War. He stressed that it would be a more fitting "monument to their dead who lie in Flanders Fields than can ever be built of marble" if the people were to turn out Coaker.[36]

In printing Morine's address, the newspapers continued their attacks on Coaker as if he was the main culprit identified by Hollis Walker. The *Advocate* in turn defended Coaker by stating that Morine and the opposition offered no better policy alternative to the relief provided by the government. The *Evening Telegram* picked up on Morine's appeal for a revival of the national solidarity and patriotism expressed during the war, to suggest that veterans should again become men of action, but now in a fight against the corruption of the Squires government. The paper urged those who had served in the Royal Newfoundland Regiment to come forward and instruct their fellow Newfoundlanders on how to defend themselves from the likes of Squires, Campbell, and Coaker, implying but never openly stating that the people should be prepared to beat back the Union Party by force if necessary.[37] The editor of the *Daily News* agreed that political corruption was a "disease" in Newfoundland that required "drastic treatment." While the editor would not suggest a specific course of treatment, a correspondent, "R.J.A.," did so, arguing that the time had come for the people to embrace the purification of the state—to free it from socialism and any other form of "atheistical or revolutionary" thinking. The best model at hand? "In Italy the Fascism of Mussolini has killed out the old Socialist party, and the result is a happy re-union of Church and State, the benefits of which are becoming more evident every day."[38]

It is not surprising that the politicians and newspapers that opposed Squires and Coaker reacted to the Hollis Walker report by reverting to the old issue of wartime sacrifice and the nobility of the Regiment, and continuing their flirtation with fascism. While openly admiring Mussolini, Thomas Nangle, as a member of the GWVA, was busy trying to establish at Beaumont Hamel a war memorial to the Newfoundlanders who died overseas, and to raise funds for another memorial in St. John's—projects he had been working on since 1922. The local newspapers regularly printed appeals from him for assistance or accounts of his activities, and these projects kept in the public eye the GWVA's goal of ensuring that veterans would have a place of honour in post-war society by encouraging people to draw inspiration from the soldiers' noble qualities so that the "spirit of selflessness, patriotism, and devotion would endure beyond the battlefields of Europe." Nangle developed a clever funding appeal that allowed people to buy unlimited shares in the St. John's memorial at one dollar per share, and provided certificates to purchasers in return. The appeal was popular, eventually raising twenty thousand dollars for the monument and giving Newfoundlanders a tremendous sense of personal attachment to the monument and, by extension, the fallen heroes of the Regiment. People in St. John's may well have remembered that, in an earlier time of crisis associated with the collapse of the National Government in 1919, the Memorial Day speeches and related newspaper editorials fostered a sense of stability by encouraging people to take "civic pride" in remembering the deeds of the Regiment.[39]

Although the opposition papers had limited success in associating Coaker with the use of relief for patronage purposes, he was nevertheless a prominent minister in the Squires government, which was receiving additional criticism for penalizing veterans through the administration of patronage. Solomon Gosse, for example, a returned soldier from Spaniard's Bay—a community in Conception Bay, not far from St. John's—wrote in a public letter on 7 April that he had lost his job as a lighthouse keeper in 1923. He had got the job in 1919 by campaigning for the Squires candidates in his district, but in the last election he had decided to campaign for Bennett's men and therefore lost his job. Gosse reminded the public that he had fought with the Regiment in almost all of its great battles, and had been wounded four times. Having read the Hollis Walker report, Gosse declared that government corruption was an offence to the memory of his fallen comrades. It was time, felt Gosse, for veterans to stand together as they "did in the fields of Flanders" to fight corruption in government and to force it to provide work for the wounded who had returned from the war.[40] The editor of the *Daily News* wrote that the Gosse affair was disgraceful, asking if "public life in Newfoundland" had "fallen to such a level that a man must be penalized for refusing to trifle with his conscience or barter his convictions for place or profit."[41]

The GWVA became more openly political in response to the Hollis Walker report. On the night of 15 April, the organization held a meeting at which Nangle (who was president that year) addressed the membership, reminding them that "we enlisted for Justice, Right and Freedom." The Hollis Walker report, he argued, demonstrated the need for veterans to improve the political morality of Newfoundland: the report had "shown us that in cases of national emergency the people of Newfoundland fall back on its ex-service men. The Walker report has only taken the lid off the pot; we want all the beans spilled and spread to public view. We want to have the whole of our Civil Service cleaned up." Nangle demanded that civil service jobs should be filled by disabled veterans who passed competency exams, rather than by the "political heelers" who were being gifted the jobs.[42] Great applause met his speech. Although he reiterated that the GWVA should not form a political party, Nangle promised that his organization would help clean up politics, calling for "volunteers to fight an insidious enemy which is lurking in many recesses in our land, poisoning its fountains and undermining its foundations."[43]

The GWVA was about to get a chance to act. In an effort to distance themselves from the misdeeds uncovered by Hollis Walker, Coaker and his Union Party members began to demand that the government press charges against Squires, Campbell, and Meaney. On 8 April, Warren announced that he would widen the investigation to include other government departments, and on 9 April, he agreed that legal action would be taken against the three. To save his own neck, Squires, who had been arrested but was out on bail, scurried to the opposition benches on 23 April with one of his Liberal Reformers, Richard Cramm, and a Union Party member, George Jones. The next day, they were joined by two more Liberal Reformers, E. Simmons and A.M. Calpin. Warren had lost the former members of government who feared a broader investigation. Cramm and Calpin successfully carried a motion of non-confidence in Warren's government, and this led to its fall. In contemplating the coming election, the *Evening Telegram* proclaimed that there was only one real issue, a moral one: "The Cleaning of Public Life in the Colony and the rebuilding of the Political fabric on the firm foundation of Honesty, Integrity and Fidelity."[44]

Warren, who had little use for Coaker, hoped to build a new coalition with the opposition to rid himself of dependence on the FPU. While the prime minister considered his options, the *Daily News*, quoting

Oliver Wendell Holmes, recommended that he look for "Tall men, sun-crowned men, who live above the fog. In public duty and in private thinking."[45] Good government required new public men who had the ability, drive, honesty, and competence to put Newfoundland's affairs on a sound footing. The Hollis Walker report demanded that such men come forward because public life had been soiled at the hands of the previous government.[46]

Warren approached leading members of the opposition, most notably Higgins, seeking support for replacing those who had been lost to Squires. The opposition, under its new leader, Walter Monroe, would have nothing to do with Coaker, and on 3 May Warren abandoned the Union Party and replaced it with Higgins and Monroe as part of his government until the general election that was to be held on 2 June. Warren's new government then lost further Liberal support, which rallied behind A.E. Hickman. Within four days, Warren's government had fallen. Hickman then formed another government, leading what he called the Liberal-Progressive Party, with Coaker's support, after the FPU president declined the opportunity to become prime minister. The *Evening Telegram*, learning that Coaker supported Hickman (whom he had previously excoriated for supporting Cashin), suggested that such unholy alliances were proof of the need for a thorough clean-up of political life in the dominion.[47] The editor attacked Coaker for trying to build a coalition to oppose Warren, calling down upon the FPU leader all the old insults: he was a "self-constituted, self-opinion-ated overlord, who preaches democracy and practices tyranny with all the methods of the Bolshevik despots." The *Telegram* asked fishers to consider how many of their fellows lived in poverty while Coaker lived in the comforts "of his castle at Port Union." It was also odd, the paper argued, that "so many petty chieftains of the Union have managed to obtain comfortable political offices, to live in luxury, to ride in expensive motor cars and to move in society while they, their comrades, have to be content with a meagre pittance."[48] Coaker's residence at

Port Union was impressive. Although called "the Bungalow," the house was an asymmetrical two-storey building in the Queen Anne style, complete with a corner tower. The house sat uphill from the plainer and smaller wood-framed duplexes, which nonetheless had electricity and plumbing, otherwise almost unheard-of conveniences for workers in Newfoundland at that time.[49]

Hickman faced Walter Monroe in the general election of 1924. The *Daily News*'s editorial position supported that of the *Telegram* on the issue of Coaker, and blamed every economic misfortune that had befallen Newfoundland since 1919 on "Coaker ideas." Indirectly boosting Monroe, the paper declared that the people required Monroe's business-man's approach.[50] Walter Monroe had the advantage of having almost no previous experience in government, thus bearing no taint of such scandals as Hollis Walker had investigated. Born in Ireland, Monroe was the nephew of Moses Monroe, and had come to St. John's to join his uncle's business interests, which included the Colonial Cordage Company, the St. John's Electric Light Company, and the Newfoundland Boot and Shoe Company. Following his uncle's death, he established a business partnership with Robert Bishop and became president of the Imperial Tobacco Company and a director of the Colonial Cordage Company—two St. John's manufacturing establishments that had benefited substantially by tariff protection. He had little sympathy for the anti-protectionist and anti-St. John's rhetoric of the FPU, as neither sentiment would sit well with the city's working class. A leading member of the Church of England in the city, Monroe had become prominent in local philanthropic work.

The main public attraction of Monroe as leader of what he called the Liberal-Conservatives in 1924—despite, or perhaps because of, his failed contest against Coaker in the 1923 general election—was the "widespread belief in his honesty and integrity and the feeling that it was desirable that somebody other than what might be termed a professional politician, should be put in charge of affairs in view of the conditions that have prevailed here in recent years."[51] Monroe was "tall and sun-crowned," the perfect hero in the fight against the "Coakerites" and the "Squirites." According to the *Daily News*, "Mr. Walter Monroe has destroyed the auction block, and refused to traffic in corruption." Monroe would have no truck with Coaker, being uninterested in using government policies to bid for Union Party support. Instead, Monroe campaigned with a simple slogan: "Clean Up; Keep Clean; And a Square Deal to All." Monroe promised to support mining development and government bounties for the fishery, but otherwise he meant to clean up government, get rid of prohibition, and reduce government expenditures.[52]

Monroe was the candidate of the St. John's business community and Archbishop Roche, but he quickly garnered the support of the city's working people too. William Linegar ran for Monroe in St. John's, declaring for the "working man" against Coakerism, unemployment, corruption, and waste. On the evening of 16 May, he sat with city candidates for Monroe's party at a public meeting in St. John's, at which Michael Cashin's son-in-law, St. John's lawyer C.J. Fox, stated that although the FPU had started as an honest organization of the fishers of Newfoundland, Coaker had "prostituted" it in politics. W.J. Browne, a student and Rhodes Scholar during the war, was running for Monroe in St. John's West, having shifted from his previous position of supporting Squires. Calling on all young men to support Monroe, Browne claimed that the election was their call to a new type of war. From 1914 to 1918, young men had come forward to fight foreign aggressors. Now, in 1924, there was a new, domestic enemy oppressing the people: political corruption.[53]

The GWVA professed political neutrality, but some of the material that appeared in its magazine was less than subtle in its criticism of Squires, Coaker, and other opponents of Monroe. Captain Jack Turner's poem "July First, 1916–1924" was a case in point. Its eight stanzas expressed Turner's belief that the fallen members of the Royal

Newfoundland Regiment would be turning over in their graves in response to the scandals afflicting Newfoundland:

> Do they sleep sound, our dead? Or do they know
> How stands today the land they died to save,
> That Land for which they were right glad to go
> And hurl their youth into a bloody grave—
> Can they sleep, when the freedom that their blood
> Bought dearly, has by lesser men been sold?
> The truth they died for trampled in the mud?
> Their country's name bartered for Judas gold?

It was impossible for the dead to rise, the poem continued, so it fell to the surviving veterans of the Regiment to clean up public life:

> So sound "Fall in!" The Regiment moves again;
> Again, back to the wall, our Country calls,
> Sore is her need today for gallant men
> To save her from the foe within her walls
> We lift the burning torch again, its light
> Shines through the cloud of shame that lies so deep
> Upon our Country's honour. One last fight
> And—that fight won—our gallant dead may sleep.[54]

Governor Sir William Allardyce had elaborated on just what light shone forth from such burning torches in his address at the Memorial Day ceremonies on 1 July 1923. Allardyce had taken up the governorship in 1922, having recently served as the governor of Tasmania and having enjoyed a long career as a colonial official in Fiji, the Falkland Islands, and the Bahamas. The governor claimed that the Newfoundland men who had volunteered for military service during the Great War had held aloft the torch of civilization against the darkness of German aggression.[55] In his poem, Captain Turner was suggesting that this torch was a political beacon that veterans should now hold aloft. A fellow author writing under the pseudonym "Newfoundlander" agreed, noting that returned soldiers were better than the average elector. The scandals, financial woes of government, and the economic problems of the dominion, he argued, could be laid at the feet of voters who "allow themselves to be deceived. They cheer the most extravagant promises, though these promises are really dishonest.... The electors have ceased to be natural." A sense of national purpose in politics had to be restored or responsible government itself would be in jeopardy.[56]

Although the GWVA did not officially endorse Monroe, one of its founders and most prominent members, Harold Mitchell, declared for Monroe in the District of Trinity. In May, it had appeared that the GWVA had blundered politically when its president, Thomas Nangle, accused the *Evening Telegram* of printing "German propaganda" because it had dared to allow coverage in its pages of Britain's Labour government's criticism of France's hard line on the issue of German reparations payments. The *Telegram* had responded by calling Nangle's letter "dictatorial" in tone, "utterly uncalled for," and "offensive."[57] Nonetheless, Mitchell stood against Coakerism and had the combination of business background, military service, and lack of previous political office that made him a star candidate. His family was in business as J.B. Mitchell & Son, a brokerage business, but he had left the business in 1915 to join the Regiment. Wounded at Gallipoli, he returned home, became active in veterans' issues, helped to organize the GWVA, and became its first president. By 1920, he had become the managing director of the family business.[58]

The newspaper supporters of Monroe reported on the election as if it were a war. The *Daily News* printed its coverage of election issues under the headline "From the Front."[59] The *Evening Telegram* argued that Coaker was guilty by association with Squires and Meaney, and declared in bold letters that Newfoundlanders' patriotic duty was to end Coaker's influence by turning out Hickman's Liberal-Progressives.[60] The electoral results in June were decisive: Monroe's party took twenty-five seats to Hickman's ten.

Coaker had decided not to run, but Monroe and his running mates Lewis Little and William Winsor won in Coaker's former stronghold, the District of Bonavista. Hickman won election in Harbour Grace, as did the FPU's J.H. Scammell in St. Barbe. Mitchell did not prevail against William Halfyard, a stalwart of the FPU, or his Liberal-Progressive running mates in Trinity. William Warren would not side with either party and won election in Fortune Bay as an independent. The *Daily News* was ecstatic about the results, declaring that "Newfoundland stands to-day vindicated in the eyes of the world. Revelations of the Walker Enquiry have borne fruit. The country has expressed its unquali-fied displeasure and disgust. The slate has been wiped almost clean...."[61] The *Evening Telegram* agreed, hailing Monroe as the "doughty champion" who would lead the "purge" of public life required by the revelations of the Hollis Walker report.[62]

Monroe had become prime minister, but his lack of political experi-ence, which had proved such an asset during the election, ill-suited him to the task of governing. He relied on A.B. Morine, appointing the latter to the Legislative Council and making him a member of cabinet. The *Advocate* lashed out against "Monroe's treachery" in making Morine such an important member of the government. Reminding its readers of Morine's role in the Reid railway deal of 1898, the *Advocate* proposed that "Monroe is only in the kindergarten class with Morine as his tutor." The newspaper refused to refer to the government as Monroe's, calling it instead the "Morine-Monroe Administration."[63] Monroe also included other prominent members of the old People's Party in his cabinet, Sir John Crosbie and J.R. Bennett, despite the fact that he had come to power as the people's champion against an old system of political corruption. The prime minister might have believed his own press, but his supporters, "far from being enemies of the old system ... were its quintessential products."[64]

The official unveiling of the War Memorial in St. John's on 1 July 1924 drew public attention away from the formation of the Monroe administration. The GWVA had played a central role in raising the funds and planning the memorial without asking for direct financial assistance from the Newfoundland government. It wanted the War Memorial to stand for future generations as a model of self-reliance and the ability to undertake public works without adding to public debt, although the Imperial War Graves Commission had actually contributed five thousand dollars to the cost as a way to mark otherwise unmarked graves of fallen Newfoundlanders.[65] The *Evening Telegram*, like the *Daily News*, would not explicitly discuss the War Memorial in the context of the recent election, but its comments were thinly veiled when it hoped the memorial would "stand through the centuries as a monument before which the fires of patriotism shall forever burn. May it remind us of the men who did not hesitate when duty called. May it be an inspiration to place love of country before all other considerations."[66] The *Advocate* would not dispute that the War Memorial called Newfoundlanders to embrace a purer political life, but in welcoming Lord Haig, who officially unveiled the monument, the paper preferred to emphasize the imperial connection cemented by the sacrifices of the men of the Regiment and the Naval Reserve.[67] In thanking Haig for his visit, and praising Nangle, who served as Haig's aide-de-camp during the visit, for his work in seeing the War Memorial built, the *Daily News* argued that the memorial was most significant as "an incentive to all that is best and truest in citizenship; a sacred place, whence must radiate the rays of selfless service, unflinching courage and the best and purest of human aspirations, if its true meaning is understood."[68]

Following the unveiling of the War Memorial, the Monroe government made clear that it hoped to deal with government debt and budget deficits through retrenchment, especially by cutting back on public employment.[69] The administration started dismissing some government employees, including the lighthouse keeper William Thorne of Hopeall, a father of two men who had died in the war, in the District of Trinity, where Mitchell and the other Monroe candidates had met defeat. The dismissal could not save money because a Monroe supporter got the job instead. The *Advocate* pointed out this hypocrisy in a government that promised to answer the GWVA's call for better treatment of veterans and their families.[70] Under the headline "back to Toryism," the *Advocate* claimed that every person suspected of voting against Monroe's candidates had to fear retaliation, even the parents of fallen soldiers.[71] Less than two months into its mandate, the Monroe government was continuing the patronage game and allowing members of government to collect fees for their services—a practice that Monroe's supporters had objected to when Squires had permitted it.[72]

Monroe's supporters struck back at Coaker by blaming him and other members of the FPU for the industrial unrest that occurred in the summer of 1924. On Bell Island, the British Empire Steel Corporation had been squeezing the miners of Wabana because of the low prices for iron ore it was getting from its German customers. In 1922, many of the workers had formed the Wabana Mine Workers' Union (WMWU), affiliated with the International Union of Mine, Mill and Smelter Workers. In August, workers on the Humber project at Corner Brook threatened to go on strike over poor pay and working conditions. One of their leaders, Alfred Prince, had telegrammed Monroe on 31 July asking for government assistance in the event of a strike. The *Daily News* called Prince "dictatorial" and "a dangerous and unrestrained demagogue." Worse, Prince was supposedly a "Coakerite" who was embroiling the naive workers of the Humber project in a "despicable plot," hatched by FPU members in the House of Assembly (K.M. Brown and Scammell), to foment industrial unrest there and on Bell Island. The *Evening Telegram* supported the *Daily News*'s allegation of an FPU plot.[73] J. Sinclair Tait, a medical doctor who had practised in Newfoundland for forty years, wrote that the Corner Brook workers risked descending into Bolshevism, which was "nothing more than revolutionary terrorism akin to German frightfulness."[74]

The *Advocate* denied that Coaker had anything to do with the labour unrest. When the Humber workers returned to work following a brief stoppage, they brought forward concerns and demanded an impartial investigation of employment conditions on the pulp-and-paper development project.[75] Throughout the summer, Coaker and the *Advocate* continued to object to the Humber developer, Armstrong Whitworth & Company, using a subcontractor, W.I. Bishop Ltd. of Montreal, to import Cape Breton workers for its project.[76] By allowing such "un-British" conduct, they said, Monroe was demonstrating that he was "by birth and environment a Tory who is entirely out of sympathy with the just demands of labour."[77] The major forestry companies required loggers, but people from distant fishing communities were reluctant to assume the high costs of travelling to low-paid jobs in distant camps. The *Evening Telegram* defended the hiring of Cape Breton loggers by arguing that the area between Grand Lake and Sandy Lake, which had to be flooded as a reservoir for the project, would need to be cleared of commercially valuable wood without delaying the overall Humber project.[78]

The *Evening Telegram* also supported the Monroe government's major policy initiative of the summer: a revision of the laws concerning prohibition. Some of Monroe's supporters had felt that efforts to get around the prohibition measures had fostered government corruption ever since they had been implemented during the war. Reforming prohibition was, therefore, a precondition for cleaning up government. The *Daily News*, otherwise a strong supporter of Monroe, was unhappy that the government introduced the Prohibition Act Repeal Bill. The bill stated that previous governments had undermined prohibition by permitting lax enforcement and evasion, especially through the use of alcohol for medicinal purposes. The Monroe government, however, did not even pay lip service to the supposed evils of liquor, and regulated the consumption of alcohol with the new Act Respecting Alcoholic Liquors, which limited adults to the purchase of one bottle a day. The *Daily News* saw the new law as a revenue grab—a peculiar way for an administration to clean up government. For once, the *Advocate* agreed with the *Daily News*.[79]

The Monroe administration was desperate for the revenue, and had to continue borrowing money for relief and public works to combat the problems of deepening depression. In August 1924, Sir John Crosbie, as minister of finance, hurriedly borrowed six million dollars to cover government expenses. The *Advocate* pointed out that the Monroe government was proving no better at making government more efficient or reducing expenditures than had been the previous government. Rather, by continuing to fire and hire along partisan lines, the government was acting worse than "the thug along the highway." "How much longer," asked the *Advocate*, "will the Churches admit to memberships and to places in the front pews these notoriously vindictive, unjust and dishonest politicians who, if they practiced in private life or business those same debauched methods of depriving honest people of their livelihood would be banished from the precincts of any reputable concern and ostracised by the community?"[80]

In October, Monroe and William C. Winsor faced by-elections in the District of Bonavista to confirm their cabinet appointments as minister of education and minister of marine and fisheries respectively. Coaker decided to challenge them on the government's record so far, especially on prohibition. The FPU leader had wanted to withdraw from politics, and had, earlier in the fall, overseen the removal of the FPU newspaper to Port Union under the formal editorship of John Scammell, to isolate it from the political contamination of St. John's. The moral issue of prohibition, however, proved too powerful a temptation. The *Daily News* closed ranks with the government, claiming that Monroe still offered the best chance of cleaning up politics. The *Evening Telegram* was happy to condemn Coaker directly for being a prohibitionist, claiming that, unhappy with his failure as "dictator" of the fishery, Coaker now wanted to dictate people's conscience. Monroe and Winsor defeated Coaker's challenge, much to the *Telegram*'s delight.[81]

By the end of 1924, the *Evening Telegram* was arguing that, with this defeat of Coaker, Newfoundland had finally achieved peace. The paper attributed all of Newfoundland's post-war economic problems and related social distress to the policies permitted by Coaker's admission to the corridors of government, beginning with the National Government in 1917 and extending through the coalition he established with Squires. In commenting on the GWVA's fund-raising poppy campaign in November, the paper claimed that "this year more than on any former occasion we should remember those who thought no sacrifice too great to make in their country's cause, for it is only now, six years after the war ended, that peace has really come. It is only now that the gaunt spectre of poverty and distress has departed, and that prosperity has returned."[82] The paper promised that, with more measures such as the repeal of prohibition, the Monroe government would soon have Newfoundland's economic house in order; the need for public relief would decrease and, consequently, so would the public debt.[83]

The *Telegram* was clearly implying that Coaker's years in government had continued the war in a new form. The first phase of the conflict had been Britain's war for liberty between 1914 and 1918, of which Newfoundland had been such a proud part. By fighting for more state intervention, particularly through the fisheries regulations, Coaker had begun a second phase of conflict, mounting another war on liberty. This war reflected the deeper immorality of Coakerism, which might be seen further in the FPU leader's bargains with the corrupt Squires. Monroe had risen to the challenge of the Hollis Walker report and would, with allies such as Harold Mitchell of the GWVA, purify Newfoundland. Or so the propaganda of Coaker's opponents would have it—and people were likely to be convinced by it in the context of constant economic distress. By the end of 1924, even Coaker was coming to the same conclusion as his antagonists: that Newfoundland politics were in need of purification. In adopting this position, Coaker's political disillusionment was almost complete. But failures of the "clean-up" Monroe administration that were still ahead did not change his attitude—they would only intensify Coaker's growing lack of faith in responsible government.

TEN

The Death
of Democracy,
1925–1934

In 1924, Squires's and Coaker's opponents wrested government away
from them, but over the next four years Prime Minister Monroe's
government did little better. Public spending, relief demands, and public
debt increased, provoking a sense of crisis and leading many more
people to believe that more authoritarian political options might be the
solution. Since 1919, the constant highly charged and public accusations
of government graft, corruption, treason, and betrayal of wartime ideals
had left little reason for anyone to feel much commitment to responsible
government in Newfoundland. When Coaker returned to government
with Squires in 1928, it was clear that the old FPU leader was disillusioned and openly admired the authoritarian politics of Fascist Italy. He
was by no means alone. The inability of the second Squires government
to calm social unrest arising from an acute public relief and debt crisis
was the last straw in the collapse of responsible government, but it was

not the reason for it. The breakdown had started in the rancour that had been fuelled by the war. By the early 1930s, politics in Newfoundland had become a death watch for liberal democracy.

The "clean-up" promises made by Monroe regarding financial responsibility proved empty in the years following his election. If anything, his government aggravated the situation with its February 1925 tax reforms: by abolishing the income tax measures established in 1918, the government became more reliant on the less stable and more direct revenue from customs. To protect St. John's manufacturing and replace lost revenue, the prime minister raised the duties on imported goods. Such a policy could not help fishers with low incomes buy more domestically produced manufactures, and it also raised their cost of living. The higher import duties protected companies in which the prime minister had vested interests, such as the Imperial Tobacco Company and the Colonial Cordage Company, as well as the margarine factory in which his finance minister, Sir John Crosbie, had interests.[1] Peter Cashin, who had won election again as a Monroe supporter, was disgusted: he knew that Crosbie had already given Monroe his opinion that the Newfoundland government was on the verge of bankruptcy. He felt the budget was self-serving and had passed on the tax burden to those least capable of paying it, so he protested in the House of Assembly. This led Monroe to ask him to leave the party if he would not change his position, and the Great War veteran crossed the floor to sit as an Independent. Other members of government who shared Cashin's view, including cabinet minister F. Gordon Bradley, followed suit.[2]

Though the government did not take effective measures to put its finances on a better footing, from almost every quarter of the press in St. John's came the advice that the people must follow models of greater self-reliance. Papers of almost every political stripe found their model in a reimagined seal hunt. Now political commentators resurrected the older view of the hunt as a defining element in a rugged Newfoundland national character, emphasizing the image of the hardy, self-reliant sealer rather than the picture that had emerged during the time of the *Newfoundland* disaster, of the downtrodden, exploited member of the industrial army who required the protection of the state. With the departure of the sealing fleet for the ice in March 1925, the *Daily Globe*—a newspaper founded in September 1924 to replace the *Evening Advocate* in St. John's, which had closed its doors as part of the transfer of the FPU's operations to Port Union—commented that sealers were the core of a hardier, more self-reliant strain of the British race, bold and brave, fearless in the face of danger and disdainful of the protections or support the state might afford.[3]

At the *Evening Telegram*, otherwise a supporter of the Monroe government, C.E.A. Jeffrey shared the *Daily Globe*'s perspective on the seal hunt, underlining the "romantic appeal" of sealers as fearless Vikings, setting out to wrest a livelihood from the elements. The editor wrote that "every loyal Newfoundlander" should be inspired by the willingness of sealers to risk the many dangers of the front each spring to earn part of their livelihoods, no matter how paltry the income might be.[4] Implicit in the paper's view was the notion that the hardships faced by the working people of Newfoundland paled in comparison with those faced by sealers, but sealers allegedly never complained and never hesitated to go back to the ice despite the many hardships they suffered.[5] If sealers put up willingly with such hardship and uncertainty year after year, Jeffrey reasoned, then other working Newfoundlanders had little to grumble about. The unemployed should demonstrate the self-reliance inherent in their race by rejecting government relief. This self-reliance should also mean that workers such as the miners of Bell Island should not strike for better conditions. In 1925, British Empire Steel Corporation (BESCO) forced striking Wabana Mine Workers' Union (WMWU) workers to take a pay cut by threatening to close the mine, something it had already done in Cape Breton. The next year, the demoralized WMWU collapsed, but workers' unrest continued because BESCO was scaling back operations and laying off workers.[6]

The newspapers suggested that people should think of the sealers or the sacrifices of the Great War rather than succumb to the divisiveness of industrial disputes. Remembering those who had fallen in war was on everyone's minds because of the press coverage of the official unveiling by Field Marshall Haig—who was well thought of in Newfoundland for the praise he had given the Regiment in the past—of the war memorial at Beaumont Hamel on 7 June. Nangle had orchestrated Haig's visit, and attended the ceremony as his aide-de-camp. The memorial sculpture of a caribou, by English sculptor Basil Gotto, and the surrounding park planned by Rudolph Cochius, had been designed to foster a strong sense of willing and courageous self-sacrifice, and to reaffirm the importance of Newfoundland to the Empire; it was to inspire a sense that any obstacle or challenge might be overcome by heroic selflessness.[7] The challenge to be faced now, according to the *Telegram*, was not war but post-war economic instability. Instead of allowing "petty personal grievances, political differences, class distinctions, and industrial disputes" to undermine their resolve, the people should fight against the desire to demand assistance from government with the same determination as the soldiers who had marched into battle against the Germans during the war.[8]

The *Telegram*'s idealization of those who had marched in battle contrasted sharply with the actual experiences of veterans locally, many of whom needed government assistance. Later in 1925, Isaac C. Morris—the St. John's businessman who had covered the NPA's recruitment drive in the press during 1915 and who had lost his son Edward in battle with the Regiment on 3 December 1917—took up the current plight of returned soldiers. Most, he pointed out, were suffering from long-term physical, mental, and/or emotional trauma as a result of their service. As bad as such problems were, they paled in comparison to the veterans' sense of having been betrayed by the society to which they had returned. Recruiters had assured every man who enlisted that a grateful people and government would take care of the men upon their return, particularly by ensuring that they had employment. However, the war had changed most of them in such a way that they were often unable to simply return to the lives and the work they had left. Veterans had pressing needs, according to Morris, and the government had a moral duty to provide for pensions, funding them through additional taxation, if necessary. Perhaps drained by his public duties, and desirous of a quieter private life, but also likely disturbed by the contrast between the idealization of veterans and their treatment, Nangle left the priesthood in 1926, and relocated to what was then Rhodesia to build a new life by starting a family.[9]

The idealization of the self-sacrificing soldier and the hardy sealer were ideological prescriptions for what the political behaviour of the working people of Newfoundland should be, whether fisher or wage labourer. Such people should be orderly and undemanding, especially by disavowing the need for poor relief or any other assistance from the government. The press, whether supporting Monroe, Coaker, or Squires, feared the people, including veterans, who might need relief. Even apparently unrelated and more positive matters, such as women's suffrage, had a darker undertone associated with this fear of the people. In 1920, the *Evening Telegram* had supported women's suffrage, not because it believed that women should have the same rights of citizenship as men, but because it liked the idea of the wives and daughters of the city's business and professional elites, who were leading the suffrage movement, having a greater say in elections.[10] Such women had parlayed their involvement in the Women's Patriotic Association and overseas nursing during the war into a demand for political rights that could hardly be resisted. The female proponents of suffrage used ideals of domestic partnership and patriotism to justify their political equality to men and to promise a greater purity in politics. Suffragettes promised to bring a more nurturing role to politics that would be untainted by the corruption that had so often prevailed among male politicians. Squires mistrusted the suffrage movement's emphasis on political purity, and he was less than enthusiastic about a movement that he saw as primarily driven by the St. John's elite, but it fit in well with Monroe's campaign promises, and women gained the vote in 1925.[11]

Purifying politics and exhorting working people to know their proper place and national duty were part of a broader trend in the mid-1920s: Monroe administration supporters and opponents alike feared the political left and admired the radical right as an alternative. Interest in fascist movements overseas continued, perhaps because there were no local fascist organizations to disrupt life in St. John's. At the end of the year, for example, the *Daily Globe* praised an English group calling itself the "National Fascisti" for raising a Union Jack over a municipal building in Battersea, London. Battersea North's MP throughout the 1920s was the Communist Shapurji Saklatvala, and the paper warned that communism, which it saw as a betrayal of true British principles, had also grown in popularity in Canada, especially among immigrants in the West.[12] The *Daily News* felt that Newfoundland required some form of strong measures because it was being swept along in the international currents of post-war crisis: depressed trade, growing unemployment, and the consequent growing interest abroad in political movements of the left, especially communism.[13]

Although it would have been unimaginable for him to do so in the previous decade, Coaker, bitter and stung by the ruthless and unfair Monroe campaign of 1924, agreed with the idea expressed by the *Daily News* that strong measures were required to deal with the political problems and unrest looming in Newfoundland. Coaker was more specific, recommending to the annual convention of the FPU in November 1925 that Newfoundland take a ten-year rest from democracy. Newfoundland had great economic potential in its fisheries and other natural resources, he argued, but these required careful public stewardship. Unfortunately, the party politics of the past thirty years had paralyzed government and catapulted it into financial profligacy as politicians tried to buy the affections of the electorate. Coaker suggested that the way out of this mess was for a government to seek election on the promise that, once in power, it would pass legislation that turned government over to a commission of nine men for ten years. These men might be elected initially, but they should be sound managers who could "produce reforms, establish industries, procure retrenchment and place the fishing industry on a sound businesslike basis." Graft would also disappear, Coaker thought, because the nine wise men would not have to worry about partisan politics thereafter for an extended period.[14] In December, Coaker wrote to readers of the *Advocate*, suggesting that Newfoundland required putting in place a new model of "government by appointed Commission" before it fell into penury, reverted to crown colony status, or—the always unpopular option in the dominion—became a province of Canada.[15]

Coaker did not see his suggestion for government by a commission as particularly subversive of democracy because he felt that the dismantling of the democratic process was already well under way due to the actions of the Monroe government. The FPU leader had been aggravated by the government's conduct in a by-election in St. John's East in 1925. One of the seats for that district was vacant, but Monroe did not want to have a by-election that might serve as a referendum on his tax reforms—reforms that had already cost him the support of Peter Cashin. Further defections were likely to follow, and the election of an opposition candidate would weaken the prime minister's position in the House. In early August, a delegation of Hickman's supporters petitioned Governor Allardyce to force the by-election. Allardyce followed the advice of his prime minister, who in turn took his cues from Morine as political strategist, and stonewalled. The governor later commented that Coaker's address about the need for a commission was "the effusion of a politically disgruntled man, who, wishing to return to politics is still smarting beneath the [electoral] blow he received."[16]

The FPU paper, which had reappeared as the *Fishermen's Advocate*, now published in Port Union, had no better view of the governor and campaigned against Morine as a dictator who, with Allardyce as his puppet, was undermining the constitutional rights of Newfoundlanders. The opposition organized the East End Electors Committee, which engaged in public demonstrations and supported Michael Cashin as its candidate. Abram Kean had been defending the role of Morine in the St. John's East by-election affair, leading Coaker to write that "Capt. Kean is welcome to the job of licking Morine's dirty face in the hope of removing some of the dirt. No one envies him his job, but many question his sanity."[17] The FPU leader was in fact struggling to find an alternative to what he saw as the disgraceful and corrupt politics of Newfoundland in the 1920s. Like other persistent admirers of the radical right, Coaker believed in the importance of national unity, but he was not ready to commit to anything more radical than the idea that a responsible government would place policy in the hands of wise men for an extended (but still limited) period so that they could make good policy without the patronage and deals that electoral success demanded, or the dirty tricks that Monroe, Morine, and their supporter Kean seemed capable of.

Coaker's growing disillusionment with liberal democracy stemmed primarily from his anger at the Monroe-Morine alliance's political subterfuge, such as in the St. John's East by-election affair. The *Advocate* kept up its criticisms of anyone who supported the prime minister, including Robert Duff of Carbonear. By the spring of 1926, Monroe's majority in the House of Assembly had disappeared as more disaffected members of the government followed Peter Cashin across the floor to sit with the opposition in protest over the government's financial measures. Monroe's government and Hickman's Liberals each had seventeen supporters, with William Warren's votes as an Independent keeping the government alive. Duff, a prominent Conception Bay businessman, sat as a Liberal, but on 29 June 1926, Monroe enticed him across the floor with a cabinet position. This was the sort of wheeling and dealing that Coaker had been condemning, but in the opinion of the papers that supported Monroe, the FPU leader's previous balance-of-power strategy and his pursuit of FPU objectives through coalitions hardly let him claim innocence against political machinations. The *Evening Telegram* put it directly, asking what right Coaker had to such holier-than-thou attitudes when he had made such "lightning changes in recent years" in his own choice of prime ministers "that even a chameleon might envy him." Coaker had dangled Union Party support before Bond and Morris. He had excoriated then supported Squires, and heaped abuse upon but now supported Hickman. Coaker was, in the *Telegram* editor's opinion, the last politician who had the right to complain about the quality of political principles in Newfoundland.[18]

For all of his professed desire for a new type of politics, Coaker could not resist entering the fray in the ongoing St. John's East by-election controversy. He had approached the East End Electors Committee about coordinating opposition to Monroe's government outside St. John's, and received encouraging information (from Ken Brown, a prominent Grand Falls labour leader, Hickman Liberal and, later, president of the FPU) that Peter Cashin was open to forming a political alliance. By the spring of 1926, five members of Monroe's government had defected to the opposition benches; as the year wore on, Coaker hoped that he might find in them the basis for another coalition that would allow him a further attempt at fisheries reform. The Monroe government was looking weak: its prominent members had proved self-interested in their management of public finances and were unable to solve the country's public debt problems. Commenting on the upcoming Armistice Day ceremonies in November, the *Daily News* mourned the dejected condition of public life in Newfoundland, suggesting that the "ideals" of the war years eluded people, and that "the brotherhood of the trenches has not found its way into our daily lives."[19] Monroe's promise in the previous election had been "Clean Up; Keep Clean; And a Square Deal to All," but his government was proving just as self-interested as any prior administration.

The Monroe government had failed to provide a square deal to all; it had not managed to alleviate the need for public relief to the unemployed and had given reluctant support to the private and ineffectual Charity Organization Bureau, an organization led by the local business and professional community to deal with social problems. While Monroe's supporters in the press blamed poor public morale for the government's troubles, Peter Cashin held Monroe and his supporters fully responsible. In January 1927, Cashin wrote to Coaker proposing an alliance on behalf of the "common people of this country" against graft; he claimed "there is not one man who occupies a position of trust in the present Government who has the interests of Newfoundland at heart.... The present Prime Minister is totally incapable of filling that position of trust conferred on him two or three years ago, and [has] prostituted his position in every way...."[20] It had taken less than three years for the Monroe government to be described in exactly the same way as the Squires government amidst the scandal of the Hollis Walker revelations.

Though the social, economic, and fiscal problems of Newfoundland had come to appear almost insurmountable, good news still happened in the dominion, but even when it did, Monroe appeared unable to respond positively. In 1927, Newfoundland won a dispute with Canada over boundaries in Labrador through arbitration by the Judicial Committee of the British Privy Council, but not before the dominion endured the public spectacle of the Monroe government trying to sell to Quebec its rights to most of Labrador for thirty million dollars. Most politicians thought the sale of Labrador might be the answer to Newfoundland's financial problems, but it was Monroe who explored the possibility, including the spectacle of even cutting the original asking price in half, preserving only fishing rights along the coast for Newfoundlanders. The Monroe government also lapsed back into the same old desperate efforts to attract foreign investment in forestry and mining development through tax concessions, as had Squires in the case of the Humber project. As Monroe's reputation deteriorated, Coaker saw no problem in rebuilding an alliance with Squires, who had been rehabilitating his image partially by again becoming grand master of the Orange Order and by fending off prosecution for matters arising from the 1924 scandals. In May 1928, nine members of the opposition, led by William Halfyard, announced that they sat as members of a new Liberal Party led by Squires. In July, Monroe resigned and turned the government over to his business partner and cousin Frederick Alderdice. On 29 October 1928, the Liberals won the general election through a political partnership of Squires, Coaker, and Peter Cashin. All three were elected, and Coaker became a minister without portfolio while Cashin became minister of finance and customs.[21]

Coaker and the newspapers were appalled at the state of government upon his return; even his own FPU supporters were content to demand patronage of Coaker. Nowhere to be found were the idealized grizzled veterans of the ice floes, the sealers whom the press liked to hold up as models of risk-taking honest livelihoods earned independently of government, with the same bravery as those who died in the trenches of Europe.[22] All of the appeals asking people to live up to the heroic sacrifices of the trenches by foreswearing patronage or government assistance had been in vain, or at least that was Coaker's view, as well as that of the newspapers that normally opposed him.[23]

Just before the election, Coaker had complained about the role of "bribery and corruption" in politics, by which he meant that voters expected patronage in return for their votes. Coaker too had hoped for a purer politics to arise from women's suffrage, arguing that "the women's vote will have to stamp out rascality. It is in their power to stand up for right and they will."[24] This hope was naive in that women's suffrage could do nothing to stem the tide of ever-mounting demands for public relief. Such demands forced the new Squires government to borrow more money, thus adding to the existing public debt burden. Indeed, the situation had become so bad that the government had almost no capacity to deal with crises, such as the one that occurred in November 1929 when a tsunami struck the Burin Peninsula, causing more than one million dollars in property damage, the loss of at least 27 lives, and leaving many families without homes or the means of subsistence as winter approached. The government sent a relief ship with some supplies, but relied on private donations from Newfoundlanders and Labradorians, as well as from Canada, the United States, and England, to provide the assistance it could not afford.[25] By the end of the year, Coaker was again pleading for women to help clean up the political mess by demanding an elected commission of six people to govern for ten years. Such commissioners would be able to rise above the current political "game of give and take," which compelled even the best-intentioned leaders to bribe people for support. People never wrote to government to suggest policy improvements or to ask for funding for worthy projects, Coaker asserted, but rather wrote in an "evil" quest for personal self-advantage. Only a commission that did not have the immediate worry of facing the electorate at the polls could do what was "right" and "moral" rather than what the people willed.[26]

Such statements from a minister of the government did not surprise those newspapers that supported the opposition. The *Evening Telegram* had pointed out that, although the Squires government had won many seats, it was little more than a ragtag coalition of factions cobbled together through "compromises and concessions, which have not been conducive to harmony, and have exposed the individual members of charges of sacrificing their sense of public duty for the sake of personal gain."[27] True to form, the *Daily News* greeted Coaker's "doleful and despairing" message by suggesting that the FPU leader wanted "the establishment of a sort of dictatorship" because "he would, of course, like to be a part."[28] The *Telegram*, however, was less antagonistic, thanking Coaker for his "frankness and courage" in voicing what was on many people's minds: that the only way Newfoundland could move forward to a better future was through "the suspension of our constitution, and ... the appointment of a commission with power to administer the affairs of the Colony until such time as political sanity has been restored."[29]

Coaker's state of mind about the problems meant that he was likely to be further disappointed as he set out to work on new regulations for the fishing industry through 1930. Once again, in an effort to secure mercantile support, he had watered down his proposals so that they were not worth much. However, there was little appetite for fisheries regulations in Newfoundland, as the poor international market conditions drove down prices for fish and forestry products, the main staples of the Newfoundland economy, especially in terms of generating employment. Growing public debt—fuelled as ever by the financial demands of the railway, the ongoing attempt to pay back money borrowed for the war, and the constant demand for poor relief—meant that the government was in a poor position to borrow the money it needed to meet even more demands for relief from the unemployed and the indigent. In the fishing industry, fishers and merchants struggled over credit: merchants tightened access to it, and fishers began to avoid paying debts by dealing with competing firms or, on occasion, by beginning to trade for themselves. Everyone was looking to the government for financial assistance, even as leading members of the business community blamed economic problems on reckless government spending. The condition of the poor was appalling: about one-third of the Newfoundland population depended on public relief, which usually took the form of men exchanging labour on public works for tea, flour, pork, and molasses. As distress grew, so did public anger, so that during the summer of 1931, Prime Minister Squires feared "Red tendencies" among the crowds of unemployed people in Conception Bay and St. John's who demanded better relief.[30]

Although still a cabinet minister, Coaker minced no words about how he felt about the political situation, revealing his own depressing slide into contempt for the common people and liberal democracy. He denounced the people as becoming morally bankrupt, tracing it back to their support for the railway patronage of Morris's People's Party victory in 1909. The people had become used to government providing them with work and relief, and always demanded more rather than less.

"All Governments have given way to this universal demand," Coaker declared. "The representatives did their part in abetting it and the people stood ready to crucify any candidate prepared to denounce such insanity or plead for economy." Squires, Monroe, and Alderdice used money to buy off the masses, and the result was "madness, political depravity, frivolity of the most debased quality." There was only one solution: electoral politics must be ended and anyone who agitated publicly for more relief measures should face imprisonment so that the government could get on with cutting the public debt.[31] As good as his word, Coaker became the architect of the Squires government's retrenchment measures. The opposition newspapers did not criticize them, but berated Squires for failing to provide alternate employment through economic development. The *Daily News* ridiculed the prime minister's promise to "breathe the breath of life" into yet another pulp-and-paper development on the Gander River, describing the failed negotiations as an example of Squires's "blighting, chilling halitosis."[32]

The relief crisis was but one manifestation of the Squires government's increasing inability to meet all of its financial obligations. It also could not cope with the day-to-day running expenses of government, including hiring and equipping more police to control protestors, nor could it meet the huge interest payments on the public debt. The Squires government turned to four Canadian banks, but especially to the Bank of Montreal, hoping without luck for a bailout similar to the one given after the Bank Crash in 1894. At Squires's behest, the Canadian government convinced the Canadian banks to lend Newfoundland more money, and in exchange, the Newfoundland government accepted a representative of the Canadian banks to control the use of the funds since the banks feared that Canada's credit would suffer if Newfoundland defaulted. In desperation, the elected government had surrendered control over its spending.[33]

The *Evening Telegram* greeted the news of the banks' loan with the headline "Newfoundland Saved from Default," but warned that

Newfoundland's day of reckoning had come; there would have to be deep cuts in government spending.[34] Coaker too felt that the day of judgment was at hand, and that many people, whether old allies or enemies, were responsible for the dominion's financial mess. The days were long gone when the leader of the FPU would have sympathized or made common cause with labour leaders such as James McGrath of the Longshoremen's Protective Union (LSPU). No longer serving as president of the LSPU, McGrath continued to advocate for the poor of St. John's, which made him a likely candidate for jail as the type of troublemaker Coaker now decried. The Newfoundland government continued to cut spending, hiring Montreal businessman R.J. Magor in late 1931 to organize a much reduced relief system. Since the 1920s, unemployed workers in St. John's had been organizing under the leadership of unionists such as McGrath to fight for employment and against cuts to relief. In the early winter of 1932, McGrath was often at the head of delegations from the Committee of the Unemployed, attending its protests against Magor's more miserly relief plans. The spectacle of poorly fed and clothed workers on able-bodied relief projects during winter prompted a Committee of the Unemployed, chaired by McGrath, to petition the government for better conditions in February 1932. By 11 February 1932, marches organized by the committee protesting relief cuts led Prime Minister Squires to call McGrath a "gangster" because of his leadership of the committee. McGrath responded by a public letter denouncing the prime minister's relief measures.[35]

In the meantime, Peter Cashin was becoming increasingly uncomfortable with Squires's arrangement with the banks and with the prime minister's conduct. On 1 February, Cashin resigned as minister of finance, and on 4 February, he rose in the House to accuse Squires of having falsified cabinet minutes to conceal his misappropriation of funds, including five thousand dollars from monies provided by the War Reparations Committee. There were further allegations that business colleagues of Squires had benefited from improper payments. The news was sensational, seeming to be a repeat of the scandals of 1924, and prompted a riot at Government House by the unemployed a week later. Unrest spread to the north side of Conception Bay, where many of the miners who worked at Bell Island lived when not employed in the mines. Further austerity measures led to more protests through March.[36] The *Evening Telegram* condemned Squires as a shameless looter of funds that should have been used to assist veterans, their dependants, and the families of those who had fallen in battle.[37]

This new scandal broke over the political scene with a greater fury than the revelations of the Hollis Walker report because the campaign for purer politics by Monroe, subsequent failures to live up to such promises, worsening economic problems, and the ongoing histrionics of public debate as expressed in the newspapers had boiled the political waters of the capital. On 4 April, an open-air meeting organized by merchants and opposition supporters, including Eric Bowring, Harry Winter, and Walter Monroe, demanded an investigation into Cashin's allegations against Squires. J.H. Adams, a veteran, addressed the meeting by speaking directly to other veterans, reminding them that Squires stood accused of stealing from them and their families, and that if any one of them had been found guilty of such a crime while in service, he would have been shot.[38] Amid more allegations by Cashin, on 5 April a business-dominated citizens' committee led a march of between eight and ten thousand people to the Colonial Building, the seat of the House of Assembly. A riot ensued as some marchers fought police while others stormed the building seeking Squires, who had to flee.

The government relied on members of the GWVA and other special police to assist in maintaining order the next day, and to provide additional members for an expanded police force.[39] Although Squires had a troubled relationship with the veterans' organization, he had preserved their pensions amidst the cuts to other forms of relief. In March, the prime minister had received a number of letters from disabled veterans such as Hedley White. White had "lost a limb" during the war, and asked Squires "in the name of God and for the sake of War Veteran little children, try and figure out some other way so as the wounded returned soldiers can still have the benefit of their few dollars." A.J. Verge, who had been "suffering from shock" and blackouts since the battle at Monchy-le-Preux in 1917, made a similar request. Squires assured White that there would be no cuts to veterans' pensions for 1932.[40]

Some veterans may have assisted the government against the rioters because they supported Squires, but the more able-bodied probably wanted the employment. One of the veterans who turned out to maintain order was William Yetman, who, finding no work in Newfoundland at the end of the war, spent the years between 1918 and 1925 serving in a cavalry regiment or as a sailor in various parts of the Empire and Germany. Upon his return in 1925, Yetman took a job as ship's steward with Job Brothers, but had gone to the seal hunt in the spring of 1932. Since the end of the war, veterans occasionally took service in the hunt: in 1922, for example, Abram Kean had at least one veteran among the crew of his vessel, the *Terra Nova*, at the hunt, although the Old Man refused to provide him with a gun for shooting seals.[41] In 1932, the sealers received reports of the riots back home by wireless, and Yetman later remembered that "some people were going to hang Sir Richard Squires." The government's hiring of extra police in response to the riots finally provided Yetman with a secure career.[42]

The spring riots finished Squires's prime ministership: the House of Assembly was dissolved and an election set for early June. Frederick Alderdice, with the support of Water Street merchants, led a United Newfoundland Party against Squires, who faced the election without Coaker's support. The FPU leader had resigned from government in May, and Alderdice had his tacit backing, as long as he promised to examine the viability of an appointed commission. Coaker also did not want British civil servants to be members of such a commission, arguing that it would take them too long to get to know Newfoundland's problems. Alderdice won the general election and Squires met personal defeat at the hands of Harold Mitchell, who then served as a minister without portfolio in Alderdice's government. The new prime minister attempted to alleviate the country's financial situation by leasing Labrador to British interests for ninety-nine years, but the attempt failed. Public anger continued to mount as the government cut relief further, exploding in more riots in St. John's and across the island throughout the rest of 1932.[43]

Alderdice's supporters at the *Daily News* and the *Evening Telegram* took the opportunity occasioned by Memorial Day services during the summer to declare that Beaumont Hamel demonstrated that public discipline was at least as important as democracy. People wasted too much time in debating and disagreeing about policy, but the Regiment had proved the value in not stopping to reason why. Now was not the time for dissent, but rather for marching orderly in step towards the goal of retrenchment.[44] Somewhat ironically, the *Telegram* later chastised the GWVA for protesting against proposed cuts to pensions for its members, stating that they had to accept them with the "same spirit of sacrifice" that soldiers had demonstrated during the war.[45]

Coaker, having decided not to fight alongside Squires, had been willing to believe Alderdice's promise on the matter of the commission. However, he was completely disenchanted with the new prime minister's mercantile supporters and consequently became far more inclined to authoritarianism. He was even more bitter at mercantile opposition to his second attempt at regulating the fishery, and blamed himself for not being "cold blooded enough" to resist as a member of Squires's government in 1930. For the old FPU leader, the consequence of the failure of party government in a liberal democracy was clear: "What is required for Newfoundland and what is most essential for present conditions is a Mussolini. If a man with a soul encased in steel, experienced and not under forty years old, appeared on the political horizon in this country today as a Mussolini I would support him with all my strength."[46]

Coaker had long found Mussolini appealing, as had other prominent people in St. John's, and this had likely been encouraged by the rehabilitation of Mussolini in British eyes during the 1920s. Some conservatives had adopted a more favourable view of the Italian dictator as result of the election of the first Labour government in Britain in 1924, and many more expressed their admiration for Mussolini's handling of strikes when Britain experienced the General Strike of 1926. Internationally, Britain had not wanted to antagonize Italy because of the nations' shared role as powers in the Mediterranean. Prominent interests in the British government had come to believe that, if the choice was between fascism and communism, the former was preferable both in dictatorships abroad and as a tendency that might be counted on to appear within popular movements at home in the event of labour unrest in the mining industry. In 1925, for example, a senior government official, Sir William Mitchell-Thompson, met with British fascists who had joined the Organisation for Maintenance of Supplies, a volunteer group that would assist the government in the event of a strike. In September 1925, Home Secretary Sir William Joynson-Hicks had informed Prime Minister Stanley Baldwin that he thought the fascists would make dependable volunteers in the event of a miners' strike.[47] Coaker was less impressed initially by the possibility that a fascist regime might suppress the union movement, but he claimed that Newfoundland needed its own Mussolini to overcome the influence of merchants and industrialists in party politics. By contrast with the social unrest in Newfoundland, Coaker had witnessed the apparent Fascist miracle of new public works, industry, and social order in Italy during a visit there in 1932.[48]

Newfoundland did not get a Mussolini. Instead, it lost the political rights of responsible government. Alderdice also considered defaulting on Newfoundland's public debt, but yielded to British fears that such an action would hurt Newfoundland's and Britain's reputations and possibly Britain's credit rating. The British and Canadian governments arranged more loans for Newfoundland, but on the condition that a joint commission of inquiry into Newfoundland's financial affairs would be established, the commission to be composed of British, Canadian, and Newfoundland representatives. The Newfoundland government's lack of commitment to dominion status since 1924 had anticipated this intervention; Newfoundland governments fell behind the other dominions in asserting its right to have a say in the international affairs of the Empire that affected it. Although the Balfour Declaration of 1926 had recognized Newfoundland's status as equal to that of the other dominions, the Newfoundland government, in fact, acted much more as a subordinate of the Empire. Prime Minister Monroe, during the spring of 1927, had made it clear that he was reluctant to see Newfoundland evolve further as a dominion, stating that the Balfour Declaration was something akin to an imposition rather than a privilege. In 1931, the Squires government had proved little more enthusiastic, accepting the application of the term "dominion" to Newfoundland in the Statute of Westminster by stipulating that none of the statute's provisions for sovereign jurisdiction be extended to Newfoundland without specific request.[49]

The British appointed Lord Amulree, a Labour peer, to lead the commission. Before he left Britain, the Treasury and Dominions Office made it clear to Amulree that Newfoundland was not to default and that the British taxpayer would not be expected to underwrite the colonial treasury unless the government in London, not Newfoundland politicians, had control over the spending. The Canadian representative on the Amulree Commission, Charles A. Magrath—the former surveyor and Conservative MP for Medicine Hat from 1908 to 1911, nominated by Prime Minister R.B. Bennett—did not think Newfoundland's problems were too severe, and considered that a partial rescheduling of payments on its public debt, along with further financial help from Canada and Britain, would see Newfoundland through its crisis. That said, he also felt that the best option was confederation with Canada. However, the Canadian government was unprepared to help further. Britain remained determined to take political control over Newfoundland in the case that London was to be the source of financial help. Alderdice, who had come to feel that widespread political demoralization required a change in Newfoundland's political system, had picked Canadian banking advisor Sir William Stavert to represent Newfoundland on the commission, and the Canadian banks favoured Britain's plans to take over the direction of Newfoundland's affairs. Stavert consequently was also no advocate of Newfoundland's constitutional independence.

The precedent of the Hollis Walker report meant that the Amulree Commission was predisposed to find a people living in a society and economy that by its very nature mired them in despondency and corruption. The commission found the population demoralized by long-term neglect and reckless squandering of the colony's natural resources— "misled into the acceptance of false standards; and the country sunk in waste and extravagance." Absolute contempt for local politicians of any stripe, the commission's report argued, had been intensified by the blatant patronage practices and promises of local electoral campaigns.[50] There was no shortage of witnesses who were willing to support such views. Business leaders such as Leonard Outerbridge, the son of Sir Joseph and a Great War veteran of the Canadian army, claimed that the government was too weak to help employers break strikes by organized workers, singling out the LSPU as a particular problem. Eric Bowring claimed that the vast majority of Newfoundlanders were too illiterate to be able to exercise democratic privileges, and argued that reverting to crown colony status or empowering a commission would give the country a break from the people's influence. While they would have taken issue with Outerbridge's and Bowring's particular views, labour leaders (such as the LSPU's Michael Coady and the Journeymen Coopers Union's James Power) agreed that the political situation had become untenable, and supported a commission along the lines proposed by Coaker. In a letter to the Amulree Commission on 26 March 1933, Max Small, a fisher from Moreton's Harbour on the northeast coast, wrote that merchants and politicians had squeezed "blood money" from fishing people for years to support their fine lifestyles. He included Coaker in the ranks of merchants, pointing out that the old FPU leader now lived in fine style in the West Indies. While the poor had suffered, government members had issued dole, not to help but to further their own political careers. Small wanted a commission to free Newfoundland from such influences, but also to ensure that the working people of the country received a fair return for their labours.[51]

The Amulree Commission's report recommended the suspension of responsible government and its replacement by a commission appointed by the British government, "until such time as Newfoundland may become self-supporting again."[52] The report had the support of Prime Minister Alderdice, who, in the special session of the House of Assembly convened to debate the report, argued that Newfoundland needed "'a political holiday and a breathing space [for] working out its destiny'" and that democracy had proved "'a curse instead of a blessing.'"[53] Coaker approved of the idea of a commission, but he was unhappy with the particular form recommended by the Amulree Commission. He had expected that the Newfoundland legislature would have appointed the commission itself, and that the new body would be composed of local people.

There were, however, few voices of opposition as most prominent Newfoundlanders supported the recommendation, including the leaders of the GWVA, who hoped that the deeper pockets of the British Treasury might fund better benefits for association members.[54] In April 1930, the association's magazine had printed an editorial on the relief problem that was effectively an indictment of democracy in Newfoundland. It had argued that too many people were becoming dependent on the government for employment and assistance with matters they could well afford to pay for themselves. The people could not be blamed for such dependence because "supine and venal politicians" allowed them to think that their votes were for sale to the highest bidder. The editorial had voiced views very similar to Coaker's: that it was time for government to begin retrenchment without regard for currying the favour of the people. Government must stop acting as "fairy god-fathers for every indigent dependant who wants assistance."[55]

One of the few people who opposed the very concept of the Amulree Commission was Peter Cashin. His later memoir recalled it as collusion between the Bank of Montreal, Squires's opponents, and British officials, but underplayed his own role in the disgrace of Squires. Another opponent of the suspension of liberal democracy was F. Gordon Bradley, who, with Roland Sparks of Green Bay, constituted the last members of opposition in the House of Assembly under responsible government.[56] Despite such resistance, on 16 February 1934, Prime Minister Alderdice signed the papers that suspended Newfoundland's effective dominion status and its democracy.

By 1934, the political possibilities for a more progressive politics that Coaker had hoped for twenty years earlier were dead, and he had witnessed the establishment of a type of government that, although he had helped prepare its way, had come in a form the old FPU leader opposed. He could not have been made any happier by the complete public rehabilitation of his old nemesis, Abram Kean, in that year. Although embarrassed by the allegations concerning the *Newfoundland* disaster, Kean had continued to prosper in his profession. His longevity as a sealing commander meant that, political controversies aside, Kean had benefited from the romanticizing of the hunt that had accompanied the deepening crisis of the 1920s and early 1930s. Newspapers described him and his fellow sealing captains (such as William Bartlett) as sagacious commanders of men who "have each year been found on the bridge, as full as ever of the vigour and of high resolve to wrest from the frozen pans the wealth brought down from the Arctic regions."[57]

Kean had been appointed to the Legislative Council in 1927 and remained there until 1934. In that year, he took the steamer *Beothic* to the ice for Bowrings, and there was much speculation that he would bring back his millionth seal. He received the Order of the British Empire for the feat. The passage of time, the intervention of the war, and subsequent political battles had made the death on the ice of the spring of 1914 a distant memory. For at least some families, fatalism was also now in play. Jack Jordan of Pouch Cove, just outside St. John's, for example, was only six years old when his father Thomas perished in the disaster. Jordan later recalled that his family held "no personal grudge" against Abram Kean or his son Westbury: "It was just something that happened: was meant to be."[58] Kean was the toast of Newfoundland, congratulated by the governor, feted by the Board of Trade, and celebrated in the newspapers and on radio. If anyone bothered to ask, Kean would have told them that he approved of the Commission of Government because it would limit the influence of partisanship over policy in government.[59]

In 1934, the curtain had fallen on liberal democracy in Newfoundland. While many people had flirted with the idea of a Mussolini, the outcome was more moderate: a British-appointed commission. Frustrated at the absolute failure of his post-war attempts to spark more progressive government, Coaker had led the way in advocating a rest from democracy. Coaker was not alone in his complete disillusionment with the fishing people he had once championed. Members of the GWVA also felt that the Newfoundland public was politically demoralized, and that their demands for relief betrayed the noble ideals of the war. Union and business leaders saw things similarly. Ironically, the liberal democratic ideals embedded in the British imperial war effort had become the justification for the suspension of liberal democracy in Newfoundland.

CONCLUSION

By 1934, William Coaker's political disillusionment was almost complete. Unhappy with the particular form the Commission of Government took, and with the politics of post-war Newfoundland generally, Coaker left no doubt that he believed liberal democracy had become corrupted. He had become convinced that one of the most important agents of that corruption was the public demand for relief, which made most voters willing to abandon any potential leader whose policies did not include opening wide the public purse. This state of affairs was ideal for unprincipled politicians who would make any promise to gain election, and its overall impact was the political demoralization of Newfoundland. Nor was Coaker alone in his views; by 1932 it would have been difficult to find anyone in the dominion who would have disagreed with him. The situation, moreover, was not unique to Newfoundland: the post-war disenchantment with liberal democracy was, as a number of writers have noted, merely a reflection of a broader current rushing through Europe and the Americas and expressing itself in an interest in movements of the extreme right, such as fascism.[1]

Newfoundland was generally part of the pattern of post-war political disillusionment with the forms of liberal democracy and movements of the left that existed before the war, and consequent fascination with

the extreme right—what Raymond Sontag called the "broken world."
However, it is important to consider how such political discouragement
was manifested locally. In Newfoundland, although a post-war phenom-
enon in effect, political disillusionment originated in the terrible tragedy
that occurred before the outbreak of war in the summer of 1914. That
spring had brought death on another front, with the horrifying losses on
the ice floes during the seal hunt. While the loss of the *Southern Cross*
had led to many more deaths, the *Newfoundland* disaster had been a far
more public tragedy: there were plenty of eyewitnesses and survivors to
give accounts of the horrors that had been experienced by the lost men
at the front. The arrival of sealing vessels in St. John's with the dead
and the injured had been greeted by sombre crowds of the disbelieving.
When sorrow turned to anger at the apparent disregard for human life
at the ice, it galvanized the incipient protest that had been gathering
strength, to express itself in the political form of William Coaker's FPU
and its political arm, the Union Party.

The horrible spectacle of the *Newfoundland* disaster had charged
the political climate of the colony with an unprecedented awareness of
class. Seventy-eight men had died because of the incredible risks sealing
captains took to ensure a profitable hunt. They took these risks on
behalf of mercantile firms that owned the sealing ships, one of which,
A. Harvey and Company, had decided to remove a wireless radio from
the *Newfoundland* because it was not generating enough income as a
useful device for locating seals. It had never occurred to the firm that
the radio might be useful for any other purpose, such as ships' captains
communicating with each other about the location of their crews. The
majority report of a commission of inquiry had also found Abram
Kean neglectful in not taking proper care of the men he had effectively
summoned to his ship. Coaker had pushed this further, asking why
Abram Kean and his son Westbury were clever enough to figure out
how to communicate about the whereabouts of seals by raising a derrick
(the signal that had summoned the men of the *Newfoundland*) but had

not even thought about having a means of communicating about the safety of their crews. Although Newfoundland political culture had been informed in part by the mythology of the hardy sealer as a tough adventurer who bore any risk for the sake of an honest livelihood, the sealing disaster had suggested that such men were expendable—the cannon fodder of an industrial army sent into battle each spring for the sake of mercantile profits and sealing captains' renown. It was people's anger over this situation that had fuelled public protests and greater support for the FPU.

The class awareness that had been growing in 1914 had been neither proletarian nor revolutionary. The fishing people who provided the crews of the seal hunt were not wage labourers but petty producers in household production who were ideologically committed to a paternalistic ethos. That paternalism provided powerful ties to people of other class backgrounds, such as merchants. Throughout the nineteenth century, the dynamic and cyclical pressures of resource depletion, over-capitalization, and credit contraction in the fishery and the seal hunt had been gnawing at these bonds. Death on the ice front in the spring of 1914 was merely the most outrageous example in a long chain of insults that finally brought to light how little the paternalism of Newfoundland society was benefiting fishing people. What William Coaker led was a movement that demanded a reorganization of society and economy so that each fisher would get "his own." The FPU wanted to see the fishery put on a more secure basis and the seal hunt made safer by, among other things, state regulation. Under Coaker, the FPU had been committed to using the liberal democratic process to secure moderate but progressive reforms. He and other prominent members of the FPU, most notably Grimes, were sympathetic to the labour reformism of working-class leaders in St. John's, such as Jim McGrath of the LSPU, but they were committed primarily to the pursuit of outport interests.

The outbreak of war in August 1914 produced the conditions under which Coaker defined his progressive political platform more sharply.

The FPU leader had entered the House of Assembly the previous year as one of the most important leaders of the opposition to Prime Minister Morris's People's Party government. Coaker had opposed the organization of the war effort by the voluntary Newfoundland Patriotic Association (NPA), seeing it as an abdication of the responsibility of the people's elected government. He had also opposed the raising of the Newfoundland Regiment, seeing it as an expense the colony could not afford, and as a form of military service that would discriminate against outport volunteers. However, Coaker had spent much of the first year of the war pursuing what was to become a more personal and vituperative battle against Abram Kean over the *Newfoundland* tragedy. Only when it had become clear that the war would be a long one had Coaker realized that he risked dissipating the Union Party's support by inviting charges of waging a divisive, and therefore potentially unpatriotic, campaign against Kean. Then, throughout 1915, the news of the Regiment's deployment to Gallipoli and the reports of losses among the Newfoundlanders of the Royal Naval Reserve had made it politically untenable for any politician to risk being portrayed as undermining the war effort.

Death on another front—the near annihilation of the Newfoundland Regiment at Beaumont Hamel on 1 July 1916—had crystalized Coaker's views on what needed to be done. As wartime inflation tightened its grip through 1915, choking the well-being of working Newfoundlanders, whether outport fishers or wage labourers in the city, Coaker had joined labour leaders such as Jim McGrath in protesting against mercantile profiteering through price gouging and the sale of the colony's best tonnage to Russia. In his fight against profiteering, Coaker had argued that only better state regulation of shipping and prices could deal with the problem. The slaughter of the Regiment in 1916 had confirmed Coaker's view that the war effort could not be left to voluntarism and bourgeois charity. He had argued that the Newfoundland government must do the same as the British: regulate the economy for a total war effort and adopt policies such as a wartime profits tax to ensure that the wealthy supported the war to the same extent as working people. It was hypocritical and unpatriotic, Coaker had argued, for profiteers to oppose the conscription of their wealth even as they were beginning to support the conscription of mostly outport men for battle.

Throughout 1917, the war had provided ideological justification (patriotism) and the means (the unprecedented levels of state intervention in the economy) to achieve Coaker's goal of making government the instrument of the people, a progressive force in the development of a more equitable society. The continued sacrifices made by the Regiment on the Western Front had meant that casualty rates were outstripping voluntary enlistment rates. The spectre of the disbandment of the Regiment, combined with imperial pressure for more men at the front, had then led the Morris government to contemplate conscription. Coaker had known that the idea of conscription was unpopular with fishers, but he had seen an opportunity in Morris's efforts to build an all-party National Government that would be able to implement it. Such a government would have to take the direction of the war effort out of the hands of the NPA, and conscription of troops would have to be matched by the conscription of wealth through income and profits taxes. Even more important, by joining the government, Coaker had seen that he would gain the authority to implement regulations for the better organization of the fishery, a key component of the FPU's pre-war platform. As a minister of the subsequent National Government, Coaker had shared responsibility for the implementation of conscription in 1918 and, although this policy had forced a wedge between Coaker and his outport supporters, the FPU leader had hoped that all would be forgiven if the regulations he developed—to boost the production, quality, and marketing of fish after the war—succeeded in improving economic conditions in Newfoundland.

Coaker's regulations were not particularly radical, and his overall political platform, particularly as a member of the National Government, had essentially been that of a moderate progressive who believed that the state had a duty to intervene to protect the public interest in matters such as profiteering and industrial disputes. However, Coaker had come up against a deeply conservative mercantile community whose values reflected those of the commercial, professional, and political elites of St. John's and who rejected the right of the state to regulate beyond the bare minimum permitted in a British liberal democracy committed to a free market—unless, of course, businesses wanted the regulations in their own interests. These elites had been prepared to contribute their part to the British war effort collectively, but only through voluntarism in the form of the NPA. This emphasis on voluntarism was seen not as a weakness but as a source of great pride by people such as newspaper editor, People's Party supporter, and member of the Legislative Council P.T. McGrath, who had perceived the war effort run "by volunteer helpers, by citizens who acted for the Government and administered its funds" as a record of "patriotism and courage." McGrath declared, "It upheld, and added lustre to, the traditions of the past."[2] The NPA's inability to keep up the supply of men for the killing fields of Flanders had subsequently meant that it had to cede control over the war effort to government, and to concede that voluntary enlistment must give way to conscription, but the commercial and professional elites who had dominated the NPA remained mostly hostile to any further government regulation of the economy.

The problem Coaker had faced was that his fisheries regulations came to represent a break with traditions of the past. This representation had emerged from an intemperate and vituperative form of polemics, inspired by the rhetoric of war. In the conflict's last year, Coaker's opponents in the colonial press had taken to labelling his interest in using state mechanisms to control inflation and tax wealth as "Hunnish" or "Prussian" betrayals of the very principles that loyal and patriotic Newfoundlanders were dying for in France and Belgium.

After the war, the opposition press had kept up the propaganda war against Coaker. In their view, William Coaker was Newfoundland's own

Kaiser Bill and, somewhat contradictorily, its Comrade Coaker, leading the charge against all that was British, Christian, and decent through his "Bolshevik" attempts to regulate the fishery. Although Coaker's policies had fallen to the rhetoric of war and commemoration, he actually bore much responsibility for their failure, for he had been as quick as his enemies to pour his political spleen into the pages of the FPU's *Evening Advocate*. The FPU leader had not hesitated to label his opponents a bunch of treasonous, corrupt grafters and idiots. Then in 1920, in his capacity as minister of marine and fisheries, he had gone too far by arguing that he had the right to impose censorship on the critics of his regulations by using the War Measures Act. In doing so, Coaker had revealed that he had actually begun to embrace a more dictatorial view on the requirements of government in Newfoundland.

The failure of the Coaker regulations was significant. Fish exporters had justified abandoning them by asserting that the small dominion of Newfoundland could not hope to influence the big bad world of international fish markets. The exporters had also claimed that the undercapitalization of their firms—caused by the long years of cyclical credit overextension and business collapse that had reached a crisis point in the disastrous Bank Crash of 1894—had left them unable to resist the pressure from the banks to sell fish in disregard of the regulations. Such arguments, of course, were not only facile but condemnatory of the entire private organization of the fishing industry in Newfoundland. In Iceland and Norway, national regulation of the fishing industry in concert with a more cooperative fishing industry had succeeded in strengthening both countries' place in international markets.[3] As Rosemary Ommer pointed out in her comparative analysis of fisheries development in Newfoundland and Iceland, the very conditions exporters used in the Newfoundland case to argue against state regulation in fact demanded it.

Mercantile firms in Newfoundland, however, had shown no desire to reorganize the industry beyond their own short-term interests, and for those few who might have wanted to, the crushing burden of the past impoverishment of the industry meant that state resources would have been necessary to provide the capital and direction for an economic sector organized for the good of the colony rather than individual firms. The specific regulations Coaker had implemented in 1919–1920 and abandoned in 1920–1921 undoubtedly would have required even more support, perhaps somewhat like Coaker's proposed national banking structure—especially given that the country was facing the extremely difficult challenges of a rapidly deepening post-war international depression. Of course, the regulations did not cause the recession, but Coaker's opponents had effectively blamed them for it and accused Coaker of being dictatorial in the process. So the regulations failed in Newfoundland, while Iceland and Norway went on to use a variety of regulations to emerge from the 1930s as international leaders in the North Atlantic fishing industry.[4]

In the short term, the failure of the fisheries regulations brought profound political repercussions. Coaker had made a political alliance with Richard Squires, his old nemesis from the People's Party and the fight over the *Newfoundland* disaster, to achieve his goal of better regulation of the fishery. His facility in making common cause with former foes had allowed Coaker's opponents to portray him as an unprincipled opportunist who was willing to do anything for power, and this alleged opportunism had reinforced the image of the Prussian or Bolshevik Coaker, the despiser of the noble and sacred principles of liberal democracy and the free market that true Britons had supposedly laid down their lives for in the war. In 1923, when the scandal about bribery, misallocation of liquor revenue, and Squires henchman Alex Campbell's use of relief funds for patronage came to light, Coaker had become guilty by association, though the Hollis Walker report the next year absolved him of any wrongdoing.

By this time, Coaker had become too disillusioned by the failure of his regulations and the constant sullying of his personal reputation to continue his fight for a more progressive state. Already enjoying the trappings of personal success—a private residence in Port Union that was palatial in comparison to the nearby row houses of FPU workers, a knighthood, trips abroad, and a residence in Jamaica to name a few— Coaker began to retreat into the business of running the Union Trading Company, leaving the presidency of the FPU in 1926. Now more like the merchants he had previously fought, Coaker became remote from the hardy men of the north and lost faith in ordinary people. In the meantime, the fisheries regulations had failed and the Squires-Coaker alliance—which had supposedly been demoralizing Newfoundland politics with its overly generous and corrupt relief spending—had been overthrown by the Liberal-Labour alliance of Walter Monroe, who had run on a retrenchment and "clean up politics" campaign. However, corruption, coupled with Monroe supporters' continued bitter attacks on Coakerism, had by now done a great deal to undermine liberal democracy in Newfoundland.

The Monroe campaign had constantly exhorted Newfoundlanders to reject Coakerism by returning to the ideals of the Great War as embodied in the sacrifices made by the men of the Royal Newfoundland Regiment. Whatever complex reasons had motivated these men to enlist in the first place, the need to make sense of the horrible losses of the war through the politics of commemoration had simplified them, transforming the dead into selfless crusaders for an idealized British liberty, and veterans into foot soldiers in a new post-war battle against graft and corruption. The politics of commemoration in Newfoundland during the 1920s had encouraged veterans, and people generally, to believe that society had broken faith with those who had sacrificed overseas. In doing their duty, soldiers, sailors, forestry corps members, and nurses had set an inspiring example, and the new generation were called on to exhibit "the same kind of courage as they displayed" and to offer "the same high standard of service, applied to our everyday affairs."[5]Already having crossed swords with Squires a number of times, the veterans' organization, the GWVA, had become increasingly sympathetic to the notion that Newfoundland was adrift in a post-war morass of debased politics. While the GWVA remained officially non-partisan, prominent members supported Monroe.

The victory of Monroe and his supporters in 1924 had been pyrrhic: the almost hysterical tone of the anti-corruption campaign had done much to suggest that the task of cleaning up politics was hopeless. No less prominent people than Thomas Nangle of the Regiment and the GWVA, Coaker himself, and the editors of the capital's major daily papers had come to openly express their admiration for fascism as an alternative to the supposedly debased politics of Newfoundland. The Monroe government, which had promised to clean up politics, had failed, its members proving to be just as capable of using power for self-interest as had any government before them. By 1928, Monroe had quit and his party had fallen to another Squires-Coaker alliance.

Facing persistent domestic economic problems that were about to converge with a growing international depression, the new government had not had the means to deal with burgeoning relief and public debt. Coaker had made a half-hearted attempt at new fisheries regulations, but they had received no better mercantile support. The government had been so hampered by the burgeoning costs of servicing its debt and providing relief that it had been unable to contemplate any effective new policy initiatives. Obliged to meet its debt payments, the government had tried to cut relief. As a result, in the face of mounting public anger, Coaker had become the new apostle of retrenchment, blaming the people for being politically demoralized paupers. He had advocated a type of government that would not have to worry about popular support—a Newfoundland version of the Mussolini regime. The GWVA had not gone quite so far as to be in favour of a fascist leader, but it would have certainly agreed with Coaker about the demoralized state of the Newfoundland people. The riots of 1932 were the last straw, driving Squires from power and bringing Lord Amulree to investigate and recommend a suspension of responsible government in exchange for financial assistance to Newfoundland.

The flirtation with fascism was important, not because it was likely to succeed, but because it was an indicator of how threatened liberal democracy had been in the post-war political environment of Newfoundland. An influential theme in modern studies of British politics during the 1920s and 1930s is that, before the emergence of Oswald Mosley's British Union of Fascists, fascist movements in the United Kingdom were "quixotic and eccentric" and hardly worth explaining because of their fringe nature.[6] However, it can be argued that such fascist movements are worth studying because their failure reveals much about the political values of the time.[7] In Newfoundland, any interest in fascism was far more marginal than even the fringe movements in Britain. However, in Britain the post-war recession had been of a comparatively short duration, organized labour and the Labour Party were strong and moderate, and the Conservative Party was sound. The result of these conditions was that radical conservatives posed little real threat and attracted few to move outside of the boundaries of well-established party politics. Confidence in British liberal democracy might waver, but it did not wane. The case was much different in Newfoundland: the severity of post-war recession, the burden of public debt, and the vicious chaos of party politics came together to ensure that, by 1934, almost no confidence in local liberal democracy could be found among its people. There was, however, a great deal of confidence in British liberal democracy, to the extent that the collapse of responsible government was manifested not by a radical turn to the right but by the invitation to a British commission to come in and tidy up the political mess.

And what did this all mean for the sealers who had experienced death on the ice in 1914? In the spring of that year, Newfoundland society had seemed poised to demand not the overthrow of the existing social order but simply recognition that sealers experienced terrible treatment in their industry—that they deserved at least the protection of minimum health and safety regulations. By the late 1920s and early 1930s, however, the sealers had been reimagined. No longer were they men who had suffered appalling risks because they had no other way to earn livelihoods for their families. They had become manly thrill-seekers, the descendants of the English risk takers of the Elizabethan era who sailed out to find Newfoundland in the sixteenth century. The danger of the hunt was described as adding "zest" to an opportunity, to demonstrate that sealers sought the same risk and adventure as these explorers. Such revisionism disregarded the earlier concerns expressed by sealers, the FPU, and Coaker following the tragedies at the ice in 1914, about the need for better safety regulations in the seal hunt. The *Evening Telegram*, for example, enthused about the sealers, "Descendants of the sea dogs who could not resist the call of the unknown, they too sally forth in the same spirit, and take little count of the exposure, the discomfort or the hazards, and are concerned mainly with the opportunities which the voyage offers to display their prowess and to win out in their fight to wrest from the frozen pans the wealth which comes down from the Arctic."[8]

Such imagery had played to the masculinity embedded in the paternalism and the imperialist sense of entitlement among working men that they had a right, as Britons, to good jobs that would allow them to provide for their families—beliefs that had been so important in pre-war political culture, including that of Coaker and the FPU. In 1914, Coaker had championed sealers as a cruelly exploited group of working men who had deserved the protection of the state from shipowners and captains who cared only for their own profits and reputations as seal killers. But by 1934, Coaker had abandoned the sealers, and now yearned for a mythic past in which the strong, hardy men of the ice floes, like their fellow outport people, would rather die than yield their independence by asking the government for relief.

Newfoundland men died on two fronts between 1914 and 1918. Sealers fell in their masters' reckless and careless pursuit of profits in the seal hunt. Soldiers fell on many battle fronts during the Great War, but most notably at Beaumont Hamel in 1916. It was, however, liberal democracy in Newfoundland that was the final casualty in the bitter struggles over the meaning of these events. The autonomy of the Dominion of Newfoundland, which had ostensibly strengthened since the conclusion of the war, ended suddenly with the death knell of responsible government in 1934.

NOTES

INTRODUCTION

1. See, for example, the entry "front" in Judy Pearsall and Bill Trumble, eds., *The Oxford English Reference Dictionary*, 2nd ed. (Oxford: Oxford University Press, 1996), 557.

2. "Front," in G.M. Story, W.J. Kirwin, and J.D.A. Widdowson, eds., *Dictionary of Newfoundland English* (Toronto: University of Toronto Press, 1982), 203.

3. The notion that the rugged nature of seal hunters supposedly helped to define a special Newfoundland character had been a part of the local nationalist sentiments that developed in the late nineteenth century. It became very popular in the 1920s and found expression in George Allan England's *Vikings of the Ice: Being the Log of a Tenderfoot on the Great Newfoundland Seal Hunt* (Garden City, N.Y.: Doubleday, Page & Co., 1924). On the earlier nationalism, see James K. Hiller, "Robert Bond and the Pink, White and Green: Newfoundland Nationalism in Perspective," *Acadiensis*, 36, 2 (2007), 113–33.

4. The work first appeared in serial form in 1972 in select British, Australian, American, and Norwegian newspapers and magazines. I use the edition published by Doubleday in Toronto, 1974. Brown wrote the book, later in association with Harold Horwood, the troubled relationship and context of which are explored in Nancy Earle, "*Death on the Ice* and the Newfoundland Imaginary: Print Culture on the Periphery," *Papers of the Bibliographical Society of Canada*, 48, 1 (Spring 2010), 119–52; the popular culture of the seal hunt is summarized in Shannon Ryan, *The Ice Hunters: A History of Newfoundland Sealing to 1914* (St. John's: Breakwater, 1994), 368–96.

5. David R. Facey-Crowther, "Introduction," in Facey-Crowther, ed., *Lieutenant Owen William Steele of the Newfoundland Regiment: Diary and Letters* (Montreal and Kingston: McGill-Queen's University Press, 2002), 10.

6. G.W.L. Nicholson, *The Fighting Newfoundlander: A History of the Royal Newfoundland Regiment* (St. John's: Government of Newfoundland and Labrador, 1964), 283.

7. Ambivalence is not confined to the relationship between the province and Canada. Labradorians often feel the same sentiment about their place within the province, which did not officially become the Province of Newfoundland and Labrador until 2001. Before that, the colony, dominion, and later province were usually termed "Newfoundland," a usage reflected in most of the sources used for this book and which I will follow throughout the rest of the text unless referring specifically to matters related to Labrador.

8. Kirk Squires, "Finally," guest commentary, *Advertiser*, Grand Falls-Windsor, 10 July 2006, A11; Ernest S. Parsons, "Don't Call it Canada Day," letter to the editor, *Telegram*, St. John's, 8 July 2007, A6; Janice Wells, "A Wonderful Weekend in Town," *Telegram*, St. John's, 7 July 2012, F6.

9. Parks Canada, *The Price We Paid for Nationhood: Beaumont-Hamel and Vimy Ridge* (Ottawa: Parks Canada, 2010); Jonathan Vance, "Battle Verse: Poetry and Nationalism after Vimy Ridge," in Geoffrey Hayes, Andre Iarocci and Mike Bechtold, eds., *Vimy Ridge: A Canadian Reassessment* (Waterloo, ON: Wilfrid Laurier University Press, 2007), 265–78; Tim Cook, *Clio's Warriors: Canadian Historians and the Writing of the World Wars* (Vancouver: UBC Press, 2006), 250.

10. *Daily News*, 18 April 1917 (all newspapers cited were published in St. John's unless otherwise noted); MacKenzie, "Eastern Approaches," 356. For a recent, succinct and excellent statement of the commonalties of the Beaumont Hamel and Vimy Ridge components of national mythologies, see Sarah Glassford and Amy Shaw, "Introduction: Transformation in a Time of War?" in Glassford and Shaw, eds., *A Sisterhood of Suffering and Service: Women and Girls of Canada and Newfoundland During the First World War* (Vancouver: UBC Press, 2012), 2–3.

11. "The Anti-Confederate Song," Newfoundland and Labrador Heritage Website, www.heritage.nf.ca/law/song.html; accessed 28/01/2013.

12. "Dalton, Thomas," *Dictionary of Canadian Biography Online* [hereafter DCB], www.biographi.ca/009004-119.01-e.php?id_nbr=3342, accessed 28/01/2013; on Boulton in Newfoundland, see Sean T. Cadigan, *Hope and Deception in Conception Bay: Merchant-Settler Relations In Newfoundland, 1785–1855* (Toronto: University of Toronto Press, 1995), 141–61; Stephen J. Hornsby, *Nineteenth-Century Cape Breton: A Historical Geography* (Montreal and Kingston: McGill-Queen's University Press, 1992), 59–62; Kurt Korneski, "Development and Degradation: The Emergence and Collapse of the Lobster Fishery on Newfoundland's West Coast, 1856–1924," *Acadiensis*, 41, 1 (2012), 21–48; Terry Quinlan and Sean Cadigan, "A New Look at Confederation: Shifting Population Dynamics and Newfoundland's Relationship with Canada, 1869–1949," in Gordon Darroch, ed., *The Dawn of Canada's Century: Hidden Histories* Essay collection submitted to McGill-Queen's University Press, 2011, in press. For broader statements about Newfoundland's pre-1949 connections with Canada, see Malcolm MacLeod, *Connections: Newfoundland's Pre-confederation Links with Canada and the World* (St. John's: Creative, 2003).

13. David Macfarlane, *The Danger Tree: Memory, War, and the Search for a Family's Past* (Toronto: Macfarlane Walter and Ross, 1991), 137.

14. Richard Hibbs, *Who's Who in and from Newfoundland 1927* (St. John's: Richard Hibbs, 1927), 43–5. David Mackenzie has used slightly different figures which suggest that 5046 Newfoundlanders and Labradorians served in battle with the Royal Newfoundland Regiment, and there were 3565 casualties, including 1281 deaths. Overall, he argues, "a front-line Newfoundland soldier had a 70 per cent chance of being killed or wounded during the war." See Mackenzie, "Eastern Approaches: Maritime Canada and Newfoundland," in Mackenzie, ed., *Canada and the First World War* (Toronto: University of Toronto Press, 2005), 356–7. As we shall see, there are often variations in the exact numbers official and scholarly sources provide, but these variations should not distract us from the important point about the scale of the tragedies that will be discussed.

15. Direct quote from Mackenzie, "Eastern Approaches," 352.

16. Robert J. Harding, "Glorious Tragedy: Newfoundland's Cultural Memory of the Attack at Beaumont Hamel, 1916–1925," *Newfoundland and Labrador Studies*, 21, 1 (2006), 24–5.

17. It is difficult to be precise about the number of nurses who served overseas. The Newfoundland Department of Militia only had records of nurses who reported to the Pay and Record Office in London during the war. There appear to have been more who did not report. See Library and Archives Canada, Veterans Affairs Fonds, RG 38, vol. 439, W.V. Rendell, Chief Staff Officer, Department of Militia, to Director of Medical Services, St. John's, 25 March 1919 (my thanks to Mark Humphries for sharing these files with me).

18. The reassessment began with Jim Overton, "Economic Crisis and the End of Democracy: Politics in Newfoundland During the Great Depression." *Labour/ Le Travail*, 26 (1990), 85–124; and Gene Long, *Suspended State: Newfoundland Before Canada* (St. John's: Breakwater, 1999). The scholarly assessments they responded to were primarily S.J.R. Noel, *Politics in Newfoundland* (Toronto: University of Toronto Press, 1971), 212–20; and R.M. Elliott, "Newfoundland Politics in the 1920s: The Genesis and Significance of the Hollis Walker Enquiry," in Hiller and Neary, *Newfoundland in the Nineteenth and Twentieth Centuries*, 181–204.

19. Hew Strachan, *The First World War: Volume I, To Arms* (Oxford: Oxford University Press, 2001), 5–101; Ian F.W. Beckett, *The Great War, 1914–1918*, 2nd ed. (Harlow, Eng.: Pearson, 2007), 22–54.

20. Quotes from Joy B. Cave, *What Became of Corporal Pittman?* (St. John's: Breakwater, 1976), 153–7.

21. Modris Eksteins, *Rites of Spring: The Great War and the Birth of the Modern Age* (Toronto: Lester and Orpen Dennys, 1994), 68–90, 117–43, 175–9.

22. E.P. Morris, *Report of Sir Edward Morris, Prime Minister of Newfoundland, on his Visit to the Newfoundland Soldiers at the Front in France, July, 1916, Made to His Excellency Sir W.E. Davidson, KCMG, Governor* (St. John's: Herald Print 1916), 13.

23. Stanzas two, four and five, Frederick B. Wood, "O England, Our Brave England," *Newfoundland Quarterly*, 17, 1 (1917), 23; "Wood, Frederick Barnes," *ENL, V*, 613.

24. The case for disillusionment was most notably made by Paul Fussell, *The Great War and Modern Memory* (Oxford: Oxford University Press, 1975); for the view that a revised sense of duty rather than disillusionment was the experience of the trenches, see Eksteins, *Rites of Spring*, 179–85.

25. Mark Osborne Humphries, *The Last Plague: Spanish Influenza and the Politics of Public Health in Canada* (Toronto: University of Toronto Press, 2012), 8–9, 132–3, 155, 189–96; Gregory Kealey, "State Repression of Labour and the Left in Canada, 1914–20: The Impact of the First World War," *Canadian Historical Review* 73, no. 3 (1992), 281–314. On Flavelle, see Michael Bliss, *A Canadian Millionaire: the Life and Times of Sir Joseph Flavelle, Bart., 1858–1939* (Toronto: Macmillan, 1978).

26. James Naylor, *The New Democracy: Challenging the Social Order in Industrial Ontario* (Toronto: University of Toronto Press, 1991), 4–39, 345–7.

27. Craig Heron and Myer Siemiatycki, "The Great War, the State, and Working-Class Canada," in Heron, ed., *The Workers' Revolt in Canada, 1917–1925* (Toronto: University of Toronto Press, 1998), 11–36; John Herd Thompson with Allen Seager, *Canada 1929–1939: Decades of Discord* (Toronto: McClelland and Stewart, 1985), 19, 27–8, 35–6.

28. Judith Fingard, "The Prevention of Cruelty, Marriage Breakdown and the Rights of Wives in Nova Scotia, 1880–1900," in Janet Guildford and Suzanne Morton, eds., *Separate Spheres: Women's Worlds in the 19th-Century Maritimes* (Fredericton: Acadiensis Press, 1994), 211–32; Colin Howell, "The 1900s: Industry, Urbanization, and Reform," and Ian McKay, "The Stillborn Triumph of Progressive Reform," in E.R. Forbes and D.A. Muise, eds., *The Atlantic Provinces in Confederation* (Toronto and Fredericton: University of Toronto Press/Acadiensis Press, 1993), 155–91, 192–233; Christina Simmons, "'Helping the Poorer Sisters': The Women of the Jost Mission, Halifax, 1905–1945," *Acadiensis*, 14, 1 (1984), 3–27; Ernest R. Forbes, "Prohibition and the Social Gospel in Nova Scotia," in Forbes, *Challenging the Regional Stereotype: Essays on the 20th Century Maritimes* (Fredericton: Acadiensis Press, 1989), 13–40; Michael Boudreau, "'There is ... no pernicious dualism between sacred and secular': Nova Scotia Baptists and the Social Gospel, 1880–1914," *Nova Scotia Historical Review*, 16, 1 (1996), 109–31; Ramsay Cook, *The Regenerators: Social Criticism in Late Victorian English Canada* (Toronto: University of Toronto Press, 1985); Phyllis D. Airhart, *Serving the Present Age: Revivalism, Progressivism, and the Methodist Tradition in Canada* (Montreal and Kingston: McGill-Queen's University Press, 1992), 104–22; Nancy Christie and Michael Gauvreau, *A Full-Orbed Christianity: The Protestant Churches and Social Welfare in Canada, 1900–1940* (Montreal and Kingston: McGill-Queen's University Press, 1996); Michael McGerr, *A Fierce Discontent: The Rise and Fall of the Progressive Movement in America, 1870–1920* (New York: Free Press, 2003).

29. The experience of industrial legality in the age of "industrial voluntarism" is much more complex than this brief summary statement suggests. See Judy Fudge and Eric Tucker, *Labour Before the Law: The Regulation of Workers' Collective Action*

in Canada, 1900–1948 (Toronto: University of Toronto Press, 2004), 16–138; the most extensive study of the industrial disputes investigation acts of the era is Paul Craven, *"An Impartial Umpire": Industrial Relations and the Canadian State 1900–1911* (Toronto: University of Toronto Press, 1980). For a critical perspective, see Bryan D. Palmer, *Working-Class Experience: Rethinking the History of Canadian Labour, 1800–1991* (Toronto: McClelland & Stewart, 1992), 205–7.

30. Crain Heron, "Introduction," in Heron, *Workers' Revolt*, 3–7.
31. Ian McKay and Suzanne Morton, "The Maritimes: Expanding the Circle of Resistance," in Heron, *Workers' Revolt*, 44.
32. *Morning Advocate*, 3 January 1917.
33. Humphries, *The Last Plague*, 8–9, 132–3, 155, 189–96.
34. Jonathan F. Vance, *Death So Noble: Memory, Meaning, and the First World War* (Vancouver: UBC Press, 1997), 9–20, 27–55, 73–4, 111–125, 157, 201–32; Eksteins, *Rites of Spring*, 185, 253–93; Beckett, *Great War*, 344–436.
35. Two explanations about the nature of the argument that follows are in order. First, the place of Labrador in the Colony or Dominion of Newfoundland and the role of Labradorians in the colony's war effort have been poorly served by the histories of this era. For much of the period under discussion here, Newfoundlanders treated Labrador as a coastal area where they could find fish to catch, but otherwise took very little responsibility for the provision of government services. Island interest in Labrador had been growing since the 1890s due to a Canadian–Newfoundland dispute over boundaries that resolved in 1927 with the current boundaries between Quebec and Newfoundland and Labrador. However, most Newfoundlanders continued to think of Labrador primarily as a storehouse of natural resources awaiting development or sale for the island's benefit. Labradorians are largely invisible as a distinct group in studies of Newfoundland's war effort, except when they served as instances of romantic and ethnically stereotypical curiosity, such as in emphasis on the sniper abilities of Lance Corporal John Shiwak. Shiwak, an Inuk member of the Royal Newfoundland Regiment from Rigolet, was killed in a shell attack during the Battle of Cambrai. See Francis Patey, *Veterans of the North* (St. John's: Creative, 2003), 57. Patey's documentation of Labradorians and people from the Northern Peninsula is a useful tool from which to begin an assessment of Labrador's war effort. Second, the lack of a manufacturing base, especially in areas related to munitions and war material production, means that there was much less concern about the possibility that war might have been changing the role of women in Newfoundland and Labrador society. It may be that women engaged in more work of the fishery as a result of men going to war, but women were already highly integrated into household fish production. The economic roles of working women remained otherwise largely unchanged. Bourgeois women played vital roles in domestic support for the war effort, largely as an outgrowth of their roles in pre-war moral reform. Such roles contributed to women's suffrage. See Gale D. Warren, "Voluntarism and Patriotism: Newfoundland Women's War Work During the First World War," unpublished MA research paper, Memorial University, 2005. However, aside from a consideration of the significance of the suffrage debate in the politics of commemoration, the roles of women, like those of Labradorians, are not the direct objects of the following study.

ONE: THE NATURE OF NEWFOUNDLAND AND LABRADOR

1. Except where otherwise cited, this chapter is based on Sean T. Cadigan, *Newfoundland and Labrador: A History* (Toronto: University of Toronto Press, 2009), 3–184; Cadigan, "'But for the Loves of the Fishes': Maritime Labour and Ecological Culture in Nineteenth-Century Newfoundland," in Richard Gorski, ed., *Maritime Labour: Contributions to the History of Work at Sea, 1500–2000* (Amsterdam: Uitgeverij Aksant, 2008), 105–28; and Cadigan, "The Newfoundland of David Blackwood: A Historical Setting," in Katharine Lochnan, ed., *Black Ice: David Blackwood Prints of Newfoundland* (Vancouver, Toronto, Berkeley: Douglas & McIntyre, 2011), 71–96.

2. James K. Hiller, "Utrecht Revisited: The Origins of French Fishing Rights in Newfoundland Waters," *Newfoundland Studies*, 7, 1 (1991), 23–39; Hiller, "The Newfoundland Fisheries Issue in Anglo-French Treaties, 1713–1904," *Journal of Imperial and Commonwealth History*, 24, 1 (1996), 1–23.

3. Shannon Ryan, "Fishery to Colony: A Newfoundland Watershed, 1793–1815," *Acadiensis* 12, 2 (1983): 34–52.

4. Peter E. Pope, *Fish into Wine: The Newfoundland Plantation in the Seventeenth Century* (Chapel Hill and London: University of North Carolina Press, 2004), makes the case for the early success of the English fishery at Newfoundland in transatlantic commerce.

5. Cadigan, *Hope and Deception*, 37–50, 109–11, 148–50; James K. Hiller, "The Newfoundland Credit System: An Interpretation," in Rosemary E. Ommer, ed., *Merchant Credit and Labour Strategies in Historical Perspective* (Fredericton, NB: Acadiensis Press, 1990), 86–101.

6. Sean T. Cadigan, "The Moral Economy of the Commons: Ecology and Equity in the Newfoundland Cod Fishery, 1815–1855," *Labour/Le Travail*, 43 (Spring 1999), 9–43.

7. Cadigan, *Hope and Deception in Conception Bay*, 37–63.

8. See R. Pastore, "Fishermen, Furriers, and Beothuks: The Economy of Extinction," *Man in the Northeast*, 33 (1987), 47–60; Pastore, "The Collapse of the Beothuk World," *Acadiensis*, 19, 1 (Fall, 1989), 52–71; P. Pope, "Scavengers and Caretakers: Beothuk/European Settlement Dynamics in Seventeenth-Century Newfoundland," *Newfoundland Studies*, 9, 2 (1993), 279–93; I. Marshall, *A History and Ethnography of the Beothuk* (Montreal and Kingston: McGill-Queen's University Press, 1996), *passim*; Donald H. Holly, "The Beothuk on the Eve of their Extinction," *Arctic Anthropology*, 37, 1 (2000), 79–95; Holly, "Environment, History, and Agency in Storage Adaptation: On the Beothuk in the 18th Century," *Canadian Journal of Archaeology*, 22, 1 (1998), 101–22.

9. Ryan, *The Ice Hunters: A History of Newfoundland Sealing to 1914* (St. John's: Breakwater, 1994), 98–100, 105–06, 111–17.

10. Ryan, *Ice Hunters*, 121–9.

11. Philip Tocque, *Wandering Thoughts: or, Solitary Hours* (London, 1846), p. 196.

12. Ryan, *Ice Hunters*, 243–327.

13. Cadigan, *Hope and Deception*, Chapter 6.

14. Cadigan, *Hope and Deception*, 116–7; Little, "Collective Action," 25–31.

15. The best recent study of Methodism in Newfoundland is Calvin Hollett, *Shouting, Embracing, and Dancing with Ecstasy: The Growth of Methodism in Newfoundland, 1774–1874* (Montreal: McGill-Queen's University Press, 2010).

16. Cadigan and J.A. Hutchings, "Nineteenth-Century Expansion of the Newfoundland Fishery for Atlantic Cod: An Exploration of Underlying Causes," *The Exploited Seas: New Directions for Marine Environmental History*, in P. Holm, T.D. Smith, and D.J. Starkey, eds. (St. John's: International Association for Maritime History/Census of Marine Life, 2001), 31–65; Cadigan, "Failed Proposals for Fisheries Management and Conservation in Newfoundland, 1855–1880," in Dianne Newell and Rosemary Ommer, eds., *Fishing Places, Fishing People: Traditions and Issues in Canadian Small-Scale Fisheries* (Toronto: University of Toronto Press, 1999), 147–69.

17. C.W. Sanger, "Technological and Spatial Adaptation in the Newfoundland Seal Fishery During the Nineteenth Century," Unpublished MA thesis, Memorial University of Newfoundland, 1973, 12–53; C.W. Sanger, "The Dundee–St. John's Connection: Nineteenth-Century Interlinkages Between Scottish Arctic Whaling and the Newfoundland Seal Fishery," *Newfoundland Studies* 4, 1 (1988), 1; Ryan, *Ice Hunters*, 98–100, 105–06, 111–17.

18. Ryan, *Ice Hunters*, 65–105, 213–63; Eric W. Sager, *Seafaring Labour: The Merchant Marine of Atlantic Canada, 1820–1914* (Montreal and Kingston: McGill-Queen's University Press, 1989), 44–51.

19. Abram Kean, ed. by Shannon Ryan, *Old and Young Ahead*, 1935 (St. John's: Flanker Press, 2000), 1–9, 29; "Kean, Abram," *Encyclopedia of Newfoundland and Labrador* [hereafter *ENL*], *III* (St. John's: Newfoundland Book Publishers, 1991), 155–6; Peter Bowring, *A Thicket of Business: A History of the Bowring Family and the Bowring Group of Companies* (Stanhope, Weardale, County Durham: The Memoir Club, 2007), 14–142; David Keir, *The Bowring Story* (London: The Bodley Head, 1962); "Bowring, Sir Edgar Rennie," *ENL, I*, 233.

20. Eric W. Sager, "The Merchants of Water Street and Capital Investment in Newfoundland's Traditional Economy," in L.R. Fischer and Sager, ed., *The Enterprising Canadians* (St. John's: Maritime History Group, MUN, 1979), 75–96; "Harvey Group of Companies," *ENL, II*, 847–8.

21. Eric Winsor, "History of Wesleyville," paper on deposit at the Center for Newfoundland Studies, Memorial University of Newfoundland, 1975, 26–7.

22. Ryan, *Ice Hunters*, 306–17.

23. Kurt Korneski, "Race, Gender, Class, and Colonial Nationalism: Railway Development in Newfoundland, 1881–1898," *Labour / Le Travail*, 62 (2008): 79–107.

24. James K. Hiller, "Robert Bond and the Pink, White and Green: Newfoundland Nationalism in Perspective," *Acadiensis*, 36, 2 (2007), 124.

25. Newfoundland, *Census of Newfoundland and Labrador, 1901, vol. 1* (St. John's: J.W. Withers, 1903), Table C, "Population by Districts."

26. Mark C. Hunter, *To Employ and Uplift Them: The Newfoundland Naval Reserve, 1899–1926* (St. John's: ISER, 2009), 2–4, 21–73.

27. Sager, "The Merchants of Water Street," 75–96; David Alexander, "Development and Dependence in Newfoundland, 1880–1970," in Alexander, compiled by Eric W. Sager, Lewis R. Fischer, and Stuart O. Pierson, *Atlantic Canada and Confederation: Essays in Canadian Political Economy* (Toronto: University of Toronto Press, 1983), 3–32; J.K. Hiller, "The Origins of the Pulp and Paper Industry in Newfoundland," *Acadiensis*, 11, 2 (1982), 42–68.

28. Briton Cooper Busch, "The Newfoundland Sealers' Strike of 1902," *Labour/Le Travail*, 14 (Fall 1984), 73–101.

29. Ryan, *Ice Hunters*, 213–71.

30. Naboth Winsor, "'By Their Works.' A History of the Wesleyville Congregation, Methodist Church—1874–1925, United Church—1925–1974," 1976, 4–18, paper on deposit at the Center for Newfoundland Studies, Memorial University of Newfoundland.

31. Sandra Beardsall, "Methodist Religious Practices in Outport Newfoundland," unpublished Th.D., University of Victoria and the University of Toronto, 1996, 59, 88.

32. Eric W. Sager and John J. Mannion, "Sea and Livelihood in Atlantic Canada," and Murdo MacPherson and Douglas Campbell, "Religious Adherence," in Donald Kerr and Deryck W. Holdsworth, eds., *Historical Atlas of Canada, III: Addressing the Twentieth Century* (Toronto: University of Toronto Press, 1990), plates 23, 34.

33. "Water Street," *ENL*, V, 512–16.

34. Fred Winsor, "The Newfoundland Bank Fishery: Government Policies and the Struggle to Improve Bank Fishing Crews' Working, Health, and Safety Conditions, 1876–1920," PhD thesis, Memorial University of Newfoundland, 1996, 45–9; David A. Macdonald, "They Cannot Pay Us in Money: Newman and Company and the Supplying System in the Newfoundland Fishery, 1850–1884," in Rosemary Ommer, ed., *Merchant Credit and Labour Strategies in Historical Perspective* (Fredericton, NB: Acadiensis Press, 1990), 114–28; Raoul Anderson, "'Chance' and Contract: Lessons from a Newfoundland Banks Fisherman's Anecdote," in the same volume, 167–82.

35. Barbara Neis, "A Sociological Analysis of the Factors Responsible for the Regional Distribution of the Fishermen's Protective Union of Newfoundland" MA thesis, Memorial University of Newfoundland, 1980, *passim*. See also "Fishermen's Protective Union (F.P.U.)," *ENL, II*, 180–86; Winsor, "Newfoundland Bank Fishery," 65.

36. Patrick O'Flaherty, *Lost Country: The Rise and Fall of Newfoundland, 1843–1933* (St. John's: Long Beach Press, 2005), 249–51.

37. *The Fishermen's Advocate*, 3 June 1911.

38. Ian D.H. McDonald, ed. by J.K. Hiller, *"To Each His Own": William Coaker and the Fishermen's Protective Union in Newfoundland Politics, 1908–1925* (St. John's: ISER, 1987), 15–17; Gerald Panting, "'The People' in Politics," in Robert H. Cuff, ed., *A Coaker Anthology* (St. John's: Creative, 1986), 71–8.

39. Naboth Winsor, *The Sea, Our Life–Blood: A History of Wesleyville, Newfoundland* (Gander: BSC Printers, 1984), 112.

40. McDonald, *To Each His Own*, 25–33; "Port Union," *ENL, IV,* 401–2.

41. William C. Gilmore, *Newfoundland and Dominion Status: The External Affairs Competence and International Law Status of Newfoundland, 1855–1934* (Toronto: Carswell, 1988), 2–37.

42. Robert G. Hong, "'An Agency for the Common Weal': The Newfoundland Board of Trade, 1909–1915," MA thesis, Memorial University of Newfoundland, 1998, 20–49, 80–139.

43. The preceding discussion of the FPU in politics is based largely on McDonald, *To Each His Own*, 33–47.

TWO: THE *NEWFOUNDLAND* SEALING DISASTER, SPRING 1914

1. Ryan, *Ice Hunters*, 360–2.

2. "*Southern Cross*, S.S.," *ENL, V,* 242; for a comparative study of the *Newfoundland* and *Southern Cross* disasters, see Warren Oliver Bush, "Industrial Disasters at Sea Around Newfoundland and Historicizing Maritime Peril: 1914–1918," MA thesis, Memorial University of Newfoundland, 2012, 41–111.

3. "*Stephano*, S.S.," *ENL, V,* 302.

4. Brown, *Death on the Ice*, 3.

5. James E. Candow, *Of Men and Seals: A History of the Newfoundland Seal Hunt* (Ottawa: Environment Canada, Canadian Parks Service, 1989), 89; John Feltham, *Sealing Steamers* (St. John's: Cuff Publications, 1995), 99–102; Ryan, *Ice Hunters*, 150; "*Newfoundland*, S.S.," *ENL, IV,* 65–6.

6. "Tuff, George," *ENL, V,* 436–7; Brown, *Death on the Ice*, 22–3.

7. Brown, *Death on the Ice*, 66–8.

8. Brown, *Death on the Ice*, 68–75, 105–05.

9. Brown, *Death on the Ice*, 84–95.

10. Sandra Flueriau, "Sealing Disaster of 1914," Memorial University of Newfoundland Folklore and Language Archive, Unpublished paper, 1978, MA 78–391, 10.

11. Brown, *Death on the Ice*, 97–102.

12. Brown, *Death on the Ice*, 156–8.

13. Flueriau, "Sealing Disaster," 13.

14. In addition to Brown, *Death on the Ice*, this account relies on Ryan, *Ice Hunters*, 311–15. On the relationship between McCarthy and Hiscock, see the interview with McCarthy's daughter discussed in Joan Moriarity, "Memoirs of a Daughter," Memorial University of Newfoundland Folklore and Language Archive, Unpublished paper, 1979, MA 79–240, 6–11.

15. Quotes from *Daily Mail*, 3 April 1914.

16. *Daily News*, 3 April 1914.

17. Melvin Baker, "President Coaker's Log of His Trip to the Ice Floe last Spring in S.S. *Nascopie*," *Newfoundland and Labrador Studies*, 25, 2 (2010), 217–52, quotes from 235–7, 239; see also Ryan, *Ice Hunters*, 366–8; Candow, *Of Men and Seals*, 89.

18. *Evening Herald*, 2 April 1914.

19. *Daily Mail*, 3 April 1914.

20. *Evening Telegram*, 4 April 1914.

21. *Daily News*, 4 April 1914, quote from 6 April 1914; *Daily Mail*, 6 April 1914; W. David Parsons and E. Parsons, *The Best Small-Boat Seamen in the Navy: Newfoundland Royal Naval Reserve, 1800–1922* (St. John's: DRC Publishing, 2009), 44–5.

22. "Topsail, C.B.," *Diocesan Magazine* (June 1914), 86.

23. *Daily Mail*, 4 April 1914.

24. Quote from *Daily News*, 3 April 1914. On the newspaper, see Suzanne Ellison, *Historical Directory of Newfoundland and Labrador Newspapers, 1807–1987* (St. John's: Memorial University of Newfoundland Library, 1988), 35–6.

25. *Daily News*, 4 April 1914.

26. *Daily News*, 4 April 1914.

27. *Evening Herald*, 6 April 1914.

28. *Daily News*, 6 April 1914.

29. *Daily Mail*, 6 April 1914; *Daily News*, 6 April, quote from 7 April 1914.

30. *Evening Herald*, 9 April 1914.

31. *Daily Mail*, 6 April 1914, quote from 9 April 1914.

32. Kean, *Old and Young Ahead*, 31.

33. "Davidson, Sir Walter Edward," *ENL, I*, 595.

34. *Daily News*, 8 April 1914.

35. *Daily News*, 13 April 1914.

36. "Notes from the Editor," and "Bonavista," *Diocesan Magazine* (May 1914), 65, 68.

37. *Daily Mail*, 11 April 1914.

38. *Daily Mail*, 13 April 1914.

39. "Lloyd, William Frederick," *ENL, III*, 350–1; "Hutchings, Charles Henry," *ENL, III*, 11; "Warren, William Robertson," *ENL, V*, 511–12.

40. *Daily News*, 13 April 1914.

41. *Daily News*, 13 April 1914.

42. *Daily News*, 14 April 1914.

43. Brown, *Death on the Ice*, 249–54.

44. *Daily Mail*, 14 April 1914.

45. *Daily Mail*, 15 April 1914. For a semi-fictional account of the Coakers' family life, see Carmelita McGrath, with Sharon Halfyard, ed., by Marion Cheeks, *To Be My*

Father's Daughter (St. John's: Educational Resource Development Cooperative, 2008).

46. *Daily Mail*, 15 April 1914.

47. *Daily Mail*, 16 April 1914.

48. *Daily News*, 16 April 1914.

49. *Evening Herald*, 16 April 1914.

50. *Daily News*, 17 April 1914.

51. Noel, *Politics in Newfoundland*, 137; Hiller, "Squires, Sir Richard Anderson," *DCB*, forthcoming.

52. *Daily Mail*, 21 April 1914.

53. *Daily News*, 22 April 1914.

54. *Daily Mail*, 27 April 1914.

55. *Daily Mail*, 15 April 1914.

56. *Evening Herald*, 13 May 1914.

57. *Daily News*, 27 May 1914.

58. The Rooms Provincial Archives Division, GN 121, Royal Commission of Enquiry into the Sealing Disasters of 1914, Box 1, File GN 121.45, "Magisterial Enquiry Report," submitted by A.W. Knight to Attorney General R.A. Squires, St. John's, 16 May 1914, 7.

59. *Daily News*, 28 May 1914.

60. *Mail and Advocate*, 27 May 1914.

61. *Mail and Advocate*, 28 May 1914.

62. *Evening Telegram*, 29 May 1914.

63. *Mail and Advocate*, 16 June 1914. On the *Evening Telegram*, see Ellison, *Newfoundland Newspapers*, 43.

64. "Newtown," *Diocesan Magazine* (July 1914), 102–3.

65. Ryan, *Ice Hunters*, 318.

66. "Address of the Lord Bishop of Newfoundland at the Opening of the Twenty-first Session of the Diocesan Synod, Tuesday, June 23rd, 1914," *Diocesan Magazine* (August 1914), 114–5.

THREE: WAR, 1914–1915

1. *Mail and Advocate*, 7 August 1914.

2. *Evening Telegram*, 7, 14 August 1914; *Mail and Advocate*, 1 September 1914.

3. *Daily News*, 11 August 1914.

4. *Daily News*, 13 August 1914.

5. Hunter, *To Employ and Uplift Them*, 96–99.

6. Mike O'Brien, "Out of a Clear Sky: The Mobilization of the Newfoundland Regiment, 1914–1915," *Newfoundland and Labrador Studies*, 22, 2 (2007), 404;

Nicholson, *Fighting Newfoundlander*, 89–91, 101; CO 194, vol. 288, 1914, f. 374, Davidson to Lewis Harcourt, St. John's, 21 August 1914.

7. James K. Hiller, "Morris, Edward Patrick, 1st Baron Morris," *Dictionary of Canadian Biography*, forthcoming.

8. Nicholson, *Fighting Newfoundlander*, 93–97, 102–03.

9. "Outerbridge, Joseph," *ENL, IV*, 191.

10. "Franklin, Lt.-Col. William H." *ENL, II*, 391.

11. The Rooms Provincial Archives Division, MG 136, Sir Walter Davidson fonds, Box 1, File 136.8, "War Diary 29 July–7 August 1914," 17 August, quote from 18 August 1914.

12. "Patriotic Association, Newfoundland," *ENL, IV*, 234, O'Brien, "Clear Blue Sky," 405.

13. *Daily News*, 18 August 1914; Jessie Chisholm, "Organizing on the Waterfront: The St. John's Longshoremen's Protective Union (LSPU), 1890–1914," *Labour/Le Travail*, 26 (Fall 1990), 37–59.

14. *Mail and Advocate*, 15, 21 August 1914.

15. *Daily News*, 19 August 1914.

16. *Daily News*, 24 August 1914.

17. Patricia R. O'Brien, "The Newfoundland Patriotic Association: The Administration of the War Effort, 1914–1918," unpublished MA thesis, Memorial University of Newfoundland, 1981, 1–38.

18. "Outerbridge, Joseph," *ENL, IV*, 191.

19. Nicholson, *Fighting Newfoundlander*, 104.

20. Mike O'Brien, "Clear Blue Sky," 411.

21. Patricia O'Brien, "Newfoundland Patriotic Association," 38–50.

22. *Evening Telegram*, 22 August 1914.

23. Margot I. Duley, *Where Once Our Mothers Stood We Stand: Women's Suffrage in Newfoundland, 1890–1925* (Charlottetown, PEI: Gynergy Books, 1993), 13–54; Gale D. Warren, "Voluntarism and Patriotism: Newfoundland Women's War Work during the First World War," unpublished MA research essay, Memorial University, 2005, 27; Duley, *Where Once Our Mothers Stood*, 69–70.

24. *Daily News*, 1 September 1914.

25. Patricia O'Brien, "Newfoundland Patriotic Association," 46.

26. *Mail and Advocate*, 1, 18 September 1914; S.J.R. Noel, *Politics in Newfoundland* (Toronto: University of Toronto Press, 1971), 120–22; "Bishop, Robert K.," *ENL, I*, 197.

27. Martin Middlebrook, *The First Day on the Somme, 1 July 1916* (London: Allen Lane The Penguin Press, 1971), xvii. On the Canadian situation, see John Sweetenham, *To Seize the Victory: The Canadian Corps in World War I* (Toronto: Ryerson Press, 1965), 21–40.

28. Christopher A. Sharpe, "The 'Race of Honour': An Analysis of Enlistments and Casualties in the Armed Forces of Newfoundland: 1914–1918," *Newfoundland*

Studies, 4, 1 (1988), 40; Chris Martin, "The Right Course, The Best Course, The Only Course: Voluntary Recruitment in the Newfoundland Regiment, 1914–1918," *Newfoundland and Labrador Studies*, 24, 1 (2009), 55–89.

29. A.J. Stacey, edited by Jean Edwards Stacey, *Memoirs of a Blue Puttee: The Newfoundland Regiment in World War One* (St. John's: DRC, 2002), 17–8.

30. Mike O'Brien, "Clear Blue Sky," 407–09.

31. Sharpe, "Race of Honour," 33–7.

32. Stacey, *Memoirs of a Blue Puttee*, 18.

33. David Dawe, "Newfoundland in World War I (As Seen Through the Eyes of an Enlisted Man)," Unpublished paper, Centre for Newfoundland Studies, QEII Library, MUN, date unknown but between 1963 and 1981, 3.

34. Stacey, *Memoirs of a Blue Puttee*, 18.

35. Gary F. Browne, *Forget-Me-Not: Fallen Boy Soldiers, Royal Newfoundland Regiment, World War One* (St. John's: DRC Publishing, 2010), 1–15; Brenda M. Rowsell, "William Yetman: Reflections of the Past," unpublished paper, Memorial University of Newfoundland Folklore and Language Archive, 1981, MAN 81–415, 2–5.

36. Nicholson, *Fighting Newfoundlander*, 105–12; quote from Dawe, "Newfoundland in World War I," 4.

37. *Mail and Advocate*, 16, 23 September 1914.

38. *Daily News*, 24 September 1914.

39. Warren, "Voluntarism and Patriotism," 7–8, 16; Duly, *Where Once We Stood*, 54.

40. *Mail and Advocate*, 24 September 1914.

41. *Mail and Advocate*, 5 October 1914.

42. Patricia O'Brien, "Newfoundland Patriotic Association," 52–76, 100–04; Nicholson, *Fighting Newfoundlander*, 112–16.

43. Patricia O'Brien, "Newfoundland Patriotic Association," 76–99, 174–200.

44. Quoted in Nicholson, *Fighting Newfoundlander*, 116–7; Stacey, *Memoirs of a Blue Puttee*, 34.

45. Middlebrook, *First Day on the Somme*, 22.

46. Facey-Crowther, *Lieutenant Owen William Steele*, 18–9.

47. Facey-Crowther, *Lieutenant Owen William Steele*, 30.

48. Nicholson, *Fighting Newfoundlander*, 120–31.

49. "Journal of Proceedings of the Sixth Annual Convention of the Supreme Council of the Fishermen's Protective Union, Held at Catalina, November 16th, 17th, 18th, and 19th, 1914," in W.F. Coaker, ed., *Twenty Years of the Fishermen's Protective Union of Newfoundland* 1930 (St. John's: Creative Printers, 1984), 79.

50. *Mail and Advocate*, 14 November 1914.

51. *Mail and Advocate*, 16 November 1914.

52. The Rooms Provincial Archives Division, GN8,Office of the Prime Minister, GN8/1, Box 2, E.P. Morris sous fonds, file GN8.21, Folder 4; Coaker to Morris, St. John's, 7 July 1914.

53. "Journal of Proceedings of the Sixth Annual Convention of the Supreme Council of the Fishermen's Protective Union...." in Coaker, *Twenty Years of the Fishermen's Protective Union*, 81.

54. *Mail and Advocate*, 28 October, 20, 21, 24 November, 1 December 1914; "Journal of Proceedings of the Sixth Annual Convention of the Supreme Council of the Fishermen's Protective Union...." in Coaker, *Twenty Years of the Fishermen's Protective Union*, 81.

55. *Daily News*, 1 December 1914.

56. *Evening Telegram*, 1, 4 December 1914.

57. *Daily News*, 9 December 1914.

58. *Evening Telegram*, 11 December 1914.

59. *Mail and Advocate*, 11 December 1914.

60. *Mail and Advocate*, 21 December 1914.

61. *Evening Telegram*, 31 December 1914; Candow, *Men and Seals*, 90.

62. *Mail and Advocate*, 31 December 1914.

63. *Mail and Advocate*, 28, 29 January 1915.

64. Mike O'Brien, "Clear Blue Sky," 418.

65. Nicholson, *Fighting Newfoundlander*, 127–31.

66. Letter of 3 February 1915, Fort George, Inverness-shire, Scotland, in Frank Lind, *The Letters of Mayo Lind* (St. John's: Robinson and Co., 1919), 27.

67. Facey-Crowther, *Lieutenant Owen William Steele*, 36.

68. *Mail and Advocate*, 30 January 1915.

69. *Evening Telegram*, 1 February 1915.

70. Parsons and Parsons, *Best Small-Boat Seamen in the Navy*, 94–7; Hunter, *Employ and Uplift Them*, 127–30. For a claim that the *Viknor* was torpedoed and that the *Clan MacNaughton* definitely hit a mine, see Bernard Ransom, "A Nursery of Fighting Seamen? The Newfoundland Royal Naval Reserve, 1901–1920," in Michael L. Hadley, Rob Huebert and Fred W. Crickard, eds., *A Nation's Navy: In Quest of Canadian Naval Identity* (Montreal and Kingston: McGill-Queen's University Press, 1996), 251.

71. *Mail and Advocate*, 6 February 1915; Hunter, *Employ and Uplift Them*, 99–107.

72. "Journal of Proceedings of the Sixth Annual Convention of the Supreme Council of the Fishermen's Protective Union...." in Coaker, *Twenty Years of the Fishermen's Protective Union*, 89, 93.

73. CO 194, vol. 289, 1915, ff. 18–19, Coaker to Bowring Brothers, St. John's, 11 January 1915.

74. Kean, *Old and Young Ahead*, 32–33.

75. *Mail and Advocate*, 13, quote from 19, 20 February 1915.

76. CO 194, vol. 289, 1915, ff. 16–17, Davidson to Lewis Harcourt, St. John's, 3 February 1915; Archives and Special Collections Division, Queen Elizabeth II Library, Memorial University, William Ford Coaker Papers (Coaker Papers),

COLL-009, 2.02.007; Coaker to J.S. Munn, St. John's, 2 March 1915; Coaker to Bowring Brothers, Ltd., St. John's, 2 March 1915.

77. *Daily News*, 20 February 1915.

78. *Daily News*, 23, 24 February 1915

79. *Evening Telegram*, 24 February 1915.

80. *Daily News*, 1 March 1915

81. *Evening Telegram*, 25 February, 5, 18 March 1915.

82. *Mail and Advocate*, 27 February, 2, 3, 4 March 1915.

83. "Findings and Recommendations by Commissioners Sir William Horwood, C.J., and Hon. Mr. Justice Emerson," Newfoundland, *Report of the Commission of Enquiry into the Sealing Disasters of 1914* (St. John's, 1915), 7–8.

84. George M. Johnson, "Findings and Recommendations by Commissioner Hon. Mr. Justice Johnson," Newfoundland, *Report of the Commission of Enquiry into the Sealing Disasters of 1914* (St. John's, 1915), 22–5.

85. *Daily News*, 3 March 1915.

86. *Mail and Advocate*, 5, 6 March 1915.

87. *Mail and Advocate*, 6 March 1915.

88. *Daily News*, 6 March 1915.

89. *Daily News*, 8 March 1915.

90. *Mail and Advocate*, 9 March 1915.

91. *Daily News*, 12 March 1915.

92. The Rooms Provincial Archives Division, GN8, Office of the Prime Minister, GN8/1, Box 2, E.P. Morris sous fonds, file GN8.21, Folder 4, "Fishermen's Protective Union;" Davidson to the Colonial Secretary, St. John's, 10 March 1915; Davidson to Coaker, St. John's, 10 March 1915.

93. *Daily News*, 13 March 1915.

94. See, for example, *Mail and Advocate*, 19 March 1915.

95. *Mail and Advocate*, 22, 31 March 1915.

96. *Daily News*, 31 March 1915.

97. "Notes From the Editor," *Diocesan Magazine* (April 1915), 51–2.

98. *Mail and Advocate*, 26 April 1915.

99. John Gallishaw, *Trenching at Gallipoli: A Newfoundland Soldier's Story of the First World War* (1916) 2nd ed. (St. John's: DRC Publishing, 2005), 2–3. See also Dawe, "Newfoundland in World War I," 6.

100. Letter of 26 May 1915, Stob's Camp, via Harwick, Scotland, in *Letters of Mayo Lind*, 41; "Lind, Francis Thomas," *ENL, III*, 305.

101. Nicholson, *Fighting Newfoundlander*, 152.

102. Gallishaw, *Trenching at Gallipoli*, 9.

FOUR: THE NEW FRONT: GALLIPOLI, 1915–1916

1. H. James Burgwyn, *The Legend of the Mutilated Victory: Italy, the Great War, and the Paris Peace Conference, 1915–1919* (Westport, Conn.: Greenwood Press, 1993), 5–39; for a critique of Italian leadership in the decision to enter the war, see William A. Renzie, *In the Shadow of the Sword: Italy's Neutrality and Entrance into the Great War, 1914–1915* (New York: Peter Lang, 1987).

2. *Mail and Advocate*, 7 June 1915.

3. *Mail and Advocate*, 17, 21 June 1915.

4. *Mail and Advocate*, 3 July 1915.

5. *Mail and Advocate*, 21 July 1915.

6. *Mail and Advocate*, 16 August 1915.

7. Hew Strachan, *The First World War* (London: Penguin, 2003), 99–109.

8. Strachan, *First World War*, 107–18.

9. *Daily News*, 20 August 1915.

10. Nicholson, *Fighting Newfoundlander*, 155–64; Gallishaw, *Trenching at Gallipoli*, 16.

11. Gallishaw, *Trenching at Gallipoli*, 19.

12. *Daily News*, 13 August 1915.

13. Strachan, *The First World War*, 119–22; Nicholson, *Fighting Newfoundlander*, 164–8.

14. Nicholson, *Fighting Newfoundlander*, 169–72.

15. Parsons and Parsons, *Small-Boat Seamen*, 82–91; Hunter, *Employ and Uplift Them*, 108, 115.

16. *Evening Telegram*, 23 September; 1 October 1915; *Daily News*, 22, 23 September; 5, 22 October 1915.

17. Stacey, *Memoirs of a Blue Puttee*, 57.

18. Major R.H. Tait, "With the Regiment at Gallipoli," *Veteran*, 1, 2 (April 1921), 42–3.

19. Nicholson, *Fighting Newfoundlander*, 172–7; Gallishaw, *Trenching at Gallipoli*, 32; Facey-Crowther, *Lieutenant Owen William Steele*, 81–4.

20. Nicholson, *Fighting Newfoundlander*, 173–4.

21. Facey-Crowther, *Lieutenant Owen William Steele*, 76.

22. Tait, "With the Regiment at Gallipoli," 42.

23. Gallishaw, *Trenching at Gallipoli*, 29, 82–3, quote from 48.

24. CO 194, vol. 289, 1915, ff. 14–15, Davidson to Sir Hartman Just, St. John's, 13 February 1915.

25. *Mail and Advocate*, 7, 14, 15 October 1915.

26. *Mail and Advocate*, 7, 14, 19 October, 11 November 1915.

27. "Journal of Proceedings of the Seventh Annual Convention of the Supreme Council of the Fishermen's Protective Union, Held at Mechanics' Hall, St. John's,

November 25th, 26th and 27th, 1915" in Coaker, *Twenty Years of the Fishermen's Protective Union*, 98, 101.

28. Letter of 14 October 1915, "'Somewhere' in Gallipoli," in *Letters of Mayo Lind*, 96.
29. Gallishaw, *Trenching at Gallipoli*, 76.
30. Nicholson, *Fighting Newfoundlander*, 178.
31. Gallishaw, *Trenching at Gallipoli*, 61, quotes from 76–7.
32. Gallishaw, *Trenching at Gallipoli*, 83.
33. CO 194, vol. 288, 1914, ff. 404–14; Davidson to Lewis Harcourt, St. John's, 31 October 1914; "Bowring, Sir Edgar Rennie," *ENL, I*, 233.
34. *Evening Telegram*, St. John's, 29 October, 16 November 1915.
35. Mike O'Brien, "Clear Blue Sky," 410.
36. *Evening Telegram*, St. John's, 25 November 1915.
37. *Mail and Advocate*, quote from 1, 2 December 1915.
38. *Mail and Advocate*, 8 December 1915.
39. *Evening Telegram*, 23 September 1915.
40. Mike O'Brien, "Producers versus Profiteers: The Politics of Class in Newfoundland during the First World War," *Acadiensis*, 40, 1 (2011), 46.
41. Nicholson, *Fighting Newfoundlander*, 179–80.
42. Gallishaw, *Trenching at Gallipoli*, 131.
43. *Evening Telegram*, 17 December 1915.
44. *Daily News*, 20 December 1915.
45. Letter of 30 October 1915, "'Somewhere' in the Dardanelles," in *Letters of Mayo Lind*, 103–04.
46. *The Times History of the War, XIV* (London: *Times*, 1918), 190.
47. Nicholson, *Fighting Newfoundlander*, 181–3; Facey-Crowther, *Lieutenant Owen William Steele*, 95–6.
48. Gallishaw, *Trenching at Gallipoli*, 130.
49. Peter S. McInnis, "Newfoundland Labour and World War I: The Emergence of the Newfoundland Industrial Workers' Association," unpublished MA thesis, Memorial University of Newfoundland, 1987, 36–41; Patricia O'Brien, "Newfoundland Patriotic Association," 238–40. On profiteering and the inflation crisis, see Mike O'Brien, "Producers versus Profiteers," 45–69.
50. *Mail and Advocate*, 29 December 1915.
51. *Mail and Advocate*, 4, 5 January 1916.
52. CO 194, vol. 291, 1916, ff. 41–5, Davidson to A. Bonar Law, St. John's, 11 January 1916.
53. *Mail and Advocate*, quote from 4, 7 January 1916.
54. *Daily News*, 3, 28 January 1916; "Bowring, Sir Edgar Rennie," *ENL, I*, 233.
55. *Daily News*, 4, 5 January 1916.

56. *Mail and Advocate*, quote from 6, 8 January 1916.

57. *Mail and Advocate*, quote from 10, 11 January 1916.

58. *Mail and Advocate*, 11 January 1916.

59. Nicholson, *Fighting Newfoundlander*, 185–90; Facey-Crowther, *Lieutenant Owen William Steele*, 117.

60. Facey-Crowther, *Lieutenant Owen William Steele*, 121–2.

61. *Mail and Advocate*, 20 January 1916.

62. *Mail and Advocate*, 22 January 1916.

63. W. David Parsons provides a count of forty fatalities in *Pilgrimage: A Guide to the Royal Newfoundland Regiment in World War One* (St. John's: Creative, 1994), 26–27; Parsons based this count on the cemetery monuments at the various places in which members of the Regiment were laid to rest. P. Whitney Lackenbauer lists the same dead, but identifies an additional five unknown Newfoundlanders in "War, Memory, and the Newfoundland Regiment at Gallipoli," *Newfoundland Studies*, 15, 2 (1999), 201–03.

64. Facey-Crowther, *Lieutenant Owen William Steele*, 99. Richard Cramm echoed Steele's view of the Great Flood as testimony to the special strengths of Newfoundlanders in his *The First Five Hundred: Being a Historical Sketch of the Military Operations of the Royal Newfoundland Regiment in Gallipoli and on the Western Front during the Great War (1914–1918)* (Albany, NY: C.F. Williams & Son, 1921), 41–2.

65. Lackenbauer, "War, Memory, and the Newfoundland Regiment at Gallipoli, 176–214; Stacey, *Memoirs of a Blue Puttee*, 65.

66. Nicholson, *Fighting Newfoundlander*, 193–213.

67. *Evening Telegram*, 6 February 1916.

68. *Daily News*, 8 February 1916.

69. *Mail and Advocate*, 22 February 1916.

70. *Mail and Advocate*, 23 February 1916; "Mosdell, Harris Munden," *ENL, III*, 628–9.

71. *Mail and Advocate*, 26, 29 February, 1 March 1916.

72. *Mail and Advocate*, 1 March 1916.

73. Mike O'Brien, "Producers versus Profiteers," 47.

74. *Daily News*, 2 March 1916.

75. *Evening Telegram*, 7, 8 March 1916.

76. *Daily News*, 8 March 1916.

77. *Mail and Advocate*, 8, quote from 15 March 1916.

78. *Daily News*, 7, 9 March 1916.

79. Candow, *Men and Seals*, 90–1.

80. *Evening Telegram*, 5, 20 April 1916; *Mail and Advocate*, 22 April 1916; "Devereaux, R.J.," *ENL, I*, 614.

81. *Daily News*, 4 May 1916.

82. *Mail and Advocate*, 31 May 1916.

83. *Mail and Advocate*, 8 June 1916.
84. O'Flaherty, *Lost Country*, 274; Noel, *Politics in Newfoundland*, 130.

FIVE: BEAUMONT HAMEL, 1 JULY 1916

1. *Evening Telegram*, 1, 4 July 1916.
2. *Daily News*, 3 July 1916.
3. Nicholson, *Fighting Newfoundlander*, 274; "Somme Offensive, Beaumont-Hamel—July 1916: The Outcome" (St. John's: The Rooms Corporation of Newfoundland and Labrador, 2010), www.therooms.ca/regiment/part2_the_battle_of_the_somme_part1.asp, accessed 17/01/2013. Patricia O'Brien provides slightly higher casualty rates using Newfoundland Department of Militia records in the appendices to the Journal of the House of Assembly for 1919, but notes that exact casualty figures are almost impossible to verify for the First World War. See Patricia O'Brien, "Newfoundland Patriotic Association," 138. Cave, *Corporal Pittman*, i–xx, provides the slightly higher figure of 755 dead or wounded. On 5 February 1929, J.E. Edmunds of the Historical Section (Military Branch) of the British Committee of Imperial Defence, London, wrote to J.L. Lardner-Clarke, the Aide-de-Camp at Government House in St. John's, the home and office of the governor, asking for verification of the casualty figures for the Regiment at Beaumont Hamel. Lardner replied on 22 February that 792 men of the Regiment had gone into battle on 1 July 1916, and an annotation on Edmonds's letters suggests that there were total casualties of 778 men. See Library and Archives Canada, Department of Veterans' Affairs Fonds, RG 38, vol. 440, File M-33, "Casualties—General." Again, these variations in the exact numbers of official, popular, and scholarly sources should not distract us from the important point about the scale of the tragedy of Beaumont Hamel.
4. *Daily News*, 7 July 1916.
5. Middlebrook, *First Day on the Somme*, xix–xx, 5–19; Robin Prior and Trevor Wilson, *The Somme* (New Haven and London: Yale University Press, 2005), 35–56.
6. Nicholson, *Fighting Newfoundlander*, 232–6; Middlebrook, *First Day on the Somme*, 26–7, 53.
7. Nicholson, *Fighting Newfoundlander*, 237–43; Middlebrook, *First Day on the Somme*, 48–9, 58–62; Jack Sheldon, *The Germans at Beaumont Hamel* (South Yorkshire: Pen & Sword Books, 2006), 33. On Curnew, see Browne, *Forget-Me-Not*, 60–1.
8. Peter Cashin, *My Life and Times, 1890–1919* (St. John's: Breakwater, 1976), 184–5.
9. Middlebrook, *First Day on the Somme*, 31–43; quote from Nicholson, *Fighting Newfoundlander*, 243–4; Dawe, "Newfoundland in World War I," 16–18.
10. Middlebrook, *First Day on the Somme*, 70–89. On the general problems of British and French artillery, see David Stevenson, *Cataclysm: The First World War as Political Tragedy* (New York: Basic Books, 2004), 149–51. The classic study of

soldiers' experience of the Somme is John Keegan, *The Face of Battle: A Study of Agincourt, Waterloo and the Somme* (London: Penguin, 1976), 207–89.

11. Facey-Crowther, *Lieutenant Owen William Steele*, 183.

12. Facey-Crowther, *Lieutenant Owen William Steele*, 185.

13. Facey-Crowther, *Lieutenant Owen William Steele*, 186–7.

14. Nicholson, *Fighting Newfoundlander*, 246–53.

15. Letter of 29 June 1916, France, in *Letters of Mayo Lind*, 158–64.

16. Nicholson, *Fighting Newfoundlander*, 264–5; Middlebrook, *First Day on the Somme*, 99; Sheldon, *Germans at Beaumont Hamel*, quote from 77.

17. Stacey, *Memoirs of a Blue Puttee*, 77.

18. Nicholson, *Fighting Newfoundlander*, 268–72; Middlebrook, *First Day on the Somme*, 122–89; Cave, *Corporal Pittman*, 11.

19. Letter of 16 March 1916, France, in *Letters of Mayo Lind*, 158–64. Broderick's Regimental File is available on "The Newfoundland Regiment and the Great War Database" (St. John's: The Rooms Corporation of Newfoundland and Labrador, 2010), www.therooms.ca/regiment/part3_database.asp, accessed 04/06/2012. The Rooms Provincial Archives Division, GN2/2, Royal Commission of Enquiry into the Sealing Disasters of 1914, Box 1, File GN 212.54, "Notebook with list of crew of SS *Newfoundland*"; file GN 121.48, "Sealers Agreement 1914: SS *Newfoundland*, Wesley Kean. Master."

20. Stacey, *Memoirs of a Blue Puttee*, 77.

21. Cited in Browne, *Forget-Me-Not*, 67.

22. Stacey, *Memoirs of a Blue Puttee*, 85–6.

23. The entry is recorded as 9:45, 1/7/16, "Trenches," but had to have been written at some point the next day at the earliest. The document is available as "Royal Newfoundland Regiment War Diary September 1915–March 1919 at The Newfoundland Regiment and the Great War Database" (St. John's: The Rooms Corporation of Newfoundland and Labrador, 2010), www.therooms.ca/regiment/docs/WarDiaryComplete–Sept1915–Mar1919.pdf, accessed 04/06/2012. Other reports vary, possibly listing stretcher bearers and runners, or listing survivors who returned later than at the point the observation listed in the war diary was made. See for example the *Evening Telegram*, 29 June 1929, which stated that, of all the members of the regiment present on the battlefield on 1 July 1916, "only eighty four of that number were present to answer to the roll call the next morning." The original may be found at National Archives (United Kingdom), WO/95/2308.

24. Nicholson, *Fighting Newfoundlander*, 272–4; Middlebrook, *First Day on the Somme*, 189.

25. Stacey, *Memoirs of a Blue Puttee*, 87.

26. *Evening Telegram*, 6, quotes from 7 July 1916.

27. *Mail and Advocate*, 11 July 1916.

28. *Evening Telegram*, 11 July 1916.

29. *Evening Telegram*, 13 July 1916.

30. *Daily News*, 13 July 1916.

31. *Daily News*, 17 July 1916.

32. *Mail and Advocate*, 18 July 1916.

33. *Mail and Advocate*, 21 July 1916.

34. *Evening Telegram*, 21 July 1916.

35. *Mail and Advocate*, 28 July 1916.

36. *Mail and Advocate*, 1 August 1916.

37. Noel, *Politics in Newfoundland*, 122.

38. John Keegan, *The First World War* (London: Hutchinson, 1998), 316.

39. Harding, "Glorious Tragedy," 4.

40. Haig is quoted in *Times History of the War, XIV*, 196; Harding, "Glorious Tragedy," 3–10.

41. *Daily News*, 27 July 1916.

42. *Daily News*, 4 August 1916.

43. *Daily News*, 5 August 1916.

44. *Mail and Advocate*, 4 August 1916.

45. *Daily News*, 7, 14 August 1916. The *Evening Telegram*, 8 August 1916, supported the idea of what it referred to as an Employment Registration Bureau.

46. *Mail and Advocate*, 8 August 1916.

47. *Mail and Advocate*, 26 August 1916.

48. *Mail and Advocate*, 11 August 1916.

49. *Mail and Advocate*, 22 August 1916.

50. *Mail and Advocate*, 30 August 1916.

51. Archives and Special Collections, QEII Library, Memorial University, Sir Richard A. Squires Papers, Coll. 250, file 2.12.009; Sergeant C.R. James et al. to Outerbridge, St. John's, 2 September 1916.

52. *Daily News*, 14 September 1916.

53. *Daily News*, 21 September 1916.

54. *Evening Telegram*, 21, 27 September 1916.

55. Library and Archives Canada, Department of Veterans' Affairs Fonds, RG 38, vol. 437, File M-7-4, t. 1 "Officers—Appointments & Promotions," Governor Davidson to the Colonial Secretary, St. John's, 28 October 1915 (Davidson elaborated on matters of class and Timewell in a nine-page handwritten private appendix to this letter); File M-7-4, pt. 2 "Officers—Appointments & Promotions," Edgar Bowring to Davidson, London, 21 March 1916; Davidson to Bowring, St. John's, 8 April 1916; Reserve Force Committee to Davidson, St. John's, 13 April 1916.

56. "Winter, Harry Anderson," and "Winter, James Alexander," ENL, V, 589–90.

57. *Mail and Advocate*, 1 September 1916.

58. *Mail and Advocate*, 27 September 1916; "Anderson, Hugh Abercrombie MBE," *Who's Who in and from Newfoundland, 1927* (St. John's: R. Hibbs, 1927), 166.

59. Cramm, *First Five Hundred*, 131.

60. *Mail and Advocate*, 29 September 1916.

61. *Daily News*, 4 October 1916.

62. *Mail and Advocate*, 6 October 1916.

63. Archives and Special Collections, QEII Library, Memorial University, Sir Richard A. Squires Papers, Coll. 250, file 2.12.10; Davidson to Colonial Secretary, St. John's, 13 October 1916.

64. *Mail and Advocate*, 9, 10, quotes from 11 October 1916.

65. *Mail and Advocate*, 13 October 1916.

66. *Mail and Advocate*, 18, quote from 20, 21 October 1916.

67. *Mail and Advocate*, 23 October 1916.

68. *Mail and Advocate*, 24 October 1916.

69. *Mail and Advocate*, 19, 20, 25, 26 October 1916.

70. *Daily News*, 1 November 1916.

71. "Currie, John Stewart," "Daily News, The," "Elections," *ENL, I*, 578, 581–2, 706–8; "Lloyd, William Frederick," *ENL, III*, 350–1.

72. *Mail and Advocate*, 1, 4, 6, quote from 7 November 1916.

73. Gilbert, *Battle of the Somme*, 214–5, Stacey, *Memoirs of a Blue Puttee*, 102–3; Nicholson, *Fighting Newfoundlander*, 301–23.

74. Stacey, *Memoirs of a Blue Puttee*, 112.

75. Murphy, "One Sabbath in the Trenches," *Veteran*, 1, 2 (April 1921), 54. On Nangle's early life and struggle to join the Regiment, see Gary Browne and Darrin McGrath, *Soldier Priest in the Killing Fields of Europe, Padre Thomas Nangle: Chaplain to the Newfoundland Regiment WWI* (St. John's: DRC, 2006), 4–58. See also O'Brien, "Clear Blue Sky," 409–10.

76. *Daily News*, 14, 15 November 1916.

77. Prior and Wilson, *The Somme*, 305–7.

78. "Journal of Proceedings of the Eighth Annual Convention of the Supreme Council of the Fishermen's Protective Union, Held at Catalina, December 4th, 1916" in Coaker, *Twenty Years of the Fishermen's Protective Union*, 109.

79. *Daily News*, 13 December 1916.

80. *Mail and Advocate*, 17, 29 November 1916.

81. *Mail and Advocate*, 14 December 1916.

SIX: WARS, 1917–1918

1. *Evening Advocate*, 2 January 1917.

2. The British government also created an Imperial War Conference to deal with matters other than those directly related to the conduct of the war, in which Newfoundland was represented. See Gilmore, *Dominion Status*, 47–52. On the Morris government more generally at this point, see O'Flaherty, *Lost Country*, 273–81; and Hiller, "Morris."

3. *Evening Advocate*, 3 January 1917.

4. *Evening Advocate*, 4 January 1917; J.R. Smallwood, *Coaker of Newfoundland* (1927) (Port Union, NL: Coaker Heritage Foundation, 1998), 41–2; Macdonald, *To Each His Own*, 17–18.

5. *Evening Telegram*, 20 January 1917.

6. *Evening Advocate*, 25, 26 January, 9 February 1917.

7. *Evening Telegram*, 30 January 1917.

8. *Daily News*, 8 February 1917.

9. *Evening Advocate*, 15 February 1917.

10. *Daily News*, 17 February 1917.

11. Archives and Special Collections, QEII Library, Memorial University, Sir Richard A. Squires Papers, Coll. 250, file 2.13.001; Charles Button to Squires, Lead Cove, Trinity Bay, 29 January 1917; file 2.13.002; Squires to Elisha Button, St. John's, 16 February 1917; file 2.13.003; Squires to Abraham Kean, St. John's, 5 March 1917.

12. *Evening Advocate*, 22 February 1917.

13. *Evening Advocate*, 6, 19 March 1917.

14. *Evening Advocate*, 24 March 1917.

15. O'Brien, "Newfoundland Patriotic Association," 235–75 suggests that the sentiments articulated by Coaker in the *Evening Advocate* were becoming more widespread.

16. *Evening Telegram*, 13 April 1917; *Evening Advocate*, 24, 26 March, 14, 17, 20, 25, 26 April 1917; on McGrath and the Commission see O'Brien, "Producers versus Profiteers," 63.

17. Nicholson, *Fighting Newfoundlander*, 331–5; *Evening Advocate*, 27 April 1917.

18. Stacey, *Memoirs of a Blue Puttee*, 120–3; Nicholson, *Fighting Newfoundlander*, 344–57; Dawe, "Newfoundland in World War I," 19–24.

19. Stacey, *Memoirs of a Blue Puttee*, 126–8.

20. Nicholson, *Fighting Newfoundlander*, 357–61.

21. *Daily News*, 28 April 1917.

22. *Evening Telegram*, 1 May 1917.

23. *Evening Advocate*, 12 May 1917.

24. *Daily News*, 11 May 1917.

25. *Evening Advocate*, 4 May 1917.

26. *Evening Advocate*, 22 May 1917.

27. Sharpe, "Race of Honour," 44–5.

28. *Evening Telegram*, 22, 23, 28 May 1917.

29. McInnis, "Newfoundland Labour and World War I," 101–10.

30. *Daily News*, 1 June 1917; quotes from *Morning Advocate*, 7 June 1917.

31. *Morning Advocate*, 8, 9, 12, 13 June 1917.

32. *Daily News*, 13 June 1917; *Evening Telegram*, 13 June 1917.

33. *Morning Advocate*, 14, 15 June 1917.

34. *Morning Advocate*, 16 June 1917; *Evening Advocate*, 19 June 1917.

35. *Evening Telegram*, 30 June 1917; *Daily News*, 30 June 1917.

36. *Morning Advocate*, 3 July 1917.

37. *Evening Telegram*, 5, 7 July 1917; *Daily News*, 7 July 1917.

38. Archives and Special Collections, QEII Library, Memorial University, Sir Richard A. Squires Papers, Coll. 250, file 2.13.008; Daly to Squires, Carbonear, 1 August 1917.

39. Sharpe, "Race of Honour," 27–33.

40. Martin, "The Right Course, The Best Course, The Only Course," 55–89.

41. Nicholson, *Fighting Newfoundlander*, 374–88.

42. *Evening Advocate*, 17 July 1917; Noel, *Politics in Newfoundland*, 123–4.

43. *Evening* Telegram, 26, 27, 28 July, 2, 3, 8, 17 August 1917; *Daily News*, 3 August 1917; *Evening Advocate*, 27, 28 July 1917; O'Brien, "Producers versus Profiteers," 65.

44. McDonald, *To Each His Own*, 58–64; O'Brien, "Producers versus Profiteers," 63; *Evening Advocate*, 21, 23 July 1917.

45. The Rooms Provincial Archives Division, GN8, Office of the Prime Minister, Box 9, William Frederick Lloyd sous fonds, file GN8.89, "Newfoundland Industrial Workers' Association [NIWA]"; Maurice H. Kitchen to Prime Minister, SJ, 22 June 1917.

46. *Evening Advocate*, 29 October 1917.

47. *Evening Advocate*, 30 November 1917.

48. CO 194, vol. 293, 1917, ff. 534–6, Davidson to W.H. Long, St. John's, 22 October 1917.

49. O'Flaherty, *Lost Country*, 278–84; Peter Cashin, ed. and annotated by Edward Roberts, *Peter Cashin: My Fight for Newfoundland, A Memoir* (St. John's: Flanker Press, 2012), 2.

50. *Daily News*, 4 January 1918.

51. *Daily News*, 5 January 1918; Coaker defended his position in government in the *Evening Advocate*, 3 January 1918. On Lloyd, see "Lloyd, William Frederick," *ENL, III*, 350–1; O'Flaherty, *Lost Country*, 260–76.

52. *Evening Telegram*, quote from 4, 9 January 1918.

53. Strachan, *First World War*, 227–69.

54. *Evening Advocate*, 31 July, 8 August, 23 October, 6 December 1917; *Evening Telegram*, 30 October 1917.

55. Stacey, *Memoirs of a Blue Puttee*, 142–4; Nicholson, *Fighting Newfoundlander*, 388–430.

56. Frances Cluett to Matilda Cluett, Rouen, 9 December 1917, in Bill Rompkey and Bert Riggs, eds., *Your Daughter Fanny: The War Letters of Frances Cluett, VAD* (St. John's: Flanker Press, 2006), 120–3. For more on Cluny and her overseas nursing colleagues, and a statement about the long-term ambiguities of their experiences, see Terry Bishop Stirling, "'Such Sights One Will Never Forget': Newfoundland Women and Overseas Nursing in the First World War," in Glassford and Shaw, *Sisterhood of Suffering and Service*, 126–47.

57. *Daily News*, 18 December 1917; Noel, *Politics in Newfoundland*, 125.

58. *Evening Advocate*, 7 November, quote from 31 December 1917.

59. *Evening Telegram*, 17 January 1918.

60. *Evening Telegram*, 18 January 1918.

61. *Daily News*, 25 January 1918.

62. *Evening Advocate*, 1 February 1918.

63. *Daily News*, 8 February 1918.

64. *Evening Advocate*, 1, 11 March, 5, 9 April 1918; *Evening Telegram*, 5, 28 March 1918; quote from *Daily News*, 6 April 1918.

65. Peter McInnis, "'All Solid Along the Line': The Reid Newfoundland Strike of 1918," *Labour/Le Travail*, 26 (1990), 61–84; McDonald, *To Each His Own*, 54–72; "Reid, Harry Duff," "Reid Newfoundland Company," *ENL, IV*, 562, 566.

66. *Evening Advocate*, 27 March 1918.

67. *Daily News*, 11, 12 April 1918.

68. McInnis, "'All Solid Along the Line,'" 80–4; Bill Gillespie, *A Class Act: An Illustrated History of the Labour Movement in Newfoundland and Labrador* (St. John's: Creative, 1986), 28–30; *Evening Advocate*, 15 April 1918.

69. Noel, *Politics in Newfoundland*, 125–7; Nicholson, *Fighting Newfoundlander*, 441–7; Strachan, *First World War*, 290–300.

70. Noel, *Politics in Newfoundland*, 127; McDonald, *To Each His Own*, 68–72.

71. *Daily News*, 23 April 1918.

72. Nicholson, *Fighting Newfoundlander*, 447–64.

73. Forsey to "Mother," BEF, France, 3 May 1918; Forsey to "Father," BEF, France, 17 May 1918, in Bert Riggs, ed., *Grand Bank Soldier: The War Letters of Lance Corporal Curtis Forsey* (St. John's: Flanker Press, 2007), 65, 69, quotes from 64, 66.

74. *Evening Telegram*, 27 April 1918.

75. *Evening Telegram*, 16 May 1918.

76. *Evening Advocate*, 7 May 1918.

77. *Evening Advocate*, 22 June 1918.

78. *Evening Advocate*, 27 June, 3 July 1918.

79. *Evening Advocate*, 5 July 1918.

80. Hiller, "Squires, Sir Richard Anderson;" CO 194, vol. 295, 1918, ff. 19–28, Harris to W.H. Long, St. John's, 8 January 1918.

81. *Evening Advocate*, quote from 17 May, 20 July 1918.

82. *Daily Star*, 4 July 1918; on the censorship incident see O'Flaherty, *Lost Country*, 289–90.

83. *Evening Advocate*, 22, 30 July 1918; McGrath's role in housing policy and reform has been treated in Melvin Baker, "Municipal Politics and Public Housing in St. John's, 1911–1921," M. Baker, R. Cuff, and B. Gillespie, eds., *Workingmen's St. John's: Aspects of Social History in the early 1900s* (St. John's: Harry Cuff Publications, 1982), 29–43; "Gibbs, Michael P.," *ENL, II*, 520.

84. *Evening Telegram*, 23 July 1918.
85. *Evening Telegram*, 5 August 1918.
86. *Evening Telegram*, 8 August 1918.
87. *Evening Telegram*, 23 August 1918.
88. *Evening Telegram*, 9, 19, 22 October 1918
89. Nicholson, *Fighting Newfoundlander*, 478–510. On the collapsing position of German and its allies more generally, see Strachan, *The First World War,* 303–325.
90. *Evening Telegram*, 12 November 1918.
91. *Evening Advocate*, 16 November 1918.
92. *Evening Advocate*, 19 November 1918.

SEVEN: PROGRESSIVES: PRUSSIANS OR BOLSHEVIKS? 1919–1920

1. *Evening Telegram*, 2, 4 January 1919.
2. *Daily News*, 4 January 1919; "Horwood, Reuben F.," *ENL, II*, 1038–9.
3. On international conditions, see Larry Peterson, "The One Big Union in International Perspective: Revolutionary Industrial Unionism 1900–1925," *Labour/Le Travailleur*, 7 (Spring 1981), 41–66; Peterson, "Revolutionary Socialism and Industrial Unrest in the Era of the Winnipeg General Strike: The Origins of Communist Labour Unionism in Europe and North America," *Labour/ Le Travail*, 13 (Spring 1984), 115–31. There is an extensive literature on the meaning of the 1919 general strike in Canada, but for the relationship between fears about Bolshevism and state policy in the Great War era, see Reg Whitaker, Gregory S. Kealey, and Andrew Parnaby, *Secret Service: Political Policing in Canada from the Fenians to Fortress America* (Toronto: University of Toronto Press, 2012), 71–89. For more specific discussions of the government's use of fear of Bolshevism to suppress dissent, see Daniel Francis, *Seeing Reds: The Red Scare of 1918–1919, Canada's First War on Terror* (Vancouver: Arsenal Pulp Press, 2010), *passim*; and William Preston, Jr., *Aliens and Dissenters: Federal Suppression of Radicals, 1903–1933*, 2nd ed. (Urbana and Chicago: University of Illinois Press, 1994), 208–37. The immediate post-1918 Red Scare was less severe in Britain, where the Labour Party made clear that it rejected Bolshevism or revolutionary leftism generally in favour of a moderate democratic socialism that privileged the role of parliamentary democracy in achieving change. See Paul Ward, *Red Flag and Union Jack: Englishness, Patriotism and the British Left, 1881–1924* (Woodbridge: Royal Historical Society and the Boydell Press, 1998), 142–98.
4. Cadigan, "McGrath, James J.," *DCB*, forthcoming.
5. *Evening Telegram*, 2 July 1918.
6. *Evening Telegram*, 9, 29 January 1919.
7. *Daily News*, 9 January 1919.
8. *Daily News*, 11 January 1919.
9. *Evening Telegram*, 8, 11 January, 24 February 1919.

10. *Evening Advocate*, 23 January 1919; quote from *Evening Telegram*, 28 January 1919. For more on the foundation of Memorial University College see Malcolm MacLeod, *A Bridge Built Halfway: A History of Memorial University College* (Montreal: McGill-Queen's University Press, 1990) and Melvin Baker, *Celebrate Memorial!: A Pictorial History of Memorial University of Newfoundland* (St. John's: Memorial University of Newfoundland, 1999).

11. *Evening Telegram*, 30 January 1919.

12. *Daily News*, 1 February 1919.

13. Gilmore, *Dominion Status*, 53–9.

14. *Daily News*, 7, 8 February 1919.

15. *Evening Telegram*, 17 February 1919.

16. *Daily News*, 23 January, 7 March 1919.

17. *Evening Advocate*, 14 February 1919.

18. *Daily Star*, St. John's, 3 March 1919.

19. *Daily News*, 25 February, quote from 11 March 1919.

20. *Evening Advocate*, 11 March 1919.

21. *Daily News*, 22 March 1919.

22. *Evening Advocate*, quote from 21, 24 March 1919.

23. *Evening Advocate*, 28 March 1919.

24. Arthur Selwyn-Brown, "Approaching Peace," *Newfoundland Quarterly*, XIX, 2 (1919), 1–3, quote from 3.

25. McDonald, *To Each His Own*, 74–8. Background on Roche may be found in John Edward Fitzgerald, "Archbishop E.P. Roche, J.R. Smallwood, and Denominational Rights in Newfoundland Education, 1948," *CCHA Historical Studies*, 65 (1999), 28–49 and "The True Father of Confederation: Archbishop E.P. Roche, Term 17, and Newfoundland's Union with Canada," *Newfoundland Studies*, 14, 2 (1998), 188–219.

26. Gilmore, *Dominion Status*, 72.

27. *Evening Telegram*, 4 April 1919.

28. *Evening Telegram*, 3, quotes from 4 and 10, 11 April 1919.

29. *Evening Telegram*, 17 April 1919.

30. *Daily Star*, St. John's, 1 March 1919.

31. Archives and Special Collections, QEII Library, Memorial University, Sir Richard A. Squires Papers, Coll. 250, file, 2.15.004: Elisha Button to Squires, New Melbourne, 10 April 1919.

32. *Evening Telegram*, 21 May 1919; Noel, *Politics in Newfoundland*, 128–9.

33. "Hickman, Albert Edgar," *ENL*, II, 934–4; O'Flaherty, *Lost Country*, 281–5, 296; Noel, *Politics in Newfoundland*, 135–7.

34. *Evening Advocate*, 23, 26 May 1919; "Stone, John Glover," *ENL*, V, 310–11.

35. Archives and Special Collections, QEII Library, Memorial University, Sir Richard A. Squires Papers, Coll. 250, file 2.14.001; "Star" to Dr. Mosdell, St. John's, 12 January 1918.

36. Archives and Special Collections, QEII Library, Memorial University, William F. Coaker Papers, Coll. 009, file 10.03.052; Morine to William Sampson, Jr., St. John's, 23 June 1919. Morine's earlier disputes with Coaker may be glimpsed in Morine to Coaker, St. John's, 2, 26 September 1914.

37. *Daily News*, 10, 17, 18 June 1919.

38. *Daily News*, 19 June 1919.

39. *Evening Telegram*, 30 June 1919.

40. *Daily News*, 10 July 1919.

41. *Evening Advocate*, 16 July 1919.

42. *Daily Star*, St. John's, 30 June 1919; Hiller, "Squires, Sir Richard Anderson," uses the term "political warlords"; see also O'Flaherty, *Lost Country*, 295–9.

43. Archives and Special Collections, QEII Library, Memorial University, William Ford Coaker Papers, Coll. 009, file 10.03.070; Squires to Coaker, St. John's, 23 August 1919.

44. Noel, *Politics in Newfoundland*, 144–5; Elliott, "Newfoundland Politics in the 1920s," 182–3; Edward Roberts, "Nothing Venture, Nothing Have: Mr. Coaker's Regulations," Major MA Research paper, Memorial University, 2006, 20–1.

45. *Evening Advocate*, 19, 28, 31 July 1919.

46. Robert Cuff, "The Quill and the Hammer: The NIWA in St. John's 1917–1925," in M. Baker, R. Cuff, and B. Gillespie, eds., *Workingmen's St. John's: Aspects of Social History in the early 1900s* (St. John's: Harry Cuff Publications, 1982), 48–57; McInnis, "All Solid Along the Line," 83–4.

47. *Daily News*, 30 August 1919.

48. *Daily News*, 2, 8, 22 September 1919.

49. *Evening Advocate*, 22 July, 11 September 1919.

50. *Evening Advocate*, 15 September 1919.

51. *Evening Advocate*, 18, 22 September 1919.

52. *Evening Telegram*, 22, 23, quote from 24 September 1919.

53. *Daily News*, 3 October 1919.

54. *Evening Telegram*, 6 October 1919.

55. *Daily News*, 7 October 1919.

56. "Currie, John Stewart," and "Elections," *ENL, I*, 578, 708–10; "James, Charles T.," *ENL III*, 94.

57. Browne and McGrath, *Soldier Priest*, 65–81.

58. *Evening Advocate*, 8 October 1919.

59. *Daily News*, 8 October 1919.

60. *Evening Telegram*, 17 October 1919.

61. *Evening Telegram*, 23 October 1919.

62. *Evening Advocate*, 30 October 1919; *Daily News*, 30 October 1919.

63. Archives and Special Collections, QEII Library, Memorial University, Sir Richard A. Squires Papers, Coll. 250, file 2.15.010; Meaney to Squires, Manuels, 28 October 1919.

64. Noel, *Politics in Newfoundland*, 138–42; Macdonald, *To Each His Own*, 54–85.

65. "Stone, John Glover," *ENL, V*, 310–11; "Elections," *ENL, I*, 710–11.

66. *Evening Advocate*, 20 November 1919.

67. Archives and Special Collections, QEII Library, Memorial University, Sir Richard A. Squires Papers, Coll. 250, file 2.16.006; Price, Waterhouse & Co to Squires, New York, 17 June 1920.

68. *Evening Advocate*, 18, 19, 30 December 1919.

69. "Curries, John Stewart," and "Elections," *ENL, I*, 578, 708–10; "James, Charles T.," *ENL III*, 94; Ellison, *Newfoundland Newspapers*, 43–4.

70. Roberts, "Nothing Venture, Nothing Have," 16–17.

71. David Alexander, *The Decay of Trade: An Economic History of the Newfoundland Saltfish Trade, 1935–1965* (St. John's 1977), 20–27; McDonald, *To Each His Own*, 86–105.

72. Roberts, "Nothing Venture, Nothing Have," 16–7; Noel, *Politics in Newfoundland*, 144–5.

73. *Daily News*, 11, quote from 31 December 1919.

74. Roberts, "Nothing Venture, Nothing Have," 27; Noel, *Politics in Newfoundland*, 144–5.

75. *Daily News*, 19, 20 January 1920.

76. *Evening Telegram*, 3 January 1920.

77. *Evening Telegram*, 6 January 1920.

78. *Evening Telegram*, 14 January 1920; "Linegar, William L.," *ENL, III*, 306.

79. *Evening Advocate*, 6 January, 12 January 1920; McInnis, "Newfoundland Labour and World War I," 217–19.

80. *Evening Telegram*, 15 January 1920.

81. Harding, "Glorious Tragedy," 11.

82. George H. Tucker, "The Old NIWA," in J.R. Smallwood, ed., *The Book of Newfoundland, Volume* I (St. John's: Newfoundland Book Publishers, 1937), 279–81; Robert Harding, "The Role of the Great War Veterans' Association of Newfoundland, 1918–1925," BA honours dissertation, Memorial University of Newfoundland, 2003, 11–13; *Evening Advocate*, 8 January 1920.

83. *Evening Telegram*, 17 January 1920. On the Canadian situation, see Desmond Morton and Glenn Wright, *Winning the Second Battle: Canadian Veterans and the Return to Civilian Life, 1915–1930* (Toronto: University of Toronto Press, 1987), 79–80, 120–21.

84. The case for a more progressive early GWVA is made in James Overton, "Self-Help, Charity, and Individual Responsibility: The Political Economy of Social Policy in Newfoundland in the 1920s," in J.K. Hiller and Peter Neary, eds., *Twentieth-Century Newfoundland: Explorations* (St. John's: Breakwater, 1994), 81–5.

85. *Evening Advocate*, 24 January 1920; the editor made the case for Cashin bribery on 19, 20 January 1920.

EIGHT: THE FAILURE OF THE PROGRESSIVE ALTERNATIVE, 1920–1923

1. *Daily News*, 30, 31 January 1920.
2. *Evening Advocate*, 13 February 1920; Roberts, "Nothing Venture, Nothing Have," 25–6.
3. *Evening Advocate*, 8 March 1920.
4. Archives and Special Collections, QEII Library, Memorial University, Sir Richard A. Squires Papers, Coll. 250, file 2.16.007; Squires to Coaker, St. John's, 24 July 1920.
5. *Evening Advocate*, 5, 15, 22 April 1920; *Evening Telegram*, 14, 19 April 1920. On the disagreement between Squires and the GWVA, see Harding, "Great War Veterans' Association," 18–23.
6. *Daily News*, 20, 21 May 1920.
7. Roberts, "Nothing Venture, Nothing Have," 34–6, Crosbie quoted on 37; Noel, *Politics in Newfoundland*, 145.
8. *Daily News*, 21 June 1920. The Newfoundland pension rates were set out in a complex series of five classifications of level of disability by ten levels of rank of service. See Harding, "Great War Veterans' Association," 54. On Canadian pension rates, see Morton and Wright, *Winning the Second Battle*, 155.
9. *Evening Advocate*, 3 July 1920; "Robinson, John Alexander," *ENL, IV*, 612–13; "Carew, William J.," *ENL, I*, 348–9.
10. *Evening Telegram*, 3 September 1920.
11. *Daily News*, 29 July, 3 September 1920.
12. *Evening Telegram*, 31 August 1920.
13. *Evening Advocate*, 3, 9 September 1920.
14. *Evening Telegram*, 6 September 1920.
15. *Veteran*, 1, 2 (April 1921), 6.
16. *Evening Advocate*, 10, 11 September 1920.
17. *Evening Advocate*, 13 September 1920.
18. *Evening Telegram*, 24 September 1920.
19. *Daily News*, 24, 25 September; quote from 6 October 1920.
20. *Evening Advocate*, 25 September 1920.
21. *Evening Advocate*, 29 September 1920.
22. *Evening Advocate*, 1 October 1920.
23. *Daily News*, 21 October, 6 December 1920; *Evening Telegram*, 23 October 1920.
24. *Evening Advocate*, 22 October 1920.
25. *Evening Telegram*, 30 October 1920.
26. *Evening Advocate*, 15 November 1920; *Evening Telegram*, 1 December 1920; Ronald Rompkey, ed., *Jessie Luther at the Grenfell Mission* (Montreal and Kingston: McGill-Queens University Press, 2001), 327.
27. *Evening Advocate*, 27 December 1920; Coaker Papers, COLL-009, 1.04.004; "Coaker Recruits, n.d."
28. *Evening Advocate*, 11 November, 22 December 1920.

29. Browne and McGrath, *Soldier Priest*, 88–93; Harding, Glorious Tragedy," 20–1. For a more detailed history of the college, see MacLeod, *Bridge Built Halfway*, 17–18. Coaker's intervention on Nangle's behalf with Squires may be found in Archives and Special Collections, QEII Library, Memorial University, Sir Richard A. Squires Papers, Coll. 250, file 9.08.010; Coaker to Squires, Ypres, 3 March 1920 (cable); Squires to Nangle, St. John's, 3 March 1920.

30. Roberts, "Nothing Venture, Nothing Have," 41–65; Alexander, *Decay of Trade*, 20–27; McDonald, *To Each His Own*, 86–105; *Evening Advocate*, 5 January 1921.

31. Noel, *Politics in Newfoundland*, 130; Great Britain, *Newfoundland Royal Commission 1933: Report* (London: HMSO, 1933) [hereafter Amulree Report], 46–71.

32. O'Flaherty, *Lost Country*, 305.

33. *Evening Telegram*, 15, 22, quote from 24 February 1921.

34. *Daily News*, 1 February 1921.

35. *Evening Telegram*, 5 March 1921.

36. *Evening Telegram*, 22, 29 March, 14 April 1921; *Daily News*, 24 March 1921.

37. *Daily News*, 27 January, 15, 18, 21 April, 13 May 1921.

38. *Daily News*, 7 May 1921; *Evening Telegram*, 20 May 1921.

39. McDonald, *To Each His Own*, 106–113; Noel, *Politics in Newfoundland*, 147–8.

40. *Evening Advocate*, 4 March 1921.

41. "GWVA Notes," *Veteran*, 2, 1 (April 1922), 59; Harding, "Role of the Great War Veterans' Association," 22–3; *Daily News*, 2 November 1921.

42. Hunter, *Employ and Uplift Them*, 148–53.

43. "GWVA Notes," *Veteran*, 1, 2 (April 1921), 81.

44. Archives and Special Collections, QEII Library, Memorial University, Sir Richard A. Squires Papers, Coll. 250, file, 2.17.006; Murphy to Squires, Bell Island, 19 June 1921.

45. *Evening Telegram*, 15 July 1921.

46. *Evening Telegram*, 15 August 1921; Browne and McGrath, *Soldier Priest*, 93–4; Harding, "Role of the Great War Veterans' Association," 27.

47. Christian's Regimental File is available on "The Newfoundland Regiment and the Great War Database" (St. John's: The Rooms Corporation of Newfoundland and Labrador, 2010), www.therooms.ca/regiment/part3_database.asp, accessed 04/06/2012.

48. Archives and Special Collections, QEII Library, Memorial University, Sir Richard A. Squires Papers, Coll. 250, file 9.08.011; Nangle to Coaker, London, 21 May 1920; file 9.08.013: Coaker to Squires, St. John's, 1 June 1920.

49. "Commemoration Day, July 3rd, 1921. Sergeant's Memorial Unveiled by His Excellency The Governor," *Newfoundland Quarterly*, 21, 1 (1921), 25–7.

50. Robinson, "The Debt of Honour And Ways of Paying it in Part," *Veteran*, 1, 3 (September 1921), 56.

51. Arthur Selwyn-Brown, "Restoration of Commercial Confidence," *Newfoundland Quarterly*, 22, 2 (1922), 11–12.

52. Archives and Special Collections, QEII Library, Memorial University, Coaker Papers, COLL-009, 1.004.001; Nangle to Coaker, London, 12 December 1922.

53. Archives and Special Collections, QEII Library, Memorial University, Sir Richard A. Squires Papers, Coll. 250, Box 3, file unnumbered "The Great War Veterans' Association .... 1921–1922"; Gerald T. Whitty to Jennings, St. John's, 28 November 1921; Jennings to Squires, St. John's, 29 November 1921.

54. Archives and Special Collections, QEII Library, Memorial University, Sir Richard A. Squires Papers, Coll. 250, Box 3, file unnumbered "The Great War Veterans' Association .... 1921–1922"; Squires to Higgins, St. John's, 8 December 1921.

55. *Evening Telegram*, 18, 24 January, 1 February 1922. On the poor relief system, see O'Flaherty, *Lost Country*, 307–08; Amulree Report, 48–50.

56. Archives and Special Collections, QEII Library, Memorial University, Sir Richard A. Squires Papers, Coll. 250, file 2.18.003; Squires to Rev. H.T. Renouf, Bishop of St. George's, St. John's, 18 March 1922.

57. *Evening Telegram*, 3 January, 20, 25 February 1922.

58. O'Flaherty, *Lost Country*, 304–5.

59. *Daily News*, 18 February 1922.

60. *Evening Telegram*, 18, 25 March, 23 May 1922.

61. *Daily News*, quoted from 4, 5 April 1922.

62. *Evening Advocate*, 3, 8, 15 April 1922.

63. *Daily News*, 10 June 1922.

64. *Evening Advocate*, 30 June 1922.

65. *Daily News*, 17 April 1922.

66. *Daily News*, 30 June 1922.

67. *Evening Advocate*, 14 July 1922.

68. *Daily News*, 4 August 1922.

69. *Evening Advocate*, 19 August, 7, 20 September 1922.

70. *Evening Telegram*, 15 September 1922.

71. *Daily News*, 4 October 1922.

72. *Evening Telegram*, 31 January, 12 February 1923.

73. *Daily News*, 22 February, 3 March 1923.

74. *Evening Advocate*, 22 February 1923.

75. *Evening Telegram*, 27 February 1923.

76. *Daily News*, 7 March 1923.

77. *Evening Telegram*, 10, 12, 14, quote from 23 March 1923.

78. *Evening Advocate*, 9, 10, 27 April 1923.

79. *Evening Telegram*, 19 April 1923.

80. "Cashin, Sir Michael Patrick,' and "Cashin, Maj. Peter J." *ENL*, I, 380–1.

81. *Evening Telegram*, 21 May 1923.

82. "Sir William Ford Coaker, K.B.E., M.H.A.," *Newfoundland Quarterly*, 3, 1 (July 1923), 18.

83. McDonald, *To Each His Own*, 106–25; Noel, *Politics in Newfoundland*, 148–58; James K. Hiller, "The Politics of Newsprint: The Newfoundland Pulp and Paper Industry, 1915–1939," *Acadiensis*, XIX, 2 (1990), 3–19.

NINE: POLITICAL DEMORALIZATION, 1923–1924

1. Noel, *Politics in Newfoundland*, 152–63; Elliott, "Newfoundland Politics in the 1920s," 181–204.

2. *Evening Advocate*, 10 August 1923; "Walker, Thomas Hollis," *ENL*, V, 498.

3. *Daily News*, 13 August 1923.

4. *Daily News*, St. John's, 1 February 1922; Crawley, "Off to Sydney," 27–51; David Frank, "The 1920s: Class and Region, Resistance and Accommodation," in Forbes and Muise, *Atlantic Provinces*, 233–71; the link between Newfoundland and more international trends was first made by Kealey in "Canadian Labour Revolt," 34.

5. *Evening Telegram*, 23 November 1922.

6. *Daily News*, 14 May 1923.

7. *Evening Advocate*, 1, 6, 10, 11 September 1923.

8. "Sir William Coaker Reviews Recent Visit Abroad: Describes Blaafjeld's Voyage to Gibralter and Deals with Business Situation in Alicante," Coaker, ed., *Twenty Years of the Fishermen's Protective Union*, 315, 325.

9. Raymond J. Sontag, *A Broken World, 1919–1939* (New York: Harper and Row, 1971), xv, 84–5, 139; Lita-Rose Betcherman, *The Swastika and the Maple Leaf: Fascist Movements in Canada in the 1930s* (Toronto: Fitzhenry and Whiteside, 1975); Martin Robin, *Shades of Right: Nativist and Fascist Politics in Canada, 1920–1940* (Toronto: University of Toronto Press, 1992); Jean-François Nadeau, *Adrien Arcand, Führer Canadien* (Montréal: Lux, 2010); Overton, "Economic Crisis," 91.

10. R.J. Overy, *The Inter-War Crisis, 1919–1939* (Harlow, Eng.: Pearson, Longman, 2007), 67–70; Martin Pugh, *"Hurrah for the Blackshirts!" Fascists and Fascism in Britain between the Wars* (London: Jonathan Cape, 2005), 40–6, 53; Stephen R. Ward, "Introduction," and "Great Britain: Land Fit for Heroes Lost," in Ward, ed., *The War Generation: Veterans of the First World War* (Port Washington, New York and London: Kenniket Press, 1975), 4, 22–35.

11. *Daily News*, 1, 6 September 1923.

12. *Daily News*, quote from 22 September, 4 October 1923.

13. *Evening Telegram*, 25 October 1923; "Jeffrey, Charles E.A.," *ENL*, III, 103–4.

14. *Evening Telegram*, 21 November 1923.

15. *Evening Telegram*, 7 January 1924; Elliott, "Newfoundland Politics in the 1920s," 193.

16. *Daily News*, 28 January 1924.

17. *Evening Advocate*, 29 January 1924.

18. *Daily News*, 12 February 1924.
19. *Evening Telegram*, 12 February 1924.
20. *Evening Telegram*, 18, quote from 20 February 1924; *Daily News*, 1 March 1924.
21. A.A. Parsons, "The Lure of the Icefields: Newfoundland's Great Sealing Industry," *Veteran*, 3, 1 (April 1923), 9.
22. *Evening Telegram*, 7 March 1924.
23. *Daily News*, 11 March 1924; *Evening Advocate*, 11 March 1924.
24. James Belich, *Replenishing the Earth: The Settler Revolution and the Rise of the Anglo-World, 1783–1939* (Oxford: Oxford University Press, 2009), 456–73.
25. *Daily News*, 11, 13, 18 March 1924.
26. *Daily News*, 19 March 1924.
27. *Evening Advocate*, 13 March 1924.
28. *Daily News*, 21 March 1924; Noel, *Politics in Newfoundland*, 163–70.
29. Noel, *Politics in Newfoundland*, 163.
30. Elliott, "Newfoundland Politics in the 1920s," 183–90.
31. *Daily News*, 21 March 1924.
32. "GWVA Notes," *Veteran*, 2, 1 (April 1922), 59.
33. Overton, "Self–Help, Charity, and Individual Responsibility," 89–90.
34. "Editorial," *Veteran*, 3, 1 (April 1923), 5–6.
35. *Evening Telegram*, 22 March 1924.
36. *Daily News*, 22 March 1924.
37. *Evening Advocate*, 22 March 1924; quote from *Evening Telegram*, 24 March 1924.
38. *Daily News*, 29 March 1924.
39. Harding, "Glorious Tragedy," 12–13; Harding, "Great War Veterans' Association," 30–2; Browne, *Soldier Priest*, 101–16; Bert Riggs, "Cast in Metal, Carved in Stone," paper presented to the Rotary Club of St. John's Northwest, 24 November 2009.
40. *Daily News*, 9 April 1924.
41. *Daily News*, 10 April 1924.
42. *Daily News*, 16 April 1924.
43. *Evening Telegram*, 16 April 1924.
44. *Evening Telegram*, 28 April 1924.
45. *Daily News*, 2 May 1924.
46. *Daily News*, 3 May 1924.
47. *Evening Telegram*, 6 May 1924. The preceding two paragraphs, except where otherwise cited, are based on Elliott, "Newfoundland Politics in the 1920s," 193–5; Noel, *Politics in Newfoundland*, 170–7; "Elections," *ENL*, 1, 712–13.
48. *Evening Telegram*, 7 May 1924.
49. Andrea O'Brien (compiler), "Architectural Survey of Port Union, NL, Conducted by Andrea O'Brien and Debbie O'Rielly, June 15–16, 2006, Heritage Foundation

of Newfoundland and Labrador, www.heritagefoundation.ca/media/725/report-port-union.pdf, accessed 21/01/2013.

50. *Daily News*, 8 May 1924.

51. "The New Government," *Newfoundland Quarterly*, 24, 1 (August 1924), 13. "Monroe, Moses," *Dictionary of Canadian Biography Online*, www.biographi.ca/ EN/009004-119.01-e.php?id_nbr '6308, accessed 19/06/2012; "Monroe, Walter Stanley," *ENL, III* (St. John's, 1991), 599–601.

52. *Daily News*, quote from 14, 15 May 1924.

53. *Daily News*, 17 May 1924.

54. *Veteran*, 4, 2 (July 1924), 38–9.

55. "Commemoration Day, July 1st, 1923," *Newfoundland Quarterly*, 3, 1 (July 1923), 27. See also "Allardyce, His Excellency Sir William Lamond...," *Who's Who in and from Newfoundland, 1927*, 55–6.

56. Newfoundlander, "Thoughts for the Present," *Veteran*, 4, 2 (July 1924), 74–6.

57. *Evening Telegram*, 1 May 1924.

58. "Mitchell, Harold," *ENL, III*, 590–91; *Evening Telegram*, 15 May 1924.

59. *Daily News*, 23 May 1924.

60. *Evening Telegram*, 28 May 1924.

61. *Daily News*, 6 June 1924; "Elections," *ENL, I*, 713–15.

62. *Evening Telegram*, 6 June 1924.

63. *Evening Advocate*, 25, 26 June 1924.

64. Noel, *Politics in Newfoundland*, 179.

65. *Daily News*, 20, 21 June 1924.

66. *Evening Telegram*, 30 June 1924.

67. *Evening Advocate*, 30 June 1924.

68. *Daily News*, 3 July 1924.

69. *Daily News*, 22 July 1924.

70. *Evening Advocate*, 26 July 1924.

71. *Evening Advocate*, 28 July 1924.

72. Noel, *Politics in Newfoundland*, 180–1.

73. *Daily News*, 19 July, 1, 2 August 1924; *Evening Telegram*, 2 August 1924.

74. *Daily News*, 4 August 1924.

75. *Evening Advocate*, 2, 4 August 1924.

76. *Evening Advocate*, 29 August 1924.

77. *Evening Advocate*, 10 September 1924.

78. *Evening Telegram*, 25 September 1924.

79. *Daily News*, 11, 13, 18 August 1924; *Evening Advocate*, 13 August 1924.

80. *Evening Advocate*, 19 August, quote from 13 September 1924.

81. *Daily News*, 6, 30 October 1924; *Evening Telegram*, 20, 21, 30 October 1924; Long, *Suspended State*, 37.

82. *Evening Telegram*, 7 November 1924.
83. *Evening Telegram*, 31 December 1924.

TEN: THE DEATH OF DEMOCRACY, 1925–1934

1. Noel, *Politics in Newfoundland*, 181–2.
2. Cashin, *My Fight for Newfoundland*, 32–3.
3. *Daily Globe*, 5 March 1925.
4. *Evening Telegram*, 7 March 1925.
5. *Evening Telegram*, 9 March 1925.
6. *Daily News*, 6 September, 7 December 1926; Gail Weir, *Miners of Wabana* (St. John's: Breakwater, 1989).
7. Harding, "Glorious Tragedy," 23.
8. *Evening Telegram*, 30 June 1925.
9. I.C. Morris, "Some Problems of the Returned Man," *Veteran*, 5, 2 (October 1925), 17–19; Martin, "Newfoundland Regiment," 63; Browne and McGrath, *Soldier Priest*, 128–37; Edward Morris's service file is available on "The Newfoundland Regiment and the Great War Database" (St. John's: The Rooms Corporation of Newfoundland and Labrador, 2010), www.therooms.ca/regiment/part3_database. asp, accessed 20/01/2013.
10. *Evening Telegram*, 9 June 1920.
11. O'Brien, "Newfoundland Patriotic Association," 53–54; Margot Iris Duley, "'The Radius of Her Influence for Good': The Rise and Triumph of the Women's Suffrage Movement in Newfoundland, 1909–1925," in Linda Kealey, *Pursuing Equality: Historical Perspectives on Women in Newfoundland and Labrador* (St. John's: Creative, 1993), 66–162; "Earle, Julia Salter," *ENL, I*, 663; Duley, *Where Once Our Mothers Stood*, 76–95; Duley, "The Unquiet Knitters of Newfoundland: From Mothers of the Regiment to Mothers of the Nation," in Glassford and Shaw, eds., *Sisterhood of Suffering and Service*, 51–74.
12. *Daily Globe*, 26 December 1925, Overton, "Economic Crisis," 199, at fn. 67.
13. *Daily News*, 31 December 1925.
14. "Journal of Proceedings of the Seventeenth Annual Convention of the Supreme Council of the Fishermen's Protective Union, Held at Port Union, December 25th, 1925," in Coaker, *Twenty Years of the Fishermen's Protective Union*, 235–6. Although the date is given as 25 December 1925, the Convention was held in November and covered in the *Advocate*. See Long, *Suspended State*, 42–3.
15. *Fishermen's Advocate*, Port Union, 4, 11, 18 December 1925.
16. DO 35, vol. 3, 1926, f. 450, Allardyce to L.C.M.S. Amerey, St. John's, 2 January 1926.
17. *Fishermen's Advocate*, Port Union, 22 January 1926; on the by-election, see Long, *Suspended State*, 38–41.
18. *Evening Telegram*, 9 November 1916; "Duff, Robert," *ENL, I*, 651.

19. *Daily News*, 10 November 1926.

20. Archives and Special Collections, QEII Library, Memorial University, William Ford Coaker Papers, Coll. 009, file, 10.03.015; Cashin to Coaker, St. John's, 4 January 1927.

21. "Monroe, Walter Stanley," *ENL, III*, 599–601; McDonald, *To Each His Own*, 131–4; Long, *Suspended State*, 49–53; Noel, *Politics in Newfoundland*, 184–5; Overton, "Self–Help, Charity, and Individual Responsibility," 95–111.

22. *Evening Telegram*, 4 March 1927.

23. *Daily News*, 30 June 1927, 5 March, 30 June 1928; *Evening Telegram*, 2 July 1927.

24. *Fishermen's Advocate*, Port Union, 19 October 1928.

25. Maura Hanrahan, *Tsunami: The Newfoundland Tidal Wave Disaster* (St. John's: Flanker Press, 2004), 156–96; Alan Ruffman and Violet Hann, "The Newfoundland Tsunami of November 18, 1929: An Examination of the Twenty-eight Deaths of the 'South Coast Disaster,'" *Newfoundland and Labrador Studies*, 21, 1 (2006), 97–148.

26. *Fishermen's Advocate*, Port Union, 27 December 1929.

27. *Evening Telegram*, 21 December 1929.

28. *Daily News*, 2 January 1930.

29. *Evening Telegram*, 2 January 1930.

30. Sean T. Cadigan, "Battle Harbour in Transition: Merchants, Fishermen, and the State in the Struggle for Relief in a Labrador Fishing Community during the 1930s," *Labour/Le Travail*, 26 (Fall 1990), 125–50; Jim Overton, "Public Relief and Social Unrest in Newfoundland in the 1930s: An Evaluation of the Ideas of Piven and Cloward," in Gregory S. Kealey, ed., *Class, Gender, and Region: Essays in Canadian Historical Sociology* (St. John's: Committee on Canadian Labour and Working-Class History, 1988), 153–66; Overton, "Economic Crisis," 85–124.

31. *Fishermen's Advocate*, Port Union, 31 July 1931.

32. *Daily News*, 5 November 1931.

33. The Newfoundland situation bore some similarity to the Canadian case in the early 1930s, when the four Western provinces in particular hoped that the federal government would provide more financial support for the provinces' efforts to deal with the social and economic problems of the deepening depression. The federal government refused in 1933, feeling that the provinces' financial woes were of their own making. On other occasions, the federal government was willing to consider a new arrangement, but only if the provinces surrendered more control over spending. See Christopher Armstrong, *The Politics of Federalism: Ontario's Relations with the Federal Government, 1867–1942* (Toronto: University of Toronto Press, 1981), 148–59, 235.

34. James Hiller, *Confederation: Deciding Newfoundland's Future, 1934 to 1949* (St. John's: Newfoundland Historical Society, 1998), 3–4; James Overton, "Riots, Raids, and Relief, Police, Prisons and Parsimony: The Political Economy of Public Order in Newfoundland in the 1930s," in Elliott Leyton, William O'Grady, and Overton, *Violence and Public Anxiety: A Canadian Case* (St. John's: Institute of Social and Economic Research, 1992), 236–65.

35. *Evening Telegram*, 18 February 1932.
36. Overton, "Riots, Raids, and Relief," 209–30; "McGrath, James J.," *ENL, III*, 409.
37. *Evening Telegram*, 10 March 1932.
38. Long, *Suspended State*, 64–5.
39. Long, *Suspended State*, 65–8; Overton, "Economic Crisis," 107–10.
40. Archives and Special Collections, QEII Library, Memorial University, Sir Richard A. Squires Papers, Coll. 250, file, 2.28.003; White to Squires, Badger, 4 March 1932; A.J. Verge to Squires, Winterton, 9 March 1932; Squires to White, St. John's, 18 March 1932.
41. George Allan England, *The Greatest Hunt in the World* (1924) (Montreal: Tundra Books, 1975), 351.
42. Rowsell, "William Yetman," 7–11.
43. *Fishermen's Advocate*, Port Union, 27 May 1932; "Mitchell, Harold," *ENL, III*, 590–1; Overton, "Riots, Raids, and Relief," 236–65.
44. *Daily News*, 30 June 1932; *Evening Telegram*, 2 July 1932.
45. *Evening Telegram*, 26 September 1932.
46. Article 10, 21 Sept. 1932 in W.F. Coaker, *Past, Present and Future: Being a Series of Articles Contributed to the Fishermen's Advocate, 1932* (Port Union: Fishermen's Advocate, 1932), n.p.
47. Richard Charles Maguire, "'The Fascists … are … to be depended upon.' The British Government, Fascists and Strike-breaking during 1925 and 1926," in Nigel Cosey and David Renton, eds., *British Fascism, the Labour Movement and the State* (London: Palgrave, 2005), 6–20; see also Pugh, *Hurrah for the Blackshirts*, 23–33, 44–7.
48. "Notes of a Visit to Greece, 1932" in *Past, Present and Future*, np; Alexander, *Decay of Trade*, 22–4.
49. O'Flaherty, *Lost Country*, 364–5.
50. Elliott, "Newfoundland Politics in the 1920s," Peter Neary, *Newfoundland in the North Atlantic World 1929–1949* (Montreal and Kingston: McGill-Queen's University Press, 1988), 15–43; Amulree Report, 77–87, 209–14, quote from 43.
51. Long, *Suspended State*, 78–92; Short's letter is quoted verbatim at 180–5.
52. Amulree Report, 197.
53. Quoted in Long, *Suspended State*, 11.
54. Peter Neary, "How Newfoundland Veterans became Canadian Veterans: A Study in Bureaucracy and Benefit," in Hiller and Neary, *Twentieth Century Newfoundland*, 197.
55. "Editorial," *Veteran*, 8, 4 (April 1930), 7–8.
56. Cashin, *My Fight*, 71–104; J.K. Hiller, "The Career of F. Gordon Bradley," *Newfoundland Studies*, 4, 2 (1988), 163–80.
57. *Evening Telegram*, 7 March 1929.

58. Monica Lucy A. Wall, "About Cabbages and Kings: One Man's Account of Life in a Small Outport," Memorial University of Newfoundland Folklore and Language Archive, Unpublished paper, 1982, MA 83–107, 6.

59. Kean, *Old and Young Ahead*, 117–48.

CONCLUSION

1. Long, *Suspended State*, 14–15.

2. P.T. McGrath and Charles Lucas, "Newfoundland," in Lucas, ed., *The Empire at War, Volume II* (London: Humphrey Milford, Oxford University Press, 1923), 321.

3. Roberts, "Nothing Venture, Nothing Have," 41–65; Alexander, *Decay of Trade*, 20–7; McDonald, *To Each His Own*, 86–105; Noel, *Politics in Newfoundland*, 146–7.

4. Rosemary Ommer's first statement was in her classic paper "What's Wrong With Canadian Fish?" *Journal of Canadian Studies*, 20, 3 (1985), 122–42, but she later extended it into a consideration of ecological consequences in "One Hundred Years of Fishery Crises in Newfoundland," *Acadiensis*, 23, 2 (Spring 1994), 5–20. On the more positive approach to state regulation of the fishing industry see Guðmundur Jónsson, "Fishing Nations in Crisis: The Response of the Icelandic and Norwegian Fisheries to the Great Depression," *International Journal of Maritime History*, 21, 1 (2009), 127–51.

5. *Evening Telegram*, 9 November 1929.

6. Richard Thurlow, "The Failure of British Fascism 1932–40," in Andrew Thorpe, ed., *The Failure of Political Extremism in Inter-War Britain* (Exeter: Exeter University Press, 1989), 67–84.

7. David Baker, "The Extreme Right in the 1920s: Fascism in a Cold Climate, or 'Conservatism with Knobs On'?" in Mike Cronin, ed., *The Failure of British Fascism: The Far Right and the Fight for Political Recognition* (New York: St. Martin's Press, 1996), 17–26.

8. *Evening Telegram*, 5 March 1928. Similar statements may be found on 7 March 1930 and in the *Daily News*, 9 March 1931.

BIBLIOGRAPHY

PRIMARY SOURCES

GREAT BRITAIN

Colonial Office Records

    CO 194, 1914–. Microfilm copies on deposit at the Centre for Newfoundland Studies, Queen Elizabeth II Library, Memorial University of Newfoundland.

    CO 532, 1907–25. Microfilm copies on deposit at the Centre for Newfoundland Studies, Queen Elizabeth II Library, Memorial University of Newfoundland.

Dominions Office

    DO 35, 1926–34. Microfilm copies on deposit at the Centre for Newfoundland Studies, Queen Elizabeth II Library, Memorial University of Newfoundland.

National Archives

    Royal Newfoundland Regiment War Diary. WO/95/2308.

CANADA

Library and Archives Canada

Department of Veterans Affairs Fonds, RG 38.

NEWFOUNDLAND AND LABRADOR

Archives and Special Collections Division, Queen Elizabeth II Library, Memorial University

William Ford Coaker Papers, Coll. 009.

Sir Richard A. Squires Papers, Coll. 250.

The Rooms Provincial Archives Division

Hollis Walker Enquiry fonds, GN 126.

Office of the Colonial Secretary, GN 2.

 World War I records, GN 2.14.

Office of the Prime Minister, GN 8

 E.P. Morris sous fonds.

 R.A. Squires sous fonds.

 William Frederick Lloyd sous fonds.

Royal Commission of Enquiry into the Sealing Disasters of 1914. GN 121.

Sir Walter Davidson fonds, MG 136.

NEWSPAPERS AND OTHER PERIODICALS

Daily Globe, St. John's, 1924–26.

Daily Mail, St. John's, 1914.

Daily News, St. John's, 1914–34.

Daily Star, St. John's, 1915–21.

Diocesan Magazine, 1914–34.

Evening Advocate, St. John's, 1917–24.

Evening Herald, St. John's, 1914.

Evening Telegram, St. John's, 1914–34.

Fishermen's Advocate, St. John's, 1910–14; Port Union, 1924–34.

Mail and Advocate, St. John's, 1914–16.

Newfoundland Quarterly, 1914–34.

Veteran, St. John's, 1920–34.

OTHER PRINT SOURCES

"The Anti-Confederate Song," Newfoundland and Labrador Heritage Website, www.heritage.nf.ca/law/song.html; accessed 28/01/2013.

Cashin, Peter. *My Life and Times, 1890–1919*. St. John's: Breakwater, 1976.

Coaker, W.F. *Twenty Years of the Fishermen's Protective Union of Newfoundland from 1909–1929: Containing the Records of the Supreme Council since the Union's Inception, and Other Matter of Interest to Members of This Great Organization*. Reprint of 1930 ed. St. John's: Creative Printers, 1984.

Great Britain. *Newfoundland Royal Commission 1933: Report.* London: HMSO, 1933.

Great War Veterans' Association of Newfoundland. *Constitution Bye–Laws, Rules and Regulations of the Great War Veterans' Association of Newfoundland (Incorporated).* St. John's, Nfld.: Evening Telegram, 1928.

———. *Constitution Bye-Laws, Rules and Regulations of the Great War Veterans' Association of Newfoundland (Incorporated).* St. John's, Nfld.: Evening Telegram, 1928.

Lind, Francis Thomas. Edited by John Alexander Robinson. *The Letters of Mayo Lind.* St. John's: Robinson & Co., 1919.

Morris, Edward Patrick, and Walter Edward Davidson. *Report of Sir Edward Morris, Prime Minister of Newfoundland, on His Visit to the Newfoundland Soldiers at the Front in France, July, 1916, Made to His Excellency Sir W.E. Davidson, Governor.* St. John's: Herald Print, 1916.

Newfoundland, *Census of Newfoundland and Labrador, 1901, vol. 1.* St. John's: J.W. Withers, 1903.

———. *Report of the Commission of Enquiry into the Sealing Disasters of 1914.* St. John's, 1915.

"Newfoundland Regiment and the Great War." St. John's: The Rooms Corporation of Newfoundland and Labrador, 2010, www.therooms.ca/regiment/part2_the_battle_of_the_somme_part1.asp; accessed 17/01/2013.

Past, Present and Future: Being a Series of Articles Contributed to the Fishermen's Advocate, 1932. By Sir W.F. Coaker, K.B.E. Together with Notes of a trip to Greece 1932 And a Foreword by J.H. Scammell, nd, np.

The Times History of the War, XIV. London: Times, 1918.

SECONDARY SOURCES

BOOKS

Airhart, Phyllis D. *Serving the Present Age: Revivalism, Progressivism, and the Methodist Tradition in Canada.* Montreal and Kingston: McGill-Queen's University Press, 1992.

Alexander, David. Compiled by Eric W. Sager, Lewis R. Fischer, and Stuart O. Pierson. *Atlantic Canada and Confederation: Essays in Canadian Political Economy.* Toronto: University of Toronto Press, 1983.

———. *The Decay of Trade: An Economic History of the Newfoundland Salt fish Trade, 1935–1965.* St. John's: Institute of Social and Economic Research, 1977.

Anderson, Raoul, editor. *North Atlantic Maritime Cultures.* The Hague: Mouton, 1979.

Armstrong, Christopher. *The Politics of Federalism : Ontario's Relations with the Federal Government, 1867–1942,* Ontario Historical Studies Series. Toronto: University of Toronto Press, 1981.

Baker, Melvin, Robert Cuff, and Bill Gillespie. *Workingmen's St. John's: Aspects of Social History in the Early 1900s.* St. John's: Harry Cuff Publications, 1982.

Baker, Melvin, and Jean A. Graham. *Celebrate Memorial!: A Pictorial History of Memorial University of Newfoundland*. St. John's: Division of University Relations, [Memorial University of Newfoundland] for Memorial University's Anniversaries Committee, 1999.

Bassler, Gerhard. *Vikings to U-boats: the German Experience in Newfoundland and Labrador*. Montreal and Kingston: McGill-Queen's University Press, 2006.

Beckett, I.F.W. *The Great War, 1914–1918*. 2nd ed., Modern Wars in Perspective. Harlow, England, and New York: Pearson/Longman, 2007.

Belich, James. *Replenishing the Earth: The Settler Revolution and the Rise of the Anglo-World, 1783–1939*. Oxford: Oxford University Press, 2009.

Betcherman, Lita-Rose. *The Swastika and the Maple Leaf: Fascist Movements in Canada in the Thirties*. Toronto: Fitzhenry & Whiteside, 1975.

Bliss, Michael. *A Canadian Millionaire: The Life and Times of Sir Joseph Flavelle, Bart., 1858–1939*. Toronto: Macmillan, 1978.

Bowring, Peter. *A Thicket of Business: A History of the Bowring Family and the Bowring Group of Companies*. Stanhope, Weardale, County Durham: The Memoir Club, 2007.

Brown, Cassie, with Harold Horwood. *Death on the Ice*. Toronto: Doubleday, 1974.

Browne, Gary F. *Forget-Me-Not: Fallen Boy Soldiers, Royal Newfoundland Regiment, World War One*. St. John's: DRC Publishing, 2010.

Browne, Gary, and Darrin Michael McGrath. *Soldier Priest in the Killing Fields of Europe: Padre Thomas Nangle; Chaplain to the Newfoundland Regiment WWI*. St. John's: DRC Publishing, 2006.

Burgwyn, H. James. *The Legend of the Mutilated Victory: Italy, the Great War, and the Paris Peace Conference, 1915–1919*, Westport, Conn.: Greenwood Press, 1993.

Budgel, Richard and Michael Staveley. *The Labrador Boundary*. Happy Valley–Goose Bay: Labrador Institute of Northern Studies, Memorial University of Newfoundland, 1987.

Busch, Briton Cooper. *The War Against the Seals: A History of the North American Seal Fishery*. Montreal and Kingston: McGill-Queen's University Press, 1985.

Byron, Reginald, editor. *Retrenchment and Regeneration in Rural Newfoundland*. Toronto: University of Toronto Press, 2003.

Cadigan, Sean T. *Newfoundland and Labrador: A History*. Toronto: University of Toronto Press, 2009.

———. *Hope and Deception in Conception Bay: Merchant–Settler Relations in Newfoundland, 1785–1855*. Toronto: University of Toronto Press, 1995.

Candow, James E. *Of Men and Seals: A History of the Newfoundland Seal Hunt*. Ottawa: Environment Canada, Canadian Parks Service, 1989.

Cashin, Peter. Edited and annotated by Edward Roberts. *Peter Cashin: My Fight for Newfoundland, A Memoir*. St. John's: Flanker Press, 2012.

Cave, Joy B. *What Became of Corporal Pittman?* St. John's: Breakwater, 1976.

Christie, Nancy, and Michael Gauvreau. *A Full-Orbed Christianity: The Protestant Churches and Social Welfare in Canada, 1900–1940*. Montreal and Kingston: McGill-Queen's University Press, 1996.

Cook, Ramsay. *The Regenerators: Social Criticism in Late Victorian English Canada*. Toronto: University of Toronto Press, 1985.

Cook, Tim. *Clio's Warriors: Canadian Historians and the Writing of the World Wars*. Vancouver: UBC Press, 2006.

Copsey, Nigel, and Dave Renton. *British Fascism, the Labour Movement, and the State*. Houndmills, Basingstoke, Hampshire; New York: Palgrave Macmillan, 2005.

Cramm, Richard. *The First Five Hundred; Being a Historical Sketch of the Military Operations of the Royal Newfoundland Regiment in Gallipoli and on the Western Front During the Great War (1914–1918) Together with the Individual Military Records and Photographs Where Obtainable of the Men of the First Contingent, Known As "The First Five Hundred," Or "The Blue Puttees."* Albany, N.Y.: C.F. Williams, 1921.

Craven, Paul. *"An Impartial Umpire": Industrial Relations and the Canadian State 1900–1911*. Toronto: University of Toronto Press, 1980.

Cronin, Mike. *The Failure of British Fascism: The Far Right and the Fight for Political Recognition*. New York: St. Martin's Press, 1996.

Cuff, Robert H., editor. *A Coaker Anthology*. St. John's: Creative, 1986.

Cullum, Linda, Carmelita McGrath, and Marilyn Porter, editors. *Weather's Edge: Women in Newfoundland and Labrador, A Compendium*. St. John's: Killick Press, 2006.

(DCB) *Dictionary of Canadian Biography*. Volumes IV–VIII. Toronto: University of Toronto Press, 1979, 1983, 1985, 1987, 1988.

Diehl, James M., and Stephen R. Ward. *The War Generation: Veterans of the First World War*. Port Washington, N.Y.: Kennikat Press, 1975.

Duley, Margot I. *Where Once Our Mothers Stood We Stand : Women's Suffrage in Newfoundland, 1890–1925*. Charlottetown, P.E.I.: Gynergy, 1993.

(ENL) *Encyclopedia of Newfoundland and Labrador*. Volumes I–V. St. John's: Newfoundland Book Publishers, 1981, 1984, 1991, 1993, 1994.

Eksteins, Modris. *Rites of Spring: The Great War and the Birth of the Modern Age*. Toronto: Lester and Orpen Dennys, 1994.

Ellison, Suzanne. *Historical Directory of Newfoundland and Labrador Newspapers, 1807–1987*. St. John's: Memorial University of Newfoundland Library, 1988.

England, George Allan. *Vikings of the Ice: Being the Log of a Tenderfoot on the Great Newfoundland Seal Hunt*. Garden City, N.Y.: Doubleday, Page & Co., 1924.

———. *The Greatest Hunt in the World* (1924). Montreal: Tundra Books, 1975.

Facey-Crowther, David R., editor. *Lieutenant Owen William Steele of the Newfoundland Regiment: Diary and Letters*. Montreal and Kingston: McGill-Queen's University Press, 2002.

Facey-Crowther, David R., and Jerry G. O'Grady. *Better Than the Best: The Story of the Royal Newfoundland Regiment, 1795–1995*. St. John's: Royal Newfoundland Regiment Advisory Council, 1995.

Feltham, John. *Sealing Steamers*. St. John's: Cuff Publications, 1995.

Fischer, L.R. and Eric Sager, editors. *The Enterprising Canadians*. St. John's: Maritime History Group, Memorial University, 1979.

Forbes, E.R. and D.A. Muise, editors. *The Atlantic Provinces in Confederation*. Toronto and Fredericton: University of Toronto Press/Acadiensis Press, 1993.

Forsey, Curtis. Edited by Bertram G. Riggs. *Grand Bank Soldier: The War Letters of Lance Corporal Curtis Forsey*. St. John's: Flanker Press, 2007.

Francis, Daniel. *Seeing Reds: The Red Scare of 1918–1919, Canada's First War on Terror*. Vancouver: Arsenal Pulp Press.

Fudge, Judy, and Eric Tucker. *Labour Before the Law: The Regulation of Workers' Collective Action in Canada, 1900–1948*. Toronto: University of Toronto Press, 2004.

Fussell, Paul. *The Great War and Modern Memory*. Oxford: Oxford University Press, 1975.

Gallishaw, John. *Trenching at Gallipoli*. 2nd ed. St. John's: DRC Publishing, 2005.

Gilbert, Martin. *The Battle of the Somme: The Heroism and Horror of War*. London: John Murray, 2006.

Gillespie, Bill. *A Class Act: An Illustrated History of the Labour Movement in Newfoundland and Labrador*. St. John's: Creative, 1986.

Gilmore, William C. *Newfoundland and Dominion Status: The External Affairs Competence and International Law Status of Newfoundland, 1855–1934*. Agincourt, Ont.: Carswell, 1988.

Glassford, Sarah Carlene, and Amy J. Shaw. *A Sisterhood of Suffering and Service: Women and Girls of Canada and Newfoundland During the First World War*. Vancouver: UBC Press, 2012.

Gorski, Richard, editor. *Maritime Labour: Contributions to the History of Work at Sea, 1500–2000*. Amsterdam: Uitgeverij Aksant, 2008.

Guildford, Janet and Suzanne Morton, editors. *Separate Spheres: Women's Worlds in the 19th-Century Maritimes*. Fredericton: Acadiensis Press, 1994.

Hadley, Michael L., Rob Huebert and Fred W. Crickard, editors. *A Nation's Navy: In Quest of Canadian Naval Identity*. Montreal and Kingston: McGill-Queen's University Press, 1996.

Hanrahan, Maura. *Tsunami: The Newfoundland Tidal Wave Disaster*. St. John's: Flanker Press, 2004.

Hayes, Geoffrey, Michael Bechthold, and Andrew Iarocci. *Vimy Ridge: A Canadian Reassessment*. Waterloo, Ont.: Wilfrid Laurier University Press, 2007.

Heron, Craig, editor. *The Workers' Revolt in Canada, 1917–1925*. Toronto: University of Toronto Press, 1998.

Hibbs, Richard. *Who's Who in and from Newfoundland 1927*. St. John's: R. Hibbs, 1927.

Hiller, James, and Peter Neary, editors. *Twentieth-Century Newfoundland: Explorations*. St. John's: Breakwater, 1994.

———. *Newfoundland in the Nineteenth and Twentieth Centuries.* Toronto: University of Toronto Press, 1980.

Hollett, Calvin. *Shouting, Embracing, and Dancing with Ecstasy: The Growth of Methodism in Newfoundland, 1774–1874.* Montreal, McGill-Queen's University Press, 2010.

Holm, Poul, Tim D. Smith, and David J. Starkey, editors. *The Exploited Seas: New Directions for Marine Environmental History.* St. John's: International Association for Maritime History/Census of Marine Life, 2001.

Hornsby, Stephen J. *Nineteenth-Century Cape Breton: A Historical Geography.* Montreal and Kingston: McGill-Queen's University Press, 1992.

Humphries, Mark Osborne. *The Last Plague: Spanish Influenza and the Politics of Public Health in Canada.* Toronto: University of Toronto Press, 2012.

Hunter, Mark C. *To Employ and Uplift Them: The Newfoundland Naval Reserve, 1899–1926.* St. John's: ISER Books, 2009.

Kealey, Gregory S., editor. *Class, Gender, and Region: Essays in Canadian Historical Sociology.* St. John's: Committee on Canadian Labour and Working-Class History, 1988.

Kealey, Linda, editor. *Pursuing Equality: Historical Perspectives on Women in Newfoundland and Labrador.* St. John's: Creative, 1993.

Kean, Abram. Edited by Shannon Ryan. *Old and Young Ahead, 1935.* St. John's: Flanker Press, 2000.

Keegan, John. *The First World War.* London: Hutchinson, 1998.

———. *The Face of Battle: A Study of Agincourt, Waterloo and the Somme.* London: Penguin, 1976.

Keir, David. *The Bowring Story.* London: The Bodley Head, 1962.

Kerr, Donald, and Deryck W. Holdsworth, editors. *Historical Atlas of Canada, III: Addressing the Twentieth Century.* Toronto: University of Toronto Press, 1990.

Leyton, Elliott, O'Grady, William, and Overton, James. *Violence and Public Anxiety: A Canadian Case.* St. John's: Institute of Social and Economic Research, 1992.

Lochnan, Katharine, editor. *Black Ice: David Blackwood Prints of Newfoundland.* Vancouver, Toronto, Berkeley: Douglas & McIntyre, 2011.

Long, Gene. *Suspended State: Newfoundland Before Canada.* St. John's: Breakwater, 1999.

Lucas, Charles, editor. *The Empire at War, Volume II.* London: H. Milford Oxford University Press, 1921.

Macfarlane, David. *The Danger Tree : Memory, War, and the Search for a Family's Past.* Toronto: Macfarlane Walter & Ross, 1991.

MacKay, Robert A. *Newfoundland: Economic, Diplomatic, and Strategic Studies, with a Foreword by Sir Campbell Stuart.* Toronto: Oxford University Press, 1946.

Mackenzie, David, editor. *Canada and the First World War.* Toronto: University of Toronto Press, 2005.

MacLeod, Malcolm. *Connections: Newfoundland's Pre-confederation Links with Canada and the World.* St. John's: Creative, 2003.

————. *A Bridge Built Halfway: A History of Memorial University College, 1925–1950*. Montreal: McGill-Queen's University Press, 1990.

Major, Kevin. *No Man's Land: A Play*. St John's: Pennywell Books, 2005.

Marshall, Ingeborg. *A History and Ethnography of the Beothuk*. Montreal and Kingston: McGill-Queen's University Press, 1996.

McAllister, Anthony. *The Greatest of Gallantry: the Newfoundland Regiment at Monchy le Preux, April 14, 1917*. St. John's: DRC Publishing, 2011.

McDonald, Ian D.H. Edited by J.K. Hiller. *"To Each His Own": William Coaker and the Fishermen's Protective Union in Newfoundland Politics, 1980–1925*. St. John's: Institute of Social and Economic Research, 1987.

McGerr, Michael. *A Fierce Discontent: The Rise and Fall of the Progressive Movement in America, 1870–1920*. New York: Free Press, 2003.

McGrath, Carmelita, with Sharon Halfyard. Marion Cheeks, editor. *To Be My Father's Daughter*. St. John's: Educational Resource Development Co-operative, 2008.

McGrath, Carmelita, Barbara Neis, and Marilyn Porter, editors. *Their Lives and Times: Women in Newfoundland and Labrador, A Collage*. St. John's: Killick Press, 1995.

Middlebrook, Martin. *The First Day on the Somme, 1 July 1916*. London: Allen Lane/ The Penguin Press, 1971.

Morton, Desmond, and Glenn T. Wright. *Winning the Second Battle: Canadian Veterans and the Return to Civilian Life, 1915–1930*. Toronto: University of Toronto Press, 1987.

Murphy, Tony, and Paul Kenney. *The Trail of the Caribou*. St. John's: Harry Cuff, 1991.

Nadeau, Jean-François. *Adrien Arcand, Fürher Canadien*. Montreal: Lux, 2010.

Naylor, James. *The New Democracy: Challenging the Social Order in Industrial Ontario*. Toronto: University of Toronto Press, 1991.

Neary, Peter. *Newfoundland in the North Atlantic World 1929–1949*. Montreal and Kingston: McGill-Queen's University Press, 1988.

Newell, Dianne, and Rosemary Ommer, editors. *Fishing Places, Fishing People: Issues in Canadian Small-Scale Fisheries*. Toronto: University of Toronto Press, 1999.

Nicholson, G.W.L. *The Fighting Newfoundlander: A History of the Royal Newfoundland Regiment*. St. John's: Government of Newfoundland and Labrador, 1964.

Noel, S.J.R. *Politics in Newfoundland*. Toronto: University of Toronto Press, 1971.

O'Flaherty, Patrick. *Lost Country: The Rise and Fall of Newfoundland, 1843–1933*. St. John's: Long Beach Press, 2005.

O'Gorman, Bill. *Lest We Forget: The Life and Times of Veterans from the Port au Port Peninsula, World War I*. West Bay Centre, NL: Bill O'Gorman, 2009.

Ommer, Rosemary E., editor. *Merchant Credit and Labour Strategies in Historical Perspective*. Fredericton, NB: Acadiensis Press, 1990.

Overy, R.J. *The Inter-War Crisis 1919–1939*, 2nd ed. Seminar Studies in History. Harlow, England; New York: Longman, 2007.

Palmer, Bryan D. *Working-Class Experience: Rethinking the History of Canadian Labour, 1800–1991*. Toronto: McClelland & Stewart, 1992.

Parks Canada. *The Price We Paid for Nationhood: Beaumont-Hamel and Vimy Ridge.* Ottawa: Parks Canada.

Parsons, W. David. *Pilgrimage: A Guide to the Royal Newfoundland Regiment in World War One.* St. John's: Creative, 1994.

Parsons, W. David, and Ean Parsons. *The Best Small-Boat Seamen in the Navy: The Newfoundland Division, Royal Naval Reserve, 1900–1922.* St. John's: DRC Publishing, 2009.

Patey, Francis. *Veterans of the North.* St. John's: Creative, 2003.

Pearsall, Judy, and Bill Trumble, editors. *The Oxford English Reference Dictionary*, 2nd ed. Oxford: Oxford University Press, 1996.

Preston, William. *Aliens and Dissenters: Federal Suppression of Radicals, 1903–1933.* 2nd ed. Urbana: University of Illinois Press, 1994.

Prior, Robin, and Trevor Wilson. *The Somme.* New Haven: Yale University Press, 2005.

Pugh, Martin. *"Hurrah for the Blackshirts!": Facists and Fascism in Britain between the Wars.* London: Pimlico, 2006.

Pope, Peter E. *Fish into Wine: The Newfoundland Plantation in the Seventeenth Century.* Chapel Hill and London: University of North Carolina Press, 2004.

Renzi, William A. *In the Shadow of the Sword: Italy's Neutrality and Entrance into the Great War, 1914–1915.* New York: P. Lang, 1987.

Riggs, Bert, editor. *Grand Bank Soldier: The War Letters of Lance Corporal Curtis Forsey.* St. John's: Flanker Press, 2007.

Rompkey, Bill, and Bert Riggs, editors. *Your Daughter Fanny: The War Letters of Frances Cluett, VAD.* St. John's: Flanker Press, 2006.

Rompkey, Ronald, editor. *Jessie Luther at the Grenfell Mission.* Montreal and Kingston: McGill-Queens University Press, 2001.

Robin, Martin. *Shades of Right: Nativist and Facsist Politics in Canada, 1920–1940.* Toronto: University of Toronto Press, 1992.

Ryan, Shannon. *The Ice Hunters: A History of Newfoundland Sealing to 1914.* St. John's: Breakwater, 1994.

———. *Fish Out of Water: The Newfoundland Saltfish Trade 1814–1914.* St. John's: Breakwater, 1986.

Sager, Eric W. *Seafaring Labour: The Merchant Marine of Atlantic Canada, 1820–1914.* Montreal and Kingston: McGill-Queen's University Press, 1989.

Sheldon, Jack. *Germans at Beaumont Hamel*, Battleground Europe. Barnsley: Pen & Sword Military, 2006.

Smallwood, J.R., editor. *The Book of Newfoundland, Volume I.* St. John's: Newfoundland Book Publishers, 1937.

———. *Coaker of Newfoundland* (1927). Port Union, NL: Coaker Heritage Foundation, 1998.

Sontag, Raymond James. *A Broken World, 1919–1939.* New York: Harper & Row, 1971.

Stacey, A.J. Stacey, edited by Jean Edwards. *Memoirs of a Blue Puttee.* St. John's: DRC, 2002.

Stevenson, D. *Cataclysm: The First World War as Political Tragedy.* New York: Basic Books, 2004.

Story, G.M., W.J. Kirwin, and J.D.A. Widdowson, editors. *Dictionary of Newfoundland English.* Toronto: University of Toronto Press, 1982.

Strachan, Hew. *The First World War.* London: Penguin, 2003.

———. *The First World War: Volume I, To Arms.* Oxford: Oxford University Press, 2001.

Swettenham, John. *To Seize the Victory: The Canadian Corps in World War I.* Toronto: Ryerson Press, 1965.

Tait, Robert. *"The Trail of the Caribou": The Royal Newfoundland Regiment, 1914–1918.* Boston: Newfoundland Publishing Co., 1933.

Thompson, John Herd, with Allen Seager. *Canada 1929–1939: Decades of Discord.* Toronto: McClelland and Stewart, 1985.

Thorpe, Andrew. *The Failure of Political Extremism in Inter-War Britain.* Exeter: Exeter University Press, 1989.

Tocque, P. *Wandering Thoughts: or, Solitary Hour.* London, 1846.

Vance, Jonathan F. *Death So Noble: Memory, Meaning, and the First World War.* Vancouver: UBC Press, 1997.

Ward, Paul. *Red Flag and Union Jack: Englishness, Patriotism, and the British Left, 1881–1924.* Woodbridge: Royal Historical Society and the Boydell Press, 1998.

Weir, Gail. *The Miners of Wabana.* St. John's: Breakwater, 1989.

Whitaker, Reg, Gregory S. Kealey and Andrew Parnaby. *Secret Service: Political Policing in Canada from the Fenians to Fortress America.* Toronto: University of Toronto Press, 2012.

Winsor, Naboth. *The Sea, Our Life-Blood: A History of Wesleyville, Newfoundland.* Gander: BSC Printers, 1984.

ARTICLES

Baker, Melvin and Neary, Peter. "'A Real Record for All Time': Newfoundland and Great War Official History." *Newfoundland and Labrador Studies*, 21, 1 (2012), 5–32.

———. "Sir Robert Bond (1857–1927): A Biographical Sketch." *Newfoundland Studies*, 15, 1 (1999), 1–54.

Baker, Melvin and Overton, James. "J.R. Smallwood on Liberalism in 1926." *Newfoundland Studies*, 11, 1 (1995), 75–126.

Baker, Melvin. "President Coaker's Log of His Trip to the Ice Floe Last Spring in S.S. *Nascopie*." *Newfoundland and Labrador Studies*, 25, 2 (2010), 217–52.

———. "Rural Electrification in Newfoundland in the 1950s and the Origins of the Newfoundland Power Commission." *Newfoundland Studies*, 6, 2 (1990), 190–209.

Barr, William. "Newfoundland Ship Made Soviet Arctic History." *Canadian Geographic*, 99, 2 (1979), 30–35.

Boudreau, Michael. "'There Is ... No Pernicious Dualism between Sacred and Secular': Nova Scotia Baptists and the Social Gospel, 1880–1914," *Nova Scotia Historical Review*, 16, 1 (1996), 109–31.

Busch, Briton Cooper. "The Newfoundland Sealers' Strike of 1902." *Labour/Le Travail*, 14 (Fall 1984), 73–101.

Cadigan, Sean T. "Recognizing the Commons in Coastal Forests: The Three-Mile Limit in Newfoundland, 1875–1939." *Newfoundland and Labrador Studies*, 21, 2 (2006), 209–34.

———. "The Moral Economy of the Commons: Ecology and Equity in the Newfoundland Cod Fishery, 1815–1855." *Labour/Le Travail*, 43 (Spring 1999), 9–42.

———. "Battle Harbour in Transition: Merchants, Fishermen, and the State in the Struggle for Relief in a Labrador Fishing Community during the 1930s." *Labour/ Le Travail*, 26 (Fall 1990), 125–50.

Chisholm, Jessie. "Organizing on the Waterfront: The St. John's Longshoremen's Protective Union (LSPU), 1890–1914." *Labour/Le Travail*, 26 (Fall 1990), 37–59.

Crawley, Ron. "Off to Sydney: Newfoundlanders Emigrate to Industrial Cape Breton, 1890–1914." *Acadiensis*, 17, 2 (1988), 27–51.

Earle, Nancy. "*Death on the Ice* and the Newfoundland Imaginary: Print Culture on the Periphery." *Papers of the Bibliographical Society of Canada*, 48, 1 (Spring 2010), 119–52.

Fitzgerald, John Edward. "Archbishop E.P. Roche, J.R. Smallwood, and Denominational Rights in Newfoundland Education, 1948." *CCHA Historical Studies*, 65 (1999), 28–49.

———. "'The True Father of Confederation' Archbishop E.P. Roche, Term 17, and Newfoundland's Union with Canada." *Newfoundland Studies*, 14, 2 (1998), 188–219.

Harding, Robert J. "Glorious Tragedy: Newfoundland's Cultural Memory of the Attack at Beaumont Hamel, 1916–1925." *Newfoundland and Labrador Studies*, 21, 1 (2006), 3–40.

Hiller, James K. "Robert Bond and the Pink, White and Green: Newfoundland Nationalism in Perspective." *Acadiensis*, 36, 2 (2007), 113–33.

———. "The Newfoundland Fisheries Issue in Anglo–French Treaties, 1713–1904." *Journal of Imperial and Commonwealth History*, 24, 1 (1996), 1–23.

———. "The 1904 Anglo-French Newfoundland Fisheries Convention: Another Look." *Acadiensis*, 25, 1 (1995), 82–98.

———. "Utrecht Revisited: The Origins of French Fishing Rights in Newfoundland Waters." *Newfoundland Studies*, 7, 1 (1991), 23–39.

———. "The Politics of Newsprint: The Newfoundland Pulp and Paper Industry, 1915–1939." *Acadiensis*, 19, 2 (1990), 3–39.

———. "The Career of F. Gordon Bradley." *Newfoundland Studies*, 4, 1 (1988), 163–80.

———. "The Origins of the Pulp and Paper Industry in Newfoundland." *Acadiensis*, 11, 2 (1982), 42–68.

Holly, Donald H. "The Beothuk on the Eve of their Extinction." *Arctic Anthropology*. 37, 1 (2000), 79–95.

———. "Environment, History, and Agency in Storage Adaptation: On the Beothuk in the 18th Century." *Canadian Journal of Archaeology*. 22, 1 (1998), 101–22.

Jónsson, Guðmundur. "Fishing Nations in Crisis: The Response of the Icelandic and Norwegian Fisheries to the Great Depression." *International Journal of Maritime History*, 21, 1 (2009), 127–51.

Kealey, G.S. "State Repression of Labour and the Left in Canada, 1914–20: The Impact of the First World War." *Canadian Historical Review* 73, 3 (1992), 281–314.

———. "1919: The Canadian Labour Revolt." *Labour/Le Travail*, 13 (1984), 11–44.

Korneski, Kurt. "Development and Degradation: The Emergence and Collapse of the Lobster Fishery on Newfoundland's West Coast, 1856–1924." *Acadiensis*, 41, 1 (2012), 21–48.

———. "Race, Gender, Class, and Colonial Nationalism: Railway Development in Newfoundland, 1881–1898." *Labour/Le Travail*, 62 (2008), 79–107.

Lackenbauer, P. Whitney. "War, Memory, and the Newfoundland Regiment at Gallipoli." *Newfoundland Studies*, 15, 2 (1999), 176–214.

Little, Linda. "Collective Action in Outport Newfoundland: A Case Study from the 1830s." *Labour/Le Travail*, 26 (Fall 1990), 7–35.

Martin, Chris. "The Right Course, The Best Course, The Only Course: Voluntary Recruitment in the Newfoundland Regiment, 1914–1918." *Newfoundland and Labrador Studies*, 24, 1 (2009), 55–89.

McInnis, Peter. "'All Solid Along the Line': The Reid Newfoundland Strike of 1918." *Labour/Le Travail*, 26 (1990), 61–84.

O'Brien, Mike. "Out of a Clear Sky: The Mobilization of the Newfoundland Regiment, 1914–1915." *Newfoundland and Labrador Studies*, 22, 2 (2007), 401–28.

Ommer, Rosemary E. "One Hundred Years of Fishery Crises in Newfoundland." *Acadiensis*, 23, 2 (Spring 1994), 5–20.

———. "What's Wrong with Canadian Fish?" *Journal of Canadian Studies*, 20, 2 (1985), 122–42.

Overton, James. "Economic Crisis and the End of Democracy: Politics in Newfoundland During the Great Depression." *Labour/Le Travail*, 26 (1990), 85–124.

Pastore, Ralph. "The Collapse of the Beothuk World." *Acadiensis*, 19, 1 (1989), 52–71.

———. "Fishermen, Furriers, and Beothuks: The Economy of Extinction." *Man in the Northeast*, 33 (1987), 47–60.

Peterson, Larry. "Revolutionary Socialism and Industrial Unrest in the Era of the Winnipeg General Strike: The Origins of Communist Labour Unionism in Europe and North America." *Labour/Le Travail*, 13 (Spring 1984), 115–31.

———. "The One Big Union in International Perspective: Revolutionary Industrial Unionism 1900–1925." *Labour/Le Travailleur*, 7 (Spring 1981), 41–66.

Ryan, Shannon. "Fishery to Colony: A Newfoundland Watershed, 1793–1815." *Acadiensis*, 12, 2 (1983), 34–52.

Sanger, C.W. "The Dundee–St. John's Connection: Nineteenth Century Interlinkages Between Scottish Arctic Whaling and the Newfoundland Seal Fishery." *Newfoundland Studies*, 4, 1 (1988), 1–26.

Sharpe, Christopher A. "The 'Race of Honour': An Analysis of Enlistments and Casualties in the Armed Forces of Newfoundland: 1914–1918." *Newfoundland Studies*, 4, 1 (1988), 27–56.

THESES, DISSERTATIONS, UNPUBLISHED PAPERS, RECORDINGS

Beardsall, Sandra. "Methodist Religious Practices in Outport Newfoundland," ThD, University of Victoria and the University of Toronto, 1996.

Bush, Warren Oliver. "Industrial Disasters at Sea Around Newfoundland and Historicizing Maritime Peril: 1914–1918," MA thesis, Memorial University of Newfoundland, 2012.

Cadigan, Sean T. "A Nova Scotian in Newfoundland: Harry Crowe, Progressive Capitalism, and Common Property Rights in the Coastal Communities of White Bay, 1923–28." St. John's, Memorial University of Newfoundland, 2005.

Cuff, Robert H. "Quill and Hammer: Class and Labour Activism in Newfoundland and Nova Scotia, 1919–1925." BA dissertation, Memorial University of Newfoundland, 1980.

Dawe, David. "Newfoundland in World War I (As Seen Through the Eyes of an Enlisted Man)." Paper on deposit at the Centre for Newfoundland Studies, Memorial University of Newfoundland, date unknown but between 1963 and 1981.

Facey-Crowther, David R. "The Soldier's Tale: Newfoundland Soldiers' Accounts of the Great War." Paper on deposit at the Centre for Newfoundland Studies, Memorial University of Newfoundland, 1999.

———. "For King and Country: The Royal Newfoundland Regiment and the Battle of Beaumont Hamel 1 July 1916." Paper on deposit at the Centre for Newfoundland Studies, Memorial University of Newfoundland, 1993.

———. "War and Remembrance: Newfoundland and the Great War." Paper on deposit at the Centre for Newfoundland Studies, Memorial University of Newfoundland, 1996.

Flueriau, Sandra. "Sealing Disaster of 1914." Memorial University of Newfoundland Folklore and Language Archive, Unpublished paper, 1978, MA 78–391.

Harding, Robert. "The Role of the Great War Veterans' Association of Newfoundland, 1918–1925." BA honours dissertation, Memorial University of Newfoundland, 2003.

Hong, Robert G. "'An Agency for the Common Weal': The Newfoundland Board of Trade, 1909–1915." MA thesis, Memorial University of Newfoundland, 1998.

McInnis, Peter S. "Newfoundland Labour and World War I : The Emergence of the Newfoundland Industrial Workers' Association." MA Thesis, Memorial University of Newfoundland, 1987.

Moriarity, Joan. "Memoirs of a Daughter." Memorial University of Newfoundland Folklore and Language Archive, Unpublished paper, 1979, MA 79–240.

Neis, Barbara. "A Sociological Analysis of the Factors Responsible for the Regional Distribution of the Fishermen's Protective Union of Newfoundland." MA thesis, Memorial University of Newfoundland, 1980.

O'Brien, Andrea (compiler). "Architectural Survey of Port Union, NL, Conducted by Andrea O'Brien and Debbie O'Rielly, June 15–16, 2006." Heritage Foundation of Newfoundland and Labrador, www.heritagefoundation.ca/media/725/report–port–union.pdf; accessed 21/01/2013.

O'Brien, Patricia R. "The Newfoundland Patriotic Association: The Administration of the War Effort, 1914–1918." MA thesis, Memorial University of Newfoundland, 1981.

Quinlan, Terry, and Sean Cadigan. "A New Look at Confederation: Shifting Population Dynamics and Newfoundland's Relationship with Canada, 1869–1949." In Gordon Darroch, ed. *The Dawn of Canada's Century: Hidden Histories.* Essay collection submitted to McGill-Queen's University Press, 2011, in press.

Parsons, Andrew D. "Morale and Cohesion in the Royal Newfoundland Regiment 1914–18." MA Thesis, Memorial University of Newfoundland, 1995.

Roberts, Edward. "Nothing Venture, Nothing Have: Mr. Coaker's Regulations." Major MA Research paper, Memorial University, 2006.

Riggs, Bert. "Cast in Metal, Carved in Stone." Paper presented to the Rotary Club of St. John's Northwest, 24 November 2009.

Rowsell, Brenda M. "William Yetman: Reflections of the Past," Paper on deposit at Memorial University of Newfoundland Folklore and Language Archive, 1981, MAN 81–415.

Sanger, C.W. "Technological and Spatial Adaptation in the Newfoundland Seal Fishery During the Nineteenth Century." MA thesis, Memorial University of Newfoundland, 1973.

Warren, Gale D. "Voluntarism and Patriotism: Newfoundland Women's War Work During the First World War." Unpublished MA research paper, Memorial University, 2005.

Winsor, Eric. "History of Wesleyville." Paper on deposit at the Centre for Newfoundland Studies, Memorial University of Newfoundland, 1975.

Winsor, Fred. "The Newfoundland Bank Fishery: Government Policies and the Struggle to Improve Bank Fishing Crews' Working, Health, and Safety Conditions, 1876–1920." PhD thesis, Memorial University of Newfoundland, 1996

Winsor, Naboth. "'By Their Works': A History of the Wesleyville Congregation, Methodist Church—1874–1925, United Church—1925–1974," 1976.

ACKNOWLEDGMENTS

The idea for this book came from Margaret MacMillan and Robert Bothwell, general editors for Allen Lane's History of Canada series, who invited me to contribute a volume on Newfoundland. I benefited immensely from their advice and encouragement as I prepared this manuscript for publication; it was an honour to work with such outstanding scholars.

Colleagues at Memorial University stepped forward to help. James K. Hiller, professor emeritus of Newfoundland history, and Mark Humphries, a professor in the Department of History, read and provided advice on earlier drafts of this book. Mark generously provided me with access to research materials he had gathered in British and Canadian archives. Bert Riggs, the head of the Archives and Special Collections Division, Queen Elizabeth II Library, and a scholar of the impact of the First World War on Newfoundland, also read an earlier version of this book and provided constant support to my work. Charles Conway, a cartographer with the Department of Geography, prepared the maps. Lisa Rankin, interim dean of arts in 2011, provided indispensable support.

Rosemary Ommer, now an adjunct professor in the Departments of History and Geography at the University of Victoria, was a constant source of support, which included reading and suggesting important revisions to an earlier version of this work. For many years a professor of history at Memorial University, Rosemary was my teacher and graduate supervisor, and has remained my friend and colleague. Her expertise on the history of Newfoundland's marine industries is second to none.

Three students at Memorial University provided research assistance: Christopher Ryan, Stephen Walsh, and Tim Young. Tim studied with me as an honours student and was a delight to work with.

This book would not have been possible without the patient support of all the people at Penguin Group Canada who have seen me through this project: Diane Turbide, publishing director; Lisa Rundle, rights and contracts director; Mary Ann Blair, managing editor; and Justin Stoller, editorial assistant. Tara Tovell provided excellent and good-humoured line and copy editing, which made the final stages of writing a pleasure.

My partner, Bonnie Morgan, shared her research on the history of religion in Newfoundland and provided the type of moral support that may only come from family. I dedicate this book to Bonnie and my daughters Elizabeth and Margaret.

The responsibility for any error or omission in this work is solely my own.

PHOTO CREDITS

1   Courtesy of the Maritime History Archive, Memorial University of Newfoundland from an original printed in Coaker, *The History of the Fishermen's Protective Union of Newfoundland* (1920), 184.

2   Courtesy of Archives and Special Collections (Coll-137, Photo 2.01.017), Memorial University of Newfoundland Library, St. John's, Newfoundland.

3   Courtesy of the Rooms Provincial Archives Division, VA 137-27/ R.P. Holloway.

4   Courtesy of the Rooms Provincial Archives Division, VA 164-7/ R.P. Holloway.

5   Courtesy of the Rooms Provincial Archives Division, A 23-83/ J. Vey.

6   Courtesy of the Rooms Provincial Archives Division, VA 33-59.

7   Courtesy of the Rooms Provincial Archives Division, E 48-60/R.P. Holloway.

8   Courtesy of the Rooms Provincial Archives Division, VA 37-1.5.

9   Courtesy of the Rooms Provincial Archives Division, B 2-43. Used by permission © Imperial War Museum (Q 1530).

10 Courtesy of the Maritime History Archive, Memorial University of Newfoundland from an original printed in Coaker, *The History of the Fishermen's Protective Union of Newfoundland* (1920), p. 148.

11 Courtesy of the Maritime History Archive, Memorial University of Newfoundland from an original printed in Coaker, *The History of the Fishermen's Protective Union of Newfoundland* (1920), p. 96.

12 Courtesy of Archives and Special Collections (Coll-308, Leaf # 7B, Photo # 277), Memorial University of Newfoundland Library, St. John's, Newfoundland.

13 Courtesy of the Rooms Provincial Archives Division, VA 18-15.2

14 Courtesy of the Rooms Provincial Archives Division, E 35-10.

15 Courtesy of the Maritime History Archive, Memorial University of Newfoundland from Job Photograph Collection, Location No. PF-315.322

16 Courtesy of the Rooms Provincial Archives Division, A 19-21

INDEX

A

Act Respecting Alcoholic Liquors, 273
Adams, J.H., 291
alcohol prohibition, 202–203, 205
Alderdice, Frederick, 286, 289, 292–295, 297, 298
Allardyce, Sir William, 282–283, 268
American Federation of Labor, 183
Amulree Commission, 295, 297–298
Amulree, Lord, 295, 309–310
Anderson, Hugh, 143
Anderson, John, 120, 143, 183, 191
Anglo Newfoundland Development Company, 70
anti-Semitism, 212, 215, 252
Armistice, 185
Armstrong Whitworth & Company, 240, 244, 273
Arras, 158, 159, 160
Australian and New Zealand Army Corps (ANZAC), 91, 96–97, 138
Austria-Hungary, 93–94, 95
Ayre and Sons, Ltd., 193

B

Baldwin, Stanley, 294

Balfour Declaration of 1926, 295
Bank Crash of 1894, 21, 306
Bank of Commerce, xxi
Bank of Montreal, 68, 230, 239, 289, 298
Bank of Nova Scotia, 223
Barbour, George, 14, 42
Barrett, Silby, 250
Bartlett, William, 298
Barton, C.H., 49
Battle of Cambrai, 172, 175
Battle of Lys, 179
Battle of the Somme, x, 125–127, 134–137, 150
Battle of Transloy Ridge, 148
Beaumont Hamel
    British forces and, 130, 133, 138
    capture of, 150
    casualties at, 126–127, 129, 131–139, 157, 179, 203, 222, 241, 303, 312
    chaplains and, 149
    conditions at, 126–128, 137
    French forces, 138
    German forces, 124–127, 129–133, 148, 150
    memorial site, 208, 228–229, 262, 279

Newfoundland Regiment and, 126, 130–138, 156, 303

press coverage of, 134–136, 138–139

public reaction to, 134–135

Bellaventure (ship), 39–41, 46, 110

Bennett, C.F., 15

Bennett, John R., 45–46, 48, 62, 154, 155, 168, 242–243, 270

Bennett, R.B., 295

Beothic (ship), 110, 298

Beothuk (Aboriginal people), 6

Bermuda Trading Company, 13

Bernard, A.R., 108

Big Flood of 1915, 109, 113, 115, 132

Bishop, Robert K., 67, 164, 266

Blackall, W.W., 195

Blaine, James G., 26

Blandford, Sydney, 76

Bloodhound (ship), 118

Board of Trade (Newfoundland), 27

Bolshevism, 191–192, 196–197, 207, 216, 218, 254, 261

Bonaventure (ship), 110

Bond, Robert, 16, 19, 23, 26, 29–30, 143, 199–201

Bond–Blaine Convention, 26

Boulton, Henry John, xiii

Bowring (company), 12, 34, 82–83

Bowring, Benjamin, 12

Bowring, Charles Tricks, 12

Bowring, Edgar, 12–13, 66, 83, 104, 112, 115, 142, 146

Bowring, Eric, 291, 296

Bradley, F. Gordon, 277

Breslau (ship), 96

British Colonial Naval Defence Act of 1865, 17

British Empire Steel Corporation (BESCO), 278

British Empire Steel Corporation, 272

British War Committee, 113

Broderick, Mike, 131–132

Browne, W.J., 267

Brownrigg, H.J., 212, 213, 215

Bruce (ship), 110

Bulgaria, 95, 113

Bungay, Jacob, 36, 39

Burin Peninsula, tsunami at, 286–287

C

Caldwell, John, 213

Calpin, A.M., 264

Cambrai, Battle of, 172, 175

Campbell, Alexander, 204, 239, 247–248, 259, 261, 307

Canada Day, Memorial Day controversy and, xi–xii

Canadian Expeditionary Force, 73, 254

Cape Helles, 113, 125

Carew, W.J., 222

Caribou Hill, 107–108, 115, 149, 208

Carter, Frederick, 15

Cashin, Michael P., 66, 177, 182, 199–206, 209, 215, 232, 241, 243, 255, 267

Cashin, Peter, 126, 170, 244, 277, 282, 284–286, 290, 298

Catholic Cadet Corps, 62

censorship
Coaker and, 225–227, 245–246, 306

fishery and, 226–227

press criticism of, 182, 184

War Measures Act and, 104, 182, 218, 223, 225

wartime communications and, 145

Central Powers, 95, 107, 113, 124, 172, 185

Chaplin, John Fielding, 80

Charity Organization Bureau, 285

Christian, William Coaker, 235

Church Lads' Brigade (CLB), 62–63

Churchill, Winston, 96

Clarke, George, 33
Cluett, Frances, 173
Coady, Michael, 296
"Coaker Recruits," 151, 153, 173, 228
Coaker, Jessie, 52
Coaker, William Ford. *See also*
  Fishermen's Protective Union (FPU);
  Union Party.
  admiration for Mussolini, 251–252,
    254, 276, 293–294, 309
  alliance with Squires, 213–214, 222,
    286, 307–309
  "Coaker Recruits" and, 151, 153,
    173, 228
  Committee of Citizens and, 60
  conflict with Abram Kean, 114, 117,
    121, 145–146, 220, 303
  criticism of Morris government, 136–
    137, 140, 146, 153–154, 157, 161,
    163–165
  criticism of St. John's elites, 144
  ethnic discrimination and, 24
  knighthood of, 244
  Liberal-Union alliance and, 29
  National Government, 168–171, 177,
    179, 182
  political disillusionment, 300, 307–308
  political/economic views, 23, 27, 59–
    60, 77, 83, 89, 92–95, 101–102,
    106–107, 111–112, 114–122, 140,
    143, 145, 147, 155, 157, 163– 165,
    167, 168, 171–172, 174, 177, 181–
    182, 186–189, 196–200, 202, 205–
    207, 211–212, 218–219, 225–227,
    233, 235–236, 240, 251–252, 254,
    261, 273, 275, 281–283, 286–289,
    299–300, 302–305, 307, 311
  press/public criticism of, 50, 83–84,
    88, 182–183, 188–189, 191, 192,
    200, 202–204, 206–210, 213–216,
    219, 221, 223–227, 229–231, 238,
    240, 242–244, 246, 263, 265–267,
    274–275, 284, 296–297, 305–307

  religious views, 23
  Squires government and, 189, 210,
    248, 276
  SS *Newfoundland* disaster and, 33, 42,
    49–50, 52–54, 56, 58, 64, 78–79,
    80, 82, 85, 87–88, 92, 117
  Union Trading Company (UTC) and,
    25
  views on war, 63, 67, 75–76, 93, 101–
    102, 106–107, 109, 114–119, 121,
    124, 136–137, 139, 142, 145–147,
    150, 153, 160–161, 179, 181
  Walker inquiry and, 255, 258–259
coal
  mining, 231
  price of, 157
  profiteering and, 111–113
  shortage of, 112–113
Cochius, Rudolph, 279
Codfish Information Act, 220
Codfish Standardization Act, 220
Colonial Cordage Company, 266, 277
Commission of Government, xiii, xv–xvi,
  282, 287, 295, 297, 299, 300
Committee of Citizens (Patriotic
  Committee), 60, 63, 112
Committee of the Unemployed, 290
Committee of Union and Progress, 95
confederation with Canada
  opposition to, 15, 62
  possibility of, 154, 169
  support for, 15, 16, 62, 176
conscription
  in Britain, 155
  in Canada, xxv
  debate over, xxv, xxvii, xxiv, 118,
    161–162, 165–167, 172–175, 178,
    187, 218, 304
  implementation of, 177–178
  Military Service Act, 178, 180–181
  soldiers' views on, 180

Conservative Party (of Newfoundland),
15
Cook, Jessie Crosbie, 23
Corsican (ship), 195
Cramm, Richard, 264
Crewe, Albert John, 40–41
Crewe, Reuben, 40–41
Crosbie, John Carnell, 30
Crosbie, John Chalker, 30, 111, 170, 177,
182, 206, 209, 211, 220–221, 229,
232, 241, 243, 270, 277
Crowe, Harry J., 228
Crowe, Lawrence, 228
Curnew, George R., 126
Currie, John, 207, 210
Curtis, Levi, 193

D

Dalton, Thomas, xii-xiii
Daly, T.B., 166
Danger Tree, The (Macfarlane), xiii–xiv
Dardanelles, 92, 95–97, 104, 132, 148
Davidson, Sir Walter Edward, 48, 61, 63,
66, 77, 83, 88, 101, 104, 111, 135,
138–139, 141–142, 145, 167, 169
Davidson, Lady, 66
Dawe, Frank Gilbert, 69–70, 91, 127, 159
Dawe, Harry, 69
Dawe, Will, 69
Dawson, Thomas, 36, 39
de Lisle, Sir Beauvoir, 129
Devereaux, R.J., 119
dictatorship, support for, 252–255
Dominion Iron and Steel Company, 248
Dominion Iron and Steel, 249
Donnelly, James J., 107–108, 149
Duff, Robert, 283
Dunfield, Brian, 219

E

Earle, Julia Salter, 194, 231–232, 250
East End Electors Committee, 283, 284
education
post-war reconstruction and, 193–194
religious schools and, 193
teacher training, 193
war veterans and, 195
Egypt, 96–97, 107
elections
of 1889, 16
of 1900, 16, 23
of 1908, 27
of 1909, 27
of 1911, 29
of 1913, 30, 61, 147, 201
of 1919, 205, 209, 212, 247
of 1923, 247, 251, 260, 266
of 1924, 266
by-election in 1920, 212, 215, 218
by-election in 1924, 274
Ellsworth, James, 107
Emerson, George H., 77, 85, 88
Entente forces, 93, 95, 98, 113, 124–126,
129, 171–172, 177, 184–185
Exportation of the Salt Codfish Act, 233

F

Farquhar, Captain J., 34
fascism
interest in/support for, 294, 310
Mussolini and, 249–256, 262, 293–
294, 299
Firemen's Union, 146
First World War. *See also* Naval Reserve;
Newfoundland Regiment; war effort.
Armistice, 185
Australian and New Zealand Army
Corps (ANZAC), 91, 96–97, 138

Austria-Hungary and, 93–94, 95

Beaumont Hamel, 126–129, 130–139, 149–150, 156–157, 179, 203, 208, 222, 228–229, 241, 262, 279, 303

British forces, 93, 96, 98, 127–128, 148, 150, 172, 183

Bulgaria, 95, 113

Canadian forces, 60, 73, 75, 91–92, 96, 138, 166

casualties, 107–109, 123, 126–127, 129, 131–139, 157, 179, 203, 222, 241, 303, 312

Central Powers, 95, 107, 113, 124, 172, 185

conscription and, xxvii

Dardanelles, 92, 95–97, 104, 132, 148

Egypt and, 96–97, 107

elections during, 163

Entente forces, 93, 95, 98, 113, 124–126, 129, 171–172, 177, 184–185

French forces, 93, 172

Gallipoli, xv, 91, 95–101, 103, 107–109, 113–115, 138–139, 149, 156, 175, 179, 208, 303

gas attacks, 105, 108, 125, 148

Germany and, 93–97, 108, 124–127, 129–130, 148, 150, 159–160, 172, 177, 183–184, 269

Gommecourt, 123–124

Greece and, 97

hardships on home front, 109–110

inflation and, 161, 162, 217

Italy and, 93–94

Monchy-le-Preux (Monchy), 158–160, 167, 208, 292

munitions, 127–128, 129

origins of, xviii–xx

Ottoman Empire and, 93, 95

outbreak of, 59

Passchendaele, 172, 179

patriotism and, 60–61

press and, xxi, 64, 94, 101, 104–106, 106, 108, 115–116, 118, 147, 156, 157, 160

profiteering and, 110, 140, 147, 161, 206, 241, 243, 303–304

Romanian forces, 95, 150

Russian forces, 150

Turkey and, 95, 96

United States and, 171

Verdun, 118, 124–125, 127, 150

Vimy Ridge, xii, 159

Western Front, xv, 124, 137, 154, 171, 177, 185, 304

Ypres, 91, 95, 138, 148, 159, 167, 172, 177, 179, 184

Fisher, Hubert J.W., 179

Fishermen's Protective Union (FPU). See also Coaker, William Ford; fishery; seal hunt; Union Party.
   alliance with Liberal Party, 29
   criticism of Morris government, 141
   economic practices and, 27
   lawsuit by Abram Kean, 101, 102
   pension plans and, 140
   political views, 28, 54–55, 94, 95
   religious support and, 54
   SS *Newfoundland* disaster and, 47, 49–50, 52–54, 56, 87, 88
   views on war, 60, 63
   working conditions and, 25–26

fishery. See also Fishermen's Protective Union (FPU); seal hunt.
   conservation and, 10, 29
   credit and, 5, 8–9, 16, 22
   economics and, 22, 25, 27–28, 30, 224–227, 229–230
   European rights and, 2–3, 17–18, 26
   hiring practices and, 21
   international trade and, 4, 22, 26, 210–211, 220–223, 225, 227, 252, 288, 306

merchants and, 7–9, 13

political affiliations and, 27

prices and, 4, 206

profits and, 13

regulations/legislation and, 188, 206, 211–213, 215, 217–223, 226, 227, 229–230, 232, 238, 242, 245– 247, 304–309

remuneration and, 4

shortages of fish, 157

"tal qual" and, 25

working conditions, 31

Flavelle, Joseph, xxi

Florizel (ship), 34–35, 37, 41–42, 73–74, 119, 144, 146

Foley, Michael, 213

Food Control Board, 168–169

Forbes-Robertson, James, 131, 133, 159

Forestry
Humber development, 238–240, 242, 244, 272, 273

pulp and paper mills, 18–19, 68, 109, 238, 240, 273, 289

regulations, 238–239

Forsey, Curtis, 179–180

Fox, C.J., 267

Franklin, William, 63

G

Gallipoli
Australian and New Zealand Army Corps (ANZAC), 91, 96–97

Caribou Hill, 107–108, 115, 149, 208

casualties, 98–101, 103, 107–109, 114–115, 138–139, 175, 179

conditions at, 99–101, 103, 109

Newfoundland Regiment and, xv, 95–97, 107–109, 113–115, 156, 303

Gallishaw, Henrietta, 173

Gallishaw, John, 91–92, 96–97, 101, 103–104, 109, 173

General Strike of 1926 (Britain), 294

Germany, First World War and, 93–97, 108, 124–127, 129–130, 148, 150, 159–160, 172, 177, 183–184, 269

Gibbs, Michael, 183, 191

Goeben (ship), 96

Gompers, Sam, 183

Goode, William, 224

Goodwin, Albert "Ginger," 215

Goodyear, Harold Kenneth, xiii–xiv

Goodyear, Hedley John, xiii

Goodyear, Josiah Robert, xiii

Goodyear, Oswald Raymond, xiii

Goodyear, Stanley Charles, xiii

Gosling, William G., 27, 138, 183

Gosse, Solomon, 263

Gotto, Basil, 279

Grand Banks, 2

Great War. *See* First World War.

Great War Veterans' Association (GWVA), 214–216, 219, 221–222, 228, 233–234, 236–238, 260–264, 269, 272, 275, 299

Greece, 97, 113, 251, 254

Green, Charles, 35–36

Greene, W.M., 107

Grieve, Walter Baine, 218–219

Grimes, George F., 44–45, 163, 190, 196–197, 207, 209, 214

Gueudecourt, 148–149, 156, 208

Gulf Stream, 2

H

Hadow, Arthur Lovell, 132–133

Haig, Sir Douglas, 125, 127, 129, 136, 138, 150, 179, 219, 271, 279

Halfyard, William, 170, 286

Hardy, W.F., 98

Harmsworth, Alfred (Lord Northcliffe), 18

Harmsworth, Harold (Lord Rothermere), 18

Harris, Sir Charles Alexander, 182, 236, 260

Harvey and Company, 13–14, 34, 62

Harvey, Alexander J., 14, 110–112, 119

Hay, John Milton, 26

Hibbs, J.F., 74

Hickman, A.E., 200–201, 206–207, 229, 265–266, 269–270, 282–284

Higgins, J.G., 206, 233–234, 237, 243

Higgins, W.J., 247, 248, 265

High Cost of Living Commission, 164

Hillier, John, 159

Hilt Trench, 148–149

Hiscock, John, 39–40

HMS *Calypso* (ship), 44, 61–62

HMS *Clan MacNaughton* (ship), loss of, 81–82, 84

HMS *Cornwall* (ship), 203

HMS *Cornwallis* (ship), 98

HMS *Viknor* (ship), loss of, 81–82, 84

Hollis Walker report, 249, 255–256, 258–266, 270, 275, 285, 291, 307

Hollis Walker, Thomas, 249, 255. *See also* Hollis Walker report.

Holmes, Oliver Wendell, 265

Horwood, William H., 77, 85, 88, 189

Horwood, R.F., 189

Hughes, Sam, 68

Humphries, Tom, 103

Hunt, Charles E., 244

Hutchings, C.H., 50

Hutton, E.T.H., 91

Hynes, R.E., 107

I

Imperial Munitions Board, xxi

Imperial Tobacco Company, 266, 277

Imperial War Conference, 154

Imperial War Graves Commission (IWGC), 207–208, 271

Industrial Disputes Investigation Act of 1907, xxiii

Infantry Hill, 159

International Association of Machinists (IAM), 163

International Union of Mine, Mill and Smelter Workers, 272

Italy
fascism and, 276
First World War and, 93–94
fish exports and, 210–211
fishery disputes and, 226–227
government of, 210
Mussolini, 249, 262

J

James, Charles T., 158, 207, 225

Jeffrey, C.E.A., 254, 278

Jennings, W.B., 236–237

Job, R.B., 219

Joffre, Joseph, 125

Johnson, George M., 77, 86–88, 101

Jones, Sidney, 36, 39

Jones, Bishop Llewellyn, 48, 58

Jones, George, 264

Jordan, Jack, 299

Jordan, Thomas, 299

Journeyman Coopers Union, 212, 296

Joynson-Hicks, Sir William, 294

July first, meaning of, xi, 152, 165

K

Kean, Abram
Bowring Brothers and, 13
by-election of 1925, 283
conflict with Coaker, 220, 303
election of 1919 and, 205, 208
Florizel and, 119
lawsuits by, 101, 102
political appointments, 117

Prospero and, 145
public rehabilitation of, 298–299
sealing and, 12–13, 31
SS *Newfoundland* disaster and, 33–38,
    41, 47, 50–53, 55–57, 60, 64,
    77–79, 82–88, 92, 301
Terra Nova and, 292
Kean, Joseph, 12, 13, 101
Kean, Nathan, 13
Kean, Westbury, 13, 34–37, 40, 47, 50,
    52–53, 55–57, 79, 80, 299
Kean, William, 12
Kent, James M., 30
King George V (or Seamen's) Institute,
    43–44
King, William Lyon Mackenzie, xxiii
Kitchener, Lord, 92
Knight inquiry, 47, 50–51, 53, 55–56,
    77, 86
Knight, A.W., 47, 50–51, 55, 56, 77. *See
    also* Knight inquiry.
Knights of Columbus, 46
Knowling, George, 48
Ku Klux Klan, 252

L

labour relations
    attitudes on, 190
    in Canada, 190
    Labour Revolt of 1919, xxiii
    press and, 120
    religion and, 64
    strikes, 190
    in the United States, 190–191
    wages and, 31
Labrador
    border disputes, 239, 285
    Labrador Current, 2
    leasing to Britain, 293
laissez-faire liberalism, 106
laissez-fairism, xvi, xxv

Leggo, John, 126
Leggo, Sarah, 126
Legion of Frontiersmen, 62
Lenin, Vladimir, 172, 191–192
liberal democracy
    corruption of, 300
    free market and, 305
    principles of, 77, 106, 171, 186
Liberal Party, 15–17, 23, 26–27, 29–30,
    57, 164, 167, 170, 201, 286
Liberal-Conservative Party, 266
Liberal-Labour alliance, 308
Liberal-Labour-Progressive Party, 212,
    242, 247, 265
Liberal-Progressive Party, 205, 207, 269
Liberal-Reform alliance, 205, 233, 238
Liberal-Reform Party, 204, 206, 210, 239,
    247
Liberal-Union alliance, 29–30, 167, 201,
    203
Lind, Frank, 80–81, 91, 103, 108, 129,
    131–132
Linegar, William, 210, 212–213, 215,
    243, 267
Lintrose (ship), 110
liquor control
    Act Respecting Alcoholic Liquors, 273
    alcohol prohibition, 273, 275
    corruption and, 259
    liquor control board, 255
    Liquor Control Department, 249
    Prohibition Act Repeal Bill, 273
    prohibition reform, 273, 275
Little, Lewis, 243, 270
Lloyd, William F., 30, 50, 143, 167, 170,
    175, 199–200, 202
Lloyd George, David, 154
Longshoremen's Protective Union (LSPU),
    64, 112, 161–163, 177, 183, 213, 250,
    290, 296, 302
Lys, Battle of, 179

M

Macfarlane, David, xiii–xiv
Macpherson, Cluny, 105, 148
Magor, R.J., 290
Magrath, Charles A., 295
Martin, Robert, 207
Marxism, 191
McCarthy, Richard, 39–41
McGrath, James, 64, 112, 161–163, 183, 191, 205, 213, 290, 302–303, 305
McGrath, Patrick T., 47, 114, 119, 142, 158
McWhirter, H.W., 98
Meaney, J.T., 209, 259, 247–248
Megantic (ship), 96
Memorial Day, xi–xii, 165, 181, 186, 214, 222, 241, 268, 293
Memorial University College, 195, 228
Methodist Church, 9, 10, 20, 21, 54, 142, 149, 166, 178, 193
Methodist Guards Brigade, 62
Military Service Act, 178, 180–181
Mitchell, Harold, 175, 214, 221, 269–270, 293
Mitchell-Thompson, Sir William, 294
Monchy-le-Preux (Monchy), 158–160, 167, 208, 292
Monroe, Walter
    alcohol prohibition and, 273, 275
    conflict with Coaker, 243, 267
    conflict with Squires, 291
    election of 1924, 266–267, 269–271
    failure of government, 285, 309
    government debt and, 274, 276, 277
    government patronage and, 272
    government's foreign investment and, 285
    opposition leader, 265
    press criticism of government, 278
    support for, 246, 266–267, 269
    tax reforms and, 277

Morgan, Fred, 81
Morgan, John Thomas, 81
Morine, A.B., 16, 19, 50, 200, 202, 203, 206, 209, 238, 242, 261, 270, 282–283
Morris, Edward Patrick
    Abram Kean and, 57
    confederation and, 62, 154
    conflict with Coaker, 29, 57, 60, 89–90, 136–137, 140–141, 146, 153–154, 161
    conflict with sealers, 83
    conscription and, 167, 304
    death of, 170
    fishery development and, 26, 27
    FPU and, 29–30, 32, 61, 63, 141, 147
    government debt and, 153–154
    Liberal Party and, 17
    merchants and, 27, 30–31
    patronage appointments, 140
    peerage in House of Lords, 169–170
    People's Party and, 26–27, 45, 54, 303
    press support of, 29
    railway and, 16, 29, 45
    Reid enterprises and, 27, 30, 62
    resignation of, 169
    SS *Newfoundland* disaster and, 46, 48, 57, 146
    war effort and, 60–64, 67, 76, 158
    war profiteering and, 146
Morris, Isaac C., 279, 280
Morry, Howard, 132–133
Mosdell, H.M., 47, 63, 117
Mosley, Oswald, 310
Mouland, Arthur, 36, 39
Munn, John, 83
Munn, W.A., 229
Murphy, B., 219
Murphy, Leo, 149, 234

Mussolini, Benito, 249–256, 262, 293–294, 299

N

Nangle, Thomas, 149, 207, 208, 228, 234–236, 241, 251–252, 254, 262, 264, 269, 279–280, 309
Napoleonic Wars, 4
Nascopie (ship), 110
Naval Reserve
  casualties, 81, 82, 303
  enlistment in, 17, 72
  establishment of, 18
  outport communities and, 72, 116–117
  pensions and, 234
  political influence of, 209
  recruitment, 60–61
  remuneration and, 72–73, 81–82, 120
  vs. Newfoundland Regiment, 147–148
Neil, Kenneth, 37, 41
Neptune (ship), 91
Newfoundland Regiment
  Beaumont Hamel, 124, 130, 156, 303, 312
  casualties, 70, 80, 98–101, 103–109, 114, 124, 126–127, 129, 131–139, 148–149, 158–160, 166–168, 172–173, 175, 179–180, 303, 308, 312
  conditions aboard *Florizel*, 73–74
  conditions in England, 75–76
  Dardanelles, 92, 95, 97, 104
  enlistment in, 73, 105, 115–116, 147, 150, 156, 166, 173
  funding of, 71
  Gallipoli and, 95–99, 105, 107–109, 113–115, 156, 303
  medical requirements and, 69
  morale of, 102–104
  munitions and, 74–75
  pensions and, 234

  recruitment and, 151, 155
  religion and, 114
  remuneration and, 72–73, 81–82
  reputation of, 91
  training of, 75–76, 80
  volunteerism and, 147, 173, 174
  vs. Naval Reserve, 147–148
  war memorials and, 207–208
Newfoundland and Labrador
  climate of, 7
  environment and, 2–3
  immigration to, 10
  population, 17
Newfoundland Board of Trade, 27
Newfoundland Boot and Shoe Company, 266
Newfoundland Forestry Corps, 162, 166
Newfoundland Industrial Workers' Association (NIWA), 163, 165, 168–169, 175–177, 191, 205, 212–214, 216
Newfoundland Knitting Mills Limited, 163–164
Newfoundland Patriotic Association (NPA), 66, 72, 92, 115, 121, 141–142, 167, 305
Newfoundland War Contingent Association, 114

O

Ommer, Rosemary, 306
One Big Union, 215
Orange Order, 46–47, 54, 170 178, 209, 286
Organisation for Maintenance of Supplies, 294
Ottoman Empire, 93, 95
Outerbridge, Sir Joseph, 62–63, 66, 296
Outerbridge, Leonard, 296
outport communities
  employment and, 19

Naval Reserve and, 72, 116–117

seal hunt and, 6–7, 14, 80

SS *Newfoundland* disaster and, 80

vs. St. John's elites, 7, 200

war effort and, 68–69, 71–72

P

Paris Peace Conference, 194–195, 199

Parsons Alex A., 257

Parsons, V.M., 159

Passchendaele, 172, 179

People's Party, 26–27, 30, 47, 54, 56–57, 76, 119, 154, 167, 176, 183, 199, 201, 203, 207, 222, 247, 288, 303

Pope Leo XIII, 191

Porter, James, 44

post-war recession/depression
banking and, 307

debt and, 239, 258–259, 274

poverty and, 231–232

public assistance and, 232, 237–238, 241, 279

taxation and, 242

unemployment and, 218, 231, 237–239, 259–260

post-war reconstruction, xxv, xxvii, 189, 193–194, 198, 204

Power, James, 296

Presbyterian Newfoundland Highlanders, 62

price controls, 168

Prince, Alfred, 272

Prohibition Act Repeal Bill, 273

Prospero (ship), 64

public assistance
demand for, 288, 297

misspending of, 249, 259–260

opposition to, 247

post-war recession/depression and, 232, 237–238, 241, 279

pulp and paper industry, 18–19, 68, 109, 238, 240, 273, 289

R

Railway Commission, 231

railway development
cost of, 16, 18, 153

debt and, 231, 239

economic gains and, 18

employment and, 17

government takeover of railway, 248

impact of, 17

Morris government and, 16, 29, 45

Railway Commission, 231

support of, 16

Raley, Captain Arthur, 132

Randall, Isaac R., 40

Rawlinson, General, 125, 127–130

Red Cross, 132

Red Cross Line, 13, 146, 164

Reform Party, 12, 16

Reid Newfoundland Company, 46, 102, 110, 164, 197, 202, 247

Reid, Harry, 175, 176

Reid, Robert G., 16–17

Reid, W.D., 111

Reid, William, 175–176

religion
Christian progressivism, 250

employment/promotion and, 142

labour relations and, 64

Newfoundland Regiment and, 114

paramilitary groups and, 62

political affiliation and, 204–205, 209, 213

political intervention and, 10

Roman Catholic–Protestant divide, 10, 54

sealers and, 20–21

sectarian conflict and, 54

representative government, 10, 63

Rerum Novarum, 191

Reserve Force Committee, 66, 142

responsible government, suspension of, xxvii, 63, 276–277, 282, 287, 294, 297, 298–299, 310, 312

Returned Soldiers' Association, 201

Ricketts, Thomas, 185, 195

Rimouski (ship), loss of, *102*

Riverside Woolen Mills Limited, 163–164

Robinson, John Alexander, 46, 222, 236

Roche, Monsignor Edward Patrick, 48, 149, 191, 198, 200, 209, 267

Roman Catholic Church, political intervention and, 10

Ross, H.H.A., 107

Rothermere, Lord, 253

Royal Flying Corps, 228

Royal Mail Steam Packet Company, 81

Royal Naval Reserve. *See* Naval Reserve.

Royal Newfoundland Regiment. *See* Newfoundland Regiment.

Royal Scots, 98

Russia
  Bolshevism and, 172, 207
  First World War and, 150
  government of, 171–172
  oppression in, 196

S

Sailly-Saillisel, 167

Saklatvala, Shapurji, 281

Salt Codfish Exportation Act, 220, 221

Scammell, John, 208–209, 270, 274

Scarpe, Second Battle of the, 160, 167

Scimitar Hill, 98

Seal Fishery Act, 119

seal hunt. *See also* Fishermen's Protective Union (FPU); fishery.
  conservation and, 10–11

economics of, 19, 174–175

exploitation of sealers, 19

folk tradition, ix–x

hiring practices and, 21

labour organization and, 9

merchants and, 9

outport communities and, 6–7, 14

patronage and, 12

petitions and, 88

protests and, x

regulations/legislation and, 11, 32, 77, 119, 217, 219, 310–311

religion and, 20–21

resource depletion and, 11

risks of, xvii, 7–8, 14, 31, 36, 89, 90, 301, 311

sealers' rally, 88–89

sealers' strike, 19

Sealing Bill, 51

SS *Greenland disaster,* 14

SS *Newfoundland* disaster, x, 32–58, 301–302

wages and, 20

war veterans and, 292

working conditions, 7, 11, 20, 28, 31, 32, 51, 257, 278

Sealing Bill, 51

Shea, Ambrose, 15

Sheikh-ul-Islam, 95

Sheppard, Mark, 51

shipping. *See also* fishery; seal hunt.
  Bermuda Trading Company, 13
  freight rates, 146, 157–158, 164
  Harvey Companies, 13–14
  legislation and, 168
  profiteering and, 110, 111, 146, 151, 164

Simmons, E., 264

Small, Harvey, 210

Small, Max, 296

Smallwood, J.R, x, 155

Smith, Adam, 106

Smith, Canon, 65

Smith, Warwick, 163, 175

Social Gospel movement, xxii–xxiii, xxv, 106

Society of United Fishermen, 46, 178

Somme, Battle of the, x, 125–127, 134–137, 150

Sontag, Raymond, 301

Southern Cross (ship), disappearance of, 33, 43, 48–49, 90

Spanish influenza epidemic, xxv

Squires, Lemuel, 44

Squires, Richard
  alliance with Coaker, 212–214, 222, 286, 307–309
  conflict with Coaker, 143, 189
  conscription and, 166
  Daily Star and, 117
  final defeat, 292
  government corruption and, 219–220, 246, 247, 247, 248, 249, 255–256, 258–259, 261, 263–264, 275, 291, 298, 307
  government debt and, 276
  GWVA and, 219, 221, 234 237, 238
  labour relations and, 213
  Liberal-Reform alliance and, 233
  Morris government and, 76
  Orange Order and, 170
  People's Party and, 54–56
  press/public criticism of, 182, 231, 240, 243, 244, 267, 291
  relief crisis/debt, 289–292
  resignation of, 244–246, 248
  war veterans and, 219, 221, 234 237, 238

SS *Greenland* disaster, 14, 32, 35, 50, 45, 63

SS *Nascopie* (ship), 42

SS *Newfoundland* disaster
  Abram Kean and, 35–37, 41, 47, 50, 85–89, 92, 101, 301
  Bellaventure and, 39–41, 43, 46
  casualties, 33, 41, 56–57, 78, 80, 90
  charitable donations and, 46, 48–49, 57–58
  Coaker's views on, 42, 85, 92, 117
  communication failure and, 35, 38–39, 41–42, 47–48, 51–53, 56–57, 101, 301
  crew of ship, 35–37
  Florizel and, 35, 41–42
  FPU's reaction, 44–45, 47, 87
  government reaction to, 44–48, 50–51, 53, 55, 88
  investigation of, 77–78
  Knight inquiry and, 47, 50
  outport communities and, 80
  political fallout and, 59
  press reaction to, 43, 45–46, 49, 51, 53–54, 56–57, 78–79, 84, 86, 88–90
  rescue of survivors, 41
  SS *Stephano* and, 35–39, 42, 47, 83, 85–86, 101
  Tuff and, 36
  Westbury Kean and, 35–38, 50
  weather conditions and, 36–39, 55

SS *Stephano* (ship), 34–35, 38, 40, 51, 53, 55, 79, 85–86, 91, 101, 144–145

SS *Terra Nova* (ship), *Terra Nova* (ship), 44, 90, 257, 292

St John's elites, 41, 143–144, 186, 281. *See also* Water Street merchants/elites.

St. John's Electric Light Company, 266

St. John's Rifle Club, 62

Stacey, A.J., 68, 69, 99, 132–134, 149, 159–160

Stacey, Charles, 68

Statute of Westminster, 295

Stavert, Sir William, 296

Steele, Owen, 74, 75, 81, 100, 113–115, 128–129, 131, 133–134

Stenlake, W.D., 149

Stone, John G., 201, 209

strikes
  of firefighters, 158
  NIWA and, 169, 176, 177
  of sealers, 19, 26
  in United States, 157
  Winnipeg General Strike, 190

Strong, Eliza, 52

Suez Canal, 96

T

Tait, J. Sinclair, 272

"tal qual," 25, 28–29

taxation
  Bond government and, 18
  exemptions, 18
  fish trade and, 15
  income tax, 134, 154
  merchants and, 30
  Monroe government and, 277
  reforms, 277
  post-war recession and, 242
  war effort and, 153–155, 158, 164, 165, 168, 181, 303–304
  war profits and, 94, 140, 155

textile industry, 163–164, 168

Thorburn, Sir Robert, 16

Thorne, William, 271

Timewell, Henry Arthur, 80, 142–143

Tippett, Edward, 39

Tippett, Abel, 39

Tippett, Norman, 39

Tocque, Philip, 7

Transloy Ridge, Battle of, 148

Treaty of Utrecht, 3

Treaty of Versailles, 3, 199

Trotsky, Leon, 191–192

"truck," (credit practice) 5, 8

Truckmen's Protective Union, 46, 112

Tucker, Walter, 105

Tuff, George, 35–39, 50–51, 55–56, 79, 85–86, 88

Turkey, xix, 95–100, 103, 107–108, 113, 124, 185. *See also* Dardanelles; Gallipoli.

Turner, Jack, 267, 268

U

unemployment
  wartime and, 68
    Committee of the Unemployed, 290
    post-war recession/depression and, 218, 231, 237–239, 259–260

Union Party, 26, 28, 30, 54, 66, 143, 153, 163–164, 167, 169–170, 178, 181, 190, 197–200, 233, 248, 255, 261–262, 264, 284, 301, 303

Union Publishing Company, 101

Union Trading Company (UTC), 25, 170, 192, 210–211, 221, 224, 244, 308

United Fishermen's Movement (UFM), 242

United Mine Workers of America, 250

United Mine Workers of Nova Scotia, 250

United Newfoundland Party, 292

V

Verdun, 118, 124–125, 127, 150

Verge, A.J., 292

Vimy Ridge, xii, 159

Voluntary Aid Detachment (VAD), 66, 173

Volunteer Force Act, 66

W

W.I. Bishop Ltd., 273

Wabana Mine Workers' Union (WMWU), 278

Wakefield, Dr. Arthur, 62

war effort. *See also* First World War; Naval Reserve; Newfoundland Regiment.
classism and, 117
debt and, 156, 182, 192, 198
financial hardship and, 176
financing of, 66, 71, 120–121
inflation and, 84
Morris government and, 64, 66, 76, 78, 163
munitions, 70, 74–75, 91
Newfoundland's support of, 116
NPA and, 72, 84, 92, 141, 144, 153, 157, 158, 166, 303
outport communities and, 68–69, 71–72
patriotism and, 68, 70, 71, 76, 94
press views on, 65
taxation and, 153, 154, 155, 158, 164, 165, 168, 181, 303–304
women's involvement, 66, 71–72, 76, 99, 101
Women's Patriotic Association, 99, 101

War Measures Act (of Newfoundland), xxi–xxii, 66, 104, 176, 206, 212, 218, 223, 225, 232, 306

war memorials
Beaumont Hamel site, 208, 228–229, 262, 279
budget for, 208, 228–229
ceremony for, 235, 262, 271
partisanship and, 203
proposals for, 193, 195, 207
unveiling of, 270

War Pensions Act, 185, 221

war profiteering, 110, 140, 146–147, 161, 164, 206, 241, 243, 303–304

War Reparations Committee, 290

war veterans
Britain and, 253
employment and, 139–142, 144, 155, 165, 193, 198, 218–219, 234–237, 260–261, 264, 280, 292
financial hardship and, 144, 214, 219, 221, 236–237
GWVA and, 219, 221–222, 228, 233–234, 236–238, 263–264, 291
labour unions and, 139
long-term suffering, 279
pensions, 140, 142, 151, 185–186, 198, 206, 214, 219, 221, 230, 233–234, 291–293
press coverage and, 141–142
public assistance and, 260–261

Warren, William, 50, 204, 245, 248, 264, 265, 270, 283

Water Street merchants/elites. *See also* St. John's elites.
economic exploitation and, 22
elite families, 72
First World War and, 63
government's relationship with, 156
political power and, 31, 67
support for Alderdice, 292
war effort and, 65
war profiteering and, 110, 111, 117, 121, 162

Western Front, xv, 124, 137, 154, 171, 177, 185, 304

White, Hedley, 291–292

Whiteway, William V., 15, 23

Whitty, Gerald J., 233–234

Winnipeg General Strike of 1919, 190, 215

Winsor, Jesse, 242

Winsor, William C., 270, 274

Winter, Harry A., 143, 291

Winter, James A., 143

Women's Christian Temperance Union, 66

Women's Patriotic Association (WPA), 66, 72, 76, 99, 101, 106, 195, 280

women's suffrage, 66, 280–281, 286–287
Wood, Frederick B., xx–xxi
Woodford, William, 219
Workingmen's Party, 210
World War I. *See* First World War.

Y

Yetman, William, 292
Young Turks, 95
Young, Jim, 133
Ypres, 91, 95, 138, 148, 159, 167, 172, 177, 179, 184